"The prosperity of the West was buil[...]
peoples and the sweat of other peo[...]
Professor Fenelon skillfully weaves the long and thick story of [...]
Europeans and a myriad of their institutions participated in this process and
benefitted from it. After this book, no European or their descendants can
claim racial innocence. Bravo Professor Fenelon for this major contribution."

Eduardo Bonilla-Silva, *Duke University, Author of*
Racism Without Racists

"The history of capital, as Professor James Fenelon shows in this urgent and
timely new study, is the history of racism and genocide. The story is told with
great clarity, passion, and abundance of historical evidence. At a time when
global capitalism is throwing communities around the world into desperate
struggles for survival and threatening our very existence, this masterful study
is as much a powerful indictment of the past and the present of this out of
control system. as it is a dire warning of the future to come if we do not
come to terms with the legacy of racism, colonialism, and genocide in the
Americas and beyond."

William I. Robinson, *Distinguished Professor of Sociology,*
University of California at Santa Barbara, Author of
The Global Police State

"Once again, Dakota Professor James Fenelon offers a thoughtful, provocative,
and engaging history examining race and racism globally. He focuses on
Indigenous, Black, and Irish people, offering a global story of people and
systems. The book analyzes the impact of colonialism, racism, and Native
responses—past and present—of systems designed to denigrate, distort, and
exploit. Fenelon focuses on agency and sovereign responses of people faced
with rapid change and foreign disruptions. Superbly researched, elegantly
written, and wonderfully argued, Fenelon draws on original sources,
multiple illustrations, and his own experiences to offer this fascinating,
groundbreaking study."

Clifford E. Trafzer, *Rupert Costo Chair in American Indian Affairs,*
Distinguished Professor of History, University of California, Riverside

Indian, Black and Irish

This book traces 500 years of European–American colonization and racialized dominance, expanding our common assumptions about the ways racialization was used to build capitalism and the modern world-system.

Fenelon draws on personal experience and the agency of understudied Native (and African) resistance leaders, to weave a story too often hidden or distorted in the annals of the academy that remains invisible at many universities and historical societies. The book identifies three epochs of racial constructions, colonialism, and capitalism that created the USA – Indigenous nations, the first to be racialized on a global scale; African peoples, enslaved and brought to the Americas; and European immigrants. It offers a sweeping analysis of the forces driving the invasion, occupation and exploitation of Native America and the significance of labor in American history provided by Indigenous people, Africans and immigrants, specifically the Irish.

Indian, Black and Irish makes major contributions toward a deeper understanding of where Supremacy and Sovereignty originated from, and how our modern world has used these sociopolitical constructions, to build global hegemony that now threatens our very existence, through wars and climate change. It will be a vital resource to those studying history, colonialism, race and racism, labor history and indigenous peoples.

James V. Fenelon is Professor and Director of the Center for Indigenous Peoples Studies, California State University, San Bernardino. Currently he is also the Lang Visiting Professor for Social Change at Swarthmore College. His books include *Redskins? Sports Mascots, Indian Nations, and White Racism; Culturicide, Resistance and Survival of the Lakota;* and *Indigenous Peoples and Globalization* (with Thomas Hall).

New Critical Viewpoints on Society Series
Edited by Joe R. Feagin

Love Under the Skin
Interracial Marriages in the American South and France
Cécile Coquet-Mokoko

Through an Artist's Eyes
The Dehumanization and Racialization of Jews and Political Dissidents
during the Third Reich
Willa M. Johnson

**Leveraging Multigenerational Workforce Strategies in
Higher Education**
Edna Chun and Alvin Evans

Grasping for the American Dream
Racial Segregation, Social Mobility, and Homeownership
Nora Taplin-Kaguru

Who Killed Higher Education?
Maintaining White Dominance in a Desegregation Era
Edna B. Chun and Joe R. Feagin

The Spanish Language in the United States
Racialization, Rootedness, and Resistance
Edited by José A. Cobas, Bonnie Urciuoli, Joe R. Feagin, and Daniel J. Delgado

Indian, Black and Irish
Indigenous Nations, African Peoples, European Invasions, 1492–1790
James V. Fenelon

For more information about this series, please visit www.routledge.com/
New-Critical-Viewpoints-on-Society/book-series/NCVS

Indian, Black and Irish

Indigenous Nations, African
Peoples, European Invasions,
1492–1790

James V. Fenelon

Routledge
Taylor & Francis Group

NEW YORK AND LONDON

First published 2023
by Routledge
605 Third Avenue, New York, NY 10158

and by Routledge
4 Park Square, Milton Park, Abingdon, Oxon, OX14 4RN

Routledge is an imprint of the Taylor & Francis Group, an informa business

ISBN: 978-1-032-32450-0 (hbk)
ISBN: 978-1-032-32448-7 (pbk)
ISBN: 978-1-003-31508-7 (ebk)

DOI: 10.4324/9781003315087

Typeset in Bembo
by Newgen Publishing UK

Contents

---

1 This book is comprehensive over a sweep of 500 years of history, with a world-systems analysis undergirding it. After an introduction, each chapter is chronologically laid out according to the central theses, with primary analysis over early Native nations, supported by case studies, and documentation, that extends into the Irish as exemplary of "becoming white."

    I (we) have been working on and off on this project since 1997, first proposed with more emphasis on "Indian and Irish". Then, I was back from an insightful trip to Ireland, especially Northern Ireland. I developed a foundational thesis, and supporting arguments, into a broader analysis of understanding racism under historical/comparative systems through racial classifications of three primary groupings, Indigenous people as Indians, African-descent people as Blacks, Irish-descent people as Whites, with ethnicity coming into play as construction of whiteness, racial and census typologies, especially of Latino-Hispanics, and variable classification schema of contemporary America.

Standing on *Stolen Land* with *Stolen Hands*: Prelude to Chapter 3 the Black

3   The *Black*: 1620–1790 Institutionalizing Racial Codification

Personal Statement as Preface to Chapter 4: Walking Race and Empire in America

4   Three Revolutions: 1776–1790 Three Races in a New State

Illustrations, Charts and Tables

Foreword

Joe Feagin, Texas A&M University

In this pathbreaking book about the clash of global worlds, James Fenelon, a leading scholar of Indigenous studies, makes evident the systemic racial oppression that began with European imperialism in the 15th century. This imperialism rapidly expanded its invasions of non-European lands across the Atlantic and Pacific over subsequent centuries, and is continuing in the present day. As Fenelon succinctly notes, these quite different human worlds came into conflict beginning

> in the year 1492 using a Roman Julian calendrical system. From this contact into conflict would emerge a modern world system ... of European dominance and power, building to industrial capitalism from four foundations – first, taking of vast new lands and valuable resources from Native Nations ...; second reduction of whole populations into race-based slave labor ...; third, creation of agricultural to industrial capitalism using new, unequal transoceanic trade systems; and fourth developing of global economies through corporate-state relationships that colonized the world.
>
> (p. 5)

Unlike most analyses of this globalized imperialism, Fenelon systematically names the names of numerous elite European men—soon self-defined as white capitalists and their mostly white political and religious allies—who generated and maintained it. Especially too, he begins with and features the Indigenous leaders (soon racialized by Europeans as inferior "savages") who resisted these many European invasions. Indeed, he frequently calls out the absurd Western parochialism wherein there is little recognition that

> Hundreds of nations ranging from great civilizations to relatively small (transhumant) nomadic societies existed throughout the Americas for thousands of years easily comparable to those of European origin, or those preceding on the African continent, and relative to the most ancient largest civilizations of China and India.
>
> (p. 7)

Fenelon's naming these names and presenting critical details mark a signal contribution to social science studies because only certain of these actors and decision-makers, mostly white and European, in most Western-presented historical dramas are given this extensive attention. Too many of them, especially those not white and resisting European invasions in the past and present, are actually missing or are hidden beneath a prose of vague if not derogatory nouns.

In each historical era and for each historical case Fenelon examines four basic aspects—(1) the agency demonstrated by key European invaders and by Indigenous and other human societies resisting their oppression, (2) the dominant and subordinate institutional structures created in the process of the racialized exploitations and resistance, (3) the specific conflicts and other major interactions involved in these globalizing encounters and (4) the processual timeframes of these racialized exploitative events.

In his probing chapters Fenelon makes clear that the central exploitative problem of the last half millennium of human history is elite white men. Early in this era, and enduring to the present, they have created and aggressively maintained what can be termed the *elite-white-male dominance system*. Including capitalistic, political, religious and military leaders, this white male elite has long ruled rapaciously, undemocratically and globally, yet often remains nebulous or concealed to those it routinely dominates. I have suggested the importance of particular systemic-oppression framework empirically and theoretically for decades, and in my view much future social science research should follow in Fenelon's paths to detail the world-scale operation, dimensions, and impacts of this elite-white-male dominance system. It has long destroyed "life, liberty and the pursuit of happiness" for billions of the planet's people.

Over centuries most people invaded and exploited by the mostly male European and European American imperialists have been non-European. This invasive imperialism and colonization have been guided by an aggressively predatory and Eurocentric framing that views white European men as having a God-ordained *right* to conquer new areas, kill or "civilize" the "savage" inhabitants and violently seize their lands and labor in the name of assertively virtuous and superior European goals and culture.

Naming names and detailing who these decision-makers are, both invaders and those resisting their invasions, changes the character of how we understand and interpret a half millennium of radical global change. In Fenelon's detailed social, political and geographical mapping we are no longer lost in a cloud of ambiguous nouns or passive tenses. We see in detail many male Europeans, and most are indeed male, making lasting humanity-changing decisions with concrete inhumane motivations. Most centrally, we observe and understand how these European elites, including male capitalists and their political and religious enablers, have long operated out of what can be termed a *predatory ethic*, an ethic and associated racial framing that have long assumed that powerful European men have the right to steal the land and labor of others to use for their individual and collective gain.

Interestingly, significant discussion of the motivation of these European invaders and land/labor thieves, and more generally of their generative home contexts, has frequently focused on motivational issues such as their "Protestant ethic." For instance, the influential sociologist Max Weber famously wrote of the "Protestant ethic and the spirit of capitalism," arguing that the rise of certain types of European Protestantism facilitated or fostered the great expansion of entrepreneurial capitalism in certain European countries. However, in considering the history of the aggressively globalizing European imperialism and colonialism chronicled in this book, one can speak more accurately of the aforementioned *predatory ethic* as the real and enduring "capitalistic spirit," as the recurring motivation behind the massive, centuries-long expansionist agendas and operations of European imperialism.

Wise about such historical assessments, in the early decades of the 19th century the political-economist Karl Marx succinctly detailed the world-shattering significance of this predatory imperialism:

> The discovery of gold and silver in America, the extirpation, enslavement and entombment in mines of the aboriginal population, the beginning of the conquest and looting of the East Indies, the turning of Africa into a warren for the commercial hunting of black-skins, signaled the rosy dawn of the era of capitalist production. These idyllic proceedings are the chief moments of primitive accumulation. . . . [C]apital comes dripping from head to foot from every pore with blood and dirt.[1]

The original German commonly translated as "primitive accumulation" is perhaps more accurately translated as "original accumulation"—that is, as referencing the first large-scale generation of "capital" on which subsequent centuries of capitalism have been built. While Marx never developed this key insight in his further work, here he clearly saw the world-scale reality of the predatory, rapacious, anti-human character of the birth of modern capitalism.

As Fenelon demonstrates well, the early and later expansion of Western capitalism was firmly constructed on the great wealth generated by the violent seizing by European capitalists and their acolytes of the land, other natural resources, and labor of non-European peoples, eventually in most sectors of the globe. This "original accumulation" remains important to modern capitalism, again as Fenelon demonstrates throughout this book. The Marxist-Feminist scholar Silvia Federici has argued that this extensive exploitative accumulation of white male capitalists beyond western borders has been essential to capitalism not only in the past, but now continuing well into the present, and likely into the future. This ever globalizing capitalism "has been able to reproduce itself ... only because of the web of inequalities that it has built into the body of the world proletariat, and because of its capacity to globalize exploitation."[2]

A constant dimension of this globalization is the scale and extraordinary character of the white male violence involved. Throughout Fenelon's book we observe how central to Western capitalistic imperialism and colonization is organized white male violence, violence typically generated and buttressed by various types of state violence. As noted previously, the central oppressors in this original, and subsequent, capital accumulation and associated human destruction were for the most part aggressively masculinist European men— especially capitalistic entrepreneurs, top religious leaders and leading nation- state and associated military officials. But they did not act just as individuals. They headed up extremely profitable, world-changing companies—many soon formalized as corporations—and other religious, military, and political organizations engaged in this predatory human destruction.

Another key dimension in this half millennium of European and European American globalized imperialism is just how racialized it quickly came to be, a key feature for which Fenelon provides many examples. Numerous scholars have quoted the aforementioned lines of Marx's *Capital* in their analyses of modern capitalism's expansion, yet few have noted well the key dimension of racialization, one that Marx himself did not emphasize.

One of these few, the astute African American sociologist Oliver C. Cox, was the first U.S. scholar to develop a systematic analysis of the role of white- seized labor and land in North America and overseas in creating the capital- istic world and its associated systemic racism:

> Seizing the labor of non-Europeans in North America and elsewhere is actually the beginning of modern racial relations. It was not an abstract, natural, immemorial feeling of mutual antipathy between groups, but rather a practical exploitative relationship. . . . As it developed, and took definite capitalist form, we could follow the white man around the world and see him repeat the process among practically every people of color."[3]

In Fenelon's savvy analysis he follows exactly this admonition, following the white man around the world exploiting and racializing people of color:

> Race, and therefore racism as we know it, began shortly after 1492. Around Columbus's journey, indigenous peoples – 'Indians' – were given special subordinate status as a 'savage' or inferior and uncivilized 'race' of people. Within a few decades, European colonial expansion over the Americas developed immense stratification systems including slavery, colonization, genocide, and cultural domination with race as a primary marking feature.

(p. 21)

Central to capitalistic imperialism and colonization is this highly *racialized* reality. Almost every major societal group that became central to the early (and later) European accumulation of capital in the imperialistic capitalistic system has been non-European, and each of them soon became denigrated (literally, "blackened") in an increasingly developed white racial framing of this colonialism process and of the colonial societies it constantly created. European capitalism, colonialism, and racial oppression—mostly at the behest of elite white men—thus emerge together in this particular centuries-long era and over extraordinarily great geographical expanse.

Central to this complex and extensive racialization process is what I have termed the "white racial frame." By developing this dominant racial framing, the white European colonizers and their descendants created the socially constructed reality called "race" or "racial group." As Fenelon shows, this development began with the 15th-century colonial invasions of Iberian and Mediterranean political powers, but by the 1600s the colonizers from northern Europeans areas had more aggressively racialized their imperialist efforts, being among the first to regularly color-code themselves as "whites" and those they subordinated as "reds" or "Indians," or some version of "blacks." Since this 17th century, elite and other Europeans and European Americans have institutionalized such color labels (e.g., "white," "black," "red," "yellow," "brown") for racial identities they have imposed on others. These "race" colors are not empirical observations but part of an imposed and metaphorically racialized system. As the scholar Andrew Goatly puts it,

> Those who defend the existing classifications of society, for example race/colour, in which they are the most powerful group use the language of nature to justify this classification. This is an exceedingly important motive for the adoption of power-aggression theories of nature since the celebration of the winners in a competitive struggle is useful to those in power.[4]

Clearly, the bloody and rapacious historical realities of this white racial oppression make it clear that the traditional social science concepts of racial prejudice, stereotyping, and individual discrimination are much too weak, indeed are intentionally so in their white social science origins. It takes much more realistic social science analysis, which includes the considered perspectives of people of color about institutional and systemic racism, and much stronger critical thinking about racial matters to make full sense of what has taken place since the European imperialism and colonization that began in earnest in the 16th and 17th centuries. These perspectives are well accented for the reader throughout this book.

In addition, over a half millennium the exploitative process of European and European American imperialism, colonialism, slavery, and genocide created enormously wealthy European and European American societies that gradually came to dominate much of the planet. Central to Fenelon's detailed discussions of these realities is a savvy assessment of what it has meant for Western societies to have developed in these ways, especially to be *founded on* such extensive racialized slavery and genocide. His full-throated critical analysis shows or implies how these bloody historical realities have forever shaped Western societies in ways seldom recognized, to the present day.

Indeed, one of the hardest things for white Westerners to understand is that their countries are not just riddled with institutionalized racism but are fundamentally, systemically, and foundationally white racist. That is, the racial oppression is foundational in most Western countries because for centuries they were grounded in profitable slavery and genocide. And this anti-human oppression was soon well-institutionalized, well-legalized, and well-bureaucratized. Indeed, the cases of African American slavery and Indigenous extirpation and genocide involved what are often termed "total institutions" for those subordinated. These Americans of color were early victims of Western totalitarianism—a system controlling all major aspects of their lives. Over the last half century anti-imperialist and decolonization efforts by people of color in the United States and elsewhere have begun to dismantle this racialized totalitarianism, albeit often slowly and leaving much yet to be done.

Over the last century these anti-imperialist and decolonization efforts have provided much stimulus for new or renewed critical research work by scholars and activists of color like James Fenelon. This scholarly work is increasing dramatically in the West and globally as communities and societies of color free themselves from the physical and intellectual control of white Westerners. This remains a major challenge. As Fenelon eloquently points out in describing much white scholarly malpractice,

> Beautiful societies and sophisticated civilizations of Indigenous peoples and nations in the Americas are little discussed in the socio-political histories of great universities and scholars, who represent the strong states of the western world of 1500 in observing the Renaissance, religious Reformation, citizens in Civil Society and powerfully productive economic Capitalism. Deep scholarship is developed and taught with alacrity and precision only in observing the 500 year rise and fall of colonial European Empires and American world trade systems. Similarly, the struggles and social movements of African peoples brought to be slaves, ethnic immigrants in servitude and oppressive working classes, or Asians as forced labor then banned from immigrating, are at best represented as contributing to America, at worst as inferior, while the Anglo or White immigrants are typified as builders of the nation ....

(p. 1)

Unsurprisingly, the white elites, including many elite scholars, resist substantial challenges to conventional white racial framing such as that suggested by Fenelon here. For example, currently in the United States there is an attack, engineered mostly by white male activists connected to far-right think tanks, on the *New York Times* "1619 Project" and on what they intentionally misname as "critical race theory." Both are essentially white supremacist attacks on race-critical research perspectives developed principally by scholars of color, including African and Indigenous American scholars. These highly politicized attacks on leading scholars of color and their quality scholarship signal just how radical researching and teaching an honest history of a Western country like the United States has become. Many of these scholars, as well as some white scholars also engaged in critical racial scholarship, have regularly faced violent threats, including recurring death threats. Increasingly in recent decades, the preservation of white Western racial dominance, including the dominant white racial frame and its traditional racial mythology, requires the suppression of critical social science research on white racism and, more generally, of critical thinking about many mythologized societal topics. Unsurprisingly, the original and pathbreaking research in this book, and its brave author, will be considered "dangerous" as soon as it is published.

Recent social science research indicates that critical thinking about an array of U.S. societal matters is remarkably weak in the United States. This includes the educational system at all levels. One Stanford University research team has examined the level of critical thinking among various levels of K–12 students and among college students. They had thousands of students read news-type commentaries from the internet, in the process seeking to "establish a reasonable bar, a level of performance we hoped was within reach of most middle school, high school, and college students." In their research they assessed whether middle school students "could distinguish an ad from a news story. By high school, we would hope that students reading about gun laws would notice that a chart came from a gun owners' political action committee." Most could not do so. And in their test of critical thinking among college students, they sought to determine if the students "would look beyond a .org URL and ask who's behind a site that presents only one side of a contentious issue." Most could not. The summary of their findings emphasizes that

> in every case and at every level, we were taken aback by students' lack of preparation.... at each level—middle school, high school, and college— these [student] variations paled in comparison to a stunning and dismaying consistency. Overall, young people's ability to reason about the information on the Internet can be summed up in one word: bleak.[5]

Throughout this book Fenelon presents a similarly bleak picture of (the lack of) Western knowledge about the last five centuries, in both the ordinary white population and in the white elite. He thus lays out the scholarly, and indeed ethical, admonition that

> What the social sciences must do in the 21st century after a half millennia of racialized capitalism now contested throughout the world and in the streets of the dominant state itself, facing dual threats of climate change in the Anthropocene and wars between competing nations, is recognize the struggles of the past 500 years in a balanced and truly comparative way. I can find no better method of achieving this, than present the leaders of nations and movements from all sides and diverse perspectives ....
>
> (p. 5)

Notes

1 Karl Marx, *Capital*, Volume I, trans. Ben Fowkes (New York: Vintage Books, 1977), pp. 915, 926.

2 Sylvia Federici, *Caliban and the Witch: Women the Body and Primitive Accumulation* (New York: Autonomedia, 2004), p. 17.

3 Oliver C. Cox, *Caste, Class, and Race* (Garden City, NY: Doubleday, 1948), pp. 332–333.

4 Andrew Goatly, *Washing the Brain: Metaphor and Hidden Ideology* (Amsterdam, The Netherlands: Benjamins, 2007), p. 194.

5 Stanford History Education Group, "Evaluating Information: The Cornerstone of Civic Online Reasoning," Stanford University, November 22, 2016, https://stacks.stanford.edu/file/druid:fv751yt5934/SHEG%20Evaluating%20Information%20Online.pdf (accessed December 8, 2022).

Preface(s) Four Directions

This is a story, about great swings of history with notable people as heroes or villains, living within societies that are conquering and equivocating in the face of conquest, in worlds that are changing human society and civilization, for the better or worse or both, on a planet that is now strained to the maximum by great urban centers and late stage capitalism altering the very environment – earth itself in ways that threaten humanity and other life-forms sustained over millennia in what we have come to see as a web of relations. This is a global story, where each of three powerful social systems – capitalism as the economic, colonization as political, racism as social-structural – have broken or distorted relational webs of humans, societies, environments that have guided and informed previous civilizations.

It is a story we had better listen to, and one that needs to be told in a most straightforward manner with respect for the many peoples and diverse societies from which all this has emerged. It is a story I am well positioned to tell, (with military system experience). I grew up listening to oral histories of Dakota (Sioux) relatives having fought the U.S. army to a standstill, in famous battles, meeting homeland relatives, hearing stories of how families survived. My first peacetime international gig was to Denmark and an ancestry of *Vikings*, my second was with Cubans from the Mariel boatlift, and between returns to the Dakotas, my third gig was to Haiti, learning an incredible Indigenous history of European invasion and slave revolts and experiencing deep melding of ancient African-Taino ceremony. Fourth was invitation to Shanghai, lecturing on sources of injustice and inequality in America, which the U.S. Consulate reportedly saw as "un-American" activity, followed by years in Japan and Malaysia with upriver trips to Sarawak Borneo meeting the *Iban* and *Penan* (headhunters?), later comparing these "hunter-gatherers" with the Euro-American "civilized" societies in creating a modernity that John Trudell called the great Predator. After the Miskito in Nicaragua, Ireland was the icing on my familial inheritance, where English domination went on for centuries in the countryside around Dublin, and can still be seen after the Troubles of ethnically mixed North Ireland in Derry, Belfast and Armagh.

This story includes building of the largest cities with the most complex social structures and scientific technology ever in the known universe. It also includes destruction of some of the most well-adapted Native social systems known in history, to the point of genocides, and the development of the largest, most dehumanizing slavery systems our world has ever known—both genocides and enslavement have been for profits and to amass wealth, done for capitalism. Much of this winnowing, dehumanizing of humans was conducted in the name of democracy, and for progressive civilization. We had better understand how these competing paradigms of humanity came about, in hopes that this knowledge can shed light on how our maximally well-developed society cannot curb its own greed from swallowing up all that is generous and good, like the insatiable giant *Iiyah*, or uncivilized spider-man *Inktomi* after creation of the world.

Note to This Book

This work has always been conceived, thought about and developed to be comprehensive over the 500 plus years of creating a modern world out of the Americas. I have attempted to pull it together over the years, redirected to write other works in 1992 (my dissertation, first book), around 2004 (international Indigenous travels leading to my second book), and again about 2016 (linking racial icons to racism, in my third book). As 2020 appeared on the horizon, and possible retirement or a refinishing to more creative works, long dormant in my poetry and story-telling, I took liberty with a sabbatical and various offers looming, to propose completion of this project, prepping at the beginning of the year with my works on climate change and global environment, to finally sit down and put the already written pieces together into a whole, pushing pen to paper (quite literally – all meaningful text was originating in longhand writing). And then, ominously, pandemic broke out of China near where I used to work and travel, and spread to four directions, each devastated in places and ways all too familiar with the spread of European colonization.

I was isolated in my home, with one of my two sons finishing his second year of college, which took up copious amount of time and energy to teach, virtually, and reconfigured my work, noting the pandemics of the 16th and 17th century that devastated the Indigenous nations of Turtle Island and produced a different, more vulnerable world, to conquest and colonization. I realized, like so many others, this as an opportunity to let my sons experience movement, and to envision a better world in the face of injustice and inequality, through participating in the rising marches, protests and demonstrations by "protectors" of water, land and peoples, that encompassed our nation and brought out the very issues I was writing on and over. These included a primary focus on Black Lives Matter, stressing American Indian/Indigenous nations such as at Standing Rock, along with La Raza and refugee/immigration conflicts, and renewed interest in white nationalism and racial supremacy. I am not sure whether I contracted the virus at ICE detention protests in the High Desert where we were at as I watched from afar the police fire flash-bang explosives, or during the BLM/AIM/RAZA marches in downtown Los Angeles where prisoners in the LA jail tapped out support, ending outside the mission church where genocidal colonization began, with my other son tending interest in the diverse peoples coming together under one banner.

Nonetheless, by and during the fall semester, the slightly symptomatic fatigue and mind disorientation accompanying my historic bronchial and traumatic issues from military service came to a head so to speak, and slowed down my writing and ability to focus, becoming now classic long-hauler syndromes of brain fog, waves of fatigue, inability to focus intensely for long periods of time, and later sleep restlessness, all of which interfered with writing a magnum opus. Although one night, being unable to visualize the four epochs in a half millennia of colonization, I feverishly wrote a colored chart included herein that became a guiding paradigm for the work (also with visions from ceremonial experience in the Dakotas, and on four sacred mountains …). As we strode into 2021, and needing to have some completion, I proposed breaking the book into roughly two separate works of 500 years in visage, with a sociopolitically occurring transition, often taught in U.S. history, into the colonial construction of the United States of America. The result is this first book, to be followed by another, soon, with benefit of this approach in that we can view the 13 colonies becoming independent and taking on colonizing expansion over North America using racial, class-ridden, patriarchal systems of domination from a colonial base.

I have come to see a full picture of my life's experience in this work, and its overlay with our world – old and new, European and Indigenous with African diaspora – as one and the same, like the Old ones have taught us to seek out a vision, and live our life accordingly. So I share this with the readers, in hope of finding a more just, more equitable world in the future.

Acknowledgments

This book represents the culmination of my academic career and of my personal journey, for which I must give thanks to many generous teachers and scholars who shaped my growth. I first envisioned this work during my 1981–1982 travels in Haiti (ranging from Jacmel to the south, Jeremie to the west, Hinche in central east, and Cap-Haitien to the north). I stated it in lectures I gave in Shanghai a few years later, and colored in a diverse experiential and ethnic background in Vejen Denmark, when driving around Ireland, and when I returned to the United States – California where I grew up and took my own family, North Dakota where I was born and kept returning, celebrating Indigenous roots and ancestral knowing. Acknowledging the Four Winds – *Tate Topa* – 4 Directions from the guides along my journey who inspired this book.

Upon returning to relatives in the Dakotas (grandparents in Bismarck), I found myself at the ceremonial grounds outside Little Eagle (South Dakota). An elder traditional[1] man, said to be last of the old-time *Heyoka*, took a willow stick, pointed to four directions, saying in Lakota[2] I would travel to these distant places of the world, and learn from their peoples while telling them of Native nations and my relatives. When those journeys were completed, I would return here, and tell the people – *nations* – what had been learned from these four distant peoples of the earth, completing the circle or Medicine Wheel of my life.[3] I thought perhaps this would help other peoples to better understand Indigenous relationships, concepts such as our earth mother, guiding spirits of ancestors, and the grandmothers and grandfathers who guide us spiritually[4]...

Dedicated to my second son – James Dean Phillip Fenelon – born of his Mexican, Dakota/Lakota, Gaelic Irish, French, Scandinavian and Tarahumara descent. I acknowledge Indigenous medicine leaders from Dakotas, Haiti, China, Japan, Malaysia, Ireland and Denmark; senior scholar professors of universities I attended (Mel Davidson, Caleb Gattegno, Yan Yide, Charles Willie, Joe R. Feagin, with a younger Aldon Morris, and others passed on, too numerous to mention); scholar activists (Askov Danes,[5] Mary Louise Defender Wilson of Standing Rock, Haitian houngans); those studying racial wealth gaps (especially Meizhu Lui and William Darity, Jr.); more recent luminaries (Eduardo Bonilla-Silva); co-conspirators sharing the streets (Bobby Vega, Eddie Two Rivers); and times of high conflict (resistance movement leaders, fellow U.S. Veterans) now having passed on; discussions at Northwestern (John Diamond and David Pellow) and especially my publisher, and friend, Dean Birkenkamp.[6] I include what Albert White Hat recognizes in his book *Life's Journey—Zuya*, noting it was knowledge passed down over time, eons really, by what some call the Elders, or the Ancestors, often at great expense or threat to themselves, that allows us to share what we came to know with future generations, who we fervently pray will inherit the Earth, (noting that errors or mistranslations are to my discredit alone, as are any omissions and the very critical frames I employ).

I need to acknowledge the time and support given by my university of the past 20 plus years (California State University, San Bernardino), and many wise, wonderful, and fully awake people from those years, noting the recent passing to the spirit world two great friends, Luke Madrigal of the Cahuilla and Julia Bogany of the Tongva. Many others (elder Ernest Siva) have lived their lives in respect and recognition of those who came before. I also note a year giving me time to finish, as Lang Visiting Professor for Social Change at Swarthmore College.

Remembering prayers upon sacred mountains on four continents, and across the oceans of the world, I give thanks (*pidamaya*) for that shared with me (along with tobacco to the earth), and express deep honor (*wopida*) to those who struggle for justice and peace. We are all, indeed, related. O-midakuye oyasin.

Frontispiece – "Anacaona" by Jayelle.
Vision of Anacaona – original artist rendition by Jayelle.[7]

Anacaona of Xaragua (1474–1503) is the first and most prominent Indigenous woman Leader, rising to be Head of the Councils of Xaragua (cacique or caciquess), known for resisting Spain's invasion and domination, and engaging Spanish (including Columbus) in diplomatic negotiations exchanging artful peace for food and other supplies. Spain's governor deceived and captured her, while massacring the diplomatic mission, and ordered her execution as she maintained sovereign independence of the Taino people over their homelands of Ayiti.

Notes

1   This "elder traditional man" was Chauncee Dupree from Cherry Creek on the Cheyenne River Reservation, I figure I could name in the notes, but not in the main text, to avoid stereotyping and misrepresentation, and since I do name him in my third book *Redskins: Sports Mascots, Indian Nations and White Racism* (Routledge, 2016).

2   *– tate wiyohpeyata kiya – tate wiyohinyanpata kiya – tate waziyata kiya – tate itokagata kiya –*

3   I use "nations" though I believe he said "*oyate*" but I don't remember exactly, and think some readers may find this presumptive, which is fair enough, except my life over the next decade unfolded precisely that way.

4   I originally put "to mother earth, *Ina Maka*, and the guiding spirits of the *kunci*, our grandmothers and *tunkashila*, grandfathers, considered *wakan* …" but figure that too can be considered stereotypical or quasi appropriation, except, like above, it resulted in my first book: *Culturicide, Resistance and Survival of the Lakota ("Sioux Nation")* (New York: Garland), 1998 (December).

5   Also the Dane who gave me that first edition of Henry George in long discussions in Copenhagen.

6   Students such as Seth Jeter (Swarthmore) helping to do final edits of the manuscript have proven invaluable.

7   Jayelle read the chapter excerpts and discussed Anacaona and came up with the first beautiful art piece (which had bare breasts) that we are using in the first bios in chapter 1 although for the larger picture and American sensibilities we asked her to sketch in some coverings as found in the Frontispiece, which works just as well as the original; she did this under the working name of JayeElleArt at "jayeelleart@gmail.com" jayeelleart@gmail.com

Chapter 1

Introduction

1490–2020 Racial Construction of Indians, Blacks, Whites

Introduction 1 – Two Worlds, Four Societies in Two Hemispheres 1492–1790

We begin this story, a half millennial history of four continents creating a modern world-system, where all good stories start, at the beginning. In the year of 1492 the western hemisphere, which would become known as the Americas, was rich with Indigenous nations, civilizational empires, mobile and settled tribes and complex societies as well adapted to earth as any around the world. The great continent of Africa, where humanity in all likelihood originated from, was populated by ancient and recent civilizations in addition to an incredible diversity of societies, ranging from small with far-reaching trade systems, to large with legacies of pyramid-building and expansive earthen-works. The extreme western expanses of greater Asia, including the Mediterranean Sea touching north and south, east and west, that would become known as Europe had emerged from internecine, militaristic development into diverse competing nations encompassing civilizations noted for monumental architecture and wonderful arts telling of a storied past of great empires. Leaders and movements were resplendent among all these societies from the two hemispheres, making for a good historical-comparative, sociopolitical vantage point like the eye of the eagle, from which to view the unfolding events of this worldwide story.

Beautiful societies and sophisticated civilizations of Indigenous peoples and nations in the Americas are little discussed in the sociopolitical histories of great universities and scholars, who represent the strong states of the western world of 1500 in observing the Renaissance, religious Reformation, citizens in Civil Society and powerfully productive economic Capitalism. Deep scholarship is developed and taught with alacrity and precision only in observing the 500-year rise and fall of colonial European Empires and American world trade systems.

Similarly, the struggles and social movements of African peoples brought to be slaves, ethnic immigrants in servitude and oppressive working classes, or Asians as forced labor then banned from immigrating, are at best represented as contributing to America, at worst as inferior, while the Anglo or White

DOI: 10.4324/9781003315087-1

Introduction: 1492 – Two Worlds, Two Hemispheres of Many Societies, Many Nations of 1492

Anacaona, beautiful and deeply disciplined in verbal and martial arts, dutifully performed final ceremonies preparing her for shared leadership of *Xaragua*, a rich kingdom of mountainous *Ayiti* southwestern region, stronger in the arts and Taino philosophy than the rolling lands of *Kiskeya*, the eastern region. Each of the five kingdoms, ranging from hundreds of thousands to a million residents, developed multiple townships interconnected in trade networks that extended across the seas to other Arawakan peoples on islands and coastal areas throughout the seas the Spanish would come to call the Caribbean, steeped in a prophecy of strange men bringing great change, encompassing two connected continents making up a western hemisphere the Europeans would come to call the Americas.

*   *   *

Moctezuma Xocoyotzin prepared altars for *Mexica* nobility sacrifice of *Tlaxcalans*, an enemy city-state, rebellious and independent from a Triple Alliance empire ranging throughout central valleys of what the Spanish would call Mexico, prophecy of *Quetzalcoatl* returning from an East bringing death and destruction. The central valleys were peopled by 20 millions and more, controlled by a great Aztecan capitol city Tenochtitlan, extending trade to land of Condors in the South, where *Inka* governors ruled from highland centers, and to land of the Eagles far North, civilizations of *Anasazi* preceding Canyon de Chelly inland to where *Cahokia* urban networks flourished, to sociopolitical civilizations of Mound-building peoples, multinational coalitions along the eastern seaboard.

*   *   *

Oceti Sakowin representatives from 28 council fires met on Dakota lands – *Mde'wakantowan* of the four *Isantee* oyate (eastern), *Illahanktowan* (northern) and *Ihanktowan* (southern), flanked by the *Teton Lakota* oyate (seven western), where leaders came to consensus on important issues facing the people, in a year of a double moon blocked from view (1492) when 'wind shakes off leaves' October. Eyapaha from their Menominee relatives brought word of visions from one known as *Deganawida* who had united *Haudenosaunee* into Confederation of five council fires or nations, reaching plurinational consent, sending diplomat *Ayenwatha* to the great waters to learn of men coming from the East. Two great gatherings, confederations of Native Nations, sent emissaries across Turtle Island.

*   *   *

Túpac Inca Yupanqui retired for ceremony in a sacred temple *Coricancha*, representing Cuzco, the regional metropole of nearly a quarter million residents and capitol for the Inka empire extending northward to the new city of Quito and southward to the mines near current Santiago, where gold was sent to ornate administrative centers, and used for trade. Many southern Indigenous nations, *Mapuche* and other tribes resisted incorporation into the mountainous oceanic power of the Inka, where spiritual leaders, *Machi* grandmothers were organized in relational family clans who met in *Rukas*, where they coordinated 300 years of resistance in lands Spanish called *Arauco* Chile, with prophecy from healers strengthening leaders like *toqui Lautaro* defeating Conquistadores, still fighting to this day.

*   *   *

Figure 1.1 Eight biographies from two worlds each with four society leaders.

Cristóbal Colón prepared for his voyage into the unknown western Atlantic, finally authorized by the Spanish Crown who had finished driving out the Moorish architects and armies that had conquered and controlled the Iberian peninsula for centuries, and while purging Spain of Jews and Muslims through massive deportation and tortures of the Inquisition. The King was willing to employ a few caravels to attempt to find trade routes not controlled by other European powers. Columbus knew of political risks from success as well as failure, earlier betrayed by the King of Portugal who sponsored him on islands off the African coast, but also made a failed attempt to cross the southern Atlantic, under the watchful eyes and prophetic ideologies of God and Country, the Church in Rome.

* * *

Rodrigo Borgia conducted Christian Mass preparing to become a Catholic Pope, in the Vatican, changing names to Alexander VI, sponsored by trade merchants, Bishops and a powerful Borgia family, needing to reward his sponsors in Spain and Italy who paid great fortunes for elections, wanting financial favors and political positions for their relatives in the northern Mediterranean. Borgia's sponsors from merchant city-states were exerting hegemonic control over shipping trade increasingly contested by Portuguese in the Atlantic, coming under threat from the routes through Constantinople first separated in the great Schism of 1054, and overrun by an Ottoman empire decades earlier, hardening centralization of church and state in Rome, with Reconquista of Iberia and northern Europe.

* * *

Charles VIII Valois, King of France and **Henry VII Tudor** of England, signed the Peace of Étaples in northern France in November 1492, launching a modern period of French and north European advancement, including early reforms of the church, monetary policy, agreements on state expansion into newly 'discovered' regions in competition with Spanish, Portuguese and later a Dutch fleet of privateers and trading companies. This logical extension of Charlemagne's defunct Holy Roman Empire produced state economies, distinct from Mediterranean powers, later engaging with American colonialism in resource extraction, militaristic land-based settler colonies destroying Native Nations, creating north Atlantic racialized African slave markets, Protestant underpinnings of capitalism.

* * *

Sonni Ali was coming to an end of 25 years of rule, starting the Songhai Kings, in 1492 Africa; like earlier kings he was Muslim, although his kingdoms allowed conquered neighboring states, including what remained of the Mali Empire, to retain their cultures, as with the *Akan Ashanti* advanced economy based on gold bars and commodities traded with Moors and states of Africa. Sonni worried about Portuguese trade and forts growing along what many referred to as the new Ghana that Europeans called the Guinea or Gold Coast, building trading post coastal settlements, as at *Anomansah*, renamed in 1481, where the King of Portugal's fleet completed Elmina Castle, controlling mineral commodities and later becoming a primary port from which to ship enslaved Africans across the Atlantic.

* * *

End of the four by four on two continents – introduction by James Fenelon (May 2018–June 2020).

Figure 1.1 (Continued)

immigrants are typified as builders of the nation, whose families work hard in the land of opportunity with freedom for all (or most of them, anyway).

Leaders of Native Nations resisting invasion and occupation, Black social movement leaders of ex-slaves and oppressed minority communities and Latinx coalition leaders are not given respect to similar figures of the hegemonic, White male-dominated society, who are called Founding Fathers or great presidents, even when they rose in rebellion against the United States. Racially constructed laws of separation, slavery and suppression are rarely considered in how they created a fabulously wealthy society that rich white Americans could credit to themselves.

Figure 1.2 Great Indigenous leaders of the Americas, around 1492. (a) Anacaona – Cacique of Xaragua (original artist rendition). Original artwork by Jayelle (jayeelleart@gmail.com) to replace Cacique (Chief) Taina, indigenous of Hispaniola, from Irving's book, Vida y Viajes de Cristobal Colón. Public domain source: Vida y Viajes de Cristobal Colón. (b) Mochtezuma II – Aztec ruler. Houghton Library, Public domain, via Wikimedia Commons. (c) Ayenwatha – Haudenosaunee confederation. Related names: U.S. Department of the Army Ray, ArthurCassedy, John Irving, AAment, James EDavis, Roy TascoHolman, Emily ElizabethSchneider, Thomas FranklinRosenthal, James, field teamPrice, Virginia B, transmitterOtt, Cynthia, historianBoucher, Jack E, photographer Lavoie, Catherine C, project manager Price, Virginia B, transmitter, Public domain, via Wikimedia Commons. (d) Túpac Inca Yupanqui - Inka emperor. Incialemantos, CC BY-SA 4.0 https://creative commons. org/licenses/ by-sa/4.0>, via Wikimedia Commons.

Figure 1.2 (Continued)

What the social sciences must do in the 21st century after a half millennia of racialized capitalism now contested throughout the world and in the streets of the dominant state itself, facing dual threats of climate change in the Anthropocene and wars between competing nations, is recognize the struggles of the past 500 years in a balanced and truly comparative way. I can find no better method of achieving this, than present the leaders of nations and movements from all sides and diverse perspectives, as we have started in the introductory chapter of this book.

Two worlds, complex societies among the great diversity around the globe we call Earth, stood ready to come into contact and conflict, in the year 1492 using a Roman Julian calendrical system. From this contact into conflict would emerge a modern world-system (Wallerstein, 2004) of European dominance and power, building to industrial capitalism from four foundations – first, taking of vast new lands and valuable resources from Native Nations (Thornton, 1998); second, reduction of whole populations into race-based slave labor (Cox, 1959); third, creation of agricultural to industrial capitalism using new, unequal transoceanic trade systems; and fourth, developing of global economies through corporate-state relationships that colonized the world.

While Euro-American domination has created a hegemonic history of how these world-shaping events came to be, and "western" philosophies of higher education have perpetrated mythical constructions of simple

Figure 1.3 Leaders of the European – West African half hemisphere around 1492. (a) Cristóbal Colón – Navigator to Americas. Sebastiano del Piombo, Public domain, via Wikimedia Commons. (b) Henry VII – King of England. Public domain, via Wikimedia Commons. (c) Alexander VI (Borgia) – Roman Catholic Pope. Cristofano dell'Altissimo, Public domain, via Wikimedia Commons. (d) Sonni Ali – King of Songhai empire. Original artwork by Josif Collazo (7/27/22) from related Wikimedia Commons imagery.

political democracies and competitive economies (Wolf, 1982) in social fact, the modern world-system relied on massive genocides of Native peoples (Stannard, 1992) and construction of racialized slave markets (Resendez, 2017) trading across continents and oceans (Davidson, 1980) that along with vast wealth transfers and complex hierarchical social structures helped to create the global capitalism we know today (Arrighi, 1994).

That is the story or essence of this book – that we must start by reorienting these worlds into equal footings grounded in the societies and civilizations that preceded them.[1] We begin by observing four well-developed societies in the Americas in contrast or comparison to four highly structured societies in the western Euro-African regions of the world. In many ways, this initially becomes a contrast of Caribbean with Mediterranean societies, with northward growth that evolves from large systems of tributary conquest, commonly backed up by religious ideologies, into great colonizing systems that perpetuate European forms of civilization above all others, creating supremacist ideologies that rationalize and undergird these world-systems of racism. These hegemonic states' economies, often going to war with one another, produced mercantile, industrial and ultimately global corporate capitalism (Robinson, 2016), under the ideologies of Euro-American or western civilization.

We can take two observations from this – first is that European political expansion was global from its onset 1492–1542, and second that economic domination and growing capitalism in these time frames is predatory and maximizes unequal exchange and inequality at its start. However, we get ahead of ourselves in this story – we need to start with straightforward comparisons of these two worlds, but unlike western oriented beginnings with Columbus and Christian states of Europe, we should (equalize) our stories to begin with the social worlds of a western hemisphere (Mann, 2011) using theory from Indigenous peoples (Deloria, 1995, 1979) and French West Indies racial perspectives (Frantz Fanon, 1952; Aimé Césaire, 1955), the East (Edward Said, 1978) tempered in elimination of Native Nations (Deloria and Lytle, 1984) that Eric Wolf (1982) titles "people without history."

Hundreds of nations ranging from great civilizations to relatively small (transhumant) nomadic societies existed throughout the Americas for thousands of years easily comparable to those of European origin, or those preceding on the African continent, and relative to the most ancient largest civilizations of China and India. These Indigenous nations (on "Turtle Island")[2] civilizations and Native societies (of the Americas) need to be re-humanized and understood within the same constructs that social science has developed for its western civilization origins.

At least four locative perspectives toward Indigenous peoples, nations, empires or societies, fully developed as advanced social systems, or conversely in close relations to earth and nature, represent both the diversity

---

Ayiti – Bohio – Kiskeya

The large island of 1492, known to its Taíno-Arawakan inhabitants as Ayiti in the West, Bohio in the Central region, and Kiskeya in the East, held well-organized communal societies composed of five caciquats (nations or kingdoms) – Marién, Maguá, Higüey, Maguana, and Xaragua. Each caciquat was governed by a cacique (council leader or chief). Christopher Columbus renamed the island Española (Hispaniola) meaning "little Spain" in December, 1492, after he anchored off the northern shore. Christmas Eve near modern Cap-Haïtien, his flagship Santa Maria sank off an inlet Columbus later named La Natividad. The Taíno cacique, Guacanagarí, allowed Columbus to leave 39 men behind at the settlement of Natividad, who systematically abused the locals in their search for gold, and taking of women and girls. On his return with an invasion fleet in 1493, Columbus found the fort destroyed and moved a coastal base of operations 70 miles east to establish La Isabela, the first permanent Spanish settlement in the Americas.

There were between 2 to 5 million Taíno people living within the five nations in 1492, with other estimates of 5-7 million (Stannard, 1992; Sale, 1991), and revisionist estimates below a million, downward numbers made 200–500 years later (see ch.2 notes v, vi, vii). The first European eye-witness observer Bartolomé de las Casas, estimated more than 3 million Taíno over the island, which appears to be confirmed in Columbus's logs that count a thousand inhabitants of most villages, a few thousand in many and three thousand in at least one central township with a cacique, where he observes "densely populated" areas with "cultivated" lands and a "beehive" of townships. Already partially depopulated through conquest, enslavement, disease and domination, a 1496 census run over Kiskeya half of the island, counting only the healthy labor force above 14 years of age, found 1.175 million persons, when extrapolated to children and doubled seems to support a minimum of 3 million residents, two to three years after invasion.

Columbus and other chroniclers found the Taíno to be physically well-formed, generous to a fault, gregarious people living in the most beautiful environment with an abundance of food sources, so that they refer to it as paradise and superior to social life in Spain. Later they would learn of deeply artistic and creative people of Xaragua, under the leadership of Bohechío with his poetess warrior sister Anacaona married to the more martial leader Caonabo of Maguana, and of trading partners within the Marién, Maguá, and peaceful Higüey nations. The sea or ocean going canoes that rescued the Santa Maria ranged throughout the Caribbean, with great growing fields and fisheries, hatcheries, forests, granaries and domesticated animals. Women held household control and could rise to leadership and governing councils, with all persons having civil rights and universal education for children from families irrespective of social position. Minerals were surface mined for purpose, used as ornaments, and possessions were shared with no suffering or poor among the villages. Warfare was rare and primarily defensive, with great care given to families and relatives, seeming to practice the cardinal virtues of their more northern neighbors – reciprocity, generosity, bravery, and fortitude. Sufficient rainfall and fresh water combined with incredibly rich soils for an agricultural productivity out-shown only by the social structures with regard for all members of their society.

Ayiti was as close to human social paradise as existed anywhere in the world of 1492.

Figure 1.4 Ayiti – Bohio – Kiskeya (Española in 1492 Caribbean).

and the sophistication of the two continents we call the Americas, and strongly resist a European invasion followed by colonization, to defend their ways of life.

First, and foremost, are complex Arawakan societies of the Caribbean, especially large island nations of *Ayiti* or *Kiskeya*, with sea trade routes throughout the region, vast forests and agricultural systems including surface mining systems, and incredibly dense and diverse sociopolitical relations that allowed for local leadership to work for communities while part of a larger nationalist coalition. These are easily equivalent (though different in shape and structure) to late-15th-century Mediterranean societies, who would come in conquest and domination.

Second, in stark contrast, are highly centralized city-states (Triple Alliance under Azteca empire) in central Mexico, with one of the largest urban capitals in the world, standing armies, universities and vast trading networks to the northern continental and southern coastal continent regions (to the Inka) of nearby nations and societies. The Aztecan alliance are like Greek city-states, preceded by Toltecs, Mayan or Teotihuacan urban complexes, equivalent to the Roman or Egyptian temple pyramid building societies centuries earlier in Euro-Asia Africa.

Third, far north and eastward, are extremely sophisticated sociopolitical confederations of five or more nations called the Haudenosaunee, creating a quasi-democracy of bicameral governance that provided a common defense and internal solidarity while allowing different cultures and societies to coexist in peace and mutual prosperity, giving wealth and stability to a region previously full of internecine warfare, with great influence over the surrounding nations. This confederated alliance is equivalent to many city-state alliances of the ancient world.

The fourth social system represents de-centralized peoples, living in sometimes mobile communities, yet able to mobilize forces resistant to invasion and domination, in environments of southern regions of the American continent from coastal, riverine and plains peoples of the Mapuche to mountainous redoubts of Pehuenche, with a deep spirituality close to the earth in four directions, the cosmos and ceremonies that reflect their far northern relatives awaiting arrival of the horse to change their social relations forever. Both in adaptability and mobility these peoples, like those from the Dakotas, are perhaps equivalent to the Mongols, or the strong pre-conquest Gaelic Irish centuries earlier, and their Norse relatives in Scandinavia.

We will return to these peoples, nations, civilizations and societies – and many others in the Americas – when we more fully understand the European (and African) peoples and nations that will invade, destroy, dominate and exploit this hemisphere, and in their wake build wealthy countries that came to colonize much of the world over a *longue durée* of the last 500 years.

The Axes of European Nations, Mercantile Capitalism and Colonization

There are four major axes of powers around 1492 that are central to the development of conquest capitalism, racism and colonialism over the first era of the invasions of the Americas.

First and foremost is a newly emerged Portugal – Spain complex of the Iberian Peninsula, engaging in competitive expansion westward over the Atlantic, including agency of Columbus. Second is a centralization of Catholic religious authority in the Vatican, Rome, returning from Constantinople in building a state-based, quasi-imperial Christianity, at least partly made from great mercantile trade in the Mediterranean, and helping to launch the European Renaissance. Third is France, having controlled the Vatican as Europe's largest country economy, increasingly turning to and fighting England and other northern European powers, creating socio-economic relationships of empire, stoking the Protestant revolt or revolution, realigning relations between church, state and capital that would forever alter growing hegemonic systems on a global level. The fourth critical development, a direct outgrowth of the early Mediterranean expansion, is penetration of the northwest African coastal nations, and empires, over resource exploitation, including human slave labor for plantations, connected to a very destructive colonialism that would erode the internal social structures and sap the economic bases of African civilization.

Europe – America cross Atlantic hemispheres of 1492

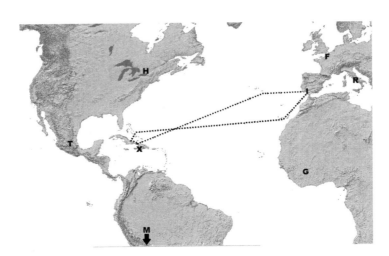

Figure 1.5 Europe – America (4×4 nations, Columbus voyage) transatlantic, 1492. Map adapted by Juan Aviles, graduate student at CSUSB.

H = Haudenosaunee nations (five or six) and O = Oceti Sakowin nations (seven or 28)

T = Tenochtitlan (Aztecs Triple Alliance, city states and nations, tributary)

X = Xaragua of Ayiti (Hispaniola as central Caribbean power)

(M) I = Inka (Cuzco) empire, and M = Mapuche (south to Chile, S.A.)

--> dotted line = Columbus roundtrip (Spain to Hispaniola)

I, S = Spain, and I = Iberian peninsula (Spain and Portugal)

F = France (northern, near Étaples) and E = England (British Commonwealth)

R = Rome (Vatican over Catholics as Mediterranean power)

G = Songhai (Ghana old kingdom) empire

Figure 1.5 is a map of bi-continental Atlantic hemispheres, four nations by four nations on both sides.

Historical Analysis: Methods (Approach Issues) and Theories (Social Problems)

There are four major problems[3] with social science research that considers long-term (*longue durée*) development of racist-capitalist systems in the modern world-system – first is a lack of **original agency** by Indigenous and other oppressed "people of color;" second is general failure to observe **nations**, empires or civilizations in the Americas preceding European invasion, likewise as induced back into African history; third is lack of **structural observation**[4] by Euro-American theorists relying on colonialist writings; and fourth is a continual devolution to a **savage versus civilized** dichotomy, especially when counting and criticizing Native-American (Deloria, 1995) and African societies (Mills, 1997). These four problems lead to massive denial or distortion of the social sciences (Graeber and Wengrow, 2021), especially works on genocide, family – gender roles and the effects of life-long enslavement over generations. They are also dismissive of contributing effects of stolen land and slave labor on developing capitalism.

To avoid such problems, I begin this book with the agency of Indigenous leaders from well-developed societies around 1492 comparatively historicized with Euro-African leaders, starting with the great *caciqa* Anacaona of the Xaraguas of Ayiti, where Europeans first invade, where Native Nations first resist, where the first racialized enslavement occurs, where the first major acts of resistance occur and the first successful revolts take place. We also consider how Mochtezuma II existed in a complex Aztecan society with a nobility from three different ruling nations overseeing a truly great city connected to one of the world's most developed trading empires that is taken down by the Spanish with violence that spreads along with disease across Latin America, creating new stratified ethnic populations. We observe the mythical historical agency of Deganawida as ancestral teaching of *Ayenwatha* who would unify the Five Nations of the *Haudenosaunee* into a powerful confederation that may have served as a governance model for the United States. When in communication with plurinational *Oceti Sakowin* they operated like the United Nations. And we see leadership agency in toqui Lautaro who successfully resisted and defeated conquistadors coming to Chile, helping to keep Mapuche society alive for 500 years, so that today they resist political domination by transnational corporations.

Let us turn to each of the Euro-African geopolitical arenas in turn, noting our explanation through applying limited agency theory to Columbus in the Portugal/Spain complex, through Borgia popes as the Catholic nations dominate using the Vatican in Rome, through Charles VIII Valois of France and Henry VII Tudor of England by making international treaties, and finally through Sonni Ali by acting among the last of the powerful (Songhai) Kings along the Guinea, Gold or Ghana coast of Africa. In each of these cases, the agency of the political leaders is only guided or understood by their relationship to the nations they rule or answer to, and in regional conflicts that create opportunities and tragic consequences for such fortunate sons.

By 1492 Portugal had been independent from the Moors for well over 200 years and, as documented and authorized by the Catholic Church (which gave Prince's rights to rule), independent from Spanish claim for 350 years. Portuguese ships had begun to control ports and some islands off the northwestern African coast, and developed a sugar trade monopoly on Madeira, with increasing traffic in the southern Atlantic. Portuguese merchants traded goods across the Mediterranean, and throughout Europe. One navigator from Genoa, Cristobal Colon (Columbus), had married into a noble family who controlled Porto Santo off Madeira. Between that and trips to trading ports such as Elmina, Columbus had observed how enslaved workers were brought to sugar plantations, increasing corporate profits for the nation, and heard of times and proposed routes to cross the Atlantic to reach East Asian trading partners, even as mariners had rounded the Cape of Good Hope into the Arabian seas.

The Moors, who extended Islamic civilization establishing university centers in Cordoba with trading fleets and an occupation of southern Spain, were driven off the Peninsula by 1492. Along with Portugal and coastal routes to Lisbon, Spain completed its independent Reconquista, becoming extremely martial and suppressing Jewish and Muslim peoples in the region. Cristobal Colon (Columbus) as an outsider had been driven out of Portugal a few years earlier, after pitching his version of proposed routes to the Orient. The emergent states of Iberia explored the Atlantic from the sociopolitical views of a Mediterranean environment. As we will see in the following chapter, conditions for creating transatlantic trading markets were nearly perfect, as were the means of creating inferior races, relating to the use of slavery and ethnic purges, and Columbus was well prepared for that project.

Mercantile systems for investment in trade were developing in northern Europe at the same time, the prelude to capitalism (scholars note Flemish and certain northern city-states of the Italian peninsula as finance centers).

Slave markets and slavery existed throughout Mediterranean societies, evident in Spain, and in Portugal with their increasing trade in north Africa that resembled the trans-Saharan slave trade of the Moors and other Arab states (Davidson, 1980: 59). Although there began to be racialization of African slaves held or taken by Portugal (Kendi, 2016), like Moors and Arabs, their earlier relationships with powerful African kingdoms, as by Musa I (Mansa Musa) of Mali, said to be among the richest of world leaders, maintained diplomatic ties with African royals. Along with standing armies of other African kingdoms and trade caravans through territory controlled by warlords, we can be certain that any denigrating racialization of African slaves were not so accorded to African leaders and heads of state like Sonni Ali, who presided over strong economies and state trading routes from the African interior to coastal lands.

Even after 1492, the French, English and even the Dutch were not (yet) engaged in slaving, while Portuguese and Spanish slave markets were primarily domestic. The mercantile system that was growing in western Europe controlled most trading operations, and would adapt to enslavement of Native peoples in the Americas and Africa, by expanding markets into central economies. Most states operated under Crown authority, which like official trade and other titles relied on the authority of the Catholic Church expressed through edicts and Bulls issued by the Vatican, authorized by Popes considered to be religiously infallible. Renaissance social change along with growing economies were already calling into question Crown – Church – Capital relationships, which were amplified after 1493 with the potential for conquest wealth from the Americas. While Madeira would serve as an island model, European nations created new forms of social control, extraction, profiteering and wealth accumulation through the process of colonization. Thus the interdiction of Papal authority from a corrupt Vatican would be most concerned with states gaining power and riches under the church authority.

These large systems were developing into racism for labor exploitation and land takings, mostly on the island level, under sovereignty by a Crown authorized by the Catholic Church. Control over important markets, such as sugar, was becoming another critical component. When word came back to Europe upon Columbus's return to Spain, the western European world stood ready to develop the most extensive systems of conquest colonization ever known, which used race as its central organizing principle, and was backed up by a religious justification associated with European sovereignty. Moreover, new forms of risk capital and accumulation would arise alongside banking, insurance, investment and wealth controlled by companies or corporations also linked to state sovereigns.

First Signs: Capital – Colony – Race

The first signs of developing Race in conjunction with trade, capital investment, slavery and colonies, could be found in two powers emerging from the Iberian peninsula – Spain in throwing off the last Moorish occupation in the deeply martial Reconquista, and Portugal, in growing trade links along the Northwest African coast and outlying islands.

In the first pre-capitalist modes on Madeira, the Portuguese used Canary Islanders, (described more like Caribbean Indians than Africans), where slaves could be gotten along islands and coastal ports that Europeans had developed, in what was later called the Gold, Guinea or Ghana coasts. Although picking up in number and economic power, this was little more than sea-going routes for trading human slaves, spices, valuable minerals (gold) and other assets, that Arabs had conducted from frontier-like areas of the inner kingdoms for hundreds of years. (Madeira pre-capitalist formation, see: Moore, 2009 and 2010).

"…slave trade of the Portuguese differed little from the trans-Saharan trade of the Moors," (Davidson, 1980:59), while Spain limited most enslaving to domestic markets.

Slaves from inner Africa could be seen as Black, (Kendi, 2016) or as Beastlike, although they were infrequently explicitly described that way. Slave markets and systems, including those found in Portugal and Spain, were not racially exclusive or driven – in fact lighter skinned European looking girls fetched some of the highest prices in these markets (Portugal 1492 had mostly traded in African Blacks). The racist ideologies linked to the construction of a less or uncivilized African was imported from the Americas after initial invasion with a development of racialized colonies. Actually Spain initially enslaved more Native populations as Indians than Africans as Blacks, which only started in earnest after 1518, coinciding with the early and massive disease depopulation. Spanish governors like Nicolás de Ovando persuaded Queen Isabela not to reinforce African slaves as they would resist and escape to join Taino forces, though that policy reversed in a decade.

However, Portugal had coastal ports and island slave populations already in place, and were more decisively expeditious in developing southern transatlantic slave shipping markets to Brazil which reinforced an initial enslavement on a massive scale of Indigenous peoples inland, with added problematics of conducting such operations on a land-based continent rather than islands. We need to understand the transoceanic systems of colonial enslavement and racism so as not to typologize or stereotype African nations and societies at the time, which the social sciences demonstrably do by the 20th century. Similarly scholars looking back have placed the first Black African slaves into North America at 1619 and afterwards, that is also demonstrably inaccurate, with slave uprisings occurring in Caribbean and Brazilian areas as early as 1519, usually done in conjunction with Native resistance forces, and various racialized policies including enslavement appearing in the Spanish held Floridian territories, most interestingly around St. Augustine. We will revisit these ethno-histories later, especially on establishing trading of enslaved Africans in 1619, but more in the context of its relationship to developing capitalism which initially emerges out of sugar plantations on the Madeiras (Moore, 2009), with sugar exported to European countries as trade commodities (Korzeniewicz and Payne 2019), controlling exchange prices and trading routes (Manning, 2019), as precursor for transatlantic trades including human beings (Conniff and Davis, 1994; Davidson, 1980).

Figure 1.6 First signs of capital – colony – race (Madeira – text box).

I have constructed these partially historiographic accounts from combinations of methodological approaches outside of the constraints of traditional social science inquiry, so in no sense are they simple additives to a so-called "canon" of European thought. We will return to the canon later in this chapter; however, in terms of methodology, after attempting to both make careful citation and to construct arguments related to previous scholarship, I realized this was slowing me down, and to an extent limiting holistic inquiry to configure to existing paradigms. In order to make a comprehensive, 500-year (or herein 250–300 year) analysis, I would need to proceed constructing this work in constant review of existing literature and paradigms (Graeber and Wengrow, 2021: 515) within more of a fully informed "flow" that I will relate at chapter's end to globalization. This is also a positionality statement, as a bi-cultural person with experiences in diverse nations of the Americas further informing my writing (Fenelon, 1998: 96–104; Fenelon and Hall, 2005).

In terms of a "canon" extension of the constrained, directive social science described above, with additional constraints imposed by modern universities, scholars must either draw from this body of knowledge or must defend their use of any other modes of inquiry or sources of knowledge (Connell, 2018). The best allegory I employ here is my experience with bilingual/multicultural education in the United States, where additive models were challenged and gradually (not everywhere) replaced by new models that centered other ways of knowing, and other geographic locatives, (i.e, Indigenous worldviews, see Chilisa, 2020; or Afrocentricity). When conducting experiential reviews, opening my mind to different psycho/socio-linguistic languages (Fenelon and LeBeau, 2006; Fenelon and Alford, 2020), I came to see original linguistic and sociopolitical geographies of differing peoples that not only shaped their worldviews, but also had been quite consciously suppressed or eliminated from the "canon" with such efficiency (Grosfoguel, 2013; Morris, 2022; Go, 2020) that merely entertaining such worldviews was considered unacceptable, or even heresy.

As Graeber and Wengrow state at the end of their magnum opus – rather than giving one's take on all (or even most) of the "scholarly views" of the modern world, or to "refute every existing interpretation" along with strengths and flaws of their arguments (514–515, futility) – I am going to "map out what we (I) think really happened" (Burawoy, 2013, 2021) over a half millennia of European conquest and colonization leading to an America that becomes the globally dominant hegemon bereft of the Indigenous societies upon which it was built. I do this while noting my own positionality, Indigenous perspective, experiential insights (Morris, 2022) and a worldview based on my experiences both internationally and inter-culturally.[5]

The Need to Reframe Colonization and Modernity with Genocide Studies

An area of applied social theory, very much discussed and developed in all disciplinary areas, is – has been – genocide and related topics, including ethnocide and settler colonialism, with much of my dissertation and first book on the Culturicide of Native Nations (using a single case study Lakota Oyate or Sioux Nation).[6] Some scholars (Gerald Horne, 2020) typologize colonizer's societies (and their historical location) making comparative analysis across broad timeframes very difficult if even possible. However, by using policy constructs and laws we can show how Hitler and the Nazis borrowed extensively not only from the Jim Crow South (even mainstream historians like Frederickson have long acknowledged) but also from "America's Red man" in destroying them according to law, creating reservations, which look a lot like early Nazi camps. Race and racism scholars had long been on top of this, when the Yale legal scholar Whitman came up with Hitler's American Model: The United States and the Making of Nazi Race Law (James Q. Whitman, 2017) that found the offending passages in the United States and their connections to the Nazis. This turns out to be important in trying to identify these trends and political actions over time that don't originate (but are refined) in Calvinism (transferred to both Anglican and American Protestant sectors generally) and passed along, some say intensified the anti-Jewish (and Muslim) laws and policies in late 1400s Spain, as in Duneier's Ghetto (2016), or in Winant's (2001) The World is a Ghetto. Thus ideologies related to White Supremacy, Black subordination and Native suppression are locked into a history of genocide and domination.[7]

Carnoy (1994) points out, "Throughout U.S. history, dominant groups have attempted to impose a set of values and norms ('ideology')[8] on subordinate groups." Trigger identified distortions of native peoples, originating from ideological self-interests of newly dominant groups: "As a consequence of ever more ambitious European projects to seize possession of American lands, native people were represented increasingly as savages, irredeemably bellicose, and the inveterate enemies of civilization" (1986: 255; Fenelon, 1998: 31)

Weber (1965) finds these are "institutionalized" within larger sociopolitical structures called nations, states and empires (conquering nation-states). These socially interactive "institutions" become the instruments of domination (Fenelon, 1998: 36).[9] Therefore, discussion of genocide is defined as the death of many people, with both intent and purpose, and is then applied to Culturicide policies. So in "genocides against indigenous peoples" Kuper (1985) states a complaint brought to the U.N., under the formal charge of genocide, which:

...alleged that the following violations led to the wholesale disappear-ance of the group: enslavement, torture, killing, massacre, withholding food and medicine, and destruction of cultural traditions. The response of the Paraguayan minister of defense was to deny intent. There had been victims and victimizers but not the intent: hence one could not speak of genocide. The admission that there had been a group destruc-tive process was coupled with the assertion that the process had been launched quite innocently.

(Kuper, 1985: 151)

Kuper uses examples from Brazil that eliminated native people "for exclu-sively economic reasons ... to take possession of the lands..."[10] and then states that "All the genocides of colonization would dissolve" without considering "any special animus" on the part of the perpetrators, using this reasoning[11] (1985: 151).

Jennings (1975) develops a discussion of the "cant of conquest" in Kuper's terms, with "rationalization for the invasion and conquest of unoffending peoples" of indigenous North America along the east coast leading to a his-torical "suppression of facts." Jennings describes Europeans as "highly com-petent in the skill of conquering other peoples" (15) ending with "They invaded and displaced a resident population" (38; Grosfoguel, 2016; Fenelon, 2016).

Stannard (1992) describes depopulation rates at the 95%, "working rule of thumb," and "destruction of Indians of the Americas was, far and away, the most massive act of genocide in the history of the world." Kuper, Stannard and the United Nations found: (281) "In light of the U.N. language – even putting aside some of its looser constructions – it is impossible to know what transpired in the Americas during the sixteenth, seventeenth, eighteenth, and nineteenth centuries and not conclude that it was genocide" (see: Fenelon, 1998: 39–40).

Horowitz identifies the need to "place these broad types (measurement scale of life and death) within a framework of state power rather than cul-tural systems," because it is state repression that applies the mechanism, and because cultural systems are the target, although the state can instrumentalize culture. By identifying policy as the unambiguous practice of that state power, we more precisely define models that transmute to other analysis and transfer to case studies of differing cultural systems. The question of instrumentation is critical to the choice of methodology. Horowitz (1982: 44) finds "Social systems provide a continuum; it is only when one examines the poles of the continuum the extent of differences in human organization becomes apparent"[12] (Fenelon, 1998: 44). I provide analysis from my last book "Redskins" concluding chapter (7) that ties together the genocidal location of the terms, and connects it to both Frederickson's "three racist regimes" in terms of their (symbolic) flags, and so trace the flow of these racialized ideologies and icons (images) through four epochs (Winant, 2001: 19–21) in global formation:

> The root of Redskins is the initial ideological stereotype of the Hispaniola savage, the fearsome enemy icon of the colonial conquests, the Hostile other of the Plains wars, and finally the caricature of the once feared but now mocked dangerous Other, compliant in being released in the gladiator's arena and told what an "honor" it is that the dominant spectators have chosen this image over the animals and undead violent gangs from the past.
>
> (Fenelon, 2017: 121)

These images and flags are not only commonly found among supremacist groups across the nation, but were ostentatiously flown during the January 6 insurrection assault on our capitol, making a direct line from colonialism to the present day.

Methods and Analysis

As demonstrated above in using genocide and settler colonialism, multi-modal problems arise in developing consistency when identifying, selecting and employing mechanisms of colonization and domination, and evidence to prove, or demonstrate, the intentionality of genocidal regimes. Therefore, we use legal and social policy constructions as prima facie evidence in demonstrating the colonizer actions, as well as intentionality. I observe policy constructs or groupings (clusters) within each epochal time period. These laws and policies reflect the movement toward racial supremacy in colonization, and the rise of supremacist ideologies in each time period, that act as direct evidence that the dominant actors – whether state, colonizer, government organization or movement group – were intentional and designed to destroy social systems and take life.

We also must demystify, or demythologize, these laws and policies, in order to determine their intent or objective (i.e., 1493 Papal Bull, colonial race laws, Louisiana Purchase, restrictive citizenship rules and civil rights laws; Bhambra and Holmwood, 2021; Itzigsohn and Brown, 2020; Fenelon and Defender, 2004). We question terminology employed or grand historical narratives that impose ideologies that may not be accurate. For instance, the Reformation (when named so) and Enlightenment (of, by and for who?) coincide with the Royal African Company (slave-trading) developing in between these time periods (e.g., see Chapter 3). Another evidentiary case would be genocidal wars conducted by English colonies, renamed to insurgent or resistance forces as in "King Philip's War" or to nonexistent inter-racial coalitions in Bacon's Rebellion (McGee, 2021). Both of these occur during the 1670s directly between the Reformation and Enlightenment time periods.

Such omissions are replicated in the U.S. expansion of the Northwest (Southwest) ordnance that included Indian Removals as operative genocide, with the land replacement of plantations, notably cotton, using slave labor, intensifying both racial policies (of enslavement) and genocide. Finally we have the outstanding example of California, where a renaming from the second epoch, from the Mission period disguising a violent colonization process, is/are actually intensified to true genocide by the United States, which was until recently in complete denial (Fenelon and Trafzer, 2014), that the University of California recently recognized in conferences held at Berkeley in 2020. Again, we observe a continuity of dominant and exploitive practices by western colonizers operating under the ideologies of progressive civilization that is far more likely to bring death and destruction to the Native societies in its path, than any evolutionary development.

The last point we need to make before proceeding to the discussion of the precursors of race and racism, and projecting a new set of frames and models for understanding and analysis of our modern world-system, is about the origins of the initiating voyages of conquest and colonialism, viewed comparatively with the Indigenous world of the Americas and its Pacific rim.

Navigation and Exploration of the World's Peoples and Civilizations

Kendi does an analysis of the grand explorations (conducted by Europeans before 1492) a huge service by identifying the chronicler of Henry the Navigator (2016: 22–25), who describes African slaves in such denigrating terms, an early racial identity imposed by Arab traders on their captives. However, the greater issue about to unfold is also connected to Prince Henry, who as a young man had commanded the Portuguese forces taking of Ceuta in 1415, an important port along the North African coast.

In addition to gaining access to trade routes for gold, textiles, animal and plant life, spices and sundry other valuables, Ceuta held libraries of the coastal maps of Africa, the Mediterranean Sea, Arabian sea, Indian ocean, parts of the Atlantic and parts of Asia (this is contested).[13] And similar to a treasury of knowledge the Moors had at Cordoba's universities were maps and navigation systems the Chinese had for much of the world. Henry's elder brother, Dom Pedro, returned to Portugal with maps including the east coast of Africa and recovered copies of Ptolemy's *Geographia* showing the world to be a sphere (while also contested, the main point is this knowledge existed), also mapped by the Chinese, based on Admiral Zheng He's treasure fleet travels on the oceans of the Asian world (Yamashita, 2006)[14] where some maintain they also traveled the southern Pacific around 1421.

Besides the navigational and cartographic knowledge needed to round Africa to India, and to establish a base of operations off Madeira, the Portuguese had enough information to consider a westward voyage across the Atlantic, to Cathay. Paolo Toscanelli (Markham, 1909: 136, 153) indicates this knowledge in letters to other explorers illustrating (supported by an otherwise specious scholarly excerpt)[15] the maps and geographies accumulated by Nicolo da Conti and shared (throughout the 1420's and later) through the libraries of Florence, Venice and the Vatican.

Thus it was Portugal that stood positioned to break the Ottoman grip on trade routes to China, attempting the dangerous Arabian Sea and Indian Ocean, while planning a voyage westward to reach the wealth of Cathay and the Indies. And it was Columbus who was present for some discussions, having visited Madeira's wealthy sugar plantations and the African coastal ports of Elmina and Guinea. Being rebuked by the court clerics in Lisbon, and betrayed by the King's ill-fated attempt to cross from the Cape Verde Islands (Markham, 1909:85), Columbus took agency to the monarchs of Spain, also in control of vast knowledge banks of Al Andalusia (the Moors), biding his time and place to request support for the epic journey across the Atlantic.[16]

A few major points about other societies with advanced seafaring technology should be made at this juncture of our analysis. First is that Zheng He's fleets of some hundreds (140?) "leviathan" ships, flagships much greater in magnitude than the caravels under Columbus, were indicative of a truly great empire (Frank, 1998) that might have produced a global economy easily the coming size of Europe's colonies, had it not gone into an isolationism, withdrawing and erasing global knowledge (like a "Dark ages" withdrawal in post–Roman empire collapse).

Second is that Polynesians were regularly crossing the Pacific ocean with great navigational precision long before Europeans did or could, but did not formally create conquest colonies.

And a third consideration is that the Taino Arawakans had ocean-going canoe vessels, manned by up to 80 paddles, with trading abilities and routes across the Caribbean, as did Indigenous peoples along California coasts, notably in my next book, the Tongva on nearby Pacific islands.

We bring these up as counterpoints to the great unfolding of transatlantic voyages, followed by invasions and colonization that were imprimatur to the rise of European, and then American civilizational powers creating capitalism, racism and globalization in their wake.

Introduction II – Time Periods, Precursors and Origins of Race and Racism

A nation created out of genocide and slavery, and the work of the newly dominant group.

Our nation was born in genocide when it embraced the doctrine that the original American, the Indian, was an inferior race. Even before there were large numbers of Negroes on our shore, the scar of racial hatred had already disfigured colonial society. From the sixteenth century forward, blood flowed in battles over racial supremacy. We are perhaps the only nation which tried as a matter of national policy to wipe out its indigenous population. Moreover, we elevated that tragic experience into a noble crusade. Indeed, even today we have not permitted ourselves to reject or feel remorse for this shameful episode. Our literature, our films, our drama, our folklore all exalt it. Our children are still taught to respect the violence which reduced a red-skinned people of an earlier culture into a few fragmented groups herded into impoverished reservations.

(Martin Luther King Jr.)

Mediterranean peoples had long developed systems of conquest and domination, including Egyptian, Greek, Persian, Carthagian and Roman empires,[17] to name a few, as well as large trade systems ranging across at least three continental regions. Some peoples were enslaved, and others were destroyed to the point of genocide, during these large sweeps of historical conquests. During all these civilizations, peoples from nondominant nations and ethnic groups would often be subordinated and treated differently from members of the dominant group. We can see these patterns across biblical times in the region, often with different ethnic peoples living next to each other, and some serving the dominant group, some pressed into slavery and others forced to pay exorbitant taxes or tribute to the government of the dominants. In this era, ethnicity could mean people from other religions, languages, national origins, tribal communities and even from other cities. However, very little social structure existed that used physical descriptors to encapsulate large numbers of people into singular categories, a "race" of people, and then discriminate against them by associating negative and inferior characteristics to all members of a constructed group.[18]

Race, and therefore racism as we know it, began shortly after 1492. Around Columbus's journey, indigenous peoples – "Indians" – were given special subordinate status as a "savage" or inferior and uncivilized "race" of people.[19] Within a few decades, European colonial expansion over the Americas developed immense stratification systems including slavery, colonization, genocide and cultural domination with race as a primary marking feature. By the early 16th century, replacement slave populations were brought from Africa, extending visible skin tone subordination along with ethnic origin into newly colonialized societies. Extremely oppressive race-based enslavement systems began to include both indigenous Indians and imported ex-Africans. The early 17th century integrated existing racial slavery systems for Blacks and Indians in the Americas, with institutionalized subordination by the English into the forms that we know today – race-based slavery for Blacks of African descent, genocidal domination for Indians of indigenous peoples.[20] These are the systems the United States inherited and built into the country we have today. Coming from these elite Anglo-fied systems are white ethnics – Irish, Italians, Germans and Jews – and other racial classification systems that have no foundation in science, but are socially constructed for elite domination, stratification and wealth production.

Capitalism in Racial Formation

As would be the case for many new nations (Iberian wars, U.S. Revolutionary War), state monies are often depleted after wars or major social upheaval, so the "post conquista' Spain that launched the Columbus expedition was especially hungry for development. Wealth was then held in primitive forms in that most accumulation was primarily controlled through sovereigns in their physical riches, valuable holdings or treasuries (Tilly, 1985: 169–170).[21] Spain itself was such a product of wars, conquering states and political kingdoms employing taxation systems, mercantile trading and legitimation through conquest of further wealth taking and production. The Castilian Crown of Spain funded three small ships as risk capital to attempt to find a shorter route to wealthy trading kingdoms of Cipango, Cathay or fabled riches of the East Asian *Indes*, developing transoceanic mercantile trade commerce in the process (ultimately by conquest).[22] This was an early simple form of global capitalism, created by forcefully taking Native "Indian" lands and natural resource wealth, and transferring it to Spain and other European countries.

Portugal had started early mercantile capitalist systems in sugar plantations by forming Madeiran trade monopolies (Moore, 2010) with capital separated from production, for faraway markets in Europe and the Mediterranean. Sugar changed agricultural markets and food consumption on a continental scale, requiring shipping across multinational regions, enrichment through banking investments and creation of secondary multiplier effects in port cities. Forced slave labor systems using people taken from the Canary islands and later along the African coast greatly reduced labor costs and problems such as uprisings or revolts. Racial systems on an island with coerced labor dynamics driven by capital markets caused island deforestation, changing local eco-spheres and depleting resources in relatively short periods of time. When such systems were replicated in the Caribbean, "world magnates" developed similar dynamics (Korzeniewicz and Payne, 2019) and great wealth for companies with no environmental concern.

Protestant 'reform'ation allowed northern European nations to create trading companies with wealth held separately from the state or sovereign with ability to tax, legalize land takings and militarily defend the new relationships. These systems are evident in English land-takings at Jamestown, sponsored by British East India companies renamed to the Virginia commonwealth, (Chapter 3) and Plymouth company settler colonies renamed the Massachusetts commonwealth, controlled through banks and corporate holdings, racially delegitimizing previous inhabitants – Indians – similar to and borrowed from the *InterCaetera* Papal Bull of 1493.

Time Periods – Introduction to the Four Epochs (longue durée)

The rise of racism correlates well with the rise of capitalism through different temporal periods. We identify four such periods – using metaphors for racial epochs – Indian, Black, White Other. The **first** would cover the time from 1492–1620 racial construction of "Indians" and "Blacks" with conquest and enslavement by the Spanish and other European powers. This begins after Columbus returns from his first trip to the Caribbean, later called the Americas, and European powers have grand debates and power struggles over which countries will have dominion over these new lands, especially after Columbus describes how easy they would be to conquer. This describing the inhabitants of the islands as *Indios* or Indians, culminates in the 1493 Papal Bull calling them "savage" and "uncivilized" giving Columbus and conquistadors rights to Discovery and conquest. Herein Indian becomes Race in formation (Omi and Winant, 2015), wealth begins to create mercantile capitalism under transoceanic colonization, which transfers vast mineral, forest and agricultural riches using primitive human trafficking to reduce labor costs to an absolute minimum. This period goes on for more than 100 years, and includes peoples ripped from African nations to be turned into Black slaves in the new world, lasting until English colonies begin a long transition from enslaving Indians and Blacks as people, into new forms of enslavement and destruction, beginning about 1619 or 1620 in Virginia. Portugal and Spain dominated this first broad racial epoch leading to people called Indians or Blacks, thereby treated as inferiors, as a means of exploitation, probably the greatest wealth transfer (intercontinental) in world history, producing surplus and capital fueling empires based on massive agricultural resource extraction and early industrializing of wartime economies.[23]

The **second** time period extends roughly from about 1620–1790 with England institutionalizing racial codification for its American colonies and nations. This process took shape from 1620 until 1690 (or 1705), creating a category for Blacks to be enslaved and all that followed, Indians as savage tribes or enemy nations to be destroyed or removed and poor whites as indentured.[24] Laws and policies were constructed to enforce new racial systems,[25] greatly enriching English aristocrats, companies and plantation owners with slaves, as well as larger colonies taking vast land tracts from Native Nations and incorporating them into colonial holdings. This system became increasingly centralized until the American Revolutionary War took over about 1783, give or take a few years. Key issues were that the English and Americans created and maintained permanent racial categories, deeming some people to be inferior to the supremacist English elite.

During this time, agricultural labor systems including vast and systemic race-based slavery, gradually transfers into urban-based industrial labor, which begins huge social change processes that would alter the world, producing urban growth (worker populations in U.S. cities) and early industrialism employing wage-labor forms of exploitation, and an intransigent working class. However, plantation-based agricultural production would continue as a mainstay along with resource extraction that would intensify and fuel industrialism. Concomitant with industrial growth of economies was urban growth on a massive scale across the globe, first under forms of colonization and later as transnational global capitalism that relies on strong, centralized states often waging wars for hegemonic domination.[26] Global colonization transforms into capitalism growing from resource and wealth transfers from colonies into the core economic powerhouses that also controlled early urban industrialism.

The **third** grand epoch of race and racism correlates with the American ideologies associated with the early and developing United States, starting in the 1770s with clear constitutional foundations for Blacks as slaves and Indian tribes and peoples as enemy nations set in by 1790. The next 100 years were increasingly preoccupied with a racial classification of "Whites" replacing or supplanting early Anglo-Saxon dominant groups that had excluded Irish, Jews, Italians and other white ethnics. This created national hegemonic dominance by race borrowed from English legal and social systems, which also had deeply encoded race, gender and class. These intersectional systems also influenced political construction of the country's citizens.

By the 20th century, after the Civil War had emancipated Black slaves but gave way to the Jim Crow south and similar systems throughout other western states, and after depopulation of Indian peoples and destruction of Native Nations by 1890, the United States of America had a racially divided and stratified system allowing for differential treatment and laws based on one's race. This system continued through the 1930s into global conflicts that became World War II, including de-emphasizing contested colonization into global struggles over capital and geo-economic hegemony.

In order to fully understand the hidden complexity of social forces in creating the United States during its expansion over North America, we must consider a *longue durée* immigration, in all its human and social dynamics – that of white ethnic immigrants, black coerced migrants, exploited nondominant migrants and Indigenous peoples. These are all interactional systems, producing the largest conquering/enslaving genocides the world has known (Fenelon 2016), constructing the most massive race-based slave systems of labor exploitation ever developed, (Cox, 1948) and greatest movement (immigration) of peoples across hemispheres and oceans, fueling 500 years of racialized globalization. The singular myth of a "Nation of Immigrants"[27] belies and denies inherent racism (Grosfuguel 2015, 2011) of only signifying dominant groups. Later immigration and internal migrations continue this process, with the Gaelic-Catholic Irish in two or more major time periods, per O'Hearn (Beatty et al., 2016)[28], Chinese and East-Asian pan-ethnic collapse of half the world's peoples, and recently of Latinx (Hispanic) peoples, especially in Mexican, Caribbean and Central American migrations and internal displacement, (many Indigenous peoples as well) mostly for labor purposes (Golash-Boza 2015).

By dividing the history of race in America into four distinct but related periods, we can reconstruct how we understand the social forces of migration or immigration, broadly defined. Here is one take (Fenelon, 2021) on that revisualization:

Immigration in this model includes Elite replacement and building of a main population as social construction – domination, that can be viewed as invasive (including language, cultural transformation), and as reinforcement

	Immigration/Migration	All Migration as demographic change
1 IMMIGRATION		Movement of people to other regions, nations
	Invasive	voluntary, forms cultural supremacy
	Reinforcement	Dominant and subordinated populations
2 MIGRATION		People moving across differing regions
	Coercive	Labor (indentured servitude)
	Forced, captured	Labor (enslaved, subordinated)
Settler Colonialism		Settlers moved into colony
	Internal (migratory)	People move into or expand over a region
	Internal (coerced)	People forced to move as servants, for labor
Displacement		Internal colonialism, neo-colonialism
	Forced, captured	People removed and moved for labor or land
	Genocide (removal)	Peoples destroyed or removed for conquest
		Created-constructed racial-ethnic populations

Figure 1.7 Comprehensive immigration model for 500 years (table: Fenelon, 2021).

Model for an interactive developmental visualization of immigration processes in the Americas: (Demographic processes identified in 400 to 500-year modern world-system of America)

(of dominant population). More broadly infused migration can be viewed as coercive (indentured servitude, non-citizen labor) and as forced (enslaved, captured, ethnic subordinated). The model now contains settler colonialism[29] as internal migratory (coerced, captured), and what is termed displacement (forced captured, removed), and genocide. All peoples are recognized within their subordination or dominance, and we can observe building of trans-national capitalism as a central, unifying force during all four stages.

The **fourth** and final epoch of racial construction in the Americas, which continues to the present day, takes shape in Europe's borrowing of U.S. systems of racial rather than ethnic codification and suppression, evidenced in the Nazi's suppression of Jews as biological inheritance rather than an ethnic or religious construct. After World War II uncovers the Holocaust race genocide at its worst (Fein, 1979) the United States asserts capitalist control of markets under ideologies of development and progressive notions of democratic freedom and justice, creating opportunities for Civil Rights Movements (Morris, 1984) and other challenges to nationalist racial systems, even as new race systems were evolving in South Africa as Apartheid, and globally in North-South dichotomies and in exploitation of immigrant labor. Intersections of race with urban class and internal colonialism were or are met with denial of racism (Bonilla-Silva, 2009). This period takes shape in the late 1930s, moves into formal processes in the 1950s South Africa and 1960s globally under a guise of neoliberalism in places like Chile, Latin America, markets in S.E Asia, India and some argue in wars in Asia and the Middle East, (Palestinians vs. a dominant Israel), exemplified in linking an African American President to "third world" countries (Bush, 2009).

The estimated periods of the **Major Epochs of Racial Construction**, extended to modernity, can be viewed within the lens of world-systems analysis.[30] Wealth from natural resource extraction and labor exploitation, massive land conquests and global trade systems enrich first European nations, then Euro-Americans. Conquest colonizers target explicitly valued actions or resources: over land in the 1492–1622 racial construction of Indians and Blacks for conquest and enslavement and the 1620–1790 institutionalization of racial codification to build colonies and nations; over labor of Indians, Blacks and (Irish) white ethnics to 1890; over resources of Blacks and white ethnics into the late 20th century, and a hardening of global racial classification to maintain hegemonic dominance over industrialized economies into world capitalism.

Within the *longue durée*, the simplified targets are over "Indians" – conquest for land; over "Blacks" – slavery and labor exploitation; over "Whites" – race and nation-building and over the global "Other" – empire and race for an industrial economy. Racialized structures are formed through at least four different epochs, and now seen through the lens of globalization. The 21st century is aligned along a polarized North-South of developed and "under-developed" divisions of people and societies.[31] In other words, poor, suppressed countries (as ex-colonies) are made up of what some analysts call "people of color" with racial connotations, while richer, dominant countries are European or Euro-American, with East Asian exceptions. Resistance is crucial from a global onset (i.e., escaped slaves in Haiti) and continuous through today as found in the U.S. marking Black Extremists identity and Native "Jihadists" in 2017.[32]

European dominant systems, taking centuries to develop, began in colonizing conquests over the Caribbean and then the Americas, where first indigenous "Indians" and later enslaved "Blacks" made up the lower orders of labor, with European-descent peoples making up labor and ruling classes, most of the merchant and upper-end working classes, and later the middle classes.

These systems and grand epochs must be seen as a whole complex – actually can only be seen as a whole – modern world-system since the development of capitalism is (partly) reliant on the great wealth surplus generated from resources taken by conquest and colonization of the Americas. Similarly a massive urban industrialism is fed by these resources and products (i.e., cotton) and develops markets for their industrial production (i.e., cheap textiles, iron goods, war machinery for continued conquest and colonization). Thus racialized conquest enslavement develops and institutionalizes profits from cheap labor and a racialized global division of labor. All three components develop concomitantly moving through phases of conquest, colonization and global capitalism, leaving a divided world – by colony, race and ethno-national class lines.

Structural Racism Theories (Using Race Critically) of Modern World-Systems

Many scholars place the origins of race in the ancient western world (Back and Solomos, 2000; Hannaford, 1996), while others have identified more recent origins, especially in the English colonies that produced the forms adopted by the United States, (1619 Project, 2019) critiqued as earlier by Horne (2020). Frederickson observes a "seedbed" for modern racism in Spain (2002) before, during and after the 1492–1502 Columbian voyages, and traces the evolution of racist ideologies from Black – White dichotomies in Virginia and the United states to policies implemented by racist regimes of the 20th century such as Nazi Germany and South Africa. Kendi (2016) places the origins in the mid-15th-century slave markets of Portugal (Winant, 2001), again primarily driven by a 20th-century racial dichotomy seen through anti-racism work. Others find emphasis in pastoral versus structured agricultural systems in colonial domination (Smedley, 1993) over the Irish (1999), as others have socially based ethnic discrimination (Steinberg, 1989; Montague, 1997), or scientific racism reifying race identification (McKee, 1993) published in 1776 by Blumenbach (Gould, 1981) into racial classifications.

This important and relevant literature (Elias and Feagin, 2016; Hochschild, 1995) often uses contemporary forms of analysis through various lens looking into the past – recent and further back into colonialism. As Duster (2015) pointed out even on the genetic level, this view usually means inducing racial categories of the late 20th century into societal interactions or historical treatment when these terms or identities did not exist, at least by definition or name. Genetic studies have advanced to the level where vast migrations of people across great continental land bases can be identified, but as all scientists now agree there is no measure to determine 20th-century racial categories (Phelan, Link and Feldman 2013) just as there is no way to determine biological race markers other than through descendancy (TallBear 2014). This leaves us with identifying the large social structural formations that produce the racial categories employed later for quite specific reasons for stratification dominance (Bonilla-Silva, 2015; Cox, 1948), land and labor exploitation (Barber, 2020) and supremacist systems that reinforce them (Bush, 2009, 1999). We also observe that these systems (Duneier, 2016), as Feagin and Elias (2011) observe, are coterminous with the modern world-system (Wallerstein, 2004) that is clearly formed in the "long 16th century" (Wallerstein, 1974) extending into the 20th century (Arrighi, 1994) having entered into decline in the first decades of the 21st century.

Therefore, while respecting the voluminous scholarly literature on the origins of race and racism (Bethencourt, 2013), we place analysis on systems that produced race categories in formation (Omi and Winant, 2015), during the centuries preceding the legally hardened 20th-century forms, extending into the 21st century (Bonilla-Silva, 2015; see Feagin systems, 2009; Winant, 2001). In this we observe growing global dimensions of race and racism, from its onset around 1500, that continued through the concomitant transitions into colonialism and capitalism that mark all contemporary systems of racism (C. Wilson, 1996) and structures globally (Cox, 1959; DuBois, 1961) covering a full half millennia (C. Robinson, 1983, 1980).

Of course, settler-colonialism discourse has started to dominate some disciplines (Glenn, 2015; Steinman, 2016) sometimes in referent to racialized capitalism (DuBois, 1940; as if any other form existed). Scholars often apply the "settler" term to many other analytical forms or theory – capitalism, the state, even universities, and so on[33] – which further complicates theoretical and structural analysis, since it is unclear when a person or people are no longer settlers, if they ever were (Allen, 1994). Within the Indigenous studies field this is a relatively pernicious problem, which McKay, Vinyeta and Norgaard (2020) attempt to resolve by reconciling forms of settler colonialism with critical race theory from a sociological perspective of racism.

We must note, as this book illustrates, that when settler-colonialism is instituted in the English colonies (Wolfe, 2006) of North America (foothold before going global) there are three primary powers – the State as Colonizer, Company as trading force and demographic notions of settler. This quickly becomes racialized in Virginia and Massachusetts, (see Chapter 3). In all other instances and processes of colonialism, the state (Crown, colonizer) and the corporation (company, trading house, investors) remain dominant players as power brokers, while settlers are racialized into a dominant population. Intersections of settler groups and racial stratification (Cox, 1948) are intimately and structurally induced and maintained by racialized colonial elites, (Lachmann, 2020) and later institutional and socioeconomic elites (Feagin and Ducey, 2017).

Studies of identity, policies and laws (Coates, 2019; Goldberg, 2002), scientific formations (Duster, 2015) and humanities-based frames (Okihiro, 2016[34]) will continue to inform how race and racism have manifested itself in western societies, even as we come to understand large, societally based formations that produced global racism over the last five centuries (Blaut, 1993, 1992; Robinson, 1983, 2001) in colonizing empires (Steinmetz, 2013; Go, 2009).

Boundaries of knowledge production around this intersection of rising capitalism, colonialism and systemic racism, imposed by social theorists and disciplinary perspectives (Morris, 2015; Graeber and Wengrow, 2021), can be challenged from within these disciplines. This includes a foci on (settler) colonialism (Go, 2016; Magubane, 2004) relating to contemporary empires (Steinmetz, 2013), as in formation moving toward hegemonic dominance (Robinson, 2016).

For example, a panel at recent American Sociological Association meetings – Race, Colonialism and Empire: New Histories of Sociology[35] – considered the Caribbean colonies reflexive relationship with the French elite and revolution, where growing (white) supremacy of colons from Haiti and Martinique (Guadeloupe) insisted on suppressing African leadership and the restoration of slavery. This ultimately forced Napoleon's hand in sending colonial fleets to retake colonies, and to protect Louisiana territorial claims (Persaud, 2021), precisely the end topics of this book (Chapter 4). This begins the next book (Chapter 2) where supremacist forces come to fruition in European colonies and are baked into institutional structures of the early United States (Feagin, 2000; Bonilla-Silva, 1997, 2015; Grosfoguel, 2016; Morris, 2022).

Another panel challenging dominant narratives – The Sociology Curriculum Worldwide: Decentering the Canon based in Colonialism and Settler Colonialism[36] – looked at how the same forces are presented in a "Canon" of the discipline by its foundational theorists, now being challenged by scholars from the global South (Santos, 2018) and nondominant sectors (Chilisa, 2020; Alatas and Sinha, 2018). They observed how systems develop or mature in the United States into racist, exploitive control over labor (enslavement), and in North American genocidal land takings (thereby denying "inherent" sovereignty; Fenelon, 2002, 2016). Another panel[37] – Global W.E.B. Du Bois and the Sociology of Colonialism – brought discussion into frames of globalization and theories of racism applied to coloniality (Quijano, 2000). So both the social sciences and humanities stand ready to advance this dialogue to the modern day, where racism, nationalism and socioeconomic domination are part of a critical discourse on global dimensions of capitalism, colonialism and racism in America (Morris, 2022).

Finally, critical race theory frames (Crenshaw, Gotanda, Peller and Thomas, 1995; Delgado, Stefancic, 2012) prove most effective in taking historical systems into account in contemporary world society (McKay, Vinyeta and Norgaard, 2020). This is evident in many reactionary forces (Bell, 1995) responding to, denying, dismissing and often nullifying these discussions, recently through expressing hegemonic histories with so-called "founding fathers" frames that restate a mythical past with an appreciation of racial dominance (Fenelon, 2021).

The president of the United States, as I wrote this, had attacked critical race theory by name, denied the underpinnings of the 1619 project, dismissed the critical discourse of racial minority leaders and nullified the progressive agenda of the civil rights movement by calling for a "1776" curriculum that stresses the nation's founders, such as President Washington, Thomas Jefferson and James Madison. These founders were slaveholders (Feagin, 2000) wanting genocidal expansion of the country – with European immigrants' "good genes" for a supremacist foundation (Blow, 2020) discussed in my next Book (Phelan, Jo C., Bruce G. Link and Naumi M. Feldmana, 2013).

Our discussion of the origins of race and racism is not meant to be comprehensive or complete; rather we have outlined many of the central theories and approaches for understanding racism. This work finds that race and systems of racism arise in formation from the social structures of domination and discrimination, which develop concomitantly with colonialism and capitalism, during European expansion over the Americas, and then globally, of the modern world-system. Ideologies and cultural practices also arise during these formations over the last five centuries, which exact social change that reinforces the dominant group, state or socioeconomic forces. Although not fully definitive for a unified theory of race, we can observe that racist ideologies, policies and practices appear to come from the structures put into place by colonizing forces, rather than the opposite.[38] Race and racism develop at the same time as capitalism and settler colonialism as they morph into the United States and its racial-ethnic stratification, perhaps best represented as a racial wealth gap (Lui, Robles, Leondar-Wright, Brewer and Adamson, 2006). We proceed through the case study–rich chapters for each of the major timeframes, or epochs, with that theoretical understanding as its basis.[39]

Return to Intersection of Race, Capitalism, Colonization and Ethnicity

European and later Euro-American ruling classes profited from vast land and resource takings, and later through industrialism, by controlling all aspects of trade and development, utilizing ideologies of savage or "uncivilized" for Indigenous (Williams, 2021) and of inferior "uncivilizable" for African descent peoples, later extended to most non-Europeans. From the onset race and structured racism were global systems, colonizing much of the world, and were instrumental in producing sharp labor and ruling class divisions among emerging world powers.

However, some scholars and analysts persist with identifying a development of the color lines occurring in Virginia and other English American colonies over the 17th century, starting about 1620 and through to 1670 and relatively complete about 1690, with some stating that indentured "whites" and Blacks lived on somewhat equal terms and co-mingled across the lower end of the social system. While this may have been true for some, but not all people in Virginia, hard-core racial enslavement systems were already developed in Caribbean European colonies, such as Hispaniola later Haiti, and were even larger in Brazil with the greatest number of Black slaves imported from Africa. All of these countries also racially enslaved and genocidally destroyed indigenous peoples as Indians, fully 100 years before the English colonies began to mature in North America (Horne, 2020). Race and racism were already operating on a continental if not hemispheric scale with different systems borrowing and replicating methods of exploitation and suppression, spilling over into other time periods, (1750 – German Dutch immigrants "sold" as indentured [Mittelberger, 1754: 72–76])

Another set of problems rise in the study of race and racism in the Americas and globally appear when we describe comparative means of suppression and exploitation, such as is done with Irish immigrants in the English colonies, and with the Catholic Irish (and so many others) within an Ireland dominated by England and Protestants (O'Hearn, 2001). After conquering systems were in place (Penal laws), England began assimilation through coerced education, (school systems) and civic laws on work and property ownership, maintaining class boundaries while suppressing ethnically and racially defined peoples. However, when Catholic Irish (Gaelic) immigrated to America they were immediately faced with extreme color line divisions —enslaved, exploited Blacks and suppressed yet surviving Indians – which many tried to overcome by seeing their racial identities as "white" downplaying their ethnic background (Allen, 1994; Ignatiev, 1995). While Irish and other eastern/southern European peoples faced ethnic discrimination, their relative position as being European-descent and thus white was far above the primary racially suppressed peoples (Blacks and Indians), leading to a hardening of racial lines even as ethnic origins were lessening. More on this later, for now we want to identify these processes as global phenomena, taking shape in Latin America and European colonies around the world.

Basic Points and Precursors to Racism

Racism is often used to describe the hostile or negative feelings of one ethnic group or "people" toward another and the actions resulting from such attitudes.[40] We need to remember, based on our structural analysis above, that these hostile attitudes are formed by elites for the purposes of bene-fiting from basic divisions of labor, land acquisition and ideological control over a population. Of course, there is often preexisting intense prejudice toward certain groups, which can be a precondition for full flowering of racism as an ideology (Frederickson, 2002).[41] One problem with discourse around "settler colonialism" is that it demonizes the settlers rather than the home country and colonial elites who managed the transition from Indian to Black to White.

Societies moved from ethnic differentiation, where one could learn a different language, change religion, become a citizen of another nation-state, to where some folk, based on inclusion in a supposedly inferior race, could not make changes to remove stigma and any limitations.[42] (When Spain instituted Jewish expulsions in the 1492 Alhambra Decree, some *conversos* were suspect and had to undergo purity tests.) Racism sees "them" as different from "us" in ways that are "permanent and unbridgeable" (Frederickson, 2002), with race understood to exclude and oppress the Other, and racial separation as a key component of the global division of labor.

We observe how the Iberian Reconquista starts the expansion of racism around the world. The great colonizing nation Spain acted like a seedbed for many Western attitudes toward race. Conflict with the Moors heightened religious zeal and increased discrimination against Muslims and Jews, in Spain and other Mediterranean nations. Both religion and appearance of ethnic differences were operative in Spain, but were not clearly delineated if people changed religions, as found in the increasingly violent actions of the Inquisition. Anti-Semitism became racism when a "belief took hold that Jews were both intrinsically and organically evil" (Frederickson, 2002), which manifested centuries later with the Nazis borrowing from earlier racialized systems.

Portuguese island plantations off the Atlantic west-African coast also developed early race consciousness, if not actual racial groups, which would feed the Brazilian slave systems.

Religious and national elites manipulated medieval beliefs about Indians of the New World that they were "monstrous races" or subhuman "wild-men." This made the inferior status of Indians much easier to produce in the main population. It also supported the basic dichotomy between civilization and savagery that characterized imperial expansion (racism) beyond the European continent. As the Inquisition raged in Spain and Europe, those who could afford certificates of "pure" Spanish and Christian bloodlines produced another precursor of racism. The (Spanish) doctrine of *limpieza de sangre* (purity of blood) caused ancestry laws to arise in a "New World" conquest and modern racism to develop based on descent, yet also created the restraining Laws of Burgos in 1512, retooled in the 1542 New Laws.[43] While Spain never fully mastered an institutionalizing of essentialist notions of race, the English did – creating immutable racial categories for enslavement and ongoing racial subordination in its American colonies.[44]

Race and therefore racism are roughly around 500 years old, emerging shortly after the Columbus voyages, and are still existent today, albeit in different forms. Although individual racists may well be ignorant and reactionary, systems of race and racism are the exact opposite – carefully constructed to maximize profit and control. Religion intersects with racism in the Papal Bull justification of racial slavery and genocide in the Americas, with 16th- and 17th-century Spain providing Western racism a "segue between Middle Ages religious intolerance and naturalistic racism" of the modern era (Frederickson, 2002). The result comes to be racialized immigration, along with coerced migration, in building the colonies of America.

We know there is no genetic basis to racism, although there is rationalization that unequal treatment is natural. There is no basis to identify biological race differences outside skin color, and even that system is often ambiguous. Skin color has no significance of any racial subspecies and is not evidenced in scientific studies, although scientific racism during the 18th, late 19th and early 20th centuries tried to prove otherwise, causing American racism to be somewhat unique.

Racism began before the United States was formed, first in Iberian colonization and later in the English colonies, and was an important part of the constitutional process, especially for the slaveholding states. English law allowed for an exclusion of subordinated ethnic-racial groups, (Irish Catholic) foreign nationals and women, making intersectional race, gender, class systems of discrimination (Collins, 2016). Denial of citizenship rights for Blacks, Indians and Women was central to the early U.S. unequal treatment toward gendered racial-ethnic minority groups. This system of racism was 'institutionalized' in the English colonies of America (17th century) and perpetuated in the United States. Therefore, depending on the aims of the dominant group, race is constructed differently for each of the following groups — "one-drop rule" for Blacks, (kept in slavery), a blood quantum for Indians to be eliminated as nations and a racial "purity" for Whites, including the previously excluded white ethnics, such as Irish or the Italians.[45] Later, we will identify a racial triad chart – White, Black, Indian – described in my next book.

It is only through studying these systems and deleterious effects on people, along with their residual presence in modern society, that we can start to overcome (our) racist past. Effective remedies to end racism, therefore, do not include a focus on "colorblindness" that allows denial, as in the tenet "If ethnicity is thought to derive from the blood or the genes, those of the wrong ancestry can never be accepted as sons and daughters of the nation" (Frederickson, 2002),[46] evidenced in the Nazi treatment of the Jews and the U.S. treatment of Indian peoples. Remarkably, we recently saw ancestry claims[47] in a contemporary "birther" movement that denied Barack Obama as a "true American" that placed his origin in a country of color – Kenya (his father) or Indonesia (his mother lived in, briefly) – while using his middle name "Hussein" in isolation, even though he was born in Hawaii, with his mother's parents from Kansas. This is why people continue to believe such outlandish racist frames (Feagin and Ducey, 2017).

Omi and Winant see racism as "social formation" that becomes a "political project" creating structures of domination based on essentialist categories of race. (Feagin redresses these as racist systems reproduced in various time periods. I call them racist re-formulation periods using different forms of essentialism.) This is especially clear as Frederickson identifies three major racist regimes of the 20th century – White Supremacy attained its fullest ideological/ institutional development in the southern U.S. Jim Crow South in 1880s–1950s, Nazi Germany between the start and end of the 1940s World War II, and South Africa between postwar years of early Apartheid to the 1980s. To reiterate, White Supremacy emerges from a colonial context to become a

SIMPLIFIED NORTH AMERICAN RACIAL NAMES and DOMINATION MODES

RACE or ETHNIC group name/term	POLICIES and primary domination mode
Indian – Indigenous, native, "savage" red	Genocide, slavery, elimination, colonialism
Black – African-origin, negro, (d-terms)	Slavery, labor subordination, suppression
White– European-origin, Anglo, (Irish, etc.)	Migration, super-ordinated, citizens/settlers
Asian– East Asia origin, "yellow" (Chinese)	Migration for labor exploitation, suppression
EURO-AMERICAN race/ethnic groups	HEGEMONY hemispheric, global
Latino – Mexican, south-American, brown	Colonial sovereignty, socioeconomic
Oriental – Middle East, Arab, Asian generic	Immigrant, historical enemy, trade partner
Other (global) – non-western or minority	Colonialism and stratified neo-liberalism

Figure 1.8 Simplified North American racialized names (categories).

global nationalist context in the United States, then Nazi Germany, and then in South Africa, as we will observe in the coming chapters and the next book.

Within racist regimes, Fredrickson (2002) defines the institutionalizing features of overtly racist regimes, as — (1) having an official racist ideology, (2) producing anti-interracial marriage laws, (3) segregation of inferior group, (4) lack of political office or power for minority group members and (5) unequal access to social institutions. We add genocidal elimination to these constructs. Racist systems (epochs) have differentiated systems for conducting highly racial subordination, achieving supremacy in the colonies and later in the United States — with blood quantum for elimination, hypo-descent rules for inferior group maintenance and purity rules for the racially white who might otherwise experience ethnic discrimination. Importantly, continuing well into 20th-century laws, the 1896 Plessy v Ferguson (Supreme Court) decisions found racial segregation to be legal, and formalized racial blood descent laws as delineated above.[48] Racism is thereby reproduced in U.S. laws and policies through the 20th and into the 21st century.

These names and modes are neither comprehensive nor categorically critical constructions; however, they emerge from sociohistorical locations of the American expansion over the West. Conquest and colonialism of the Americas by European powers produced these racialized and essentialist terminologies, while we observe their formation (in various "oid" racial categories). It becomes important to note that Ethno-nationalist differences were primarily used in historical Europe from whence racial terms emanated, where race is often connoted for ethnic differences (see Irish for Gaels under English colonization, Jews under German Nazi genocide and so on), whereas phenotypical skin color and bodily features are the dominant mode for definition and discrimination in North America and the United States, gradually infusing into colonialism, becoming global into Africa, Asia and the Pacific, and ultimately variations in Latin America.

The complexity of these interactive and interdependent systems of racial formulation, capitalist development and globally operating state hegemons, along with deep ideologies, makes it necessary to map out (Swedberg, 2016) the epochs and case studies for the big picture. We do this in the following section of this introductory chapter — Methods and Approaches — which apply to each chapter in a consistent, straightforward manner. First, let us recover how social theories and adapted methodologies interact with critical analysis over time and space.

A Word on Theories and My Approach toward Critiquing the Canon

We have covered a lot of ground in the introductory section of this book. This has special significance over my lifetime of responding to critics and supporters, to media reactionary work and in respect to social theorists who influenced my development (see: Morris, 2022: 2–4).

First let me address world-system analysis. After I presented "From Peripheral Domination to Internal Colonialism: Socio-Political Change of the Lakota to the Standing Rock 'Sioux'" at ASA 1996 in Washington, D.C. (Fenelon, 1997), I was approached by two world-systems scholars[49] about publishing the work in the *Journal of World-Systems Research*. We stayed colleagues for the next two decades where I interacted (published) with various scholars working in this area, ending in a presentation with Immanuel Wallerstein at the 2017 PEWS meetings at Texas A&M appearing to confirm the legitimacy of the Immigration as Racial Dominance Since 1492 work.

That presentation was introduced by Professor Joe Feagin, whose race and racism work greatly influenced my own, extending from my initiation with Charles Willie at Harvard, and going on to work with Aldon Morris at Northwestern (social movements), Matt Snipp and Gary Sandefur (at Wisconsin) and tangentially with other great scholars on racism (Eduardo Bonilla-Silva).

During other ASA and PEWS conferences, I interacted with critical scholars (William Robinson) over capitalism and genocide, where I drew from the scholarship of Cedric Robinson, W.E.B. DuBois, and many others (Oliver Cromwell Cox and the list goes on infinitum) extending that to colonialism first using C.L.R. James's work on Haiti, furthering that to Frantz Fanon and Aimé Césaire, (whom I briefly met in Martinique) and a host of scholars working on Africa and Asia. Also, I interacted with and learned from Chinese scholars and leaders for the Shanghai Institute (for foreign languages) and Japanese business and corporate leaders, in the mid-1980s.[50]

Finally I began to interact and learn from the global transnational scholars out of sociology, especially after Empire dinner conversations at the ASA conference in Las Vegas, of all places. Sociologists were advancing social theory concerning colonialism and empire (Julian Go, others) when I revisited important works linking sociology with empire,[51] finding passages that seemed to underscore the approach in my upcoming book. This writing stressed empirical observations or findings, using mechanisms that would work for overarching epochs identified in my 500-year analysis, and possibly improve or reconstruct some of the social theory around racism, settler-colonialism and the rise of racialized capitalism in the modern world-system.

> these political, economic, cultural, and social determinants should not be understood as mutually exclusive. Michael Mann, like Max Weber, rejects the idea of transhistorical general laws and pseudoexperimentalist comparison in favor of a more historicist (Steinmetz, 2011a) strategy that identifies contextual patterns and contingent concatenations of mechanisms as the sources of imperial strategies and forms (Bhaskar 1986). …
>
> (Steinmetz, 2013: 45)

Steinmetz goes on to say we should search out "empirical features" and or "causal mechanisms" (45) that we can compare across empires, societies and (I add) systems, which are different in formation and development during the periodic epochal conquest colonization of the Americas. The approach I employ uses concepts and suggestions noted and in the last ASA conferences special sessions on *Critiquing the Canon*. This appears especially relevant as the 1619 to 1776 debates rage, along with attacks on Critical Race Theory and with White Supremacy on the rise.

These hot controversies revolve around criticisms of and defensive postures toward a set of readings that actually make up the so-called Canon of social theory (Alatas and Sinha, 2018) deeply concerned with what all seem to identify as (however generic or specious in character) the "foundations" of America, including colonialists as Founding Fathers of the United States.[52]

This and my next book should prove informative to this grand debate, because it offsets works like The 1619 Project (Hannah-Jones and New York Times, 2021)[53] without feeding into the dominant narratives concerning 1776 and the Founding Fathers. Basically conservative and liberal political groups and their scholarly constituencies are engaged in far-reaching battles over what constitutes the foundations of America, without bringing up Native Nations or Indigenous Americans, who lived upon the land long before any Europeans arrived (Deloria, 1995).

In this approach, we need to use laws and social policies with identified cases (Ragin, 1992) as an evidentiary (empirical) base that otherwise is highly contested, and to show a global understanding of how mechanisms of colonialism, capitalism and transnational globalism created a world that cannot, even for its survival, contain itself or the effects on a planet on which we all live.

Methods and Approaches toward Each Epochal Chapter

Each of the epochal chapters will have four major foci over the exemplary cases, including:

Agency – use select people (elites[54] see Payne, 2020) as exemplary of the racial struggles, resistance and success or their survivance, with strong focus on the **original agency** practiced by Indigenous, African and "people of color" (Morris, 2022; 1492 worlds)[55]

Structural – dominant and subordinate social structures,[56] or institutional mechanisms, created or used to maintain profiteering through racial exploitation (changes in each epoch)

Event/Place – particular interactions, conflicts, developments, ongoing relations (unequal) that, while individually unique, share some characteristics of structures (event history[57])

> **Processes/Timeframes** – processual (Abbott, 2016), chronological frame world-systemic time, of formations, formulations, relevant to capitalism, colonization and racism in America.

The primary consideration is that exemplary cases, places, narratives, racial groups and global processes cannot be fully understood, or analyzed, in isolation from other interactive systems (Wallerstein, 2004), peoples, nation-states or modalities (Wolf, 1982; Lachmann, 2020).

These are, even at the onset, transoceanic and transcontinental processes and places, peoples and societies. In social fact, they are global, almost immediately, so that by the mid to late 1500s Drake and others are in the northern Pacific, as Magellan circumnavigates the world and Cook, others etc. are sowing the seeds of colonial domination and western penetration from Europe, east and west and in search of riches from the global south. Of course, oceanic trade had gone on earlier (Figure 1.9 Bali calendar with Arab traders and Indian Sanskrit), in Southeast Asia long before, as had regional junk traders, with great Chinese fleets also approaching the African Cape of Good Hope, Polynesians circumnavigating the Pacific Ocean, and Indigenous peoples across the Americas, and North Asia, for centuries, even thousands of years before Europe.

Each set of world-systemic developments, such as the Spanish sweeping across the Caribbean into Central America, and setting off similar penetrations or violent invasions by other European powers, creates incredibly powerful if not explosive social change – events and wars, genocides and new populations, great wealth and grinding poverty – that can be viewed within timeframes that we can, if careful, grasp as a whole. It is only until

Figure 1.9 Balinese calendar, 1,000 years ethno-nation overlay (courtesy James Fenelon).

they all begin to fully merge into truly global processes – colonization and capitalism – that we can observe these, and racial formation or structural formulation, in world-systemic time (Chase-Dunn and Grimes, 1995).[58]

That these systems, which create the modern world, are directly related to the formation of "races" of peoples proves to be fundamental to the development of capitalism and later global domination. These complex systems are best understood in timeframes – epochs – that cohere together in a meaningful narrative of globalization as a founding premise (Graeber and Wengrow, 2021).

Herein we must reimagine world-system history in terms of European expansion, invasion, colonization and occupation of the Americas, and hegemonic dominance over North America, and then most of the world – moving through two world wars and two world hegemony "wars" – which bring us through five centuries to the transnational capitalism of the 21st century. Social scientists now see a globalization process (certainly transatlantic colonization and a double hemisphere occupation by world powers was global from the onset and still is) through the lens of Flows (Castells, 1989; Giddens, 2013; globalization see Steger, 2017). These flows include: capital resources, people (enslaved, immigrant, Indigenous, racialized), technology, information and cultural or structural systems, any of which greatly complicate the presentation of this work, which tries to tie all of this together. As presented earlier, we employ four great epochs of time, in simplified names, to show flows of globalizing systems of invasion/conquest, colonization, (two overlapping stages), mercantile to industrial capitalism and then global dominance through neoliberal capitalism – each epoch closely related to racial-ethnic formation as racial dominance.

These epochs are interrelated to the growth of capitalism, which becomes the dominant global economic system by the 20th century (Robinson, 2014, 2020). Further complicating our analysis is the rise of newly identified systems such as neoliberalism (Chomsky and Pollin, 2020) that definitively grew out of deep, racist constructions of the English colonies into the United States as world hegemon (see: Wallerstein, 2004). Since we have identified construction of two large systems of racial exploitation (genocide for land, enslavement for labor) as critical components for the development of capitalism, we must include the early trading fleets of the Spanish, Portuguese, French, Dutch and English empires (see: Wolf, 1982; Go, 2009; Frank 1998).

We must visualize these continental and then global developments, flows, using time periods easily identifiable from their primary characteristics, and with a minimal number of exemplary case (studies) that illustrate the basic interactions of their spatial-temporal location as cases, and also where we can observe their connectedness to identified globalization processes (Go, 2020). I developed a chart on this: Figure 1.10 – **Methods and presentation of four major epochs** – Colonization of America, where I

Epoch Name/Time period   Case 1 (in time)   Case 2 (in time)   Case 3 (time)   Case 4 (time) a

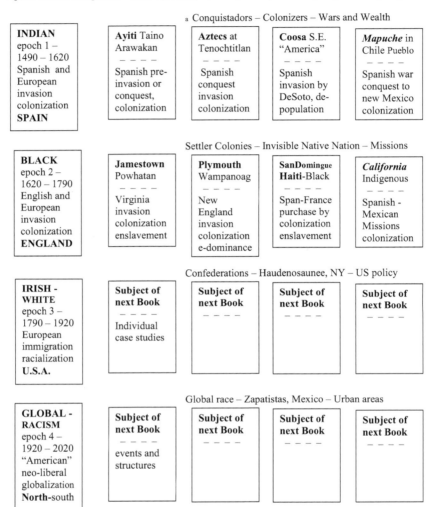

	a Conquistadors – Colonizers – Wars and Wealth		
INDIAN epoch 1 – 1490 – 1620 Spanish and European invasion colonization **SPAIN**	**Ayiti** Taino Arawakan – – – – Spanish pre-invasion or conquest, colonization	**Aztecs** at Tenochtitlan – – – – Spanish conquest invasion colonization	**Coosa** S.E. "America" – – – – Spanish invasion by DeSoto, de-population	*Mapuche* in Chile Pueblo – – – – Spanish war conquest to new Mexico colonization

	Settler Colonies – Invisible Native Nation – Missions		
BLACK epoch 2 – 1620 – 1790 English and European invasion colonization **ENGLAND**	**Jamestown** Powhatan – – – – Virginia invasion colonization enslavement	**Plymouth** Wampanoag – – – – New England invasion colonization e-dominance	**SanDomingue Haiti**-Black – – – – Span-France purchase by colonization enslavement	*California* Indigenous – – – – Spanish - Mexican Missions colonization

	Confederations – Haudenosaunee, NY – US policy		
IRISH - WHITE epoch 3 – 1790 – 1920 European immigration racialization **U.S.A.**	**Subject of next Book** – – – – Individual case studies	**Subject of next Book** – – – –	**Subject of next Book** – – – –	**Subject of next Book** – – – –

	Global race – Zapatistas, Mexico – Urban areas		
GLOBAL - RACISM epoch 4 – 1920 – 2020 "American" neo-liberal globalization **North**-south	**Subject of next Book** – – – – events and structures	**Subject of next Book** – – – –	**Subject of next Book** – – – –	**Subject of next Book** – – – –

Figure 1.10 Methods and presentation of four major epochs – Colonization of America (chart).

provide a simplified **Epoch Name**/time period along with at least four cases for each epoch – **Case 1** (Haiti) – **Case 2** (Mexico, New England) – **Case 3** (America as the U.S.) – **Case 4** (California, global cases); (see Ritzer, 2010; Ragin, 1992).

Epoch Name/Time period **Case 1** (in time) **Case 2** (in time) **Case 3** (time) **Case 4** (time) a

Mode of Presentation

Each content-rich chapter representing these epochal changes will use at least four case studies set apart in text boxes, which can be used separately from the global systemic approach herein. One set – Ayiti to San Domingue to 19th-century Haiti to late-20th-century Haiti – is found in each epochal era, as fully representative of the 500-year-period of study. Breaking the presentation into two books illustrates the critically important pivot point of the creation of the United States, identified in Chapter 4 as "three Revolutions and three Races in a new State." The United States did not exist in the 16th century, yet became a world hegemonic power by mid-point of the 20th century.

Another important presentational and methodological concern, which first came to my attention when reading Vine Deloria Jr. (1973 and 1979, then again 1995 and 2005) and later influenced by graduate studies mentors (Sara Lawrence Lightfoot and Charles Willie at Harvard) as well as Indigenous spiritual leaders (Chauncey Dupree, Mary Louise Defender) underscored now in disparate fields such as quantum physics and psycho/socio linguistics, is the personal experience and presence of the observer in any field of study (I write of this in my unpublished manuscript –Ideological Dominance Through Symbolic Icons: Los Angeles 1992). Because of this and the explanatory power of an author's experiences "in the field" rather than the research library or some metaphoric laboratory (see Morris, 2022), I precede or pretext each substantive content area chapter with a "personal statement as preface" to the particular chapter.[59]

Finally, I begin each substantive chapter with Indigenous nation/Native American cases, followed closely with African American/Black and other white ethnic discussions, precisely because these perspectives and histories are either left out of mainstream, dominant analysis, completely, or are subordinated to add-on analytics, as in terms of the "canon" (Meghji, 2021). Most of the rest of mode of presentation will follow in somewhat traditional format.

Identifying Colonizing Processes, Cases and Policies Producing Racialized Capitalism

The temporal periodization of the development of capitalism roughly adheres to the four eras identified here in this introductory chapter. Mercantile capitalism grows and expands with the racialized conquest of the Americas and wealth extraction from those lands (period 1 Indians) none more powerful than silver in the case of the huge mines at Potosí becoming globalization.

Quoting Adam Smith, Flynn and Giráldez (2004) find even one of the first economists observed "the importance of silver in stimulating world trade" along with China's markets:

> The silver of the new continent seems in this manner to be one of the principal commodities by which the commerce between the two extremities of the old one [Europe and China] is carried on, and it is by means of it, in great measure, that those distant parts of the world are connected to one another.
>
> (Adam Smith, 1965 [1776], 207)

Of course, the genocidal conquest of the lands with the mines and the dehumanizing enslavement of racialized peoples to maximize profits, in this book moving from temporal period 1 "Indians" in transition to period 2 "Blacks" in the 17th century, reflect a globalization of capitalist trade, racial structures exploiting labor and transoceanic "exchange" intersecting colonization:

> We label the 1540s–1640 period the "Potosí-Japan silver cycle" because unprecedented silver mining in Spanish America (especially Upper Peru) and Japan erupted at this time, contributing powerfully to the rise of the Spanish Empire and to the unification of Japan. The bulk of the Japanese and American silver gravitated toward Chinese markets, where extraordinarily high silver prices implied global arbitrage opportunities …
>
> The global production and spread of tens of thousands of tons of silver eventually caused global silver prices to converge by 1640, by which date the price of silver had also finally descended to its cost of production. "Between 1630 and 1640, or about 1636, the effect of the discovery of the mines of America in reducing the value of silver, appears to have been completed" …
>
> (Smith, 1937 [1776], 192)

It was during this first silver cycle that a global economy was born. During this 1540s–1640 cycle the "Columbian Exchange" and the "Magellan Exchange" led to staggering ecological consequences that unfolded over multiple generations. The intense profit motive – centered on the global trade of silver and manufactured items – had unleashed unintended ecological consequences throughout planet earth. In turn, ecological and demographic time lags impacted back upon international trade via fundamental alteration of both factor markets and end-markets throughout the world.

> (Flynn and Giráldez, 2004: 30–31)

What Wallerstein (1974) and others called agricultural capitalism – sugar, tobacco, peanuts, spices, crop exports like potatoes and corn, and cotton – may have started in the 16th century, but their boom economic growth transforming the world conforms better to the second time period (Blacks), with massive transoceanic enslavement of Africans in the 17th and 18th centuries for exploiting plantation labor (Wallerstein, 1980; Cox, 1959; C. Wilson, 1996).

Transition to industrial capitalism begins into the 19th century and is near full blown by its peak into the 20th century, completing the racial genocides toward Native populations, continuing the enslavement and then the subordinated labor exploitation of Africans as Blacks, with an increasingly oppressive reliance on class divisions to exploit the white working class (Allen, 1994) primarily in cities and factories using new immigrants such as the Irish (period 3) feeding global markets of textiles, food sources, timber products and ironworks that become the basis for empire and colonizing wars (Go, 2011; C. Robinson, 1980; Wolf, 1982).

New forms of global capitalism emerged after World War II where the multinational corporations (with roots in English privateers and trading companies) join with hegemonic states to control market economies, rather than drawing from colonial holdings (most of which moved for independence on their own). These forms of neo-liberalism (controlling markets and trade) employed hegemonic relations (i.e., the Washington Consensus) to profit over transnational processes that resembled earlier racial regimes when exploiting labor internally (Hechter, 1999; Jim Crow South, U.S. urban segregation) and when exploiting international divisions of labor, inequality and unequal positions of power (i.e., the global South and/or third world countries; Winant, 2001; W. Robinson, 2004). Violence was critically important (R. Collins, 2008) in these temporal periods and racialized regimes (Robinson, 2014) relying on ideological justifications of supremacy extending from the Papal Bulls through colonization and racialized capitalism.

Papal Bulls, Colonization, Capitalism of 500 Years

Papal Bulls were typically issued to reinforce Church positions on important social issues of the day and to fix sociopolitical policies and treaties over land disputes and international trade relations. The aforesaid Papal Bull 1453 (and 1454) was to authorize or justify policies or laws in newly taken lands from foreign, non-Christian nations, especially Moors from the Reconquista by Portugal (soon Spain as well); for new Inquisitions against non-Christians (Muslims, Jews, pagans, etc.) and to justify taking of slaves from these same nations, notably when from Africa.

While the 1493 *Intercaetera* Bull was primarily issued to extend these same reasons to the newly "discovered" Caribbean islands of the Americas (which will be discussed in the next Chapter 2), it did not include the Northern European nations that had increasing conflicts with the Vatican.

Later, it is specific Bulls and church laws, such as the selling of Indulgences and its connection to corruption over money transfers and national treasuries, that are challenged by Protestant Reformation claims, directly related to transatlantic trade and colonization (see Chapters 2 and 3).

This is why the so-called Doctrine of Discovery (doctrinaire in Deloria, 1995), used to subjugate Indigenous nations in the Americas, has limited explanatory power. Catholic Church rationales were rejected by colonizing countries undergoing the extremely violent transition to Protestant systems (England, Netherlands, "Germany" and France), yet the reasonings and ideologies of Discovery were retained (through periods 2 and 3 from 1620 to 1790 on to the 20th century).

We have established that Papal Bulls were issued in order to divide the spoils of conquest and colonization of the mid and southern Atlantic, pointedly by giving legitimacy and early monopoly over the west coast of Africa (and inadvertently the Brazilian east coast of South America) to Portugal, and all lands and seas further west into the Americas, specifically what became the Caribbean, to Spain, both with hopes of reaching the riches and markets of China. Gold and silver, buoyed by agricultural and natural resource extraction and development of plantations also for export to European markets, flooded the economic systems of the Iberian powers, and (as we establish in Chapter 2 following), began intense competition and conflict between state powers operating out of Europe, over these markets and riches, moving formally into the growth of violent mercantile capitalism. Competitive oceanic fleets were accompanied by the formation of companies and corporate structures answering directly to European states. Besides the legitimation of conquest colonization provided by the Vatican Catholic authority, ideologies were developed that rationalized the very violent destruction of Native populations, the takeover of entire continents, creation of vast markets and initial transatlantic slave trading systems that became central features of capitalism. Thus large global systems of racism were concomitant with capitalist colonization using shared ideologies of European civilization (Blaut, 1993; Wolfe, 1992; W. Robinson, 2016; Fenelon, 2016).

Deloria and Lytle are careful to see both church and state powers in naming the Doctrine of Discovery and Prince's Rights to Conquest (1984). Much later the well identified doctrinaire notions of "discovery" are employed in English law, deployed in its birthright nation the United States of America (Chapters 3 and 4), and in terms of conquest (Chapter 2 see Conquistadors) are also used militarily in colonization (Chapter 3) while invoking new ideas of dismissing Indigenous societies as pagan and primitive, therefore not nations or sovereigns (arguments made in Chapter 2 and in the treaty of Westphalia). Part of this dismissal or denial of violent invasion and Native Nations resistance can be found in emphasizing "settlers" (not state colonizers) overtaking Indian tribes as "savage" and uncivilized, used ideologically to connect to "western" civilization (religious domination). We discuss this in Chapters 3 and 4, (and further in my next book).

Many scholars and most historians observe this as early globalization, as others see globalization only through the lens of capitalism, thus placing it in the following 17th and 18th centuries, with some identifying the early 19th century as firmly capitalist globalization, with stable currencies and commodity trading markets reaching across the world. When we are fully inclusive of Indigenous peoples or nations already having crossed the Pacific, it is easy to defend the birth of globalization in the 16th century, leading to world social change on every level.

> Connection of the Americas to the rest of the world yielded ecological and social transformations of sufficient profundity that Alfred Crosby (1986, p.271) has depicted the post-15th century global exchange of flora, fauna and diseases as "a revolution more extreme than any seen on this planet since the extinction at the end of the Pleistocene."
>
> (Flynn and Giráldez, 2004: 31)

Moreover, gold and especially silver were flowing across oceans and causing growth of markets, currency exchanges and investments in the first corporate or company systems, as delineated in Chapters 2 and 3 of this book. However, the largest markets for silver, and gold, were actually in China and other East Asian countries, which could now be reached across the Pacific Ocean from the Americas. Thus some economic historians identify the birth of globalization as world capital in 1571, when Spain took the port of Manila and began the silver trade with China (Flynn and Giráldez, 1995, 1997, 2002). As we will identify in Chapter 2, silver mining literally changed global economics, and required both conquest modes by the Spanish conquistadors, and powerful colonizing racisms for enslaved labor by Spain and Portugal, later England, Dutch Netherlands, France and so on.

We see this played out on grand levels in Spanish conquest–colonization over Caribbean islands and coastal regions, extending over Central America, using Catholic Missions (church) under presidio governments (state) with military power (conquest, domination) for profiteering from land, resources and agricultural development and extraction (for capital economics). Racism is found in subordinating /destroying Indians through *encomienda* and *repartimiento* ethno-national systems of exploitation, where the church rejected early formal dehumanization and enslavement of Native peoples, complicating racist systems of slavery and genocide as argued in the church's Burgos Laws and Valladolid debates (see Chapter 2), which limited the formal policy systems of racial enslavement and exploitation.

The English had no such limitations – Protestants' ready-made notions of predestination and the Elect for ethno-racial supremacy and the (utterly) depraved for racial subordination, freed state and church from seeing full humans when undertaking genocide and slavery during colonization (Chapter 3) and new state formation (Chapter 4).

This is the analytical explanation for what happens in California, with Spanish incursions in the late 18th and early 19th centuries – although highly destructive of Indigenous cultures in the Mission system and toward Native Nations in presidios and military domination – attempting to rationalize their policies as "saving" or converting Indians, (Chapter 3 resistance, rebellion and ultimately survivance for some). When the United States takes over mid-century, it immediately employs genocide of Native peoples in the newly minted state (Fenelon and Trafzer, 2014), and racial apartheid toward all other non-white races, immigrants and ethnicities (Chapter 4). Indigenous peoples are wiped out, exterminated, from 60% to 80% during this period, rationalized by calling them dehumanized "diggers" and savages, while non-whites are exploited as racial minorities (without citizenship) until well into the 20th century (Wong, 2015; chapters 2 and 3 within the next book).

California, supposedly the most progressive state in the United States, denied it conducted genocide (Norton, 2020) under U.S. policies (next book), dismissing its racist suppression and segregation, (next Book chapters 2 and 3), even as it became an economic powerhouse (Darity, 2017) with democratic institutions as strong as anywhere in the so-called free world. How can this be?

And a final rhetorical question with profound implications for a future of American democracy, is the "post-civil rights movement" United States, which has gone beyond racism in its own eyes (Bonilla-Silva, 2009) both in 2016 somewhat successfully and 2020 unsuccessfully, conducting racially polarized presidential elections, often with racist language expressed by party nominees (Trump)? This was followed by a physical assault on the capitol (Jan. 6, 2021) heavily influenced by race and class.

This book provides an explanation for the deep conundrum of the intersection of 525 years of invasion, colonization, capitalism and systemic racism. It is also a first step toward a unified theory of race and racism, within the largely capitalist modern world-system. Through understanding how these processes and practices came to be, and how interwoven they are with neoliberal capitalism, we can see why our current system is willing to ignore poor and racially oppressed people, can deny the very humanity of countries struggling with deep poverty and global inequality and dismiss threats to human civilization and the entire world from capitalist-induced Anthropocene climate change to the racial stratification of advanced western societies. We now turn toward that story.

Notes

1 Equalizing the social science discussion means comparative-historical analysis between the two worlds of 1492 Americas (North, South and Caribbean) and the Euro-African (Europe, Africa and Mediterranean).

2 Many Native traditionalists refer to North America (sometimes all the Americas) as Turtle Island.

3 Although far from an exhaustive list, these four are most applicable to the discussion in this book (one).

4 Similar to Agency noted above, the problem is not lack of structural observation by Euro-American theorists about Euro-American colonialism, just the opposite, is strong reliance of that while ignoring or denying social structures of Indigenous and African nations, Morris (2015) shows how DuBois identifies structures in 19th and 20th century Philadelphia (1899); see Bonilla-Silva (1997) on internal institutions of racism in the United States, (Rethinking racism: Toward a structural interpretation. *American Sociological Review*, 62(3), 465–480).

5 Increasingly in cultural studies and when conducting ethnographic, community-based and qualitative research, engaged scholarship identifies the researcher positionality (their own social location), Indigenous perspectives, (either an own Indigenous affiliation or that as an ally), experiential (observations arising from one's experiences), and worldview (this is contested, but I used the analysis I present in my Culturicide book, Fenelon, 1998: 31–32, 96) based on my lived experiences both internationally and interculturally.

6 When I first explored the dynamics of genocide in my dissertation, and later in depth for my first book on culturicide as a subset or policy-practice on a continuum, at least for Native nations and Indigenous societies, I looked at most everything out there, especially sociology, and I ended using Fein's well-defined process-oriented work, mostly on the Holocaust, with an eye toward both Horowitz who was generalizing more broadly, and especially Kuper who had a wonderful international take and used many examples better suited to my analysis, such as those that took place in South and Central America. When I finished the dissertation in 1995 and went to John Carroll contracting for the book and started working on that, Goldhagen's Hitler's Willing Executioners broke out and an intense debate arose, probably linked to the nature of German society and perhaps laying Protestantism into a simplistic model based on Luther's origination, thereby sticking the debate only in Germany. However, in realizing Goldhagen's simplification of social (and political) movements (realizing that there were not only significant resistance forces in Germany, itself and among the nondominant groups), I like to think about Jo-Jo Rabbit these days (by a Maori screenwriter btw) but also implications from movies like Schindler's List (of course reading up on the Frankfurt School and a host of others, but I like movies when they work). I revisited Horowitz's model, which did use a continuum, and realized its most basic flaw in typologizing societies instead of policies and practices, which I then incorporated into all of my analysis, in that societies and powerful social forces and movements can quite literally change the direction of whole nations and more, which is why I use a continuum with genocide on one far end and (coercive) assimilation on the other, Culturicide in the middle and only using policy

practices as my prima facie evidence. This is a perfect model application for colonizing actions such as in the Americas (seems to be implied if not discussed in much work) and works fairly well in tracking out the intensifying Nazism of let us say 1932 (when I tell my classes Jews were rather well positioned in northern European countries, even if a history of pogroms still smelled 1933), through 1935 Nuremberg laws, 1938 Kristalnach and ending in the 1942 Final Solution and near perfect example of genocide. (The main reason I bring it up is to demonstrate how a fairly well-balanced society could devolve into the most extreme forms in a 10-year period, something I tell them we had better be on the watch out for in the United States.)

7

> In 1493, word of a "new world's" vulnerability spread throughout Europe (Lunenfeld, 1991), starting an important discussion on theology, conquest, peoples, indigenous societies and the very nature of civilization... Colonialization on this massive, potentially continental scale, required an integrated, multi-dimensional approach that could sweep aside the laborious process of negotiating with the indigenous peoples... The first such tone-setting edict came early on, as the Inter-Cetera Papal Bull of 1493, sent from the ubiquitous Catholic Church. This theological position statement placed the Native peoples in quite inferior positions, requiring European civilization dominance. Expeditions to a "new world" therefore had "just" cause to conquer, control and civilize in the name of "God and Righteousness." They fell to their task with undisguised vigor.
>
> (Fenelon, 1998: 7)

8 The definition of ideology that I use is described by Thompson (1990: 48) as an extension of Marx and Mannheim, in that "Ideology may be regarded as the interwoven systems of thought and modes of experience which are conditioned by social circumstances and shared by groups of individuals, including individuals engaged in ideological analysis."

9 Strickland (1992) found "American Indian policy has been characterized as "genocide-at-law" promoting both land acquisition and cultural extermination." While destructive policies easily qualify as Culturicide, tendencies to radicalize arguments occur if actions are couched in and defended by theories of benign assimilation and/or gradual civilizing processes with attendant human "losses" in cultural and demographic terms.

10 United Nations, H.R. Communication no. 478, Sep. 29, 1969.

11

> The same issue arises in different form in the mass annihilation of civilian populations in times of war, when the argument is advanced that they are being annihilated, not because they are members of the particular group to which they belong but because they are enemies.
>
> (Kuper, 1985: 151)

12 Although I agree with an idea that we must identify both societal types and social systems, I argue that it is precisely at this point that we must return to the anthropological constructs... Here we see interplay between at least three such disciplines: political science (state power), sociology (domination structures,

bureaucratic networks) and anthropology (culture, systems), which taken together constitute a now classical problem identified by Wolf (1982: 4–23) as the separation of the social sciences.

13 Note we are not supporting any claim of world circumnavigation, nor even of the Atlantic. However, like Jesuit linguistic sources on the Americas, or other destroyed sources such as the codexes held in Tenochtitlan, Menzies points toward cartographic and oceanic knowledge (Menzies, 2002: 386–390).

14 Yamashita, Michael. 2006. *Zheng He: Tracing the Epic Voyages of China's Greatest Explorer,* White Star.

15 Also leading to claims of a map of the globe in 1492.

16 The primary problem was distance, in that most geographers and scholars posited the globe more accurately, entailing a long journey to cross to Cathay. Columbus disingenuously purported a smaller globe and thus shorter travel time and route, which could (or would) have been fatal except for the Americas where he made landfall.

17 The Roman Emperor Septimius Severus is a strong example of discussions around race, slavery and dominance, having risen up through the ranks of childhood in Africa, apprenticeships in Rome and then governance, military and ultimately in power struggles over outlying provinces run by Centurions, causing him to be in a position to take the control of Rome and become one of its most popular rulers, yet often depicted in white marble statues and with flowing words that seem to decry his African heritage (as being Black, which is transmuted back into history). "Lucius Septimius Severus: the Black Emperor of the World" Edward L. Jones, in *A Turbulent Voyage, Readings in African American Studies,* edited by Floyd W. Hayes III (Collegiate Press, 1992: 96–110).

18 See earlier biblical passages for evidence of this – for instance, try to figure out individual's races without knowing their ethnic group or national origin, such as Ethiopian, or the Wise Men or Kings from the East, much less any fair-haired and light-skinned "barbarians" from the north.

19 Language ideologies with very real racial outcomes are first enunciated in the "savage" of the Papal Bulls, stays in use through the next two centuries as used against Indians, and continues to be powerful in documents such as the Declaration of Independence and the U.S Constitution (see chapter 3, ending, and chapter 4, the beginning, in this volume, extending to the end of the "Indian Wars" 400 years later in the 1890s, chapter 5, and its extension to ideologies and icons such as Redskin (Fenelon, 2017)

20 Marked separation by social institutions, although addressed by Las Casas and other Spaniard priests in the 1500s, is developed in epoch 2 the Black, dividing racial enslavement processes for Blacks as differing from the Indian, found in laws and policies from 1620 to 1690, noting that enslavement for Indians continued well into 1700s as well as related practices throughout Latin America (Resendez, 2017).

21 Tilly, Charles (1985). "War Making and State Making as Organized Crime". In Peter Evans; Dietrich Rueschemeyer; Theda Skocpol. *Bringing the State Back In* (Cambridge: Cambridge University Press. pp. 169–191).

22 Actually, the primary funding came from a rich Venetian merchant, representing others, to whom Columbus first reported to in his famous letters of March 13th, 1493, distributed to the Vatican and around the world.

23

(agricultural labor (primarily rural) gradually transfers to Industrial labor (primarily urban) beginning the social change processes that would alter the world, producing urban growth (worker populations) and industrialism employing Wage Labor for the working class (and nuclear families, reliance …)

(Fenelon, 1998)

(however, plantation-based agricultural production would continue (today) resource extraction would intensify to fuel industrialism.) (Concomitant with this industrial growth of economies is urban growth on a massive scale across the globe, later transnational global capitalism that relies on strong, central dominant States, see China 21st century calling it state capitalism …)

24 This is also when a kind of invisibility starts to imbue western social theory and history, in that all descriptors begin to discuss or bring up Indians, usually without reference to the designated nation and when they are named deeper references are dropped as western societies advance over the continent, naming vast territories under whichever European colonizer had penetrated the region, explored it or sometimes claimed it without either form of recognition. The United States institutionalizes this in the Louisiana "Purchase" of 1803 and continues to do this type of disappearing until 1890 and the last resisting nation is vanquished.

25 Note that valuable colonies connected to Eurasia continental areas, such as India, have internal populations that must be nullified or mollified, else they will rise up in resistance, limiting overall profits from colonial trade, while combined genocidal conquest and disease depopulation in the Americas allowed for settler colonialism replacement and therefore total social control over imported racialized slave populations.

26 These social forces continue into the 20th century, forging and bringing down global economies and states, finally merging into state capitalism in China in the 21st century.

27 www.ontheissues.org/Nation_of_Immigrants.htm

28 From an interview with Denis O'Hearn, in: Aidan Beatty, Aidan, Sharae Deckard, Maurice Coakley, Denis O'Hearn. 2016. " Ireland in the World-System: An Interview with Denis O'Hearn." *Journal of World-Systems Research*, 22(1): 202–213.

29 Settler colonialism has been accepted and employed, or deployed as a theoretical construct, for a few decades, with increasing usage and reference within various disciplines and the academy. However, the word "settler" carries various ideological constructs associated with civilizing and thus deeply racialized, that remains undiscussed, so we use the term with caution and concern for its continuance into racialization processes and thus racism.

30 With 1 as Indian – conquest capitalism for land and labor, 2 as Black – mercantile capitalism for labor, resources, companies; 3 as Irish (white ethnics) – industrial capitalism for production, distribution, (North – South) labor, resource colonialism; and 4 as Global Other, with global transnational capitalism running the world economy.

31 Many refer to this as the Global South that works roughly over the colonization centuries, but has become more problematic with the rise of China and sectors of India.

32 Resistance being crucial from the onset – La Navidad in Haiti, decades of Resistance including Anacaona followed by Enrique – first signs of maroons and maroon-age – all continuous through Black Extremists identity marked by the U.S. Justice Department in 2017 and Indian "Jihadists" through 2018.

33 I have seen it listed after people's names when doing Indigenous studies where Native descent people name or list their tribal affiliation or nation – i.e., John Smith, settler.

34 Common Ground: Reimagining American History, by Gary Y. Okihiro (Princeton University Press, 2001), *Third World Studies: Theorizing Liberation* (Duke University Press, 2016).

35 The panel had certain authors (Raewyn Connell, Amin Perez) specializing on these topics.

36 Organizer: Aldon Morris, with Sujata Patel, Julian Go, Zine Magubane and Xolela Mangcu.

37 Anaheed Al-Hardan, Gurminder K. Bhambra, with Connell, Julian Go and George Steinmetz.

38 This point was inferred from the beginning of this work in the 1990s and written into the test four years ago; however, Steinmetz (at ASA 2021) quoted Bourdieu in it is "the colonial situation that makes the racist," which we firmly agree with, adding the caveat that these are social structures creating, shaping and maintaining racism.

39 Karida Brown at the same ASA conference panels referenced above did a quick analysis of Cedric Robinson on Black Marxism seeing his application of racial capitalism (started by the ANC) refers to English colonization of Wales and Ireland preceding that of the Americas.

40 Frederickson (2002) as taken from many earlier scholars on racism.

41 We need to see the ideological origins and development of Nazi racist ideology over a 10-year-period, 1932–1942, from the rise of the Nazis to Nuremberg laws 1935, through Kristallnacht 1938 on to the Final Solution in 1942.

42 I often refer to the old movie Ben-Hur to my classes, since the main character goes from a leading Jewish family, wealthy in Jerusalem, to being sold into slavery under warship chain gangs, to saving the Roman Centurion's live, becoming a freeman in Rome with great success, and finally returning to Jerusalem where the Romans and Jews are persecuting Jesus as the Christ, with a phenomenal chariot race unrivaled to this day.

43 Burgos Laws of 1512 were first, followed by New Laws of 1542, after Valldolid assembled as Laws of Indes.

44 It is important to note that while English colonial law institutionalized racism for Blacks (see chapter 3 for this), England never encoded nor institutionalized racial slavery laws in their home country.

45 These are hypo-descent for Black, blood by descent for Indian, and lack of (col-ored) blood for White (pure). Painter (2011) and some other scholars identify crazy census definitions, and anthropological terms, to critically place ethnic as a common replacement for race from the 1880s through the 1920s, but in

practical usage ethnic came to mean cultural differences, especially from non-Anglo-Saxon Europeans (targeting the Irish).

46 Frederickson is referring to how Nazis (and others) used the idea of inherited "genes" of ethnicity or race to deny nationalist constructs in what becomes Fascist states, thus as "sons and daughters" of the nation.

47 It is precisely because most "white" Americans are already predisposed to be suspect of racial origins that a candidate could use this as a platform to launch a successful run for the presidency, even though it was untrue.

48 This is not stressed enough, in that the Supreme Court first had to decide if Plessy was Black, having only one African American great grandparent. (partly why he could sit in a whites only railroad car, and why his supporters used him as a precedent test case, making the legal loss all the more powerful), reinforcing the one drop rule.

49 Thomas Hall and Chris Chase-Dunn for the *Journal of World-Systems Research* they helped build.

50 I was teaching and designing language teaching programs for the Institute, where they asked me to give three talks on the origins of inequality and injustice in America (especially on Indigenous peoples and racism) in 1984.

51 George Steinmetz's seminal work Sociology & Empire.

52 What is Critical Race Theory? – AIER Episode 255: What is Critical Race Theory? (December 31, 2021) Retrieved on 1/3/2022 at www.aier.org/article/what-is-critical-race-theory/.

53 Let me be clear on having general praise for the 1619 Project and the intense debates and discussions it has generated, even if some work is overextended or exaggerated, and most of it employs a black to white binary.

54 Elites are from both the dominant invasive societies and those leading resistance and/or liberation movements. While this could use further elaboration on extending elite analysis (see Payne, 2020 review of Lachmann, 2020), specifically over "Dutch, British, and U.S. empires – in which colonial elites …" had influence "on the metropolitan political-economy" and "institutionalization" of hegemonic powers. Payne goes on "Lachmann upends the faulty binary of 'structure' and 'agency' to demonstrate how actions of elites at earlier points in time constrain the options available to elites at later points in time." Of course, this only considers elites from the dominant or successful group or nation, which explains the problem with comparing this to an extension of 'path dependency' to "how such paths are produced, reproduced, and upended." Social movements have much to say how they are upended.

55 Two other points need to be made here. First is that we must use the concept of "elites" from both the dominant and resistant groups (which can coalesce later) to be properly comparative. Second is that we are observing history from contemporary viewpoints knowing how the conflicts turn out, and thus predicating our analysis on just such results. This appears to be a problem in both comparative-historical methods and world-systems analysis.

56 Bonilla-Silva, Eduardo. (1997). Rethinking racism: Toward a structural interpretation. *American Sociological Review*, 62(3), 465–480.

57 Event history analysis should be an excellent fit for modeling purposes (Box-Steffensmeier and Jones, 2004) with "event history data structures"; however, the epochal periods described herein have vastly different sets of conditions,

problems shared with world-system analysis (Chase-Dunn and Grimes, 1995) especially when considering the formation of the United States (1776–1790) from 13 colonies on the east coast of North America, to continental dominance (around 1890) and then hegemonic dominance (post 1945) including conducting war, controlling economies, and long-term effects from the transition of colonialism into capitalism and ultimately the neo-liberalism of the 21st century. Controlling for decolonization and sovereignty (Strang, 1990) works in specific timeframes (1870–1987) to an extent.

58 By world-systemic time I simply mean that time periods as epochs must be taken in relation to large systems that interact over extensive duration, usually considered in centuries. There are many other contentious aspects to world-systems analysis that I, for one, simply set aside as not particularly useful for a half millenarian whole.

59 While I had already decided to do this albeit somewhat hidden or embedded, like substrata of a main argument, and had already moved to have an actual preface statement to each epochal chapter, I must note and praise Aldon Morris's presidential address, as delineated in his 2022 ASR article "Alternative View of Modernity: The Subaltern Speaks" where he cites W.E.B. Du Bois (1903) and C. Wright Mills (1959) emphasis on using personal experience, biography and the social structures we describe in theoretical terms, as being integral to good sociology.

Indigenous Journey in Haiti – Personal Statement as Preface to Chapter 2

Haiti was new to me when I accepted a teaching internship there over the New Year into 1982, so I read on its tumultuous history, the Black Jacobins and the Haitian Revolution and the first Columbus invasions. When I finished teaching at Port-au-Prince, I took a mountainous trail from Kenscoff over the *marchandes* route still with bandits and outlaws scattered on the southern side sloping down to the sea in dense forests fading to coconut-laden beaches Marigot to Jacmel, and ultimately a busy thoroughfare through mountain passes to the capitol, passing through ancient Xaragua lands headquartered at Yaraguana,[1] near steep redoubts where Native resistance fought a first war to colonial invasion. Then, I took a boat from the capitol port to the great peninsular city of Jeremie, home of poets and revolutionaries, and jury-rigged land rovers on undeveloped interior land where ancient yet modern ceremonies were underway, called *Vaudon* in the West. Intense perhaps unbelievable events through the night stripped away my Euro-American veneer, while gripping my eagle feather bison bone pipe stone choker. I asked and was enlightened to learn that *Houngan* leaders understood these traditions to have evolved from West African practices transplanted to Haiti, arising in plantations and grown from Indigenous Taino peoples of Xaragua, percolating for hundreds of years resisting and surviving conquest, colonization and capitalist domination. This motivated me to grapple with this half millennia story of Spanish then French, British and American domination, from Haiti to Mexico, and then from New England to California in the United States, employing a grounded scholarship and Indigenous philosophy of what first transpired and still lives in the lands of Ayiti …

Note

1 Leogane today.

DOI: 10.4324/9781003315087-2

Chapter 2

The *Indian*

1492–1620 Racial Construction of Indians and Blacks

Introduction

Indigenous scholars see "radical transformation of all human societies" when Europeans reached the western hemisphere. Notions of a "planetary existence" take shape, as Western Europe's nations spread over the globe colonizing and exploiting lands and peoples that were living in relatively healthy isolation. "European languages replaced tribal languages" as Spanish, French and then English became "the tongue of the civilized world, of diplomacy and trade, and finally expressions of civilized values." Through colonial administrations, "Western European political and economic interests dominated the economies of other continents" (Deloria, 1979: 1–2).

The Columbian quincentenary "confronted many whites with the uncomfortable fact … that we live in a world which has been foundationally shaped for the past five hundred years by the realities of European domination and the gradual consolidation of global white supremacy" (Charles Mills, *The Racial Contract*, 1997: 20).

This transformative act joined (Sale, 1990)

> vastly different cultures, evolving on …continents drifting apart for eons. Everything of importance in the succeeding five hundred years stem from that momentous event: the rise of Europe, triumph of capitalism, the creation of the nation-state, the dominance of science, establishment of a global monoculture, genocide of the indigenes, slavery of people of color, colonization of the world, destruction of primal environments, eradication … of species, and impending catastrophe of ecocide for planet earth.

Hispaniola, Genocide Studies Program, Yale University (10–14–20)

DOI: 10.4324/9781003315087-3

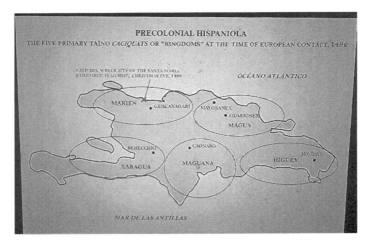

Figure 2.1 Precolonial Hispaniola. https://gsp.yale.edu/case-studies/colonial-genocides-project/hispaniola

Indigenous Taino: (Stories of *Guacanagaríx, Coanabó, Anacaona* on Arawakan *Ayiti*)

Guacanagari had finished Taino winter solstice ceremonies for his people of the Marién nation, celebrations shared with diplomats from Xaragua and Maguana, neighbors to the south and east. Word had arrived from the northern coast of strange men on a large boat coming ashore learning about the disposition of their lands and people. Emissaries were sent with gifts and greetings, as was their custom, with runners to return with the diplomats to their home nations, especially to Caonabo, cacique of Maguana and well known as a master of the martial arts. News spread throughout the lands of Ayiti, where delegations were formed to meet the newcomers.

When the foreigners' flagship foundered off a reef near the river estuary of the north, caciques sent rescue forces to off-load the crew and salvage goods. The Europeans were received with open generosity, and so Guacanagari agreed some of them could stay, if they would follow Taino laws in a respectful way. Those who had traded with the crew noted a lack of reciprocity, highly valued among the people, and a dangerous greedy interest in the soft mineral they called "oro" and young women, already reporting aggressive behavior all but unknown among Taino. The foreigners' cacique, a man they called Captain Colón,[1] who appeared to be arrogantly self-absorbed in referring to himself as coming from heaven, promised to return with word from their King across the oceans, and pledged friendship and good relations.

The hairy men who came on boats built a fortress, and started forays into the countryside, obsessed with finding the yellow mineral gold, and assaulting women and girls everywhere they went, considered to be rude and harmful to good community relations. Soon complaints began to come in to Guacanagari and he attempted to resolve the problems by referring to respectful ways among the people, which only increased the violence by Spanish in their fort. So the old cacique gathered nobles *Nitaino* and counselors *Bohiques* led by Anacaona, who conferred and sent word to Caonabó and the elite warriors of Maynerí, who met with the Spaniards and in a battle killed many of them, following to their fort and asking for surrender, even as they continued to harbor kidnapped and abused women, considered heinous by Taino morals.[2] Finally, Caonabo fought and finished them, informing his partner in marriage, Anacaona of Xaragua, of their crimes.

Captain Colón, Columbus, was incensed upon his return nearly a year later, withdrawing to the eastern Kiskeya region and setting up a settlement there. The three Taino kingdoms to the west, shocked at the Spaniards' behavior, continued negotiations with the Spanish to the east, throughout the depredations of the following years and enslaving those not fully subordinated, expanding their search for gold and the extent of their early plantations. Columbus sent special forces under General Ojeda after Caonabo who they tricked, captured and later killed shipboard. His brother Manicatex led an uprising but was defeated by cavalry. Anacaona and Bohechio entered into negotiations during Columbus's visit to Xaragua, in southwest Haiti, in late 1496. This was a first demonstration of high diplomatic art by Taino, including dance performance, during treaty relations on providing food and other support to the Spanish.

Anacaona took leadership of the Xaragua nation after the death of Bohechio, successfully resisting Spanish settler depredations from the eastern half of their island, for the next six years. Spain sent General Governor Ovando to increase colony production and pacify Indian resistance, wherein Xaragua agreed to meet, with Anacaona creating artistic political performance to show their high civilization. Ovando had secretly surrounded the meeting place, lit the buildings on fire and took the leadership captive to Santo Domingo, where they executed the men leaders. He offered Anacaona concubinage to himself or his generals, hanging her after one of the greatest resistance speeches of all time, where she noted the defilement of women, disrespect of families, greed for gold riches and debased qualities of the Spanish overlords about to execute her.[3]

Spanish and Indian – 1492–1620, Racializing "Indians" "Blacks" "Hostile" "Noble Savage"

Returning from his first transatlantic voyage to the Caribbean, Columbus initially called the Indigenous peoples he met as "*los Indios*" or in English "Indians" as the first great racial construction in world history. While southern Europeans had already absorbed supremacist ideas and images of "savage" or even "monstrous" peoples living in forests in faraway lands, this was constructed around a notion of being "uncivilized" tribes, connected to church-driven ideologies such as flesh-eating cannibals and Amazon women, anathema to the patriarchal and centralized societies arising from Mediterranean nations, and ruled by a Catholic Church centered in Rome, controlling expansive countries and doctrines about wealth, sovereignty and God.

An important element of the first expedition by Columbus in crossing the Atlantic Ocean was "risk capital" in funding three ships, a crew and supplies for a potentially dangerous voyage. Most scholars and early geographers at the time realized he would navigate half the globe[4] and thought he would find a trade route to the Indies or other areas of East Asia, perhaps even China, which was hazardous and expensive by land routes. This is why Columbus dubs native people he meets *Indios,* as people connected to lands thought to be near the *Indies.* After landing at various islands in the Bahamas and on Cuba, he stops at Ayiti (Española later called Hispaniola), to meet with people and ask about traders, and precious minerals such as gold. One of his ship's founders off Cap-Haïtien, and the local Taino-Arawak people came out in canoes to rescue the crew and salvage what goods they could. This created good relations with local governors, and Columbus observed their generosity and lack of duplicity,[5] in fact writing in his logs the infamous words "they are fit to be ruled" and that he could take much of the rich island with a small force.

Columbus left the shipwrecked crew behind on Hispaniola, asking them to find further caches of gold and other sources of wealth besides the vast stands of Mahogany forests that the French would later see as the richest forest lands in the world. After embarking for a return voyage, Columbus stopped along shores and took other Taino people captive, including young women for his sailor's enjoyment, to show off to the courts of his royal funders. These Arawakan people were subsequently sold in the slave markets of Seville. Thus the first indigenous peoples carelessly dubbed "Indios" as a racial group were also first to be sold as race slaves in the "old world." Selling of Arawakan peoples to Iberian slave markets continued for the next decade of conquest. The courts of Europe exploded with the possibilities of riches and conquest upon his return, turning to the Vatican to settle new disputes on which nations could lay claim to the new lands, preparing for an expected onslaught over peoples and places in the so-called "new world" even though the nations of peoples and societies were never engaged in any of this discussion, since they were dubbed Indians racially, and therefore inferior in all ways. The Vatican responded with a series of Papal policies, most pertinent being Papal Bull *inter caetera* of 1493, declaring "… that barbarous nations be overthrown and brought to the (Catholic) faith itself …" and that Columbus "… **discovered** certain remote islands … wherein dwell many peoples living in peace, going unclothed, and not eating flesh …" and

Española – Hispaniola – Santo Domingo – 1 2-1

Taíno canoes from the seaside capitol of the Arawak caciquat Marien nation helped rescue crew and salvage cargo from the sinking Spanish caravel off their northern coast in December, 1492. After his first trip to the Caribbean and having met a great many Indigenous Taíno-Arawakan peoples on Ayiti, Bohio, or Kiskeya and leaders of the five caciquats (nations or kingdoms), Columbus composed a letter which would be replicated and sent throughout a Europe eager to hear about the "New World" and ending in the powerful Vatican in Rome, where he referred to the peoples he encountered as "los Indios" – Indians – and thus launched the racialized term for millions of so many diverse peoples and societies. Spain and Portugal negotiated with the Pope, Alexander VI, producing the InterCaetera Bull of 1493 giving authority to claim lands inhabited by "savages" (uncivilized pagans) that he and other captains "discovered" and subsequently planted flags of their sovereign sponsors, unleashing three hundred years of conquest and colonization.

Taíno cacique Guacanagarí respected his nation's obligations as host for the Spanish at Natividad, who raped women and assaulted villagers in seeking gold, so requested assistance from a strong cacique of Maguana, Caonabo, who killed the recalcitrant crew refusing to obey the local laws. When the Columbus led invasion fleet (seventeen ships, over 1400 soldiers and settlers, attack dogs and horses) returned to Española (Ayiti) in the Fall of 1493, Spanish retaliatory raids were countered with resistance in the west, leading to Caonabo's capture and death, while Spanish reinforced settlements on the eastern half of the island, shipping hundreds of Taíno people to Spain to be sold as slaves, and forcing many thousands into gold mines, or to work plantations. Massacres of resisting Taíno forces were accompanied by mass killings documented by priests, (Bartolomé de las Casas and ad hoc historians), many so brutal and extensive that revisionists accused las Casas of creating the Black Legend of Spanish hostilities, though the stake burnings and other group tortures were also depicted in the Inquisition and later in Protestant killings. One Taíno cacique of the Higüey nation, led his people to Cuba to escape the brutal genocide, commenting when the Spanish arrived later, he'd rather go to Hell if invaders went to Heaven.

By 1502 depopulation from conquest wars, enslavement, genocide, disease, starvation, suicide, had reached 90% or more, from 1.75+ million to less than 175,000, (see notes v, vi, vii) with primary resistance in mountainous Xaragua. Attempted transfer of enslaved Taino from other islands did not work either, so Spanish monarchs instructed the incoming governor, Nicolás de Ovando to get slaves from Portugal (mixed ethnicity and race) and to pacify the resistance led by the great poet warrior Anacaona. Ovando began the slave trade to Santo Domingo, and set up meetings with leaders of Xaragua, headed by the delegation of Anacaona who presented their oral arts. Soldiers surrounded the site, enflamed the delegates, killed the security, and took four leaders to trial and shooting death, with Anacaona refusing concubinage and hanged in public. By 1512 to 1516, between 60 to 30 thousand Taíno remained in the lowlands, with resistance forces in some mountain areas, another near 90% death rate. By 1518, when missionizing smallpox killed more, so when Enriquillo's wife Mencía was raped by the Governor, and he led successful resistance as Guarocuya for another fourteen years, only a few thousand were left fighting from 1532 to 1542, 99% depopulation documented by Bartolomé de las Casas. Within fifty years of initial contact, Spanish invasión and colonization had torn apart one of the most beautiful societies on earth, Ayiti, to total genocidal destruction, in a search for gold, wealth and land that would be copied again and again for hundreds of years, creating the modern world of the Americas by 1992.

Figure 2.2 Hispaniola 1492–1502 and 1512 (text box). *Española – Hispaniola – Santo Domingo.*

that "In the island and countries already discovered are found gold, spices and many other precious things of divers kinds and qualities."

Thus Columbus on his second and subsequent voyages launched racially driven conquest of the Caribbean lands and peoples, categorized under the world's first fully racial term, with an express purpose of finding wealth and building rich and powerful bases from which to construct trade and colonies for the European nations supporting the colonizing fleets and invasion forces. On his second transatlantic voyage were 17 ships, soldiers, attack dogs and "settlers," designed to take Hispaniola for the Crown of Spain in the name of a Pope designating him Grand Admiral over the Seas, giving him carte blanche as governor of the new lands and peoples.

We must note this invasion force, stopping at Borinquen (Puerto Rico) for supplies and sexual feasting on the local population, was clearly sent to conquer, pillage and plunder, build an initial base to seek gold and enslave a rather peaceful and unprepared people. While Caonabo had been dispatched to curb the excesses of the 39 crew left at Natividad (to seize the wealth, women and control of the island, this leading to their death), the Spanish did not alter their plans for invasion and domination one whit because of this, only relocating their base to the eastern half of Hispaniola, which was easier to contain and launch their conquest. Columbus had Ojeda (Spanish soldier-general) seek out Caonabo as the first major resistance leader, capture and kill him through treachery as well as conduct pacification measures including many massacres and the burning of Taino townships that failed to produce the required slave labor or resisted raping of women. Resistance would continue in all the provincial nations, especially in southwestern Xaragua, for a decade until the Governor General Ovando was dispatched with strong military reinforcement and a slave contingent to replace the surviving Taino, for total pacification of the entire island, starting around 1502 through 1503 and many years beyond.

Spaniards fell to conquest with ferocious vigor, requiring all males and whole families to slave in gold mines, and putting down any resistance with mass execution and public torture, (Golden et al., 1991) quickly taking over Hispaniola, and island areas. Spaniards and settlers were given a superordinated status over all Arawakan peoples, now simply called *Indios* as a race.[6] Existing Taino social structures, some being the most egalitarian known to the world at the time, including women as heads of household and in some cases as cacique leaders, were decimated, with resistance such as that by Caonabo, and after him his wife the great Anacaona, woman head of state executed by Governor Ovando, defeated by brutal tactics and through treaty treachery, practices that would continue to be employed by the Spanish throughout the entire Caribbean. Many ex-soldiers and settlers would form militias into a countryside in rampant forays for gold, sex and food. By 1506 many Taino and other Arawakan societies on Hispaniola were destroyed, or relocated to maintain resistance, turning Indians into slaves, servants and laborers for life, also greatly reducing the future workforce. Uprisings on Borinquen in 1511, Cuba 1512–1517, and 1516–1519 by Taino throughout the island, decimated Indigenous populations. Smallpox decreased Taino numbers even farther in 1518, with brutal mission oppression. A major resistance struggle was started by *Enriquillo*, Anacaona's nephew, in 1519 that raged successfully for 14 years (Altman, 2007).

Many scholars and *Bartolome de Las Casas* place the preinvasion population of Hispaniola around three million, with conservative estimates under a million (one new DNA study[7] agrees) and others at several million, and an informal census of adults about 1496 counting more than a million and a half in the Spanish-controlled areas alone.[8] By the early 1500s these numbers were below some few hundred thousands, attrition through death and destruction and disease, so that by 1522 there were fewer than 30,000 Taino and other Arawakan peoples on Spanish Hispaniola, and within 50 years, let us say 1542, only surviving pockets of resistance in the mountains and small Taino groups could be found, meaning a complete genocide had been accomplished with de-population rates in excess of 98%, the highest the world had seen.[9] This was the first land base of European invasion, and similar destruction through conquest was happening throughout the Caribbean and coastal areas of the Americas. The first racially based genocide was accomplished in the half century of what Europe called advent of a "new world" that political economists identify as roots of the modern capitalist world-system. During that time transatlantic slave markets were created to partially replace a disappearing labor force.

Race, Gender, Class Intersections of Colonial Violence and Law

Spanish invaders and colonists were, at first, taking property held by people now called Indians, including sexual abuse, rape and family subordination in *encomienda*, as colonizing violence without legal or social restraint. Analysts and historians have different takes on these actions, especially on sexual assaults, which resemble the denying and reinterpreting of genocidal actions already discussed. During Columbus's second voyage, one of his oligarchic investors Michel de Cuneo self-reported in a letter to his financial supporters a kind of sexual braggadocio, when Columbus "gave" him an exceptionally pretty, naked, young woman:[10]

> While I was in the boat, I captured a very beautiful [Cannibal] woman, whom the Lord Admiral [Columbus] gave to me. When I had taken her to my cabin she was naked — as was their custom. I was filled with a desire to take my pleasure with her and attempted to satisfy my desire. She was unwilling, and so treated me with her nails that I wished I had never begun. I then took a piece of rope and whipped her soundly, and

she let forth such incredible screams that you would not have believed your ears. Eventually we came to such agreement, I assure you, that you would have thought she had been brought up in a school for whores.

We can learn from this interaction of self-described kidnapping and rape, using it as a study, two cultural practices of the Taino on Bohio and apparently the Carib from West Indies islands. First, that women clearly had the right to say No! – they had say over their own bodies, to use today's parlance (we will find evidence of this with Mexica, Coosa Mvskoke, Mattaponi Powhatan, Wampanoag, Tongva, Onondaga Hodenosaunee, Lakota and Dakota women in future chapters). Second, although self-reported rape, we see the Taino must have had healthy sex relations, within comparison to Spanish high society Catholics, when she is thought of as having advanced sexual arts from a whore house (see evidence at Jamestown and Plymouth English colonies, with captive narratives extending across the western frontier of the Americas). Background reporting from Columbus's log supports this, when he sends out (his first journey) a reconnaissance patrol to get Taino captives to find information on local areas of Ayiti (Dunn and Kelly, 1989: 221). (Where, by the way, his men found a township of a thousand homes and at least three thousand people (229) surrounded by cultivated fields interspersed with managed forests.) The patrol reports that everyone ran off or fought them, (no wonder here), and so they brought back a "very young and pretty" naked girl, who told them the local dispensation by talking with the captive women from Juana (Cuba) they already held on the ship. Later, Columbus remarks that the locals must be "jealous" with their women who had been hidden away. An alternative explanation is that the Taino, who despised sexualized assault, were protecting their women and girls. We bring this up in the book as a corroborated first instance, or set thereof, of sexual violence that will continue through each of the racial epochs, by Europeans then Americans, but which is rarely reported as such, usually it's only alluded to when observing the good Christians of Jamestown, Plymouth, California Missions and "frontier values" of the old West.

We also observe violent intersection of race, gender and class position that is reproduced throughout five centuries, covered by seeing Natives as uncivilized, hyper-sexual, savagely self-interested groups, who cannot or will not assimilate to dominant society, driving conservatives of Christian faith. No doubt many religious and political leaders were such men (remember, it is a patriarchy), perhaps including Junipero Serra (self-flagellating when coaxed by sin), John Rolfe (married Pocahontas out of goodwill), Thomas Jefferson (fathering children by Sally Hemming), John Fremont (California presidential candidate), George A. Custer (Native women prisoners), California politician, (36th governor, presidential candidate), and so the long list goes, to Jeffrey Epstein and Donald Trump, 45th President of the United States. Later,

Harriet Martineau calls these "blinders" of the good Christian women of Southern slavery, markers of a society unable or unwilling to see its own racialized sexual dominance and patriarchy. All these conquest policies are affirmed and justified by the Church's religious ideologies put into law and theology.

Finally, we see how the Catholic Church struggled with this internalized racialized violence, initially by colonists reporting excesses through the Dominican order, leading to the arrest and imprisonment of Columbus (this may have been partly political, but it shows full knowledge of atrocities). As it continues, the Church sends investigators, leading to Montesino's 1511 speech (below) on Hispaniola, another trial in Spain, and the Laws of Burgos passed 1512, imperfectly practiced but set in place and renewed in the New

---

The **Long Arc of the Doctrine of Discovery – Part 1: Catholic Spain**
Through religious edicts, laws, social policies, political ideologies, (of Christian world)

1 PRE-EUROPEAN INVASION
1453/54 Papal Bull – 1490 Bulls on Inquisition (Spain, Portugal – Catholic countries) Anti- Muslim (anti- Jew) designates non-Christians (Africans) as pagans, can be enslaved;
1492 Papal Bull – re-authorizes **Inquisitions** (Spain: Isabella I,[a] Alhambra) prelude to Race.

2 SPAIN'S CATHOLIC CONQUEST
1493 Papal Bull – *Intercaetera* – extends all the above to *Indios* as savages, non-Christian – Discovery employed as rationale for riches, lands, insinuates conquest (taking land)
1494 Treaty of Tordesillas – amended 1496, dividing hemisphere between Spain and Portugal from points farther west, giving Portugal Brazil "discovered" later (see 1506 claims)
1512 Laws of Burgos,[b] (encomienda re-established leading to) **New Laws of 1542**
1550 Valladolid (debates) Missions used conversion, becomes **Laws of the Indies**
Elizabethan edicts – James I – Penal Laws of Ireland (Culturicide, see 1932-42 Nazis)

Figure 2.3 The long arc of the doctrine of discovery – Part 1: Catholic Spain.

a Queen Isabella I of Spain oversaw Jewish expulsions (300,000 with about 175,000 forced out, great property loss, became an economic disaster) and was the first European monarch to make (sovereign) land claims in the Americas.
b The New Laws were the results of a reform movement in reaction to what were considered to be the less effective, decades-old *Leyes de Burgos* (Laws of Burgos), issued by King Ferdinand II of Aragon on December 27, 1512. These laws were the first intended to regulate relations between the Spaniards and the recently conquered indigenous peoples of the New World. These are regarded as the first humanitarian laws in the New World. They were not fully implemented because of opposition by powerful colonists.

Laws (*Leyes Nuevas*) of 1542, banning slavery, and grand debates at Valladolid in 1550, ending in the Laws of the Indies.

> Tell me by what right of justice do you hold these Indians in such a cruel and horrible servitude? On what authority have you waged such detestable wars against these people who dwelt quietly and peacefully on their own lands? Wars in which you have destroyed such an infinite number of them by homicides and slaughters never heard of before. Why do you keep them so oppressed and exhausted, without giving them enough to eat or curing them of the sicknesses they incur from the excessive labor you give them, and they die, or rather you kill them, in order to extract and acquire gold every day.
>
> (Antonio de Montesinos, December 21, 1511)

The Burgos Laws (35 legal restraints, establishing "rights") began to change, at least on the surface, some of the worst tendencies of Spanish conquistadors, ship captains and colonists. Dominican priests and friars initiated these when on Hispaniola, precisely because of genocidal attacks by governors and investors, and their settler colonists, whom the Franciscans befriended thus becoming dominant in the local church authority. The story of Bartolome de Las Casas, going from a brutal Colonizer *encomendero* to Catholic priest, and when denied communion coming completely to Dominican position (which was simply Indians were human, had souls, therefore rights after being Christianized) is instructive of the deep debates by newly colonizing forces – Church (moral justification), Crown (monarch authority), and Colonists (settlers) – which reflected the demand for wealth from plunder, plantations and land/labor acquisition.

Reports of assaults and depredations on Cuba and even later on mainland Mexico, Peru and Chile contributed to this conflicted dialogue between Catholic Church law and theology, with the Spanish Crown maximizing wealth accumulation and Spanish Colonists (settlers) wanting ever more land and titles. This was reflected in de Las Casas' famous quote:

> ... (In 1508) there were 60,000 people living on this island (Hispaniola), including the Indians; so that from 1494 to 1508, over three million people had perished from war, slavery, and the mines. Who in future generations will believe this? I myself writing it as a knowledgeable eyewitness can hardly believe it ..."
>
> (Las Casas, 1538; Josephy, 1992)

Colonists had taken action a number of times against both church and state positions arguing Indian rights and treatment that included arresting Columbus, attacking Dominican priests, especially after they returned with the Laws of Burgos in 1512, hardening encomienda systems with new rules and intensifying racial divisions between Spanish and other colonists, Indians and Native Nations (if in existence) and Africans brought to be plantation slaves.

Spanish forces had invaded Mexico and toppled the Aztecan alliance at Tenochtitlán, followed by military advances northward and southward, and spin-off Conquistadors Coronado, northern Mexico and the Southwest, Pizarro in Peru and the Andes taking down the vast Inkan trading empire across northern and western South America, with excursions into North America, (De Soto, for instance). The forces building empire and seeking wealth drove Spain and other countries in different directions – continued colonized racial hegemony over Caribbean islands, (starting to be contested by northern European countries) and Spanish land grants over regions, resources and peoples within newly conquered territories, now encompassing New Spain.

We will return to how labor in many forms – slavery in mines and farms, pueblo control over farmlands, transportation and project temporary enslavement and creation of townships – began to shape the expansion of Spain's dominion over vast territories using highly adaptable laws and policies, and fluid concepts of race, ethnicity and national origin. For Caribbean island Indians, the previously banned encomienda system was used over the falling number of survivors along with growing number of African slaves, to produce highly profitable sugar plantations, along with other commodity crops mostly meant for European markets. Rights advocates like de Las Casas went back and forth from courts in Spain and the Vatican, to colonial holdings both on islands and interior areas. Las Casas attempted an idealized system in Venezuela, but at the last moment local *encomenderos* and Bishops engineered slave raiding attacks on local villages and interior tribes, who retaliated and thus made the ventures too dangerous. Las Casas did manage to address the horrific treatment of *Kichwa* and other peoples of the conquered Inka, so that an arresting force under Crown and Church authority actually killed Pizarro, but replicated the same systems less directly dealing with deadly strategies. Similar conflicts spread in Chiapas, Mexico, Panama, Nicaragua and other conquered or colonized areas. Dominicans and Church groups argued against the renewed *encomiendas*, slavery, and deeply oppressive treatment of surviving Indian peoples successfully, getting New Laws (of Burgos) passed in 1542 to end the practices. Catholic hierarchy effectively acknowledged the first universal Human Rights within these laws, titling Las Casas as Defender of Human Rights and Indians (people), with Souls and societies.[11] Five or more of the rights, broadly grouped, include:

- Indians had to pay tribute to *encomenderos*, only if they worked, and were **to be paid wages in exchange for their labor** (however, those wages could be any amount).

- Indians were to **be taxed** fairly and treated as if they had **rights** (rarely followed).
- New laws prohibited using Native people to work in the mines (where many had died) unless **necessary**, and then ostensibly under similar working conditions as Spanish mine workers (high crimes allowed slavery, just like the United States 320 years later).
- Public officials or clergy with *encomienda* grants were ordered **to return** them to **Crown** officials (only the viceroy could establish *encomienda*) also rarely implemented.
- *Encomienda* grants would not be passed on via **inheritance**, but would be cancelled upon the death of individual *encomendero* (meant to effect distribution of land, important to note lands were not given back to Indians, going to settlers, or like California to *rancheros*).

For our purposes, we need to note that Natives were referred to as Indians by the law, racially.

We will redress these rights and their uneven or misapplied applications, or lack thereof, after the next few sections of this chapter. We need to note the increasing numbers of Africans brought by many European enslavers into the Caribbean islands and coastal areas. The first on Hispaniola were being treated differently than surviving Indian populations, especially when near resistance forces such as Enriquillo in the Xaragua region, and the concepts of Black slaves and mestizos as peasants were being developed, later spreading throughout Latin America. Dominicans took a position that individual Indians had to be baptized, converted, Christianized before they had such rights. Franciscans argued that whole groups (villages, tribes) could be collectively baptized, then their labor or social position could be justified in different ways.[12] These competing racialized systems of differentiating between two types of Indians, Africans and other Christian-borne Europeans or mixed-race folk, began to shape the Caribbean islands, and would become the foundation for Mission systems in California, mestizos in Mexico and Africans in plantations throughout the colonies. These became the greatly variable racial laws and remain a counterpoint to the highly institutionalized forms English colonies would undertake and pass into policies. Later in this chapter we consider the great number of racially enslaved Africans brought to the Americas, and forms of quasi-slavery practiced in Spanish-held regions.

The continued differences between some Catholic denominations, such as Dominicans, and Crown interests in expanding colonies versus Colonists interests in getting land and labor cheaply as possible continued to build until the Crown and Church decided to end the debates, once and for all, calling all interested parties and their representatives together in 1550 Spain. The Crown was as concerned with growing resistance and independence of the *encomenderos* leading colonists settlers, as they were with religious and social justice toward Natives.[13]

Valladolid Debates – Crown, Church and Colony[14]

The Valladolid debates (1550–1551) were held in the Colegio de San Gregorio, in Spain, under the auspices of King Charles V,[15] with opposing camps offering theological and sociopolitical arguments on Native "Indians" and Spanish colonization of America. Bartolomé de las Casas, Catholic Priest (Dominican) and Bishop of Chiapas, led a group arguing that Natives were free and "true" men in a natural order, and thus deserving of rights accorded to those converted to Christianity, using his Catholic theology. Juan Ginés de Sepúlveda, Spanish humanist scholar, led those theologians, landowners and colonists who argued Indians were "barbarians" deserving natural slavery because of their cannibalism, sexual practices and slaughter of "innocents" under Aristotle-an thought and logic about Natives who commit "crimes that offend nature." Las Casas reinterpreted the canonical law finding monarchs were responsible for controlling *encomenderos* and officials with power over Indians, seen as humans with souls, who could be brought to God, peacefully (called missions).[16]

Although both sides claimed to have won the debate, little changed in the ongoing militaristic expansion over Indian lands and their coerced submission to labor for the profits of colonizers and settlers. Spain and the Catholic Church acknowledged the basic human rights of Natives in the Americas, banning slavery and unjust imprisonment or punishment, even as they skirted the same problems with the *encomienda* system practiced by overlord *encomenderos*, often reinforced with African slaves brought by shipping *assientos* given by Spanish authority. These grand debates represented European and Christian theology, as well as colonial powers spreading throughout the Americas, and stand as counterpoint to morality and justice issues arising by Protestant colonizers in North America for centuries to come, coming to a perfect head in California with its Catholic Mission past countered and dominated by Protestant governments instituting slavery-like systems and genocidal taking of Native lands, through to the 20th century. We must keep this in consideration for English and later American institutionalization of slavery and genocidal expansion in Chapter 3 (Black), Chapter 4 (revolutionary America) and next Book Chapter 2 (Irish or White) where governments and scholars claim not to have knowledge of preexisting systems,[17] and rely on the same old arguments of savagery versus civilization.

Ayiti Arawakan Resistance – Missions to Mountains – Enrique's Rebellion

Another area of paramount importance in understanding how systems of colonization interact with peoples who are exploited and oppressed, enslaved and exterminated, suppressed and dominated is that of resistance, survival (sometimes) and revitalization. On the first order, we have a first and foremost example of ethno-national successful resistance that will inform all other resistance, rebellion and revitalization movements over the next few centuries – Enrique's Rebellion on *Ayiti* (*Xaragua*) from 1519 to 1533. This will mark (1) a first major rebellion by those partially assimilated into an invading or dominant society, (2) armed resistance camps reached out to other enslaved/oppressed Natives, (3) interracial movements' common objectives, (4) attempts at military counter-insurgency search-and-destroy forces, (5) trial agreements and treaties to de-escalate, subdue rebel forces, (6) betrayal after successful negotiations to end hostilities and (7) a first attempt by colonizers to separate out races and ethnicities, from joining social movements. Different colonizers and rebellious or resistance forces will employ similar tactical repertoires, strategies for suppression and successful outcomes or continuing resistance – within Chapter 3, English colonies against Native Nations and enslaved workers, in Chapter 4, the United States taking over Indian tribal Nations, suppressing slave revolts and quelling immigrant and ethnic unrest by the lower classes, and next Book with global hegemony over Indigenous peoples, ex-colonies as third world countries and internal uprisings or rebellions over progressive issues.

Enrique, born *Guarocuya* around 1500, orphaned after his father, cacique *Magiocatex*, and great aunt Anacaona were killed by General Ovando along with eighty other *cacique* leaders, was brought up in a monastery and educated as Enriquillo in the first Spanish mission system. Bartolomé de las Casas was his mentor in Christian thought, and he rose to be a foreman of sorts with his bilingual/bicultural presence among the Taino. A young son of an encomendero named Valenzuela became his master, and in jealousy stole Enrique's horse and then assaulted his wife, publicly to rub salt into the wound. Enrique reported the crime, was rebuked, so he journeyed to Santo Domingo for justice. There the Junta would not take his word over a Spaniard, although they agreed it was criminal, and said nothing could be done. Enrique confronted them, saying:

> Christians … are bad men, tyrants, who want only to usurp the land of others and only know how to spill the blood of those who have never given offence.
>
> (Josephy, 1994: 129)

Outraged that laws did not apply to educated Indians, and being instructed on his past, including his caciques' relatives resistance and execution, along with his ancestral birthright, Enrique left for his traditional homelands in Bahoruco, with his wife, of noble *Nitainos* birth, *Naborias* who knew the Bahoruco range, and priest-healers known as *Bohiques* who became his advisers. When Valenzuela and militia colonists came after him, they were defeated multiple times yet treated with respect and let go when captured. More Natives and others, indentured mestizo settlers and African slaves escaped from sugar plantations and gold mines, joined his forces in the mountains, eluding soldiers sent by Spain to capture him, killing a captain and his team. Although skirmishes continued, Enrique's forces were constantly on the move in mountainous areas they knew better than the colonists militias. Spanish authorities did not consider the so-called "war of Bahoruco" – named for the mountainous area in which Enrique and his people were located – to have begun until 1523, four years after Enrique and his followers first took flight (Altman, 2007: 598). Captains de Vadillo with 300 armed men, and Ortiz with another 300 all failed, until Captain Hernando de San Miguel, after years on the campaign, eventually made contact with Enrique (599), and started peace negotiations, although the first in 1528 fell apart when the Captain brought a significant fighting force with him, breaking the conditions. Before that de San Miguel had conducted slash and burn campaigns, destroying crops, killing farm animals and setting homes afire, to get the insurgents, who could not be defeated in battle, to come in for the good of their people. The next time they managed to talk with Enrique, successfully, was five years later, with a different set of conditions and stronger offers of a peaceful settlement, but even then, Enrique never drank or ate with them.

Finally, in 1533 after 14 long years of resistance movements of what appeared to be the strongest military forces on earth, and with the assistance of de Las Casas and Enrique's women relatives, with the support of local townships, the two sides met and agreed to terms. Enrique and his people would be allowed to settle as a free and independent community on lands of their choosing and receive material aid in livestock and equipment. In return, Enrique would hand over to Spanish authorities fugitive Africans or Indians who subsequently attempted to join him, (Altman, 2007: 598). Actually this last point is disputed by some accounts, who say Enrique never did come down from the mountains, and always refused to surrender Indian fugitives,[18] although he may have agreed to return escaped Africans who "subsequently" joined his force. What is very clear in these Crown authorized negotiations is that Spanish *encomenderos* and government officials were deeply concerned more about a growing African population from escaping and joining resistance forces, which is where the maroons originally come from. This would continue for the next 100 years in the Caribbean, and find strong similarities with the English colonies (Chapter 3) and the slave-holding republic of the United States (Chapter 4).

Another final point is about the racial-ethnic mixtures of the population of Hispaniola, which is also indicative of future colonizing operations. For instance, a lot of the patrols set against Enrique and Tamayo (another maroon resistance leader) were composed of "Indian – African" conscripts, and Captain Barrionuevos' "ablest and most experienced" seasoned patrols had an "equal number of indigenous servants (*indios domésticos*), as well as guides … and two (women) relatives of Enrique's "whom he has trusted on other occasions" (Altman, 2007: 604).

Hispaniola demographics had become diverse, though still oppressive (Altman, 2007: 608–614):

> With the drastic reduction of the indigenous population and the departure from the island of so many Spaniards who headed for more promising destinations on the mainland, in the 1520s Hispaniola already was on its way to becoming a fairly insignificant backwater of the Spanish empire, with **little wealth and a mostly mestizo and African population**. The mestizo group had grown steadily since the beginnings of Spanish settlement.
>
> (608)

> As indigenous populations dwindled in the Caribbean, **Spaniards imported hundreds and then thousands of African slaves** who very soon proved even more difficult to control than the region's native inhabitants. Rather than signaling initiation of a period of relative peace on Hispaniola, the peace accord concluded with Enrique instead marked a shift in Spanish concerns away from the remaining indigenous population and toward the Africans. In October 1535, barely two months after Enrique's death, the audiencia requested a reduction in the tax on gold so that the mines would not be abandoned "which would provide occasion for the blacks to revolt which would be difficult to suppress."
>
> (609)

We observe the demographic transition beginning on Hispaniola, directly related to genocidal death rates and Native resistance movements, with the rise of enslaved African labor imported to build plantation and mining operations by Spanish authorities with increasing mixed-race groups, mestizos, positioning as small land owners or middleman managers.

> By mid-1540s **complaints about Africans and fears of disorder and rebellion** on their part were proliferating. In July 1543 Melchor de Castro, notary for the mines, claimed that no one wanted to look for new mines because of danger from rebellious slaves ... Castro had personal experience ... of controlling slaves, since in early **1522 his estate had been attacked** and he had been wounded participating in suppression of **an uprising launched by** twenty Wolof-speaking **slaves on the sugar estate** of Diego Colón that quickly spread to other areas. Twenty years later **the island's slave population, estimated in 1542 at 25,000 to 30,000,** together with possibly **two or three thousand maroons,** might have been twenty or thirty times the size of the Spanish group. There is little question that by this time Africans far outnumbered Spaniards, Indians, or mestizos.
>
> (Altman, 2007: 608–614)

Here we find the critical element in racial systems development on Hispaniola leading to Haiti, with similar demographics growing throughout Caribbean islands, with violent suppression of rebellion and clear understanding of population management along racial formation lines.

> Spanish officials readily found parallels between the **growing threat from rebellious African slaves and Enrique's revolt**. Audiencia judge Licenciado Cerrato wrote to the crown September 1544 "it would be preferable that there **weren't so many ladino slaves born** in this country, because they are a bad nation, very daring and badly inclined, and they are the ones who mutiny and make themselves captains. The bozales aren't like this. The same was seen in the business of Enrique." Notably, **many escaped Africans were active in the Bahoruco**, where Enrique and his people had entrenched themselves. A Spanish patrol sent to the region in pursuit of a notorious leader named Sebastián Lemba found evidence local Indians were collaborating with African rebels.
>
> (611)

> The peace accord in itself was significant, in that it was **the first occasion**—and the last for at least two centuries—**on which Spaniards concluded a treaty with an undefeated indigenous group** that had long resisted Spanish authority. The treaty seems to have set a precedent for future dealings with relatively small, usually geographically circumscribed, groups in revolt throughout the Americas. Ironically, however, in the future these groups would be predominantly African rather than Native American.
>
> (Altman, 2007)

Spanish authorities were acutely aware of racialized resistance movements leading rebellion for other ethnic groups in their system. They also saw a danger of alliances of excluded and enslaved groups, which became intensified under the French, who simply demarcated African-only slaves. The English institutionalized separation by races, for similar reasons, in their colonies.

> The details of Enrique's struggle, his… attempts to **use the Spanish legal system** for redress of his grievances, the **alliances** that he forged with **other Indians, mestizos, Africans** on the island, the connections that he… maintained with members of Spanish society even while in revolt, and evolving views of members of the audiencia and other officials in Hispaniola as expressed in policies and opinions, all suggest that in the course of two generations a diverse and complex society had taken hold in Hispaniola.
>
> (Altman, 2007: 608–614)

Ayiti – Tenochtitlán – I: 2-2

1519

Moctezuma (II) Xocoyotzin presided as emperor of the Triple Alliance Aztecan empire, meeting in the capitol city Tenochtitlan, metropolis of nearly 300,000 strategically placed on an island in lake Texcoco, amid many smaller nations and city-states (Tlateloco) that made up broad political coalitions created by the Mexica as they climbed atop pyramids and governmental buildings shared with a ruling alepeme of Texcoco and Tlacopan states. Word had arrived from the coast that bearded men in shiny armor riding mythical beasts had landed and were advancing inland, threatening the fractured alliance he ruled over, encompassing millions of people along trade routes south to the nations aligned with Inka, and north to the Puebloan nations trading throughout the continent. The capitol included universities, arts and medical centers, vast waterworks with chinampas floating gardens, and the largest markets in the world, protected by a standing army of a hundred thousand, larger than London or Rome at the time. To the Aztecs it was the center of the universe.

Hernán Cortés, conquistador captain of a Spanish expedition to establish trade for Cuba, sunk his ships and carried out reconnaissance patrols and skirmish wars in determination to take the fabled riches of the Aztecs, relying on Indigenous Malintzin (Doña Marina), providing intelligence on the allies and enemies of the Aztecs (who would bear children for him becoming the first Ladinos). Cortés gathered allied forces to defeat the Tlaxcalans, an independent enemy city-state who then joined the Spanish army, and slaughtered the Cholulans as message to the Mexica in Tenochtitlan. Moctezuma hesitated at the threat, his counselors fearing the prophecy of Quetzalcoatl returning from an East bringing death. The Spaniards were invited to enter the city and behold its wealth and power, leading to their occupation of the central palace and looting of the treasuries of gold and silver.

The governor of Cuba Velázquez sent a large force to arrest Cortés in the spring of 1520, led by Pánfilo Narvez, who were taken by Cortés at his coastal command. In Tenochtitlán the remaining soldiers killed nobles in a celebration, and later Mochtezuma too during a protest. The new elected Mexica ruler, Cuauhtémoc gathered forces and drove Spaniards out of the city, killing many on the causeways, others drowning stuffed with heavy gold. The victory was short-lived, with smallpox ravaging the city, which the immune Spanish claimed was the wrath of God, and won their Tlaxcala allies back. In May 1521, Cortés with allied armies battled back into the weakened Tenochtitlán after a three-month siege, marking the fall of the Aztec empire, destruction of its monumental architecture, burning of codexes and libraries, and the start of the conquest of Mexico where millions died from disease pandemics, too weak to fight, like the failed Cuauhtémoc counter-insurgency.

Spanish forces conquered the destabilized and depopulated nations through enslavement, disease and domination – central civilizations of Mexico fell – the Maya, Oaxaca – all the way to Baja, millions die, church authority rises, Missions form, laws, boarding schools, destroying codexes, more pandemics, Florentine codex created by monks during plague, with after invasion effects. The conquistadors of America were launched.

Figure 2.4 Tenochtitlán 1519–1521 and 1541 (text box).

We have observed the rise and fall of an epic resistance movement against a colonizing power that along the way included interracial and cross-ethnic coalitions responding to new systems of enslavement and exploitation, and its ultimate qualified success within an expanding world-system employing racism, nationalism and early capitalism to maintain a new racial order. Perhaps as poignant an observation is that this movement began in the very year that new Spain invaded the mainland, under Cortez in 1519 toppling the Aztecs and destroying the world's great city of Tenochtitlán by 1521; and the Taino forces under Enrique ended the movement in a year Pizarro toppled the Inkan empire, destroying the world's (arguably) greatest cross-continental trading networks, where all roads led to Cuzco. To those stories of Spanish conquest (English, French, Dutch) and colonization of the Americas we now turn our analytical eyes and ears.

The taking of Tenochtitlán led to slavery of Africans, *encomienda* and *repartamiento* systems and new laws of domination. We make the following observations on how continued conquest colonization would proceed under conquistadors and colonies from Spain (and Portugal):

1   The immediate and primary wealth extraction from the Americas was PLUNDER, followed by plunder-like extraction of valuable minerals – gold and silver – with the creation of plantations – sugar, cotton, coffee, tobacco – using slave and coerced labor as if plunder.
2   Labor for plantations, mining and servile (domestic and civil) was initially using coerced and enslaved Natives, and enslaved Africans, with growing reliance on mestizo and incorporated Indian pueblos, later moving to rural/pueblo/urban (city) stratification by race and ethnicity.
3   Spanish movement into the interior (Mexico) and expansion over coastal areas benefited from conquest and disease depopulation, increasing the need for coerced/enslaved workers, especially for the brutal conditions in the mines, with increased Native armed resistance.
4   Native worker-slaves, taken under encomienda and other legal systems, were first gotten locally, then regionally and finally from distances such as with silver mines (Potosi, Palla, etc) getting slave-like Natives from as far north as regions known today as New Mexico, and as far south as Nicaragua, Panama, with similar systems developing in Peru, Chile and Columbia.
5   African slave labor could be bought under cover of *assientos* from Spanish authorities, utilizing Portuguese ships, later under Dutch and French flags (also with many revolts).
6   Investment by Dutch banks and under Netherlands authority became contentious, leading to Spain under Charles V dominion and domination over the lower provinces (Burgundy) and in support for Catholic intransigence against Protestant influences.

7   Catholics created counter-reformation policies partly in connection to Spanish laws of religious conversion and rights of Natives (Burgos and New Laws, Valladolid Laws of Indies) and broader Protestant-Catholic conflicts, such as with French Huguenots and Dutch-Swiss-German Calvinists, connected to laws on banking/investments, rights of citizens, church and state relationships and slave rights ideologies in the New World colonies.

8   Spain was seeing greater conflicts with sea forces becoming privateers under England, and European sources of colonial wealth extraction (plunder, war booty raids, insurgencies).

9   European wars and conflicts were thus connected to larger wars of colonial competition, such as the Spanish Armada defeat by England and the ex-Privateers force, by then veterans of the Mayan wars, against the Mapuche, and numerous seagoing battles over plunder.

10   The modern world-system in formation during this epochal time period is mostly driven by Atlantic European colonizing powers in high conflict over wealth and future colonial takings from the Americas, leading to mercantile to industrial capitalism, racialized labor forces, and maximal systems of human exploitation on a hemispheric scale (Native resistance uprisings).

Wealth and Colonization, Slave Markets and Capitalism, European Hegemony

Spanish holdings of land and wealth in the Americas alone were already greater than that of the Iberian homelands (also true of Portugal) with similar effects on European countries undergoing Protestant reformation. The ideology of the uncivilized and unconverted Indian was central to this wealth accumulation in Spain and throughout Europe, and supremacist ideologies surrounding colonization and the enslavement systems over Natives and Africans. Increasingly, this meant domination, incorporation through mestizo identity, destruction of Native nations, along with the development of African transatlantic slave markets for labor. These race-based systems were calling for ever-greater dehumanization of both Native and enslaved Africans, creating Indians and Blacks, in conflict over Catholic-Spanish laws on the rights of Indians.

The great social transformations of Europe – Protestant reformation; separation of states, from the Catholic church (England, Netherlands, other countries); development of corporate chartered companies for economic colonization; rise of states for hegemonic control of colony, company, and colonists in terms of its own citizenry; and the consolidation of wealth in banking and trading companies – were all connected to or were actual outgrowths of the colonizing of the Americas (and other countries around the world).

We need to see these deadly forces – (1) religious wars were killing millions of citizens in their own countries, and many millions of Native and Africans; (2) rise of hegemonic states based on wealth extracted from colonies; (3) new economic systems (not single states) were creating capitalism and (4) wars and conflicts were arising from these colonizing behemoths in Europe – more as globalizing colonies of the Americas, and around the world.

We now turn toward observing this global world-system in development, through the lens of race-based enslavement systems, depopulation demographic (collapse) from conquest wars and disease and creation of joint-stock companies as the basis for colonization and capitalism.

Many scholars and historians discount the relationship between conquest colonization with the spread of pandemic disease to non-immune populations (to the tune of millions of people). These analysts contribute to a denial of genocide or genocidal effects of such of loss of life and societies conquest wars, by lowering the numbers of Native peoples in the Americas before the entrance and invasion of European powers. They also contribute to a distortion effect, on a continental scale, of how colonies benefited from destabilized Native nations, and used their solidified colonial creation to expand over North America, destroying Native peoples, societies and civilization in the process, all the while "exporting" African peoples to be enslaved while "importing" Black peoples as racially enslaved labor for a by-then deeply racist New World.[19] We therefore must consider the early development of this (the 16th century) as connected to building transoceanic markets for enslaved racial labor to replace a more ambiguous racially enslaved and exploited Native population that is quickly disappearing, either directly or through incorporation dialectics, that end in ideologies of (unequal) assimilation for Blacks and Indians.

The African slave trade that is developed into a transoceanic, transcontinental market or system of human trafficking on the highest order, began formation in the 16th century by the Portuguese (and Spanish) in ways similar to the trans-Saharan trade of the Moors or the trans-ocean trade between East Africa and the lands of East India (Davidson, 1980: 59)[20] with a primary interest in domestic markets within mercantile systems expanding throughout Europe.

The French, English nor Dutch engaged in slaving until Natives were sold across the Atlantic followed by Africans to the Caribbean, about and after 1500, when Pedro Alvares Cabral made landfall in Brazil. The trade may have delivered a few tens of thousands of slaves to European markets before, but from then on the slave trade would increase exponentially, especially taking off in the 17th century, and within 400 years, starting with Portugal and Spain, followed by England, France, Holland, Prussia, Denmark, Sweden, Brazil and the United States of America, millions of captives were forcefully transported to the slave ports of the Americas. The early nature of African–European connection was utterly deformed (Davidson, 1980: 63), and relationships of African countries and peoples with the colonies and later the countries of American continents would continue deforming the human and social relationships of peoples fully racialized and treated as if chattel property on the lower end, or vaulted with supremacist ideologies and privileges on the upper levels of a stratification system by race and gender.

The conquest of Mexico, suppression of the Latin American Maya and toppling of Incan trade empire all produced initial great plunder wealth for Spain, raiding the treasuries of these civilizations as they tore down their cities and took over trade routes to make roads for military and political colonization. The aforesaid 15th-century Papal Bulls of the Roman Catholic Church, dividing the Atlantic world in half, granted Portugal a monopoly on trade in West Africa and Spain the right to colonize the New World in its quest for land and gold, and less discussed, Indigenous labor. Pope Nicholas V had buoyed Portuguese efforts in the Romanus Pontifex of 1455, giving Portugal's exclusive rights to territories it claimed along West African coasts and trade from those areas, with rights to invade, plunder and "reduce their persons to perpetual slavery" in the name of Christ. This was followed by the 1479 Treaty of Alcáçovas dividing the Atlantic Ocean and other parts of the globe into two zones of influence: Spanish and Portuguese.

When Pope Alexander VI (Borgia) issued the 1493 Bull, the Crown (especially Queen Isabella) invested in Christopher Columbus's exploration to increase her wealth and ultimately rejected the enslavement of Native Americans, claiming that they were Spanish subjects. However, Spain established an *asiento*, or contract, system that authorized the direct shipment of captive Africans for human commodity trading in the Spanish colonies in the Americas, thereby averting the laws of Burgos and those from the 1542 New Laws and later the Vallodolid debates.

The **Asiento de Negros** system involved contracts between the Spanish Crown and noted foreign merchants for exclusive rights to deliver African slaves to Spanish American colonies, allowing Spain as an Empire to indirectly engage in the transatlantic slave trade, not from African embarkation ports, but under trade monopoly rights of importation to foreign merchants. This quasi-capitalist system involved nations with greater influence in that part of the world – first Portuguese and Genovese, and afterward the Dutch, French and British. Lacking territorial rights in Africa, the Spanish *asiento* contracts were issued for specific African ports and slave ships to import slaves to Spanish ports in Caribbean and coastal America, and were financed by foreign merchants and investment banks, increasing the competitive interests from other countries – Netherlands, France, England – with geopolitical power to develop their own trade systems.

Thus the transatlantic slave trade started in the mid-16th century, relying on capital investment and international commerce of human trafficking, with nations and privateers warring over economic interests with direct profiteering from conquest colonization. The Portuguese ran their own system directly to Brazil, but also contracted out for the *asientos*, while the Spanish empire relied on contracting out the enslavement delivery system, with foreign investment, that competitive nation-states began to take over, using chartered companies that fueled development of mercantile colonial capitalism (Chapter 3, English colonies). While the Spanish would develop alternative forms of coerced labor, slavery by any other name (Reséndez, 2016), including early forms of debt peonage and types of indentured "just war" captured prisoners,

Figure 2.5 Great resistance leaders of the Americas after 1492 in epoch 1. (a) Enrique (*Guarocuya*) – Taino resistance. Ponytail88 at English Wikipedia, CC BY-SA 3.0 http://creativecommons.org/licenses/by-sa/3.0/, via Wikimedia Commons. (b) Bartolomé de las Casas – Spanish (priest-ally). Unidentified painterlabel QS:Les,"Pintor no identificado"label QS:Lde,"Unbekannter Maler"label QS:Len,"Unidentified painter"label QS:Lit,"Pittore non identificato"label QS:Lfr,"Peintre non identifié", Public domain, via Wikimedia Commons. (c) Cuauhtémoc – Aztec ruler (last resistance). Cbl62, CC BY-SA 3.0 https:// creativecommons.org/licenses/by-sa/3.0, via Wikimedia Commons. (d) toqui Lautaro – War Leader, Mapuche. Español: Tríptico de "El joven Lautaro" de Pedro Subercaseaux – Errázuriz Pedro Subercaseaux, Public domain, via Wikimedia Commons. Great Women Leaders of the Euro-Americas after 1492 in Epoch 1. (e) Anacaona – Ayiti-an prisoner. Cacique (Chief) Taina, indigenous of island of Hispaniola. Picture in Irving's book, Vida y Viajes de Cristobal Colón, page 193. Public domain source: Vida y Viajes de Cristobal Colón. (f) Lady Cofitachequi – Head of Cofitacheque. Here is Timucuan wedding procession as example, Houghton Library, Public domain, via Wikimedia Commons. (g) Isabella I – Queen of Spain (Castile) Spanish patriarchs dominate Native matriarchs. Museo del Prado, Public domain, via Wikimedia Commons.

Anacaona – tricked
and then taken
prisoner – was forced
to walk in chains to
the capitol court, tried
and given a very brutal
execution - here she is
depicted as European
like...

Figure 2.5 (Continued)

The Lady of Cofitachequi was brought to meet DeSoto in magisterial procession, she gave pearls and other wealth to them, allowed the leaders to stay in her home, yet was met with treachery, kidnapping, and exploitation...

Figure 2.5 (Continued)

The Spanish seemed particularly bothered when they ran into women leaders in the Americas, although Queen Isabella I was the first to support and even engineered the first decade of invasion, colonization and domination. Anacaona was given a special execution of hanging, while their attempts to kidnap and coerce the lovely "chieftainess" of Cofitachequi failed with her escape (and since the guide to capture their grand woman leader had committed suicide rather than give her up). These leaders met the Spanish with composure, generosity and a remarkable openness, yet were only uncivilized or savage women to conquistadors who otherwise answered to their own Queen, in many ways proving how powerful the racial icon Indian was.

other European powers would increase their involvement in slave trading and enslavement within their colonies. These struggles would greatly influence conflicts and religious wars on the European continent, which would then direct colonization patterns for the next 200 years.

Starting at the turn into the 16th century, we observe more than 100 years of slave market development, truly global at its start – crossing oceans, continents and hemispheres, controlled by the Iberian nations at first, and financed by still other nations in the Mediterranean waters and the low countries of central Europe. These enslavement systems had only one goal – maximizing profits from plantations and mines in the newly colonized Americas that were also producing great plunder wealth making its way back to state treasuries and, more importantly, into banking and investment houses, developing the economies of Europe at a feverish pace.

Two other major social changes came into sharp conflict during this same time period – religious authority centralized in the Mediterranean was being questioned and challenged; and, nation-states were amplifying centuries-old conflicts into wars of position with the express purpose of building stronger colonizing forces for coming conquest invasions in the Americas. Spanish hegemony over this expansion into the Caribbean and surrounding American land base had made them, along with their Iberian neighbors the Portuguese with a burgeoning slave trade, the wealthiest nations in the western world. At the same time, the Dutch Netherlands, Prussia and growing financial systems in Denmark and England were becoming economic powerhouses, even as these countries were building fleets for colonial trade and navies for oceanic warfare.

Colonization of lands and civilizations produced great wealth from resource extraction (silver/gold mining, timber, fur, animal products) and development of plantation agriculture (sugar, coffee, cotton, tobacco) for export to Europe. Both of these processes required huge shipping fleets and inexhaustible sources of cheap labor in addition to settlers. Enslavement market systems were critical components of the 16th-century development of invasive colonialism and wealth transfer to Europe, and would prove even more so in the 17th century.[21]

Intersections of (1) far-reaching shipping fleets and warring navies, from (2) very strong colonizing European nations with powerful economies, using (3) extra-national capital investment and banking and (4) massive immigration of colonists, indentured settlers and enslaved workers together caused the global growth of Europe and American colonies, spanning the Atlantic, three continents, and overtaking trading routes across the known world. This would forever alter most political-economies for the next 400 years.

One of the more influential developments of this era was the advent of commodification of sugar, begun with slave labor over the Madeiras (Moore, 2009), with Columbus in full view, so that he brings sugar-cane stalks to the Caribbean in 1493, enslaving Natives on plantations. Originally a luxury product, sugar transformed European diets, economics and sociopolitical relations between social organizations and countries (Muhammad, 2019). Physically demanding and dangerous field labor for sugar manufacture (only to be outdone by cotton the next century) required and controlled cheap labor (enslavement systems being efficient, if on a large scale) and large trans-oceanic markets for moving a captive labor force. Race-based slavery for sugar in the Americas provided the needed conditions to change coloniza-tion, with European investment. "The true Age of Sugar had begun — and it was doing more to reshape the world than any ruler, empire or war had ever done" (Aronson and Budhos, 2010; from Muhammad, 2019).[22]

Perhaps the biggest effect came from the Circuit or Triangle Trade arising across the Atlantic, with resources and wealth flowing out of the Americas, into Europe and later mostly England, where manufactured goods would be shipped to various colonies in Africa, Asia and America, over the four cen-turies following Spanish penetration (see magnates, Chapter 1).[23] Millions of African lives, families and social developments were lost or destroyed in enslavement systems for sugar and other agricultural products, with similar or greater destruction of Native societies.

These social forces – developing slave markets across the Atlantic, deeply oppressive colonies in the Americas over sugar and related products, nation-states pushing plantations – built state colonizers throughout the mid to late 16th century, both in size and scope.

> … in 1592, trying to meet a demand for slaves that was rendered prac-tically inexhaustible by the holocausts of those who died, the court spewed up a monster of an assiento. No longer a question of delivering a few hundred African captives to the Americas, the new license was for the **transport of 38,250 slaves, delivering 4,250 captives a year**, stipulated to at least **3,500 a year** to be **landed alive**. … and **not to include**: "mulattoes, nor mestizos, nor Turks, nor Moors' …"
>
> (Davidson, 1980: 66) [bolding mine]

The transformation of the slave markets, from Native locals initially for the West Indies, and the mines of Central America during mid-century, to replacement labor from Europe and gradually, from Africa where formal large scale slave trafficking would become exclusively racialized, would be relatively complete by the turn of the century, although continued enslave-ment over Native peoples in the Americas would continue for another 130 years or so, and indentured/indebted forms of quasi-slavery continued into the creation of the United States. The transatlantic slave markets would devastate three continents and change political economies throughout the world, as controlled or directed by European colonizers, "… began by enslaving the populations they had found, the 'Indians' that death robbed them of, followed by ranks of 'indentured' or near-slave workers from home, that would not suffice, until they applied to Africa and saw their problems solved" (Davidson, 1980: 63).

Part of why the Spanish proclamations on the export of slaves kept shifting was precisely because of changing patterns of racialization in relation to the growing Atlantic slave markets. Noted earlier, many early slaves coming from the Iberian markets and North Africa were "white" and female, (Rumanian) girls[24] fetching the highest prices. Governor Ovando in 1503, having put down Xaraguan resistance, complained that black African slaves were too difficult to control. He appealed to end African slave exports and Queen Isabella consented, although the African slave trade picked up again in 1510 under royal orders, in groups of 50–100, and rudimentary institutions began to form after 1519 (note Enrique's rebellion).

> The first notable African slave revolt in Hispaniola broke out in 1522, so by 1532 the Spanish had established a special police for chasing fugitive slaves … Nothing could stop the trade, there was too much money in it for the courts of Europe.
>
> (Davidson, 1980: 65)

By mid-century, Spanish attention had moved to Central and South America, while holding on to those Caribbean islands already colonized (where Spanish is spoken today). As French, Dutch and Danish forces moved into the colonizing region and slave markets (with British privateers), the Spanish formalized the *assiento* permits, limiting them to so-called Guinea slaves to avoid use of Christianized persons that had been banned in the Laws of the Indies. The Iberian royals were living off the slave trade, which was spreading to other European monarchs, at least partly because of the Crowns merging, and as noted the rise of protesting religious minorities causing greater separation from the state banking structures arising from merchant contracts.

At the end of the century of building enslavement systems, 1500–1600, clear racial boundaries had emerged, with complicated Spanish systems including African, Native and Mestizo descent (Hall and Fenelon, 2009: 64–70), hardened but not fully defined Portuguese systems in Brazil and southern Atlantic islands, and the northern European powers honing in on African slaves for the American markets. Slave rebellions and coalitions with existing Native national forces were becoming a problem (as already noted with Enriquillo), with individual nations starting to develop institutions for social control of plantations and worker populations. With Britain, France and the Dutch eyeing North America, dreaming of opportunities for plunder and great wealth infusion into their treasuries, another major factor was about to explode over the continents colonizing scene – sudden and holocaustal disease depopulation of Native nations.

Similar to what we have seen with the Spanish *conquista* colonization, as at Tenochtitlán, when Native peoples began to die in large numbers from pandemics that do not kill Europeans, this fit rather neatly into the dominant justification that their God favors them, a supremacist ideology. As we are about to see, this would be even stronger among reformed Protestants from England, with their notions of "predestination" and the "depraved" as an expression of God's will, which is further supported by the older biblical concepts of "wilderness" both in the lack of civilizations' affects and ideologies of wild savages. We will have to consider these overarching philosophies with their linkage to Manifest Destiny (Chapter 4) and global concepts of the Other (next Book), just as we are moving toward understanding the depopulated areas that English colonists were moving into (Chapter 3). For now, though, we have to also look at overall environmental effects at such massive loss of agricultural ecologies managed by Native nations across the continent, and changes wrought from the incoming Europeans in building large plantations for production of crops as commodities, and later townships and cities for developing capitalism.

> The 'disappearances' of Indigenous people led to a demographic paradigm shift, and to notable shifts in the global carbon cycle. In the 'Great Dying,' Koch, Brierley, Maslin, and Lewis (2019) find a demographic loss due to pandemics of millions (56)[25] of people in the Americas by 1600, which led to a loss or destruction of landscapes of indigenous societies, increasing carbon uptake and secondary succession of forests, that led to a lowering of global surface temperatures in the two centuries prior to the Industrial Revolution. The sustainable, agricultural activities of Indigenous civilizations and their highly diverse ecoregions were all destroyed. When these populations (20+ million in Mexico's central valleys alone) 'disappeared' due to conquest death and spread of disease, so did their agricultural systems, leading to a reforestation that reduced carbon uptake (i.e. sequestration), and thus cooled the region and ultimately the globe.
>
> (Fenelon and Alford, 2020)

The English colonization forces were entering into less or depopulated regions they typified as wilderness, sometimes without strong towns and nations, and so they could double down using Spanish Catholic notions of God's will with wilderness, along with the core Protestant doctrines of predestination and election (discussed later, this chapter, Chapter 3 and the next Book).

Many Native nations, more remote tribes and great civilizations fell under invasion, disease and the technologies of colonization, typified as *Guns, Germs and Steel* (Diamond, 1997), followed by the great enslavements, first by Spanish (and Portuguese in South America) closely followed by African slaves, markets built into transoceanic systems, much enslavement over mining (wealth transfer) such as the great silver mines at Potosi (Weatherford, 1988).

> More than the market for any other commodity, the silver market explains the emergence of world trade. China was the dominant buyer of

---

DeSoto – the Great Dying – and the Coosa I: 2-3

1500s

We have observed how Hernando Cortez conducted the retaking of Tenochtitlán only after smallpox ravaged the Aztecan resistance forces that had earlier driven him out of the city. Pandemics raged across Mexico and Latin America, reducing some 25 million people to less than 2.5 million in the central valleys alone. The Florentine Codex (Rodriguez, 2020) closely documents later pandemics as well as great loss of culture and social organization, including the resources to resist conquest colonization.

"The diseases did not merely spread among American Indians, kill them, and disappear. They came, spread, and killed again and again… There may have been as many as 93 serious epidemics and pandemics of Old World pathogens among North American Indians from early 16th to the beginning of the 20th century (Dobyns, 1983). 1520 is when the first probable epidemic of Old World disease invaded North America. It was smallpox." (Thornton, 1987:45). Later:

Hernando de Soto landed in western Florida, 1539, with a large invasion force advancing through many Native nations – the Timucua, Acuera, Apalachee, Kasihta (Muskokean) – kidnapping leaders such as the Lady of Cofitachequi when they would not submit leaders, (similar to Anacaona) and laying a swath of destruction across the southeastern region of North America. They reached the vast, rich agricultural lands of the Coosa (Josephy, 1994: 148-50), leaving behind a sick servant, and advanced wars against the Mobile, Chickasaw and other Mississippian peoples until challenged by the Sun King of the Natchez. De Soto died from illness, and his forces went downriver harassed by Indian Nations all the way. Sixteen years later, another Spanish force sought to colonize Coosa kingdoms, but they could not find their vast agricultural domain, as pandemic sickness swept through their country, killing old and young, venerated and worker alike, so the Coosa were now gone.

We can understand that the terrible and continental depopulation from diseases is both intimately and interactively connected to conquest and colonization in the first hundred years of European invasion of the Americas.

The early massive American Indian depopulation created not so much a virgin territory to be conquered by Europeans as a land widowed by early epidemics: "Europeans did not find a wilderness here; rather, however involuntarily, they made one… The so-called settlement of America was a resettlement, a reoccupation of a land made waste by the diseases and demoralization by the newcomers" (Jennings, 1975).

"Thus the first four centuries of contact between North American Indians and Europeans and Africans – later Americans – developed into two very different demographic histories, one of unprecedented decline, the other of unprecedented growth." (Thornton, 1987:59)

The Great Dying created both demographic and societal collapse across the Americas, with environmental and ecosystem degradation accompanied by weakening of nations.

There were between 92 to 120 million Native people living over the western hemisphere, before 1492, with some estimates of 140+ million (Stannard, 1992:11), with revisionist estimates millions lower, but still demonstrative of a population loss of 85 to 90%.

"The great death raged for more than a century. By 1600, after some twenty waves of pestilence had swept through the Americas, less than a tenth of the original population remained. Perhaps 90 million died, the equivalent, in today's terms, to the loss of a billion. It was the greatest mortality in history. To conquered and conqueror alike, it seemed as though God really was on the white man's side." (Wright, 1992:14)

Figure 2.6 DeSoto – the Great Dying – and the Coosa (text box).

silver. On the supply side, Spanish America (Mexico and Peru) erupted with unprecedented production of the white metal. Conservative official estimates indicate that Latin America alone produced about 150,000 tons of silver between 1500 and 1800 (Barrett 1990), perhaps exceeding 80% of the entire world production over that time span.

(Flynn and Giráldez, 1995: 202)

Ironically, much of the initial investment monies operating as mercantilism was from relocated Jewish lenders in Genoa, or Amsterdam, having fled the Spanish Inquisition also culminating in 1492. Between a third to a half of the capital profits ended up outside Spain.

Accompanied by plantation economies – sugar, coffee, tobacco, potatoes, indigo, cacao – (Weatherford, 1988) raw wealth flowed to Spain and Portugal, and capital wealth flowed from investment banking to Dutch, French and British holdings, with silver and other mineral wealth also flowing eastward in new global markets, opening after the 1571 Spanish taking of Manila in the Philippines. The year 1571 also marks Francis Drake's first raid on the Pacific Ocean side of Panama, where silver and gold were transported to the Atlantic markets, or to a growing Asian demand. These raids, proving more difficult than the privateer raids in the Caribbean (later this chapter), were just as lucrative, with more than the royal fifth going to the Crown of England, who then authorized further raiding to find the South American source of such phenomenal wealth. Drake did so, conducting one of the greatest Spanish galleon takedowns of all time, out of the port city Arica (now Chile) in 1579. The silver out of Potosí alone changed the economies of Europe, bringing silver bar currencies outside of the monarchy into trading houses around the world. Unfortunately for the Native people of the remote Andean region, this great wealth came at the cost of countless lives of laborers, some estimate it to be in the millions, after the Spanish used a **mita** system to compel Indians to work in the mines, not unlike what was done in Hispaniola. The rise and fall of Potosí reflects the early patterns of mercantile capitalism.

> *"For the powerful emperor, for the wise king, this lofty mountain of silver could conquer the world."* So read the engraving on an ornate shield sent by Spain's King Felipe II in 1561 as a gift to the city of Potosí, in what is now southern Bolivia ... The *conquistadors* ... did find a mound of silver so large it would turn an isolated Incan hamlet into the fourth largest city in the Christian world in just 70 years, fund the creation of the most advanced industrial complex of its era, and define economic fortunes from China to western Europe ... ... At its peak in the early 17th century, 160,000 native Peruvians, slaves from Africa and Spanish settlers lived in Potosí to work the mines around the city: a population larger than London, Milan or Seville at the time. In the rush to exploit the silver, the first Spanish colonisers occupied the locals' homes, forgoing

the typical colonial urban grid and constructing makeshift accommo-
dation that evolved into a chaotic mismatch of extravagant villas and
modest huts, punctuated by gambling houses, theatres, workshops and
churches … High in the dusty red mountains, the city was surrounded
by 22 dams powering 140 mills that ground the silver ore before it was
moulded into bars and sent to the first Spanish colonial mint in the
Americas. The wealth attracted artists, academics, priests, prostitutes and
traders, enticed by the Altiplano's icy mysticism. "*I am rich Potosí, treasure
of the world, king of all mountains and envy of kings*" read the city's coat of
arms, and the pieces of eight that flowed from it helped make Spain the
global superpower of the period.

(Greenfield, 2016)

Some anthropological historians see Potosí as the "first city of capitalism"
(Weatherford, 1988), because of its immense influence on currencies and
trading houses around the world. At the end, Potosí was reduced to little
more than 10,000 mostly poor, struggling miners, a wasted landscape of
colonial exploitation of natural resources, people and once great Inkan
Native societies.

Meanwhile, back at the fort, New Spain was driving north from
conquering the Aztecs, where the greatly reduced and destabilized tribal
nations were vulnerable to militant colonization and its side effects of quasi-
slavery and domination. Beginning with Coronado, Spanish forces would
invade tribal lands, often pitting Indian nations against each other in the
spirit of Cortez, but always leaving a violent wake of death, destruction and
domination. At the same time, great forests were leveled, ports built, roads
followed Indigenous routes, amid a downfall of the Incas, covering much of
the western South America regions, which led to a rapidly expanding set of
colonies, and more silver mines in Mexico that would compete with Potosí
in terms of overall numbers, at least of Native people forced into labor.

One set of resistance wars were by the Caxcanes, who played a major role
in the Mixtón Rebellion (1540–1541) and what Nahuas, now aligned with
the Spanish, called the Chichimeca War (1550–1590), where the adversaries
of the Spaniards later became their allies against Zacatecos, and other tribes.
The major force under Coronado, backed by thousands of allied Native
nations, including the Tlaxclalans (who helped fight the Aztecs), continued
invading lands north and west of the central valley into the lower southwest of North America, and other renamed territory. This became a lawless
region, ignoring the Burgos Laws or the Spanish Crown and Catholic
Church prohibitions on slavery. Labor was needed at the mines, and however shortened their lives were, many Indians were compelled to provide it
themselves, or neighboring tribes. Andrés Reséndez calculates that slave-like
conditions encompassed millions of Native peoples in a variety of methods,
including pseudo *encomiendas* from the Caribbean. Indians could be accused

of crimes and sentenced to hard labor for many years. For those forced to work at the mines, they might never return, with forms of the *repartimientos* employed again, along with debt peonage (note these would be used on U.S. plantations, and after the Reconstruction era, see next Book).

Two great processes were about to change the racialized demographics of the western hemisphere and thus the world – one was the invasion of the Americas by colonizing powers and diseases unknown to peoples Native to those continents; the other was waves of immigration by European colonizers and enslaved peoples from Africa spreading through the entire hemisphere. The English were hard upon the heels of the Spanish in terms of colonization and race slavery. "By 1561 Queen Elizabeth invested royal money in the Guinea trade. Even so, in 1564 French crews and their country, unlike England, specifically condemned the trade in slaves" (Davidson, 1980: 61). English reports that "Negroes were very good merchandise in Hispaniola ... caused captain Hawkins to put off the coast of England in the month of October 1562 ... to the coast of Guinea, and got in his possession the number of three hundred Negroes at the least ..." Piracy of hundreds more from Portuguese slavers, continued to where he "sailed over the ocean sea unto the island of Hispaniola, selling some part of his Negroes ..." then going from port to port trading for "hides, ginger, sugars, and quantities of pearls, commodities he sent to Europe for great profits" (Davidson, 1980: 68). It is important to note Hawkins, along with Drake, Newport and soon even a young Smith partake of piracy and selling of Black slaves long before there are any permanent colonies along the eastern seaboard of North America. Like that of the privateers, this lack of formal lawmaking allowed the English Crown an aura of plausible deniability. However, the trade in African slaves in all its brutality was well known to English sea captains.

All this was the start-up for

> the 'Great Circuit' trade that was to dominate the commerce of the Atlantic for many years, with export of cheap manufactured goods from Europe to Africa; purchase or seizure of slaves on the Guinea Coast and transport across the Atlantic; the exchange of slaves for minerals and foodstuffs in the West Indies and Americas; and, lastly, the sale of these raw materials and foods in Europe.
>
> (Davidson, 1980)

For this triangular system, the third (and biggest) profits were realized on the "sale of American and West Indian cargoes in Europe." This marketing of slave-grown American or West Indian products in Europe, especially of sugar, in tandem with mining, became very big business, and later built the commercial supremacy[26] of England and France during the 18th century (Davidson, 1980: 68).

The Rise of Racism and Religion in Rationalizing Slavery – Both Sides of the Atlantic

The long 16th century proved critical to the rise of structural and early systemic racism within the vanguards of slave markets on both sides of the Atlantic and the transportation modes to get enslaved people into profitable property at their destination ports. As we have seen, religion in the guise of the Vatican over the Catholic Church in European countries laid the guard rails and rules of destination over the initial transatlantic slave systems, and the white supremacy that would follow. The great religious wars of Europe also rationalized slavery in different ways, with Protestants supporting settler colonialism in its infancy, and genocidal capitalism in their colonization of the Americas. The supply side of the system, the colonizer, broke up traditional cultural systems and many times the African nations that had coddled them, with vast effects on the west coast and interior of the African continent, including the Songhai empire and its principal trading city of Timbuktu.[27]

Just as Sonni Ali had worried over, the Portuguese had taken islands off the Gold Coast and developed them into trading posts, mostly for gold, the most prominent being Sao Jorge da Mina 1487 named El Mina (the Mine), sending great amounts of gold a year to Lisbon's royal treasury, later exchanging African slaves from other regions for the gold.

> The Akan goldfields proved to be a source of such wealth that the Portuguese crown decided to place the gold trade under direct royal control and to construct a fortified base on the coast to fend off rival European traders. In 1482 … the fortress (Sao Jorge da Mina) was acclaimed to be 'the first stone building in the region of the Ethiopians of Guinea since the creation of the world'. By 1487 El Mina was sending 8,000 ounces of gold a year … By 1500 the annual trade had reached about 25,000 ounces, a significant proportion of the world's supply … To finance their purchase of gold, the Portuguese began to participate in the domestic slave trade of West Africa … … to act as middlemen in the slave trade, acquiring slaves in the 'slave rivers' of the Benin coast and selling them to Akan merchants at El Mina … By 1500 the Portuguese were shipping on average about 500 slaves each year to El Mina in exchange for gold.
>
> (Meredith, 2014: 98)

Numerous scholars have documented the elegant townships and kingdoms of West Africa during this time, mentioning the Wolof, Akan, Ndongo and people from Kongo kingdoms, Timbuktu and many other nations interacting with Portuguese. Some reported a remarkable symmetry with what Columbus wrote in 1493, as late as 1611 agents from England's East Indian Company said:

Peru – Inka – Amazonas I: 2-4a

Inka emperors Túpac Inca Yupanqui and his son Huayna Capac, had often stayed
at their mountain ceremonial center, Machu Picchu, until the elders passing
in 1493, where they would reminisce on extensions of the Incan empire,
Tawantinsuyu, over the four directions suyu, of provinces under their administrative
control: Chinchaysuyu (north to Quito), Antisuyu (east, Amazon), Qullasuyu
(south to Chile) and Kuntisuyu (west to the Pacific), with many millions of peoples
in hundreds of small nations, the greatest trading network in the world, with
waterworks, agricultural systems and architecture of the highest order. Thus, it was
natural he would get his sons, Huáscar and Atahualpa, together to discuss news
that Spanish conquistadors had entered their territory in 1524, and that he was ill,
hoping to name the next Sapa Inca to contain the growing threat.

When Pizarro led conquistadors into Peru in 1532, a war of succession between the
sons had erupted, weakening the unity of the empire, along with dreaded European
diseases. Atahualpa had risen to prominence, and followed custom of diplomacy in
sending golden treasures to Spain, inviting them to meet (de Soto brought word)
in Cajamarca, without his armies. Pizarro had priests read the Requerimiento and
demanded Incans accept the rule of King Charles I and convert to Christianity.
Atahualpa refused, so the Spanish attacked, taking Atahualpa hostage. Incan leaders
offered great amounts of gold and silver ransom, which they delivered, but upon
news of Huáscar's death, the Spaniards killed Atahualpa, installed a figurehead and
militarily conquered the kingdoms of Inka, destroying all that stood in their way,
including the accumulated knowledge of the empire, just as Cortes had in Mexico.
So the advanced civilization of the Inka and all its wealth was lost to Spain.

Chile – Mapuche – I: 2-4b

Mapuche coalition forces, strengthened by the healing counsel of their traditional
Machi, meeting in Ruka for organized resistance, defeated and defended their
homelands against Incan armies sent to extend their empire to the south, near
the BíoBío River before 1500. When the Spanish invaded in 1550 these loosely
organized communities re-coalesced into fighting forces headed by toqui (war
leaders) Lautaro and Caupolicán – defeating Spanish troops under Pedro de
Valdivia, 1553, including use of horse light cavalry and weaponry, said to have forced
the conquistador to drink liquid gold for death. Defeated by treachery in 1557,
Mapuche won treaty rights yet continued to fight in the Arauco War until 1598
and in sporadic conflicts for over 300 years, a resistance formed by refusing forced
labor like the Inca used mita system in horrific mines (like Potosi) to serve Spanish
overlords. Like the Lakota on the northern continent, Mapuche have continued
to resist domination and colonization, resurrecting their fights against Pinochet's
fascist takeover, struggling to this very day to maintain traditional relationships to
the land and sacred lifeways.

Figure 2.7 Peru – Inka – Amazonas: Chile – Mapuche (text box).

I have never seen a better land in my life … The climate is very
healthy… (with) our people sick, all regained their health and strength
within twenty days … we found the natives of the country to be very
courteous and tractable folk ….

(Meredith, 2014: 129)

While slavery was beginning to destabilize the balanced African nations, especially those that were engaged in trading gold and slaves, traders and ship captains and European political powers still had to negotiate these deals with strong leaders, many equivalent to the royalty of Europe, that were not (yet) racialized as inferior or subordinate (as a singular race) to colonizers entering their lands. On the other side of Atlantic slave markets growing in the 16th century, racism toward Indians once defeated or destroyed as nations was becoming apocalyptic along with strictly racist use of African slaves and Natives dying in the many thousands (Horne, 2020).

The growing maritime power of England was not to be outdone, even if it would be technically hampered by the Vatican's Papal Bulls which left them out of the mix in the Caribbean. So, it was auspicious when Protestant revolt and Catholic resurgence gave King Henry the opportunity to divest England from the traditional Church and create his own in the Crown's interest:

> ... 1517 was of monumental significance for the evolution of the apocalyptic events then emerging in the Americas and Africa ... ... it did seem initially that predominantly Catholic France and soon-to-be Protestant England were more than willing to consort with the Turks ... It appeared as well that religious wars would erupt between Protestants and Catholics, ... reinforced when in 1521 the Edict of Worms called for complete suppression of Luther's teachings ... ... may have fueled the flames of anti-Semitism, spurring more migration across the Atlantic ...[28]
>
> (Horne, 2020: 65–66)

Protestantism became associated with high levels of preexisting ethnic discrimination.

Moreover, we can formatively link declarations of supremacy by the English with the colonizing economic interests in the Americas, and manipulation of minority group investment:

> The unperceptive observer in the 1530s could have easily concluded that because London was enmeshed in internecine crisis as Spaniards began to approach the vast and golden territory they called California, leaving mayhem in their midst and weakening the indigenes as they had to confront a surging republic by ..., that all this meant England was forever doomed.
>
> Yet, for an ambitious Henry VIII in London, breaking with the Catholic Church made sense, the need for divorce and remarriage aside ... ..seceding from Rome ... for further mercantile adventure ... needing financing to bolster the apparatus of the state ... he did not hesitate to employ murderous tactics against foes. ... In 1535, several prominent

Carthusians, a Catholic religious order, were dragged (Negro-style) across London from the Tower to Tyburn, now Marble Arch, where they were half-hanged, disemboweled, quartered, and beheaded. In nationalist London, the hegemonic line was to reject the "Bishop of Rome" but, as well, to despise the words of the "heretic" Martin Luther.

(Horne, 2020: 66)

Methods of execution of heretics and rebels for Protestant England and Catholic Spain were transported to the American colonies, with the added improvise of it all being "God's Will." With the first importation of African slaves to Hispaniola in 1518 followed by larger imports with predictable uprisings in 1522 until 1533 and the end of Enrique's revolt, and the fall of Tenochtitlán in 1521 and conquest of Mexico along with news of great wealth taken from the Inka connected to first reports of Ponce de Leon, and Coronado and De Soto's violent incursions into North America, religious justification needed to be sublimated to Crown colonizing tactics to dehumanize, and violently subjugate, the Native and African slaves who manned the mines and plantations of the colonies. Protestant ideologies of the "depraved" (or damned) bolstered by the Elect domination of colonial governance provided that rationalization.

Spaniards were enduring revolts by thousands of organized indigenes in Darien, a province of Panama. Predictably, in 1537 Africans revolted in the heart of New Spain... there was an acute shortage of Spanish women... and the number of mestizos grew, the Crown fretted that this would simply fuel dreams of secession. The situation cried out for a "whiteness" project, curbing religious sectarianism and inviting settlers from various European polities... but it would take the scrappy underdog Protestants to embark on this pragmatic route. ...the mass liquidation of indigenes increased the odds of Spanish colonialism prevailing. But working against Madrid was its intensifying rule of the Netherlands, dominated by the Crown for decades, which drove numerous refugees into England. This flow increased beginning about 1550... contributed to a "whiteness." Tellingly, Antwerp... had one of the largest populations of Africans in Europe.

(Horne, 2020: 80–81)

Even as Charles V permitted more African slaves to be brought to the Americas, Spanish forces were becoming more interracial when penetrating the inner continental areas, with such notable figures as "jet-black" Estevan (Estevanico previously enslaved Moroccan), joining slave-hunting southwest expeditions, previously invaded by Coronado burning hundreds of *Tiwa* at the stake, undertaking "seizure and rape of indigenous women" while calling the resistance Turks (83), one famously called "the Turk"

(Josephy, 1994: 163). De Soto also employed an "estimated four hundred African and indigenous enslaved" that he used in epic battles against the Mobile in 1540 (Horne, 2020; Josephy, 1994) that were left behind after De Soto died and the remaining Spanish fled to the Mississippi River and on to Cuba.

The Calusa of beautiful southwestern coastal Florida, with Venetian-like canals and domiciles, resisted Ponce de Leon's attempted invasions in 1513 and again in 1521 when he died, under their leader called Carlos who kept independence for their kingdom even as Spanish women helped to create diversity among their peoples. The Calusa continued resistance until French forces entered northeastern coastal areas to build Fort Caroline for the Huguenots (Protestants) with close relations to local Native Nations (Josephy 1994: 137). The Spanish sent conquistador Pedro Menéndez de Avilés to subdue the French and build St. Augustine, the oldest continuously occupied settlement of European origin in the contiguous United States. Admiral Menéndez destroyed the Calusa capitol Calos and resumed mastery over the Spanish galleons of the great Armada de la Carrera (Spanish Treasure Fleet), leaving *San Agustín* to become a multicultural city, invaded and burned by privateer Francis Drake during the Anglo-Spanish War (in 1586) with Native and African refugees joining Spanish and some French to rebuild once again. Attacks against the Jamestown colony in 1611 caused retaliation, including tribal Nations, temporarily ending in the 1663 charter by Charles II of England (Getting ahead of our story). Spain reclaimed the town, holding it on and off during various raids by French and British forces until the 1763 Treaty of Paris traded control back to England, which held it until the second Treaty of Paris in 1783 declared the United States independence, returning control back to Spain. Finally in 1819, Andrew Jackson took Florida for the United States, causing wars with the local Creek and Miccosukee, and later with the multiracial Seminole. Thus, St. Augustine represents the racial and ethnic diversity, along with a rough freedom, of all the peoples and races making up America. We describe all this in Chapters 3 and 4 herein, and in my next Book.

> Ethnic discrimination became a social force in Peru and Columbia, where a wealthy Jew was burned at the stake even as Christians stole treasuries from the Inka, rationalizing discovery in the "*roots of slavery, white supremacy, settler colonialism, and capitalism*" (Horne, 2020).

Race on the African Supply Side of Transatlantic Slavery

We do have to note, once again, the disastrous effects on many African nations and peoples from the supply side economics of the transatlantic slave trade and an invasive colonialism that was becoming more racialized with every decade's and in century markers of European domination. Portuguese sugar plantations became central to an international traffic in slave from nations like Kongo through intra-African trade during the 1500's:

> The demand (for slaves) grew ever stronger. Kongo slaves were sent to Sao Tome not just to work on plantations but to transit camps to await shipment to other destinations: the Gold Coast, Madeira, the Cape Verde Islands and Portugal. A Portuguese account noted in 1507, in addition to some 2,000 slaves working on plantations, the island held 5-6,000 slaves awaiting re-export. Between 1510 and 1540, four to six slaving ships per year were kept busy hauling slaves from Sao Tome to the Gold Coast alone.
>
> (Meredith, 2014: 103)

Here we note northern European treaties, such as that made by Henry VII Tudor of England with Charles VIII Valois, King of France in the Peace of Étaples in 1492, wasn't just about putting a focus on colonizing objectives, it was as much or more over an Irish resistance against England's developing plantation economies in Ireland (and Scotland). These conditions, including early reforms of the church, monetary policy and agreements on state expansion into "discovered" regions, were ripe for the growing transatlantic slave markets in competition with Spanish, Portuguese and later a Dutch fleet of privateers and trading companies.

England was making investments in the West African trade through deployment of "privateers" such as William Hawkins, as early as 1530 and in 1540 for ivory, gold and spices, and in 1550 (an ominous year for debates on slavery), three English captains (Wyndham, Lok and Towerson) brought back similar profits and the observations on the growing slave trade, but neither France nor England had markets in slavery (yet), unlike Portugal and Spain (Meredith, 2014: 116). England pursued its interests in all areas of profiteering, including slavery, through the use of Privateers operating under their own flags, but out of English ports under letters of marque with a "royal fifth" going to the Crown and development of shipping (fighting) fleets that bounded Atlantic and Pacific trading markets and potential colonies. John Hawkins (all in the family) was sponsored by new 'adventurers' in the 1560's to make direct slave trading trips to Angola and Kongo, which he traded and pirated away from other ships up to Sierra Leone, making three such profit-making voyages to Caribbean ports with slave markets. Over the 16th century and well into the 17th century when slave-holding colonies would be fully realized, English privateers and companies would invade, defend and often develop the racist slave-trading markets of global colonization, especially over North America, that created incipient capitalism and the modern world-system.

Indian to Black, Catholic to Protestant,[29] Spanish to English, Mercantilism to Capitalism

The ideologies of conquest for (capital) profits under justification (aegis) of God's will changed Europe and thus American colonization in deep and powerful ways still not entirely understood in the academy (see chapter end, and conclusions on Christians in the next Book).

First, news of the first Columbian trip spread throughout European countries who had long awaited such news (followed by Vasco de Gama and others reaching the actual Indies) generating competition between these already war-like states. Since the Papal authority had been returned to Rome from Constantinople, where it had become a state-based if not empire-driven religion (in fact the head of the Holy Roman Empire) – Church, State, Capital (trade) – became inextricably linked together in an unholy trilogy of conquest colonialism (by Europeans).

Second, revolutionary religious thinkers (and social activists) such as Martin Luther challenged this growing troika as corrupt (Catholic) on many levels – the individual Christian as moral behavior, the social forces of Church in colonization conquest and the State in exercising religious power and accumulating wealth. Herein, practices such as the buying of Indulgences were being criticized, along with the selling of Inheritance rights such as the *limpieza de sangre*, (purity of blood by descent) in the Spanish Inquisition, and were further linked to a profligate and greedy church-state linkage empowered by vast wealth transfers from the Americas (however, Protestants as Calvinists developed their own supremacist ideology – not yet white).

Third, concepts of non-Christian Indian "savages" (making its way to the U.S. declaration of Independence in that very language) initiated new ways to justify conquest enslavement and colonization by/thru religion, through geographic and phenotypic typologies that became race, and systemic racism as a core method of organizing the modern (new) world.

This intersection of systems of domination – capitalism, colonialism and racism – became central to European (and later American) societal development and philosophic thought, especially in terms of western civilization and ideologies of social evolution (Eurocentric), (Deloria, 1984) further linked to stratification systems employing these very concepts (terms) – free markets, colonial elites and white supremacy. Also, early forms of Protestantization correlated with the power of northern European nations rejecting Catholicism more because of its control by the Vatican having issued Papal Bulls giving colonization rights to Spain and Portugal.

Religious wars followed, predicated by growing colonization competition between powers (Christianity and Colonial warfare, see below, end of chapter and Conclusions in next Book).

These ideologies produce rationalization – in political, economic and religious (cultural) thoughts – that undergird the European American takeover, especially in the following chapters when explaining the race-based enslave-ment system (the Black) and the continuing conquest colonizing in the Mission systems (the Indian), often seen in the struggle between Catholic and Protestant colonizers. It is also self-evident in the fourth chapter (Irish or White ethnic) in such massive social policies as the Louisiana "Purchase" expansion and in the Manifest "Destiny" ideological practices culminating in the California genocide.

Renaissance to Racism and Religion

The Renaissance of Southern Europe was indeed a reawakening of sorts mostly of what we could call Mediterranean cultures, that were coming under further influence from the Moors and the less passionate yet scien-tific culture of a still rising Islam evidenced in the Ottomans. And, even as the greatest civilization of the time, China (Ming dynasty) was entering into retraction, its knowledge and highly developed arts were seeping into Europe through trade and leftover influences of the Mongols' earlier expan-sion into what is now thought of as southeastern Europe, the western reaches of central Asia. This infusion of Roman-Greco and Asian developments into and out of Charlemagne's empire was deeply beautiful, immensely complex and monumentally productive with great visual arts achieving new heights, accompanied by new military systems and martial arts that began to trans-form the feudal countryside into stratified urban landscapes of competing powers, often deeply violent, that were becoming centered in cities.

Religion (large society based, less individual spirituality – Telemachus by Fénelon[30] later as an example or alternative form that never took hold) and social reasoning of what would become known as western civiliza-tion, less driven by monotheistic Gods or prophets and more as a prime source for authority (Weber, 1961) and justification, were connected or woven into the economic structures of wealth distribution. We must con-sider this observation, dangerous as it became and still is (leading to charges of heresy) when seeing vast changes occurring in Europe at this time, when there is a shift from Mediterranean centrality through Charlemagne's cen-tral western Europe to the northern countries and their peculiar corporate industriousness.

Like the Renaissance, this leads to the Reformation that is unfortunately as martial and political (militaristic and statist) as it is religious. Western Christian society does not desire to study or understand this interconnected-ness of social-artistic, military-political, philosophic-cultural and religious-economic nexus of human social forces (because it later separates them functionally and analytically, including in great universities, see Wallerstein, 2004, Steinmetz, 2013).

Martin Luther can nail his 95 theses to a church wall, and other denomin-ational leaders can take reformist principles and adapt them to the societies, and that is quite possibly a wonderful thing. However, religion, as we observed in the advent of Constantine's fusion of Roman and Christian (forces) into state-based authority, ending in the Vatican, is also an important means of social organization that can be shaped to the objectives of state and empire.[31]

Spain, and to an extent Portugal, had been vaulted into world empires because of the wealth being extracted (what Marx calls primitive accumulation) from the Americas, and oceanic trade routes to the Orient, or Asian markets. This was done in conjunction with a central Catholic authority of the Vatican, as Protestant forms arose in northern Europe, challenging church authority, excesses and corruption, so that nation-state forces took notice and began to interfere in the directions the new religion took.

France, a once and future Catholic country, became deeply embroiled in these religion wars, even as the wealthy Spain had taken control of some of the Netherlands, notably the banking and investment branches (that were growing mercantile capitalism). England, having solidified its Channel borders with growing maritime markets over Ireland, the North Atlantic and the Baltic Seas, was deeply jealous and covetous of the great wealth being taken out of the Americas. The Protestant religious uprising, or revolt, provided a perfect opportunity to break with the Catholic Church and build new wealth-seeking economic structures. About the same time as this break occurs, or the fractures arise from (religious) fissures, the creation of economic enterprises separated from religious justification and state treasuries, began to form, especially in England, whose aim to penetrate Asian markets began to envisage easterly trade routes, through Russia, as well as long-term developments in North America.

Here we must recover the convoluted path that Christianity takes in its role of becoming a state religion and returns with the Roman capitol to a centrality of Rome, where it is when the Iberian states start the invasion, conquest and colonization of the Americas. Over the following century, the nexus of power moves to northern Europe, where Church, Crown and Company authority – and means of operation – are separated, giving rise to capitalism.

We observe a number of important points of transition and change in reviewing these church policies and positions in their relations to European powers and colonization.

Growth of power and wealth of Spanish colonization, authorized by the Catholic Church, caused strong responses from the now competitive northern European powers. France, evolving out of the Holy Roman Empire mindset, and still possessing the greatest land-base and citizenry of Europe, was strongly Catholic in the center and south, but was leaning more toward reform like that growing with the Protestants around them to the north and west. This also reflected their colonizing ambitions, as they were more diplomatic with Catholic Spain.

313 – Roman Emperor Constantine makes Christianity **state religion** in the Edicts of Milan

449 – Ecumenical Council at Ephesus, Pope Leo I delivers 'Tome' asserts Papal **supremacy**

800 – Charlemagne is crowned emperor of the **Holy Roman Empire** by Pope Leo III.

1054 Great Schism – Eastern Orthodox and Western Catholic **churches separate**.

1095 – 1205 Crusades to recover Jerusalem and Holy Land, **anti-Muslim** Papacy

1305 **Papacy moved** to Avignon in dispute with Philip IV of France.

1378 Papacy **returns to Rome** (Vatican re-established)

1453 Constantinople falls to the Ottoman Turks 1452 – anti-Muslim papal bulls on **heathens**

The Vatican using the authority of Papal Bulls reinforcement of political divisions of the coming conquest profits had divided the Atlantic theater into south-eastern region to be run by Portugal, and a less-defined (but more expansive) western region, including the Caribbean, run by Spain (**1493 Bull** for discovery conquest by Spain; 1494 dividing Atlantic between Iberian powers).

1496–1502 various Bulls, Treaties, Edicts on **sovereignty** declare Church position – conversion of Indians, just war, slavery, Inquisition (Isabella I), **rules of engagement** (confirming *assientos* companies to human-traffick) in New World, including slaves/indentured.

1511–1515 Dominicans and other Catholic orders (Franciscans less so) support **Burgos Laws**

1517–1521 Martin Luther (95 theses) Protestantism rise as resistance, reforming movements

1534 **Act of Supremacy** passed – Henry VIII becomes supreme head of the English church. (Catholic / Vatican authority no longer needed for colonization in Americas)

1537 Pope Paul III papal bull *Sublimus Deus* **opposes enslaving** Indians declared "true men"

1542 New Laws (**Human Rights** for Indians, African slavery ignored – *assientos*, conquest)

1545-63 Roman Catholic **counter reformation**, Spain takes Netherlands (banking)

1550 – Valladolid debates, (Human) Rights of Indians established – *Encomienda* allowed – dissonance between Christian values and **State colonial practices** (African slavery)

1520s–1556 Netherlands **banking**/investment of Spanish fleets, colonial mining and resource extraction, rakes in huge profits – religious conflicts increase over money (taxes, value)

1556 – 1579 Spain inherits/invades Netherlands over church control/corporate profits (overseen by Catholic authority) **Religious wars** erupt in France (1562–1598) and colonies (1565).

Figure 2.8 Religious changes to state and company (chart: corporate control, capitalism).

1555 – 1599 England, followed by Dutch, French other Europeans creates (secular) Companies (incorporated by Crown charters) which **do not answer to** either **Christian authority**
1558 – **Supremacy Act of 1558/59** – Queen Elizabeth loyalty oaths to Crown over Church
1600 – 1620 or 1624 England moves for Crown authority over American colonies (company run) **separating Church** authority from **political/economic** issues of colonization

1555 Peace of Augsburg ends German religious wars.
1611 Publication of the King James Version of the Bible.
1618–48 Protestant/Catholic conflict in Germany (Thirty Years War) – Westphalia treaty.

Figure 2.8 (Continued)

Prussia and the Netherlands were more continental powers, thus less wedded to colonization, except that the Dutch were investment banking the Spanish fleets and mercantilism, which was causing conflict over wealth transfers, a situation that would intensify with capitalist colonies.

England had the most to gain by separation from Catholic authority, and was best positioned to compete in overseas ventures in the Caribbean and North America, and thus moved early for a supremacy clause and to create their own state church authority, later developing the companies that would be the basis for international corporate capitalism throughout the colonization time periods, and beyond to the 20th century.

Separation of church and state was as much separation of economic adventurism in companies from church (values and philosophies), clearly evident in Spain and the Vatican struggling with rationalizing slavery for those converted or baptized. The Crown continued to take the royal fifth until taxation systems could be put into place, and accounting systems could correct for company or corporate profit-making, which was state-held wealth – whether plunder or colonizing sources – in treasuries under nationalist control. When we observe how massive enslavement and market systems develop under international investment schemes, and how they profit from depopulation under settler colonialism, it is easier to see how such non-Christian actions on global scales can or could be rationalized and accepted, or simply made invisible, to a Christian hierarchy.

We see the strong interactions between state colonizers, religious rationalization, and early company or corporate profit-making from colonies that employed race-based transoceanic slave marketing, ethnic-based coerced and voluntary immigration, and genocidal conquest over the Americas. We next turn to see how these same interactive systems – Church, Crown, Company – develop from colonizing mercantile and agricultural capitalism (Chapter 3) to new state systems of international corporate trade and industrial capitalism (Chapter 4 and the next Book).

Rise of Protestant Christianity – Three to Four C's (Church, Crown, Colony to Company)

Initially, we need to make three itinerant observations of the rapid growth of Protestant Christianity in northern Europe, which fundamentally changes and shapes the colonization of the Americas. Although the different groups and denominations of Christians critical of Catholics vary somewhat in their early development, and a lot in later centuries – the early Protestants had begun the long, slow road to violent separation from Catholic hierarchies linked to hierarchies of the state, or Crown – they all started and stayed on a trifold path: emphasis of private property or the near worship of land ownership (these concepts are linked to colonization, in an availability of owning land, taken of course from the Native occupants); socio-religious use of the Elect and Predestination (and a counterpart the Depraved) – that are replaced with Elite and Supremacy (first national elites, then racial supremacy); and a growing worship of wealth – individual and in the developing banking, investment houses and trading companies of Europe. These would be in perfect colonial form in Virginia and in Massachusetts, becoming New England.

White Christian Domination and Supremacy over 500 Years

What we have to acknowledge is the powerfully disparate political voices in play over this social movement and broader implications of the formation of the United States of America.

(Similarly, later we see international forces in the removal, or coup, of Evo Morales in Bolivia, where virtually every component of Indigenous struggle and resistance is in play).

Another note is to see empire, for this book, and its religious precedence, in the Justinian emperor (in Constantinople later Istanbul) who is revered both as political head of the (Holy) Roman Empire, and as a Saint. This is another juncture for the Catholic religion, so that when Columbus gives news of the America voyage, and its vulnerability, reaches Europe, about 1493, the Pope in the Vatican is key to planning and policy for the upcoming conquest and invasion, hardly the province of a religious leader unless we recognize the traditional power, landed in the Christian religion, in the papacy. The political (or at least its rationalization) and the religious (or at least its power to affect social reality) were joined, first by Constantine, then centralized by Justinian, and then returned to Rome and the Vatican.

This earlier juncture was absolutely critical in the issuing of the Papal Bull of 1493, *Intercaetera*, conjoining these two major social forces with the economic, that of trade and plunder of conquest. The next juncture, also a schism in the church, is a rise of Protestantism, within three decades, that challenges the new orientation toward the centralization of political-religious order with the economic, first leading to various denominations connected to

Supremacy noted in the Catholic Church headquarters in Rome (Vatican)
Superiority-supremacy of the Conquistadors and Catholic operations in the
colonies
Supremacy noted in the Protestant Reformation writings against Catholic
hegemony
Supremacy Act by King Henry (VIII) against Vatican using the Church of England
Supremacy Act by Queen Elizabeth (I) with the Crown over the Church of
England
Superiority and later Supremacy in both Jamestown and Plymouth colonies
Supremacy developed in the U.S. Constitution (and Declaration of Independence)
We can see how racial superiority can be found in the acts of supremacy, which
views the world in terms of investments, and wealth however gotten or ill-
conceived, connected to the Privateers, (operating for the Crown) racialized
colonies and then corporations.

Figure 2.9 Supremacy and superordination.

early growth of mercantile capitalism in northern Europe (thereby church being sublimated to state, and to economic power), and by the early 17th century in the American colonies and elsewhere, the rationalizations for and toward colonialism and racism.

This last point is also critically important in observing a relationship between Christian supremacy with racial supremacy and the political-economy of colonial domination. The shift from religious supremacy to racial dominance becomes complete in the ex-colony of the United States, which sees itself as a quasi-evolutionary extension of political progress out of northern Europe, and also as an extension of religious authority and Christian civilization, associated as much with the Mediterranean as strictly European cultures.[32]

We return to this discussion in upcoming chapters. Three categories – political (Crown), economic (Colony to Company) and religious (Church) – are evidenced in evangelical Protestant churches over the next three centuries. Each of these structural categories are used to invent, reproduce and reify supremacy (white supremacy), in ethno-national and racialized systems of stratification and hierarchy. We find the evidence of their origins in the previously identified policy constructs from the 16th into the 17th centuries:

The Indigenous as Indian

The great diversity of Indigenous peoples in the Americas – whether seen as nations, tribes, empires, communities or other sociopolitical coalitions – remains a quandary for the social sciences that resort to essentialism and simplistic models of justice based on European societies. From 1493 onward, even as European nations developed concepts of sovereignty and the first rudimentary forms of capitalism through extensive resource extraction and colonization of the Americas, Native nations were systematically dominated, destroyed and distressed into subordinate positions, increasingly termed as tribes and as hunter-gatherers after larger social systems were dissembled. Ideologies and practices of criminal and social justice were based solely on states from Europe, found in the early and continuing Missions of the Spanish, which could and did include enslavement, genocidal living conditions and impoverishment of the once well-off Indigenous societies, who for thousands of years had traded and interacted, and yes, sometimes warred. Similar systems of domination were developed by the English that were considerably more exclusive, based on growing notions of race subordination and supremacy, as found in the Praying Towns of New England and Protestant dominance in the Virginia colonies. Rather than violent assimilation into highly stratified societies, Anglo systems began to rely on large-scale immigration of "settlers" into their North American colonies where genocidal death rates were driven by diseases producing monumental depopulation in many regions. The Crown colonies became stronger and increasingly independent by the mid-18th century, having outlawed religious and sociopolitical systems of justice for all Native Nations that were increasingly, and derisively, labeled collectively as Indians, although many treaties had been signed by what appeared on paper to be equals. Laws on property ownership, religious practices, use of languages, family formation and most other social spheres of colonial life were entirely based on European states in growing systemic capitalism and early industrialism.

Resistance by Native Nations within the orbit of the colonizers was suppressed through the wars and internecine violence produced by the Europeans. As the United States, Canada and various Latin American colonies revolted and gained a modicum of independence, they reproduced and renewed these laws, improving them in culturicide and genocide of Native Nations, often in defiance of or conversely in denial of treaties the new states made with individual indigenous peoples even as they were collectively treated as Indians, as Aborigines or other terms of subordination. For the next 250 years, all social practices – political, economic and cultural – employed maximal suppression of the Native Nations (500+) and many indigenous communities to the extent that populations of settlers, slaves and racialized elites became 90%+ of the peoples on North America.

Peoples fighting for survival, reorganizing or in resistance (mentioned here):

Taino Arawak – Mayan – Aztecan – Mapuche – Puebloan
Coosa (Cherokee) – Timucua – Mabila – (Mvskoke-Creek)
Inka (Quechua – Kwicha) – Guarani – Pamunkey (Powhatan)
Lenape (Delaware) – Haudenosaunee (confederation) – Wampanoag

All forms of progress and civilization were based on what became Euro-American societies, usually referred to as a New World although leaving any reference to Nations and Societies existing in the western hemisphere before conquest and colonization completely out of any discussion, sometimes referring to their mostly European origins as the Old World. Treaties and mutually agreed upon laws and perceptions of justice were entirely under the purview of the new colonial constructions, that now saw themselves as Countries and as States in their own right, that gave little to no recognition to preexisting Indigenous societies. Treaties were interpreted solely to the benefit of the new postcolonial countries, and were debased and dismissed entirely or partially in stages with the same effect of destroying or totally dominating Indigenous systems of social control and justice, replacing surviving native peoples.

The African as Black

The Black is developed as slave trading across the Atlantic, specific focus on African countries and sources of slaves, on the African coast, the mid-Atlantic voyage (along with embarkation ports acting as staging areas prepping the previous people to be treated as cargo) as a thinning or "seasoning" in preparation to be sold upon landing as valuable cargo, and then again in markets to individual owners, usually first in Caribbean port areas (Hispaniola) to enslavers and for export to other markets, and on to plantation owners. The racial label is a dehumanizing process, (Patterson, 1982). Here we identify various islands run by different European countries or mixed colonizers, their ports, such as Barbados, or Martinique (French) or Dutch islands, the Bahamas, or the Spanish in Cuba and in Hispaniola, with mines and sugar plantations.

Resistance – revolt – rebellion are seen as revitalization movements – renewed slave populations first observed in Puerto Rico in 1511 and Haiti in 1522, with uprisings in Brazil about that time, other revolts occurring throughout Latin America and even North American attempted colonies, the Carolinas in 1526 and decades later (Horne, 2020), and as noted previously around St. Augustine, with the Haitian merging of Native – African resistance, and colonizers fear of creating mestizo populations who might secede. Enslavement from the *assientos, encomiendas, repartamientos* and slave shipping transit ports also experienced revolts. Here it is best to use geographical comparative analysis – Hispaniola and its plantations with Ireland and colonization of the Ulster plantation, stressing the size and relative population displacement, showing English systems often worked without having to import labor, while the Spanish needed labor imports.

The European as White

The Spanish had, of course, as colonizers, developed supremacist ideologies regarding savagery and civilization, holding Catholics of Iberian Latin descent (*peninsulares*, see Hall and Fenelon, 2009: 68) superior to other western European countries, who collectively were thought above the base populations of the rest of the world, especially the Natives (or Indians) of the Americas, who, once conquered and under colonial domination, were considered the lowest form of human, partially with souls that could be converted, but who never could be citizens of the new land. Even as the Valladolid debates kept the Spanish from building full-scale systemic slavery, they did follow the Portuguese (who did build outright race-based slave systems) in importing African labor whenever convenient to do so.

Dutch, French and Portuguese transatlantic slavers profited immensely from Caribbean slave markets, with, as we are about to see, the growing competition of British non-Crown privateers, operating independently yet backed by English capital investments and military support when needed. The dominant English population was relatively homogenous (once accounting for Irish and other ethnic populations under early occupation), and thus became the primary population of "settlers" to the "New" world (of colonies, Indians, slaves and indentured laborers), soon known as Anglos, representative of most Protestant northern Europeans, and then finally as White.

Crown, Company and Church over Colony (of Settlers)

The rise of the Muscovy Company of Adventurers in 1555, then others, with the Dutch quickly following, for them and the growing number of private adventurers in the Caribbean, also meant taking African sea ports for slave

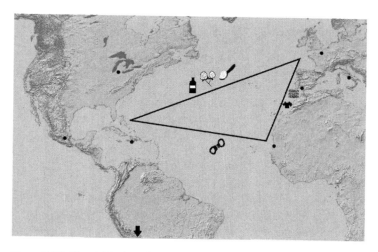

Figure 2.10 Circuit Trade – Atlantic [replaces triangular trade systems] (note: Map by Juan Aviles [graduate student at California State University, San Bernardino]).

exports to the Americas. The East Asia Company, or whatever offshoots it had, arose out of London and other English ports, followed by others, that became the London Company and afterwards the Virginia Colony, and so on it goes.

We chart a rise of incorporated companies later this chapter (Figure 2.13: Chart of **Companies)** and discuss their import – first Asia and India, at the same time North America, that were viewed as investments, connected to English Privateers (Hawkins, Drake, then Christopher Newport), and so many others, all with direct links to the Crown. Thus it was a system.

Corporate Raiders of the Caribbean

The budding relationship between trading companies, slavery and English colonialism with capitalism (mercantile) is fully evidenced in the early (trading) companies starting first with the Muscovy using English ships to the northeast with Russia, chartered and fully formed as a public private stock-held corporation in 1555 (interestingly, they used Discovery[33] in the company charters in 1551, 1555 and 1559) as the East Asia Company expanded (Dalrymple, 2019).

This coincided with Protestant financial separation of church and state with capital investment corporations (later political separation in the United States) that evoked religious rationalization supportive of private sphere wealth accumulation, relinquishing rights of responsibility over the poor or vanquished populations, and transferring those to companies, or incorporations.

Another set of relationships that would prove critical in the development of transatlantic trading companies were the privateers who raided and sometimes traded with African and Caribbean entities from the 1550s through the early 1600s, notably (Admiral) John Hawkins and (Captain) (Sir) Francis Drake. These privateers, often commanding a small fleet of pirate ships, attacked Spanish and Portuguese shipping, taking vast spoils of treasure and plunder, sharing one fifth of the profits with the Crown of England (Queen Elizabeth I at this time). This plunder was often Africans bound for burgeoning slave markets of the Americas, where the privateers would also sell their stolen human cargo. In fact, Hawkins became so proficient at this human trafficking as to be competitive with the Portuguese, Dutch and French (since the Spanish were officially banned from the African slave trade), and at times taking on slaves direct from their West African ports of embarkation, and other times engaging in oceanic warfare with cannon fusillades against Spanish fleets that were technically at peace with England.

On one such slave trading and pirating trip from England to the Guinea coast and on to sell the Africans to plantations in Panama and nearby areas, Hawkins enriched fleet was caught in extreme storms off Cuba, and he had to land in

Spanish ports near the provincial capital Veracruz, where he ran into a Viceroy fleet of warships, barely escaping himself with added crews from his sinking ships. Having no food, they dropped off nearly a hundred of the salvaged crews in Mexico, near Tampico, where they went on an incredible journey along the coast, meeting Indian nations, dodging Spanish ports all the way to Florida, where they hoped to meet with French Huguenots near St. Augustine (North America's first, longest standing settlement). However, Native intelligence informed them of the Spanish retaking the areas along with reports of fleets and military forces identified by Indian reporters as number of masts, and flags flown, so that they made their way by land coastal routes up the East Coast of North America, through a land they called Norembega (later New England), all the way to Newfoundland where they connected with English fishing – trading vessels taking them back to England. Their journey of 1567 – including enslaving and selling of Africans to the Americas, intercolonial warfare for dominance of Caribbean mineral and agricultural markets, land trekking through Native Nations fully informed and knowledgeable of the various European colonizers in the region – was told in the pubs of London for many years by the three survivors until in 1581, when England engaged Companies to begin their American colonial invasions, the last survivor was interviewed and the story documented for information sources including disposition of Spanish ports, Indian nations, slave profiteering strategies, and land/sea topographic and geographic mapping.

This can be considered important in understanding the colonization processes, capitalist development, racial formation and coming societal institutionalization of all three social forces in the Virginia and Massachusetts colonies of (New) England. The English were operating in full knowledge and deep involvement in African slave trade networks, colonization warfare in the Americas and Native Nations in regional and continental struggles. As we are about to see, the English colonies at Jamestown and Plymouth were started by chartered companies, with both settler and enslaved (and indentured servitude, much of it from Ireland already colonized) populations, employed and exploited by Crown adventures under cover of private trading groups, specifically designed for increasing transatlantic profiteering. While the first slaves from Africa may have been sold in 1619 to English colonists, and while the first Native Nations engaged in genocidal warfare happened around the same time, both processes were well underway and well understood by the English Crown and by colonizing trading companies.

The English colonization system was thus developed with three critical components: Anglo settler populations under contract to trading companies that answered to the Crown authority but were not directly invested politically much like the trading companies operated under technical independence; direct experience of racial enslavement like the Caribbean and ethnic indentured labor exploitation (Irish); intentional agribusiness plantation and natural resource extraction strategies for transatlantic trade.

Spain as the Wealthiest Nation, Naval Warfare with England

During the same period of time before formal colonization took place, the English were engaged in protracted war and internal struggle with Catholics in France and other European states, which was reflected in the competitive and violent struggles for control of the Caribbean. This was a direct outgrowth of what has been called the French Wars of Religion that were a prolonged period of war and popular unrest between Catholics and Huguenots (Reformed/Calvinist Protestants) in France between 1562 and 1598, with an estimated three million people perishing from violence, famine or disease in what is considered among the deadliest religious wars in European history (Thirty Years' War took six to eight million lives, the largest).

Figure 2.11 Killings/burnings of Taino leaders Hispaniola (wood cuts). (a) Cruelties used by Spaniards on the Indians – Massacre of Queen Anacaona. Massacre of the queen and her subjects, by Joos van Winghe, published in 1598 in the Brevísima relación de la destrucción de las Indias, written by Bartolomé de las Casas. Wikimedia – public domain. (b) Illustration of Spanish atrocities in Hispaniola – Theodor de Bry. Note: Bartolomé de las Casas (1474–1566): Regionvm indicarum per Hispanos olim devastatarum accuratissima descriptio, insertis figuris æneis ad vivum fabrefactis. Publisher: Heidelbergae,: typ. Gvilielmi VValteri Printer: Walter, Wilhelm Heidelberg, 1663–1676 Transl. of: Brevísima relación de la destrucción de las Indias. – Sevilla: Sebastian Trugillo, 1552. *Collection Peace Palace Library, The Hague.* Wikimedia – public domain.

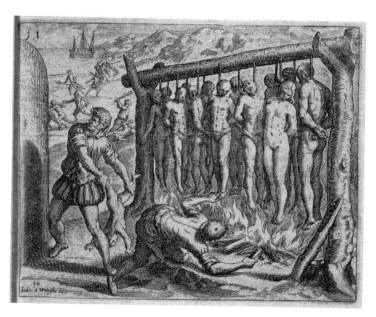

Figure 2.11 (Continued)

Colonial violence, international warfare, transoceanic trading including the slave trade, and integrated but technically separated forces of state, private companies and militaries (fleets) were involved in the rising English hegemony in America. Race both for maximized labor exploitation and genocidal expansion in land takings became critically important for England's expansionary development during the next 150–200 years of colonization in North America, subject of the next chapter.

Religion, Racism, Colonialism and the State – Part I

[This part starts an end to Chapter 2 Indians, with a long segue to Chapter 3 Blacks].

Catholicism as practiced in terms of a state religion with an ironic home (politically) in Rome, the precise empire that had done so much to suppress, torture, kill and eradicate early Christians, became increasingly violent in the Spanish reconquista, coming to a head about 1492 when the Moors were expelled from the Iberian peninsula, accompanied by deportment banning of Jews as Christ-killers, and leading to the horrors of the Inquisition being intensified. Bartolomé de las Casas watched his father and uncle go with Columbus on his second or return trip to Hispaniola, and thus viewed these horrors unfold for the next few years in his homeland and birthplace.

Inhuman execution of a mother, two daughters, and an infant at Guernsey, in 1556.   page 419.

Figure 2.12 Guernsey Martyrs, 1556. John Foxe, Public domain, via Wikimedia Commons. Here, as in the above woodcuts (the news photos of the day), we depict interpersonal violence used by Catholics, Spain or sometimes France, while bringing up similar religious and sociopolitical violence by Protestants, England, demonstrating an equivalence to what many historians and colonial apologists claim for Indian violence – scalping, torturing, burning alive (probably uncommon) and so on – which extends to American colonial forces (the rangers), and United States militias and militaries (see Sand Creek, California, killings such as Yontocket in the next book). Using such examples both undermines the Black Legend or the Saints counter-ideologies meant to sow doubt on that critical discourse, and relates directly to infant killing at the Pequot (1637) and Tolowa (1853) massacres.

Observing the purge killings, burnings and torture of the Native peoples of the Caribbean – doubling both as non-Christian and as Indians – was a somewhat logical extension of Catholic Spanish conquest. What alerts and astounds las Casas is the sheer scale of it – hundreds of thousands of human beings dying in the most awful manner – so he asks us "who in future generations will believe this (occurred)?" Indeed, historical knowledge of it is suppressed to the extent that the social sciences can easily doubt his reports and make short shrift of both the numbers and practices of the American Holocaust (Stannard, 1992), calling las Casas a gross exaggeration and the tortures as the Black Legend.

However, not only are these atrocities closely documented in Spain and in New World practices, but the struggles for religious supremacy, connected to states, was about to intensify in Europe with the rise of the Protestant Reformation. As Catholic law ordered mass executions of Protestant heretics, usually through garroting/hanging, burning and often quartering – when

Protestants came into power they retaliated with killings through hanging, disemboweling, drawing-quartering, with some unfortunates living to the end with beheading or cutting out of the heart, all as public executions to cheering crowds. England exemplified these conflicts, moving from Queen "Bloody" Mary I to Queen Elizabeth the 1st's bloody aftermath of an initially less violent transition, and moving through the colony of Ireland and to suppress insurrection in the north, especially against the Scots. Many Irish scholars refer to these very violent wars of suppression as genocide, especially that conducted by Cromwell later, exported to the Americas directly through such officers as Lane, using scorch and burn and village hanging techniques.

This becomes important in our analysis for a number of reasons, especially in that an observed "savage" public sacrifice of peoples like the Aztecs has an exact corollary in Spain and northern Europe, and in that the English transport these gruesome violent practices to the Americas, where a racialized non-Christian Other allows colonial practices to intensify religious/social/racial oppression to the point of genocide, even as historians and philosophers maintain that Puritan Pilgrim settlers were practicing religious freedom, becoming a basis for American Revolution.

While so-called settlers and religious-political leaders appear to conduct these violent operations, the power is always the state, seen in Queen Elizabeth's Act of Supremacy in 1554. Savagery is attributed to non-Christian racialized Others – Indian or Black – allowing Christian complacency and redrafting of history, with an ultimate extension found in the Protestant ideological Manifest Destiny genocides of California and elsewhere in the West of North America.

The above representations of massive Spanish burnings, torture killings and even an especially brutal child killing by tossing into fires or by decapitation (Figure 2.11b) are not only well documented in a variety of ways, but can be compared to Catholic burnings in the Inquisition states, and as pertinently in many executions of Protestant dissidents, and sometimes innocents, in the Guernsey burnings of a mother and daughters with the torture excesses forcing a pregnant victim to give premature birth, and the constables and church officers literally throwing the newborn into the same fire to die. The woodcut depiction in Figure 2.12 shows this execution with the description "Mother Catherine Cauchés (center) and her two daughters, Guillemine Gilbert (left) and Perotine Massey (right) with her infant son burning for heresy" conducted in the Channel Islands in 1556.

Figure 2.12: "Mother Catherine Cauchés (center) and her two daughters Guillemine Gilbert (left) and Perotine Massey (right) with her infant son burning for heresy" conducted in the Channel Islands in 1556.

Lest we blame Catholic excess in sole guilt for these killings against fellow Protestant Christians in the early days of the rise of the Calvinists and later the institutionalization into the Church of England, we might remember the hundreds of years of gruesome torture killings as described above against those heretics or treasonous subjects, including beheading and decapitation of those charged, followed by quartering of body parts often sent to different jurisdictions with the heads posted outside townships. The Mystic river massacre of the Pequots in 1637 and the war with the Wampanoag led by Metacom in 1675–1678 are illustrative of how these barbaric practices were conducted against Indian nations, peoples and their communities in the name of a God who completely dehumanized them without any rights. We discuss genocidal events in later chapters, but it is worthwhile to bring them up here, since they illustrate how Protestants could engage in deep violence while imploring their religion.[34]

Company Colonization by Crown Leading to Corporate Capitalism

What makes the race-based slave system of transatlantic trading, capitalism? It is the intersection of capitalists, colonization and racism, all still in early formation, with the Crown authority creation of Company profit-making ventures that launches the modern world-system.

Whether we distinguish mercantile colonial expansion by European powers over the Americas as capitalism in formation or as actual mercantile capitalism, we must identify the great trading companies becoming corporations with joint-stock holders as investment that becomes the heart and soul of capitalist control over economics. These corporate groups become start-ups using privateers as dual pirates over the open seas, who answer to Crown authority both in profit sharing and in political control and intrigue. They are perfectly represented in the slave-holding ships and captaincy of (sir) Francis Drake's raids on Spanish colonies, the admiralty of Hawkins in 1588 England defeating the Spanish Armada, and the English Armadas of 1589 and 1594.

England could sponsor raids on the near hegemonic Spanish and Portuguese fleets, controlling slave trading to America and resource extraction (gold, silver) trade back to Europe, while maintaining plausible deniability in declaring war over this trade. This too becomes a model for the next 300 years of corporate state economic expansion (more in next book).

These companies would extend their profiteering operations over the Atlantic while supporting the two bulwarks of global racism in development – labor through enslavement of African and Native American peoples, and land through conquering-colonizing over coastal areas of an entire hemisphere. And, these companies would sponsor and support the colonial beach-heads at both Jamestown and Plymouth, that grew into the Crown colonies of Virginia and Massachusetts, expanding into what we know as the 13 colonies, that became the basis for founding the United States. Relatively small perturbations aside, at least in North America, we observe

---

Company of Merchant Adventurers to New Lands – (using "Discovery"[a]) was founded in 1551 (53) (primarily to establish better trade routes with Russia (Americas) and for Northeast Passage to China).

The Muscovy Company – English trading company chartered in 1555, first major **joint stock** company, precursor of international businesses in England to finance world exploration/domination.[b]

Privateers as companies – 1577–1596, Hawkins/Drake raid Indies trading, Spanish Armada defeated 1588,[c] Portuguese/Spanish goods/slaves seized, English Armada of 1589 as joint stock company.

The East India Company – formed in 1599, chartered 1600 private investors (elites) to trade with India and environs, later controlling Bengal, much of India with private army, fleets (Queen Elizabeth I).

Dutch East India Company – formed, chartered 1602 the **first permanent joint stock** from 1612, quickly moves to take over African ports and the transatlantic slave trade to the Caribbean.

Virginia Company of **London** – chartered 1606 as a joint-stock **company** (royal charter King James I) to establish permanent colonial settlements in North America.

Plymouth Company (English joint-stock) – founded in 1606 (deployed as New England Charter in 1620) originally formed for lands north of Virginia, reformed after pilgrims land at Plymouth.

Royal Colony of **Virginia** (and **New England**) – formed 1624 – Virginia/Plymouth plantations dissolved, Jamestown and Plymouth in duress, debts paid, Crown takes control of colonies, retains corporations. Massachusetts Bay Company incorporates Harvard College as corporation in 1650.

Figure 2.13 Companies (chartered, corporate) leading to colonization capitalism (chart).

a "Mystery and Company of Merchant Adventurers for the Discovery of Regions, Dominions, Islands, and Places unknown."

b Some analysts see the first joint stock business operations (or companies) arising in China during the Song and Tang dynasties, where wealthy investors could buy into protected portions or fractions of economic enterprises, which we can differentiate by later European companies actually having stocks which can be traded or sold, also observing these were to particular individual enterprises, whereas "major" is comprehensive of companies spanning across nations, geographies and types of economies.

c Defeat of the Spanish Armada is critical, as it was linked to Spanish forces in the Netherlands defending trade routes and operations to the Americas, under assault by English-sponsored privateers. This is demonstrated by both Hawkins being an admiral and Drake a fleet captain during the defense and defeat of the Armada, and remarkably afterwards in the English Armada counteract against Spain and its fleets, led by Drake as an admiral. More relevant to this analysis should be non-declaration of war, and financing of the English Armada as a joint stock company, which is never mentioned in the historical literature. This means that the privateers are operating more like rogue companies until the great trading houses and incorporated companies arise within a decade, absolutely critical to the rise of company and later corporate capitalism in the colonization of the Americas, and elsewhere in the world.

the intersection of early capitalism (incorporated or chartered) through stock-held companies, with a new form of colonialism utilizing settlers and indentured workers as an invasive and dominant population base. And important for our study, we see a Crown or state sponsoring of hard-core structural racist systems of slavery and genocidal land takings.

England becomes the comptroller of these forces – Company(ies), Crown colony, settler Colonists – shaping these processes in distinct and self-serving ways, which develop the coming systems of capitalism, colonization and racism for the next 300 years.

These companies, as they become a basis for corporations, are considered a European invention that drives colonialism, capitalism and competitive growth of both on dual hemispheric levels, and ultimately a global colonizing expansion, through imperialism that survives decolonization to this day, as the founding for transnational corporate and neoliberal capitalism. Much of their early profiteering, at least that outside direct plundering, and crown sponsored privateer forces (from 1588 to 1606 these acted as joint stock companies themselves) arises from colonization using settlers to feed resources to the home countries, most strongly England from the Americas, and slave trading into the Caribbean and North America. It is to that discussion we will turn to in Chapter 3, the Black, where genocidal expansion over Native nations accompanies plantation slavery, sugar for growing commodity markets in Europe, and fueling a cotton textile industry and transatlantic triangular trade system that helped build capitalism.

Word: Reformation as Prelude to Enlightenment (for Who? in Chapter 3 "Blacks")

In this first fully content chapter, called Indians as the broad racial construct for the many Native Nations coming under invasive conquest and colonization, and opening the accompanying talk on Blacks as the racial construct still in formation for Africans taken from their home continent's nations to be enslaved peoples by race in the Americas, we have spent some time considering how the home nations and empires of Europe, who are conducting colonization, have changed, been inspired or have conspired to become stronger and wealthier. Most scholars call this first hundred years 1519–1619 or so, and the next hundred, as the Reformation. Yet, during this pre-Enlightenment deadly religious wars were raging across northern Europe, colonial violence rises to an extreme level, massive transoceanic slave markets are created, capitalism arises from private stock companies, and most political power is centralized with notions of sovereignty.

Yet, conversely, Christian thinking and theology is reformed, citizenship and (human) rights are codified, economies expand creating better living conditions, monarchies are replaced with parliamentary governments that are democratically oriented. These massive social changes taking place throughout Europe – the Reformation, challenging Monarchy, creation of citizenry, banking and investment, growth of technology and industry, political participation, a philosophy of the Renaissance – are later collectively referred to as an Enlightenment where free markets, liberty, democracy and morality are thought to have been borne. How can these dualities exist?

In observing initial interplay between two major martial societies – the Spaniards as Catholics, versus the Mexica as Aztecs – it is hard to cry, or even call out for either side in the final siege of the city. Both sides were known to kill large numbers of enemy combatants to demonstrate their ruthlessness in war, often considered something of a combination of bad-boy trash talking and gangland violence. Interestingly, Wright (1992) reports that the Mexica were somewhat shocked at seeing their first ritual burnings by the Spanish, being accustomed to the quick cutting out of the heart of their victims on a temple mount, although Aztec numbers appear to be higher, unless one accounts for the wartime executions and by-product killings of the Iberian powers and their Catholic counterparts (see the Crusades for earlier European examples).

Around that time (1500s) protesting reformers were arising in a mostly Catholic Europe, too, which would lead to many ritual religious killings on both sides – Catholics preferring burning at the stake after a violent Inquisition "hearing" to get at the facts; Protestants leaning towards public dismemberment or disemboweling accompanied by garroting and public parading following their own tortures to elicit a painful confession. And, similar to the Aztecs but probably on a grander scale and more riotous than ritualistic, there are the truly phenomenal slaughters of "innocents" in/over religious ideologies, such as the Saint Bartholomew's Day massacres of Protestant sympathizers in 1572 France (3,000 in Paris, France, estimates range from 15,000 to 30,000 overall) with prolonged killings in the next few decades of as many as three million, only to be outdone in wars against/for Catholic intransigence and European sovereignty, the Thirty Years War, with nearly six million Christian souls sent to Heaven, or Hell.[35] These wars were strongly associated with the Catholic – Protestant split, or schism if you will,[36] that were based on sovereignty claims (such as Spain over the Dutch Netherlands) that partly emanated from the increasingly violent (if even possible from Native viewpoints) colonial wars for plunder wealth and agricultural production related to changing mercantile capitalism. The 1648 Peace of Westphalia (Treaty), somewhat of a misnomer, did not end these wars so much as it established sovereigns as large, centralized European powers, religion-oriented in their colonial approaches. Depictions of the wars transition can be seen in the Gunpowder Plot during England's post-Elizabeth era directly preceding the first colonies formed in North America, with government executions of priests, and burning of ministers and Jews – religiously sanctioned.[37]

We need to observe these social facts, need to understand these civilizational processes, so that we don't fall into the 'primitive savagery' trap of thinking that many western historians and philosophers have set for us in using the Papal Bulls and Catholic arguments. Also we see how northern European religious reification of social domination had developed into a colonial mindset, in the Americas and around the world, that could turn a blind eye to their violent acts and policies toward Natives as less or uncivilized, and thus deserving of such deaths. Graeber and Wengrow (2021) take this reasoning a step further, when identifying the *Wendat* Kandiaronk philosopher statesman, with his "Indigenous critique" of western rational thought of the Native being "classified as a 'primitive' or 'savage' operated with a 'pre-logical mentality' or lived in mythological dreamworld" (95) becoming "projections of Western 'noble savage' fantasies." Kandiaronk maintains that his people didn't kill each other over what they believed, what God was, nor did they tolerate great poverty (critiqued as "inequality") nor try to accumulate great wealth, often at the expense of relationships with other members of their society. In other words, many Indigenous peoples practiced higher order equity with individual and familial freedoms.

Once we understand Native societies as having intelligence and forming civilizations, however, different the social structures may be, the Eurocentric perspective of progressive social evolution toward advanced societies, is called to question. Some scholars suggest that Indigenous intellectuals not only effectively critiqued European practices such as ubiquitous religious wars, extreme wealth held by elites while others starved, or top-down hierarchical autocracies even if some offices are elected (Graeber and Wenfrow, 2021), but actually changed rationalizations. Europeans borrowed from Indigenous critics, like the Haudenosaunee councils appointed by respected grandmothers and held accountable to the people as a whole. Most were deeply skeptical of western justice systems, subordination of women and broad slavery practices that condemned large parts of their societies by race and ethnicity (see Fenelon and Defender, 2004) and broke sacred treaty rights for simple economic gain (Deloria and Lytle, 1984).

Historians tend to treat the Reformation and later an Enlightenment as separate moments, or eras of religious transformation, without seeing these systems as continuous and hegemonic. Even some social scientists and theorists view religion as phenomena existing or acting outside from the state or colonizing societies. However, the European Crown states and the colonizers were key players in enacting and interpreting religious authority as a set of proactive policies. England became a premier force in this regard, declaring supremacy in the Church of England, then declaring supremacy of the English Crown over the Church, and later establishing slave-based economies, religiously sanctioned, in their American colonies.

Moreover, in the next chapter, we must figure out how religious ideologies and social practices are employed in and during enslavement by race (Blacks and Indians), where societal cognitive dissonance arising from dehumanization is judged necessary by colonizing capitalists at such great cost of human life.[38] Like looking upon a dancing, besotted dressed up Redskin, (Fenelon, 2016) not as sports fan, but upon a societal level – How can we look directly at a form and practice of deep systemic racism, unclothed in all its hideous glory, and simply not see it? We must remember this question – keeping in mind race-based slavery and racialized genocide – in the next two chapters. Reformation of What? And later, an Enlightenment for Who?

Notes

1 Christopher Columbus, Italian Cristoforo Colombo, Spanish Cristóbal Colón (born between August 26 and October 31, 1451, Genoa [Italy]—died May 20, 1506, Valladolid, Spain), master navigator and admiral whose four transatlantic voyages (1492–1493, 1493–1496, 1498–1500 and 1502–1504) opened the way for European colonization.

2 Taíno society was divided into two classes: *Nitainos* (nobles) and the *Naborias* (commoners). Both were governed by chiefs known as *caciques*, who were the maximum authority in a *Yucayeque* (village). The chiefs were advised by priest-healers known as *Bohiques* and the *Nitaynos*, which is how the elders and warriors were known.

3 Anacaona became an archetype of Indigenous resistance, in how she lived her life, led her people in war, peace and at the end in rejecting Spanish domination. The legend of this incredible speech was immortalized, in a deeply patriarchal and supremacist way, by the poet Tennyson – *Who was so happy as Anacaona/the beauty of Hispaniola/ the golden flower of Haiti …— Alfred Lord Tennyson*

4 Scholars are in general agreement that Columbus shortened estimates of the distance of the trip (ostensibly to Asia) in order to justify the expenses and potential for success. How much he distorted or misreported the data is unclear.

5 Actually, Columbus and crews had already kidnapped and held multiple Taino people, notably women and girls (which probably had been sexually assaulted), some of whom they took back to Spain (few survived) and later sold.

6 Golden, Renny and Michael McConnell, Peggy Mueller, Cindy Poppen and Marilyn Turkovich. 1991. *Dangerous Memories: Invasion and Resistance Since 1492.* Chicago, IL: Chicago Religious Task Force on Central America.

7 The article in mainstream National Geographic (Lawler, 2020) demonstrates a number of pejorative and biased points (invaders wiped out Caribbean's first people long before Spanish came; wreaked havoc on … islanders; and most pertinently that "a Spanish friar estimated that" there were 3.5 million) that are not found in the source article (Fernandes et al. 2020) which admits they did not use sample size or other standard methods to determine significance of their

estimated population sizes. Also, there is no discussion of assumptions made about migration, or descriptions of social structure, much less other anomalies in the data. The nature study, relying of course on extrapolations of DNA, does refer to the Cook & Borah study versus Henige's rambling low estimates, but does not attempt to justify it against the census Cook reports, nor other counts by eyewitnesses. The DNA analysis looks strong, the demographic findings are weak at best. Then Lawler, like many others before him, brings up the "Spanish friar" remark, meaning Las Casas, when actually he was backed by the Dominican order on site in Hispaniola and Puerto Rico, who confirmed the numbers and the atrocities (see Montecinos, herein).

8   This was about half of the island, and only counted healthy people above the age of 14, clearly a count of the labor force for enslavement.

9   Academics argue over these numbers, with some in clear denial of any over a million, without providing any rationale against Las Casas, and lower the overall number to well under a million, down to under 750 thousand, then a half million with some settling at 250,000, a number closer to 1502 than 1492, and convenient to deny or decry policies of genocide.

10 Many historians and scholars have tried to discount this, basically claiming Columbus would never have done or condoned this, with Catholic scholars making reference to his religious observations and from his log where he does report a beautiful, gentle people, sometimes stressing their total comfort in nudity, which they see as savagery. Of course, we now know that even contemporary priests and monks can exhibit this behavior, and that society always quiets it down, and virtually no one reports it in their communications or later remembrances. Essentially, this is the same denial and cover-up we see in all the forms of violence perpetrated during colonization.

11 Governors had an obligation to take care of the well-being and preserve Native Americans (referred to as *Indians* by the law). Of course, this was arbitrary and could be interpreted in self-serving ways.

Supposedly there was no motive to enslave them in the future, not by war, nor due to rebellion, nor to ask for a rescue, nor for any reason or in any way (while this meant to end slavery, it only curtailed legalized slavery).

That native Americans currently enslaved must be freed immediately, unless the owner could prove (in Spain, which implied traveling back there) the full juridical legitimacy of such a state. Encomenderos quickly made this local.

That the 'bad habit' of making Native Americans work as *tamames* against their will or without fair payment must be ended immediately (see section on New Spain and northern Mexico, or the silver mines at Potosi and elsewhere).

That only the viceroy had the right to establish *encomiendas* on Native Americans. The prohibition to establish *encomiendas* included all religious orders, hospitals, commonalities and civil servants.

That the "distribution" (of people and lands) given to the original conquerors (as a feudal lordship of sorts) should stop immediately after their death, and both land and the native people would become subject to the Crown.

12 Interestingly, 475 years later, some Christian televangelists also blessed (perhaps not baptized) whole groups or lists on electronic servers or on listserves or FAX documents, which doesn't seem all that different.

13 Interesting to note and compare this with the British proclamations in 1763 in the Treaty of Paris and elsewhere that Native Nations in the northwest territories (Ohio, Indiana, Michigan and other soon to be states) would all be respected with treaty conditions, that the colonial revolutionary forces took as frontier prize in a 1783 (Paris Treaty) designating the same territory as American colonial, and thus available for the taking, formally authorized in 1787 Northwest Ordinance by the Confederation Congress and later put into the U.S. Constitution, basically denying all nationhood rights to the lands being won in wars with France, first, and then independence from Britain.

14 It's not as if philosopher professors at the time weren't already advancing Indigenous rights and nationhood, such as Francisco de Vitoria (1483–1546; aka Francisco de Victoria) Spanish Roman Catholic philosopher, theologian and jurist, who founded just war and international law in philosophy, noting Natives had property rights and should be considered Nations that European states must negotiate and make treaties with over colonizing lands.

15 Charles V as King of a Spain gaining great wealth from the Americas, had married into Dutch royalty, and stood to gain inheritance of that Crown, which he did in five years. Like King Henry VIII of England, he used marriage laws to make a break with the Church, which was really about Supremacy over the growing colonization systems, which the banking from the Netherlands financing stood to make great profits from as the later United Provinces.

16 This turns out to be an important distinction, in there were allegations on where responsibility lay, with Church or with Crown, which continued for a hundred years. Ultimately, it is superceded by Protestant predestination of the Elect, and the non-Christian Depraved. We observe that states (crown authority) are avoiding taking responsibility for clearly intentioned actions, of genocide, enslavement and destruction of human beings on a large scale.

17 Las Casas writes up most of the history he personally experienced, and that which he extrapolated from others, along with his replication and interpretation of Columbus's first journey logs, into an epic Brief History of the Indies manuscript which not only fails to be published, but disappears for some 300 plus years, when its sudden appearance and publication also summarily resurrects the atrocities and arguments in colleges, churches and state institutions, calling to question whether it was censored, suppressed or simply set aside, so more sanguine history can reaffirm the civilizing missions of Spain, the Catholic Church, England and the other colonizers of the day.

18 These other accounts are most likely accurate, in that Altman and most other historians will only take official reports as prima facie evidence, although it was quite common to alter or even fabricate reports on military actions taken in the field to make the reporter seem more in control. Altman, Ida. (2007). "The Revolt of Enriquillo and the Historiography of Early Spanish America." *The Americas*, 63:4 April 2007, 587–614 (Academy of American Franciscan History). This was done with explorers and conquistadors all the time – in fact, Columbus reported that he left the crew behind on Ayiti-Hispaniola to take control of the island, thus managing not to report that his flagship had sunk on a reef, and he had no choice but to do so.

19 This is an important distinction, in that the exporting of African peoples to be enslaved is out of Africa, whereas the importing of Black peoples, or Negros,

as racially enslaved labor for a deeply racist America, means that some form of racialized transformation had occurred during the deadly and dangerous Middle Passage transportation.

20 Davidson, Basil. 1980 [1961]. *The African Slave Trade* (revised edition). Boston, MA: Back Bay Books, Little, Brown and Company.

21 Ibid.

22 Marc Aronson and Marina Budhos in the 2010 book, "Sugar Changed the World."

23 The circuit or triangle trade was hardly a simple three-way process of trade, changing over the centuries into dual triangles (Europe to Africa, to Caribbean Americas, back to Europe being the first; then ships from North American ports going directly to Africa, to the Caribbean, then back to north America and sometimes England) that were also changed by shipping needs, so that earlier slave ships would not meet the needs of increased trade goods shippers, who also required less infected ships for agricultural produce. While the final stage of the first circuit sometimes was not fulfilled by the same ships used in slaving, who often had ballast problems, an overall triangular effect remained.

24 European "white" girls, as those from Rumania, were mostly sold in Iberian markets, with increased trafficking in Native slaves and later the accessibility of women and girls, this part of the market fluctuated, only reinforced with African slaves later.

25 These analysts from the University of London School of Economics make an extremely conservative estimate of overall population of the Americas somewhere near 60 million, and therefore find 56 million mortality (rate). However, as we have already shown with Ayiti Hispaniola, which was likely three million, conservative numbers are often 10% so they figure from about 310,000, that fits into their picture of Native peoples, as more tribal than ethno-national or civilizational. If we take 100 million as our base number, a very rationale number, then the mortality is closer to 92 million, making it by far the greatest in world history.

26 Many of the slave ships were so filthy and not fit for cargo, especially foodstuffs, that separate shipping worked the European leg, and some captains, caught after the main harvest or growing season, had to make ballast in order to get their ships back to home port. I observe that it is precisely as market conditions improved for the product sales in Europe that this started to occur, with other changes – increased airflow and exercise for enslaved people aboard such ships, along with retro-fitting ships – that increased market sales at European and later American ports.

27 Timbuktu was one of the world's greatest cities in the 15th and 16th centuries. The intellectual center of the black empire of Songhay, Timbuktu was famed for its scholars and its social life (Bennett, 1982: 15).

28 Protestant "teachings ... may have fueled the flames of anti-Semitism, spurring more migration across the Atlantic in order to escape an increasingly bigoted Europe" (Horne, 2020: 65). Some writers see this as an inspiration for anti-Jewish Nazi Germany, but if so, it was inadvertent, not traceable to Luther, due as much to existing racism.

29 The transition toward religious ideologies increasingly divorced from the state, and rationalizing new systems of capitalist profit tied to banking credit,

investment and insurance, became structured into what has been called the Protestant revolution, that disentagled monetary holdings from state religion, and/or direct controls by the political elite, both features of Catholicism and the Spanish–Portuguese dominance over the first hundred years of dominance.

Thus, capitalism embraced and developed two key elements of systems of human bondage – slavery, genocide – along with the growth of global systems. We have a nearly unbroken straight line of supremacy by western European powers in this history. Perhaps, in formation until the 1493 Papal Bulls, after that we have the Catholic Church, extending supremacy to the Spanish Crown, then we have the Reformation in relations to two Acts of Supremacy by English rulers, King Henry VIII and Queen Elizabeth I, and then a clear transfer to the colonies of the Americas, completing the Church, Crown, Colony supremacy.

30 François de Salignac de la Mothe-Fénelon (Fénelon, 1651–1715) was a French Roman Catholic archbishop, theologian, poet and author of *The Adventures of Telemachus*, first published in 1699. He defended quietism (mindfulness) and insisted Kings had social responsibility.

31 I often use this in my classes, in repeating the ill-quoted Marxian phrase "religion is the opiate of the masses" to its probable actual application that "religion can be used to opiate the masses" as well as create political movements.

32 We can see this in constant reference to Greek philosophy and Roman law, which used to be evidenced in requiring Latin for most elite college degrees.

33 As above, the notion of Discovery had been inserted into the New World conquest, politically and ideologically, through the 1493 Papal Bull, which the English were fully aware of and probably predicated their usage from too. Starting in the 1550's and fully realized by 1600, the English used a Protestant interpretation related to companies rather than the Catholic version related to Crown authority. This allowed the Church (religious authority), the State (crown sovereign authority) and the Corporation (trading company charters) to profit from their involvement and investments, and yet to disclaim responsibility for such immoral and often illegal actions of racial enslavement and genocidal warfare. This is especially evident with Sir Francis Drake when reporting and submitting profits to Queen Elizabeth, who was engaged in brutal religious war with France and Catholics, and with the terrible consequences of the deep brutality of Hawkins with enslaved African cargo to the Caribbean, which the Crown and the Church would disavow, later staking legal claim to the Plymouth and Virginia colonies through company charters, while singing praise to God, Queen and Country, also directly stated both at Jamestown and through Massachusetts.

34 Either here, or the following, we discuss financing of Spanish, and Portuguese, ships of plunder and conquest, and the growing transatlantic slave markets, by the Netherlands banking and investment groups. Spain watches as much of its plunder wealth gets diverted to interest and debt payments, and so arranges a marriage to Dutch royalty followed by a partial invasion over those (northern) territories, where they put down bloody uprisings.

35 These social conflicts are interlinked: Huguenot "political rhetoric" had taken tone against policies of a monarch of France and monarchy in general (led in part by Calvinists (John Calvin) *Readings on the Prophet Daniel*, 1561), arguing when kings disobey God, they "automatically abdicate their worldly power" – a

change from earlier works that even ungodly kings should be obeyed. This change promoted sovereignty of the people ideology, getting fierce responses from Catholics. Even so aftermath of the massacre found widespread support for anti-monarch ideas, who previously loyal to the Crown, now called for deposition or assassination of a Godless king who had permitted the slaughter. The massacre "marked the beginning of a new form of French Protestantism: one that was openly at war with the crown.".... 1572 news reached Paris that a French Huguenot army under Louis of Nassau had crossed from France to the Netherlands and captured the Catholic strongholds Louis governed Orange and Avignon in southern France, for his brother William the Silent, who was leading the Dutch Revolt against the Spanish. Catherine de' Medici, the Queen Mother worried that Coligny's influence would drag France into a war with Spain over the Netherlands.

36 The Thirty Years' War was primarily fought in Central Europe from 1618 to 1648; estimates of total military and civilian deaths range from 4.5 to 8 million, the vast majority from disease or starvation. In some areas of Germany, deaths overall may have been up to 60% of the population.

37 I saw depictions of the wars transition with my older son watching the Gunpowder Plot miniseries in England's post–Elizabeth era directly preceding the first colonies formed in North America, with ritual government executions of priests, and burning of ministers and Jews. In talking with him (as an Anthropology major at Cal Poly), I realized how little killings and tortures inflicted by Christians were discussed, finding the same in scholarly literature.

38 Steinmetz reports in his now-seminal edited volume *Sociology and Empire* (2013) that Michael Mann thought these paradoxical forces fully emergent in the United States acting as a hegemon in the Americas and the world were like "schizophrenic" dueling versions or explanations (or rationalizations?) of the modern world works, in terms of global political-economics at the least. Fanon uses almost this exact language when describing how western dominators or colonizers used the language of democracy and freedom, even as they systematically exploited whole populations in deeply subordinated and oppressed social positions that were not included in the governance of their own lands and people.

Standing on *Stolen Land with Stolen Hands*

Prelude to Chapter 3 the Black

The rolling green forests and sparkling blue estuaries of the rich fields south east of Richmond, Virginia, along the James River's north bank let you feel land inhabited for thousands of years by Native Nations – *Pamunkey, Mattaponi* – as confederacies the Powhatan. When I arrived in fall of 1973 to join a nucleus crew of the aircraft carrier Nimitz, the largest war machine ever built, I was struck by contrasts of the land, sea and cities built by American labor, at the naval shipyard Newport News, named after the privateer captain and first governor of the Jamestown colony, commanding the horizon with its spires from great warships, churches and cathedrals. One African American mate pointed out the first plantations his ancestors labored at in centuries past even as we visited historic Williamsburg, constructed on stolen lands by stolen hands, (taking a phrase from William Barber III). Names of rivers (York) and cities (Norfolk) tell you who came to colonize in the misnomer image of the Virgin Queen, among the Chesapeake. Later, I took liberty from the USS America in Portsmouth, England, home of the colonizers, later still seeing the great fleets setting anchor in Boston harbor (*Massachusett, Wampanoag*), others at Charleston, of slave-trading Carolinas fame, likewise on lands wrested from Native Nations to build colonies and European empires. A decade later, after teaching on Haiti, I caught an old three-masted French frigate out of Martinique, learning racial dominants, Béke, had imported poisonous snakes to threaten Maroons, fugitive ex-slaves who joined forces with Indigenous resistance against colonial racism (as noted by the aging Césaire) in Fort-de-France, climbing volcanic Mount Pelée, seeing Carnival jump-up in Trinidad, Black revolutionaries on Grenada, catching a sailing ship to St. Vincent's and learning Caribbean histories on excesses of empire.[1]

Note

1 Three years in East Asia – China (P.R.C.), Japan and Malaysia – underscored how colonization processes by European countries changed the demographics and environment of continents. Recovering upon my return to the Dakotas, becoming healed by ancient ceremonies.

DOI: 10.4324/9781003315087-4

Chapter 3

The *Black*

1620–1790 Institutionalizing Racial Codification

Introduction

Scholars of color from Caribbean nations are determined never to forget "European opulence is … a scandal … built on the backs of slaves, fed on the blood of slaves, it owes its very existence to the soil and subsoil of the underdeveloped world. Europe's well-being and progress were built with the sweat and corpses of blacks, Arabs, Indians, and Asians" (Frantz Fanon, 1963).

Acknowledged by African American scholars (Isabel Wilkerson, 2020) as war crimes, dehumanization of Black slaves included many horrifying conditions from the:

> …institution of slavery was… conversion of human beings into currency, into machines who existed solely for the profit of their owners… worked as long as owners desired, with no rights over their bodies or loved ones, who could be mortgaged, bred, won in a bet, given as wedding presents, bequeathed to heirs, sold away from spouses or children to convene an owner's debts or to spite a rival or to settle an estate… regularly whipped, raped, branded, or subjected to any whim or distemper of people who owned them. Some were castrated or endured other tortures…" Geneva Conventions would have "banned as war crimes… had they applied to people of African descent on this soil.

Leaders of Native Nations (Powhatan) also saw coming invasions as destructive to their people:

> Your coming is not for trade, but to invade my people and possess my country…Having seen the death of all my people thrice…I know the difference of peace and waere better than any other Country. [If he fought the English, he predicted], he would be so haunted by Smith that he can neither rest eat nor sleep, but his tired men must watch, and if a twig but break, every one cry, there comes Captain John Smith; then he

DOI: 10.4324/9781003315087-5

must fly he know not whether, and in miserable fear end his miserable
life.

Wahunsenacawh (Powhatan)[1]

The 1619 marked an important year for the Native Nations experiencing the
settlements surrounding their peoples, as at the Jamestown area of Virginia.
Wahunsenawek had passed the year before, having met the original colonists
and experienced their intent on expanding over the countryside, with the
violent military measures that soldier-sailor acting governor John Smith
had deployed against his people. In the ensuing wars, his daughter Matoaka
(Pocahontas) was taken hostage, so the Powhatan confederacy brokered a
peace with the English colony. Matoaka later married, had a child with John
Rolfe and went to England, where she passed away on her return journey.[2]

Smaller settlements had expanded from the original, still under the
London Company operating as the Virginia (Colony) Company and other
names, associated with British interests overseas. Also in 1619, a British
privateer anchored and traded the first African (Angolan) slaves for food,
supplies and other support, thus beginning a long period of enslavement,
servitude and racial subordination for Blacks in the English colonies.[3] Of
course, this simply extended England's ongoing participation in the slave
trade, and enslavement of Africans, by English sea captains, privateers and
newly formed trading companies, all answering to or paying tithes (a royal
fifth) or taxes to the Crown.

The 1619 turned out to be a decent year for the Native Nations living
around Massachusetts, with the return of Tisquantum from Europe, where
English monks had helped him to recross the Atlantic, first having been kidnapped by British privateers in 1614 and sold into slavery in Spain. Patuxet,
his hometown, had been decimated by waves of pandemic disease, so the
Wampanoag confederacy had taken him in and debriefed his journeys among
the Hairy men from the east, where he was the next year when English
origin Pilgrims arrived and set up a township. As we will see, they were ill-
prepared to survive a winter, and were relieved to see an Abenaki diplomat
(Samoset) approach them the following year, and introduce the English-
speaking Tisquantum and their Wampanoag neighbors, who extended a
helping hand and like Virginia made treaties for peace and friendly alliance.
Like the Powhatan, the Wampanoag confederacy would realize, too late, that
the English had come to stay and extend their colonies into the Native confederacy. And, as in Virginia and throughout North America, they would
find Europeans would identify themselves from their country of origin,
while Native Nations would be called Indians, and the growing number of
enslaved Africans would be called Black, just as happened in the Caribbean.

In retrospect, the years 1619–1620 or 1621 were pivotal, only influenced
by racial fears and colonial wars associated with racist conquest. Edward
Waterhouse, secretary of the Virginia Company, wrote:

[S]uch was the conceit of firme peace and amitie, as that there was seldome or never a sword worne, and a Peece [firearm] seldomer, except for a Deere or Fowle....The Plantations of particular Adventurers and Planters were placed scatteringly and straglingly as a choyce veyne of rich ground invited them, and the further from neighbors held the better. The houses generally set open to the Savages, who were alwaies friendly entertained at the tables of the English, and commonly lodged in their bed-chambers.[4]

(Grizzard and Smith, 2007)

However good the relations between Native peoples and Colonists were in 1621 both in Virginia and Plymouth, three prime forces of Crown interests, Company profiteering and settler interests, would undo or complicate the possibilities of mutual benefits through cooperation and treaty. England would have her colony expand, the investment companies stood to make their profits and settlers had been promised a "new world" where they could become well-off landowners, requiring a violent wresting of lands from Native guardianship and destroying any resistance.

The 1622 was a high point of racial conflict in the Jamestown Virginia colony, as continued expansion of plantations into the Powhatan territories was being challenged by new leadership. *Opchanacanough* as paramount chief and his primary advisor *Nemattanew*, who was murdered by settlers, had set off a series of attacks designed to contain the settlement into a trading post. Nearly a quarter of the colonists (circa 347) were killed before the Powhatan withdrew in the mistaken belief they would negotiate new terms of the two forces. Instead, with John Smith pining to bring in a punitive military force from England that never materialized, the colonists regrouped with instructions and support from the London company, starting a slash and burn death dealing assault that destroyed food sources to generate famine, poisoned hundreds of Powhatan in meetings,[5] enflamed entire communities using attack dogs to sow deep terror, taking the most "cultivable" land across the region for colonization and driving the tribal forces into marginal lands. This process would continue for many years.

Year 1622 was just as interesting in terms of colonial-Native conflict at Plymouth, which was also extending settlements along the coast, but without strict religious parameters of the Pilgrims, who were utterly intolerant of other denominations, even calling them the anti-Christ at times.

...a sinner named Thomas Weston attempted in 1622 to found a colony at Wessagasset, or Weymouth. ...his colonists were recruited from the streets of London and were utterly godless. Their disorderly rioting soon brought them to a low condition of affairs... Thomas Morton had succeeded him... the grant of land was not to the Pilgrims, but to the seventy merchant adventurers who had financed the exodus.[6] ...

The attempt to set up an Episcopalian community in the vicinity of Plymouth was both an affront and a menace to the Pilgrims (God). ... Calling their settlement Merrymount, they set up a Maypole and danced about it with the Indians, imbibing deeply of strong waters, turning the occasion into an old Roman festival. ...Also, they sold firearms and gunpowder to the savages, together with strong waters, teaching them the uses civilization made of the several devices.

The wrath of the Pilgrims had been hot and heavy; so much so that Miles Standish was sent out with his little army to settle with the merrymakers, at their Merrymount. This he did, dispersing the disorderly interlopers with a keen professional relish in the work, and restoring the land wholly to the Pilgrim's God.

(Markham, 1909: 159–160)

This romantic history of the conflict, following extended negotiations and treaty-making with the Massasoit of the Wampanoag who controlled the nearby land base and had accepted these initial settlers because of the dispossession of Patuxet, puts an intolerant taint upon both those Pilgrims who subsequent historians have mythologized as in pursuit of religious freedom, (Markham makes clear throughout the book that the Pilgrims had no tolerance of other churches, even if Protestant) and the Plymouth Company investors in terms of social control. Subsequent 20th-century historians, however, were forced to include at least a partial study of Native nations with these internecine colonial conflicts, and developed an alternative history (still holds sway) that has the Massasoit giving permission for Standish to punish the Wessagasset colonists, supposedly in competition with an offshoot tribal nation (led by Pecksuot), "disloyal" to the Wampanoag confederation. This convenient history puts much of the blame on Native forces without considering the corporate influence of the Plymouth Company in relation to fur trade, potential tobacco and agricultural profits, and expansion of colonial interests. Instead, let us observe what Jennings finds in the critical affair:

It concerns the Plymouth colony, whose settlers engaged in the fur trade in the hope of liquidating the colony's debts. Three years after their arrival in America the Saints of Plymouth showed how to wipe out a competitor forcefully without exposing themselves to the crown's justice. The trick was to manipulate the Indians so as to achieve Plymouth's aims while diverting blame to the "savages."

A colony of adventurers sent out by Thomas Weston in 1622 had settled at Wessaguset, on the south side of Massachusetts Bay. The irritated Saints saw only trouble in Wessagusset. It was a possible (Anglican) source of religious "infection," a certain rival in fur trading, and an undisciplined hazard in Indian relations. Suddenly discovering an Indian "conspiracy," Captain Miles Standish and his small troop of Plymouth soldiery marched to "save" the Wessaguset colonists, who, however, showed a singular disinclination to be saved. One of the Wessaguset men vexed Standish by remarking, "We fear not the Indians, but live with them and suffer them to lodge with us, not having sword or gun, or needing the same." Standish promptly created a need for the same. Pretending to the Indians that he had come to Wessaguset to trade, he enticed a few of them into his hands and then massacred them without warning. After this no Englishman could be safe at Wessaguset. Indian avengers, not grasping the difference between the two colonies, took a toll of three Wessaguset men, and the rest of that unhappy community chose to abandon the site. ..refusing Standish's invitation (to Plymouth), they set sail eastward... Back in England, they proved vociferously ungrateful...

Plymouth had gained its end. ...resumed its local trade monopoly... To counter the comments of Wessagusset, Plymouth leaders sent ... Edward Winslow to propagandize for them in England. ...covered Wessaguset colonists with sanctimonious abuse and falsified events to implicate the Indians as conspirators, and to conceal the premeditation of the massacre. He succeeded so brilliantly that the facts of the affair remained buried for more than three centuries.

(Jennings, 1976: 186–187)

Wampanoag councils of course had completely different perspectives, at first allowing colonists to settle in empty village sites, then gradually resisting ongoing encroachments, but manipulated into intertribal conflicts, such as with the Narragansett, and then most ominously against Pequot communities in massacres in Connecticut territory, until their Massasoit passed away and his sons attempted to resist (Metacom), too late as earlier in Virginia and throughout the Caribbean. By now, the Crown was working with incorporated Company trading groups to build a colonial economy and political presence through encouraging English and other north European settlers to populate the new territories, wrest away land from and fight Native nations, and compete with European colonizers (France, Netherlands, Spain, Hessians and Portugal) reflected in wars back in western Europe and Atlantic coastal regions. We will return to this discussion after our historical analysis of growth of the two colonies over the North American eastern seaboard.

We have taken this time to set up a discussion of the intersection of colonialism, racism and early capitalism, and to consider some pivot points considering this sociopolitical history of three primary social forces that could have gone in different directions than they did – the Crown (colonizers), trading Company (corporations) and Colonists (settlers) – in relation to the Native nations resisting colonial invasions, along with the early ethno-racial divisions including slavery. We have observed 1620–1621 good relations between at least some colonists and Native peoples, noted in Jamestown settlements under Crown and Virginia Company influence to expand over Powhatan lands, and in the Plymouth settlements at Wessaguset where Colony and Company monetary and trading interests (paying off investors and maintaining monopoly on the fur trade) worked in collusion with Protestant religious groups to create divisions with local Native nations. Clearly, Anglican colonists at Wessaguset had created positive interactions with Indian people. Plymouth soldier leaders were sent to create divisions with Native peoples, a set of policies that would take place for more than a hundred fifty years in colonial contexts, and another hundred fifty years in the United States. What if Plymouth and other colonies had supported positive, non-divisive interactions with local Native peoples, to the extent of dancing around Maypoles and sharing lodges together?[7] What if Powhatan peoples had been encouraged to continue to visit and interact with colonists in Virginia? What if agricultural technologies and trading opportunities had been shared between Native Nations and European colonists? And finally, what if distorted mythological histories of colonial-Indian relations had not been constructed, leading to denial of the premeditated and planned colonial expansion, attributed to the Native nations and conspiracies to destroy the colonies in violent war? We may not be able to answer these questions with any certainty, but we can consider alternative trajectories for the American colonial and state development taking place over the following four hundred years.

Historiography of Jamestown Settlement Becoming Slave Colony (Arc of Discovery, Part 3)

– Jamestown Colony, Virginia Company and Crown Authority over Native Nations –

Jamestown was the first permanent English settlement in North America,[8] and was developed by new joint stock holding companies similar to the East India Company, and with many of the same players – English ship captains acting as Privateers, the Crown authority granting charters, Stockholders shaping settler-colonial laws to maximize profits, Immigrant labor being voluntary, indentured or enslaved – operating as the Virginia Company of London chartered in 1606, with express objectives of establishing settlements in North America. Companies were empowered as Corporations to govern themselves (in-country anyway, stockholders in London could determine policies and practices), so that after the 1622 Indian wars against the Powhatan confederacy,[9] colonists took on self-governance that scholars see as genesis of democracy in America, but less commonly see it as a source of

genocidal wars waged against Native Nation resistance and racial enslavement laws formalizing after Bacon's rebellion in the late 1600s.

The London Company (of Virginia) hired the famous privateer Christopher
Newport (who took plunder from a Portuguese ship returning with slave
trade riches, then burned down a Spanish town in Haiti) in 1606 to navi-
gate and captain the initial 1607 colonists into Virginia coastlands, creating
Fort James 1st settlement at Jamestown as profit-making beachhead in the
Americas.[10]

Newport returned in early 1608 with another all-male force of settlers,
to find half the colonists dead, under the leadership of the war-like soldier
John Smith having bad relations with local Native Nations, stealing their
food stores and raping women who strayed from protection. The London
merchants authorized Newport to make a Native leader a tributary "vassal"
of England, so they tried to coronate Wahunsenawek who famously refused
to bow to accept the crown, as he was "King" of many nations. After a
second resupply mission in 1609 partly failed, and the now governor John
Smith conducted further raiding on Pamunkey townships, expropriating of
lands, Wahunsenawek declared (quoted above at the start of Chapter 3):

> "Your coming is not for trade, but to invade my people and possess my
> country…"

> After a third resupply mission and possible failure of Company
> investment, Governor Thomas West (Baron De la Warr) ordered con-
> quest of surrounding tribes, so in July 1610 "Gates lured the natives
> into the open by means of music-and-dance act by his drummer, and
> then slaughtered them" in the first Anglo–Powhatan war,[11] capturing
> Matoaka (Pocahontas, or *Amonute*) daughter of Wahunsenawek, and
> holding her hostage until "all Powhatan captives be released, all English
> weapons taken by warriors [returned], and agree upon a lasting peace."
> (Vaughan, 1978)

Pocahontas was not released and later married John Rolfe, who wrote that the
way to maintain peace between the Powhatan and the English was to marry
Pocahontas, not "with unbridled desire of carnal affection but for the good
of the colony and the glory of God." After marriage, more peaceful relations
arose for a time between English colonists and Powhatan Confederacy.
In 1616, Rolfe took Pocahontas to Europe and England, to show off the
"civilized savage" and collect funding, especially for the growing tobacco
markets he had started. Pocahontas died in England in 1617, and was buried
there, leaving her son as an Indian (mixed-blood) orphan.

Relations between the Powhatan peoples deteriorated after news of
Pocahontas's death spread along with more lands being taken for townships
and agriculture. Wahunsenawek died in 1618, so his youngest brother,

Opchanacanough, became paramount leader, who with his friend war chief and advisor Nemattanew, did not believe peaceful relations with the colonists could be maintained with continued land takings, cultural intrusions and treachery in treaty negotiations.

In the summer of 1619, British ships sailed into port with human booty of African slaves, taken by privateers off Portuguese slave ships in the Caribbean, much like Francis Drake and Hawkins had decades earlier, first trading 20 for supplies and awhile later another group of the original 50 taken in battle. British colonists were well aware of operative racial caste laws in the Caribbean, although not formally in place in the Virginia colony yet, and put them to work in tobacco fields and taking care of households. Some historians note they were probably from Angola with skills in tool-making or artisanry. The Virginia colony was expanding their land base and labor force.

By 1620–1621 depredations increased, and Opchanacanough and Nemattanew began plans for an unavoidable war, hoping to shock and awe the English and contain them in a trading outpost, rather than expanding with new plantations. In spring 1622, after Nemattanew was murdered, Opchanacanough launched a campaign of "surprise" attacks on at least 31 separate English settlements and plantations, mostly along the James River, extending to Henricus.[12]

The English took revenge against the Powhatan by the use of force, surprise attacks, famine from the burning of their corn, destroying their boats, canoes and houses, breaking their fishing weirs and assaulting them during their hunting expeditions, pursuing them with horses and using dogs – bloodhounds to find them and mastiffs to attack, driving the people to flee in reach of enemies among other tribes, and "assimilating and abetting their enemies against them" while handing out **poisoned wine in peace treaty** conferences (see note 13 above). In other words, genocidal war.

The eastern seaboard of America was named Virginia from Maine to the Carolinas, although Plymouth Company had landed settlers and renamed their colony as the Massachusetts Bay Company, forming New England colonial holdings within a few decades. The corporations as companies were empowered by the Crown to govern colonies; conferred upon Virginia after dissolution of their third Charter in 1621, and hardening after the 1622 uprisings. The Virginia Company failed in 1624, but kept colonial right to self-government over the colony, establishing a royal colony as self-governing, especially in forming policies over indentured or enslaved labor, and toward Native peoples, creating a racialized early "democracy" in American colonies. This was tested in coming wars and rebellions, until the late 17th-century slave codes and Indian extermination were developed, lasting until the colonies revolted against London company hegemony and after Crown authority ended in the 1770s.

Virginia Company as Jamestown Colony Creates Two-Pronged Race Laws – Indians and Blacks

By 1676, the Virginia plantations of the Jamestown Colony had grown westward to a "frontier" with Native Nations engaged in fur trading with colonial frontiersman, who kept surveillance and geopolitical intelligence shared with colonial leaders and an elite plantation class, increasing numbers of indentured (mostly white ethnic) and enslaved (African) labor. Some Native Nations, Susquehannock, and notably the *Doeg*, after three English wars had decimated the Powhatan, fought back after land seizures, sexual assaults and other violations became intolerable.[13]

Some leaders of the plantation elite used Native resistance and a declining economy with high taxes as a scapegoat strategy to organize armed parties to challenge the Crown's official policy of respecting treaty negotiations (even when several tribal chiefs were assassinated and General Assembly declarations of war on "hostile" tribes passed in retaliation) and keeping restive populations in line, including informal militias forming in western regions of the colony. After one leader was highly criticized with his genocidal attacks on Native Nations resisting land seizures,[14] he and other colonial elites organized an alliance of European indentured and African enslaved bond-servitude militias, marched on Jamestown, burned it down and briefly expelled Governor Berkeley. London-based merchant marine ships sided with colonial government and put down the rebellion, alerting the planter ruling class of the dangerous unified mixed-race alliance, who subsequently began to mollify the white farmers and frontiersmen with lands of defeated or suppressed Native peoples, while hardening the racial caste system of slavery, driving wedges between the so-called settler colonial and enslaved colonial populations who could be united against the threat from Indian Nations.

Grievances the protest leader Bacon leveled at governing colonial elites included "unjust taxes" with advancing "favorites" to public office, "monopolizing" the fur trade with Indian nations, and assisting Natives (thereby restricting continued land takings). While these issues – taxation, government representation, trading monopolies and illegal Native land seizures[15] – would continue for the next hundred years of colonial expansion to the American revolution on these very demands, the colonial governments who answered to London merchants and the Crown of England developed and implemented two racial policies to maintain order in Virginia and other colonies: the colonists kept militias to fight off and attack Indians who resisted expansion over their lands; colonies further separated working-class whites from enslaved, subordinated Blacks, enacted in designating Hostile tribes with a "just war" reasoning, and in racially codifying slave laws for Blacks who might try to escape or rebel.[16]

Colonial elites and laws, later found in the U.S. constitutional reasoning, found it easier to mobilize peoples and militias against an "alien" race – Indians rather than Native Nations – and to divide races out of self-interest for white Christians and racial subordination for Blacks, found in the Virginia Slave Codes of 1705, that segregated white colonists and allowed enslavement laws over Blacks, thus embedding white supremacy into the colonial social institutions, that would later be the basis for U.S. political and socioeconomic institutions. These codes, developed over a decade or more of increasingly draconian laws, included:

> Slave owners property rights (racially defined), court protected free slave trading, racially separated courts, prohibitions of all Blacks from owning or deploying arms, racial employment restrictions, miscegenation and apprehension of runaway slaves.

While it is important to note the renewed centrality of racial enslavement laws and social institutions, reinforcing maximized exploitation of Black labor, that would continue to grow and evolve into racial laws of the American colonies and revolutionary government, we must also note the continued racial enslavement of Indians and destruction of Native Nations, notably strong in the Carolinas until well into the 18th century (Gallay, 2015), accompanied by frontier militias and colonial militaries to suppress Native resistance.

Three races were thereafter developed and institutionalized from the Virginia and Massachusetts colonies, which became the central race laws adopted by the fledgling U.S. revolutionary government – Indians to be eliminated as nations, removed from the land; Blacks to be enslaved and kept in subordinated roles for economic domination; and Whites as the mainstay population of colonists and later as citizens of the republic. These racist laws would be enshrined in the constitution of the new nation-state, would be defended and defined through religious reasoning and civilizational dialogues, would be embedded in the social institutions of the new racially divided society and would be the main foundations upon which the capitalist economy would be built, first as nationalism, then internationalism, and finally as neo-liberalism of the 21st century on a global level.

During this time of building plantation economies and expanding land-based economies, creating labor demand, the slave markets on both ends of the Caribbean trade, were also growing, so the basic conditions of transoceanic human trafficking were put in place – increasing supply of black Africans, shipping ports and fleets for handling the human cargo, and increasing demand for the delivered humans as chattel property to replace the lessened local slaves. This coincided with the rise of New England shipping and trading, some directly to Africa for slaves, and in competition

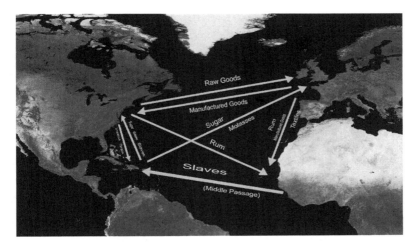

Figure 3.1 Circuit or triangular trade of the North Atlantic.

with British shipping and slaving companies, that would continue to the Revolutionary War.

Transatlantic Slave Trading and the English Colonies

The **French and English** grew bolder and were joined by **Dutchmen and Danes and Swedes,** and afterwards by **Prussians** (as the monopoly began to fold…) the **Dutch built a Gold Coast fort** of their own… these enterprises were set in train by European governments and investing merchants, with the procedure of granting a national monopoly of trade with the Guinea Coast. Such ventures were among the earliest experiments in **company formation.** Thus, the **first genuine incorporation** of English investors for the Guinea trade occurred **in 1618,** when **James I gave a charter of monopoly to thirty London merchants,** the **Company of Adventurers of London** Trading into Parts of Africa (Davidson, 1980: 71).

Here, we see the formation of company-directed trading markets across the Atlantic, including building of forts to protect enslaving and shipping operations from the African Gold Coast, through many European nations to slave-holding colonies in the Americas. Moreover, English investors were given a Crown charter for the slave trade, linking future capitalist developments in North America with enslaving of Africans as Blacks, one year before the 1619 Jamestown sale or bartering of the Angolan slave booty from a Portuguese slaver. Although the Virginia colony had not yet instituted specific race-based slave laws for Black Africans, all the necessary pieces for race-based slavery were already in place – transatlantic shipping routes including captains that brought the original colonists, company investments at both embarkation ports and point-of-sale disembarkation colonies, and Company – Crown control over developing colonial profits, needing only expansion over Indian lands, and thus their destruction as nations.

The **Dutch** were soon ahead of their rivals. Their **West Indian Company** – joining trade to Guinea with settlement in the West Indies – was **formed in 1621**, only a few years after their first appearance in West Africa [see world-systems analysis of the Hegemon, *mine*]. **The Danes** soon followed. …The slave trade, in short, was grafted little by little into a **living nexus of commercial needs** and appetites and habits (Davidson, 1980:72).

While our major concern is with English enslavement markets into North America that morph into entirely race-based institutionalized forms of Virginia, that become the basis of the United States formation, we do need to note the world-systemic control by the Dutch trading companies, backed up their principal investors who had earlier invested in Spanish and Portuguese efforts. Many analysts see these processes as hegemonic, which I do not, since the Netherlands cannot effectively impose military dominance around their global interests, but instead primarily have maximum control over banking, shipping and marketing of slaves and other "commodities" (contributing to dehumanization of enslaved Africans, later in African colonies), which make up the basis of early capitalism. We note this development is important in future capitalist enterprises – mercantile, agricultural-resource extraction, industrial and neoliberal – that correlate closely with the rise of colonizing racisms and global racialized inequalities in the four epochs identified in these books. What makes English colonization racism appear to be unique, now called settler colonialism, is concomitant development of land appropriation (called dispossession as of late) and population replacement (genocide and removal) by settler-colonists racialized as White.

In 1609, the English established themselves in the **Bermudas**; in St. Christopher in **1623**; in **Barbados** in **1625**; and thence onward to the Leeward Islands. The **French came hard** behind them, founding settlements on **Guadaloupe in 1626**, on **Martinique in 1635**, and elsewhere in following years. The **Dutch,** for their part, took the southern **Caribbean islands** of **Curacao, St. Eustatius** and **Tobago** during the **1630s**. The **Danes** occupied **St. Thomas in 1671** (Davidson, 1980: 74).

Here we observe the English developing their slave-holding island colonies in the Caribbean, starting in 1609 about the same time as Jamestown, in conjunction with their mainland holdings, which also required the suppression, dispossession and ultimately genocidal removal of Natives. Therefore, so-called settler colonialism was advancing, at least by the English since there had long been settlers involved in the waves of European invasions over the Americas, at the same time that the English were becoming more deeply involved in the slave trade, both to their Caribbean holdings which were closely contested by other maritime powers, and especially along the eastern seaboard colonies of North America. This occurs from just after the break of the century, early 1600s, into the Jamestown and Plymouth company colonies (later to be crown colonies) from 1620 and on. Many of the settlers recruited or coerced were indeed indentured as servants or farm and craft laborers, and some were treated badly, especially near the end of their servitude years which could be extended for various legal and extra-legal reasons. Nonetheless, the increasing trade and cheap labor reliance over Black slaves, borrowing extensively from a well-grounded Caribbean marketplace, compelled plantation owners and slave traders to harden the enslavement conditions, creating an intergenerational inheritance of their status and thus no foreseeable escape for those experiencing what would later be termed "social death" (Patterson, 1985) when restrictive laws were put into place for African-descent slaves only. This is why Bacon's Rebellion was such a critically important juncture in racial identification systems, and is often misunderstood by many analysts as unique to the English colonies in North America. Yes, potential coalitions of servants and slaves – whites and Blacks – were dangerous, but no more so than those of escaped Blacks with Natives, particularly severe for those escaping to Spanish held Florida. A larger problem the English were facing was competition between other slave-holding colonies, and the penetration and conquest invasion, with resulting colonization, of the westward interior regions of the continent. They resolved this by producing settler militias and pioneers who could take lands while warring with Indians even as they began to harden their slave labor force in the agricultural rich colonies.

Social, Economic and Environmental Effects of Plantation-Based Colony

The conquest and colonization of the Americas also led to the ecological transformation of newly colonized lands, establishing of (a) stratified, social order with European nations on top, and a (deep) need for (cheap) labor leading to (a/the) demographic transition based on race. The Indian had been created and stratified, after conquest and demographic collapse, into the bottom of the new colony. The European, as Christian but not yet fully white, was (marked) by national representation (i.e. Spain, France, England, etc.) on the top of the colonial order. The African, taken from their origin lands (never to return), forcibly transported to be slaves in the colonies, shared the bottom structures as the Black (Negro, or still sometimes by African nation).

We have seen the deep growing developmental formation of the races, and the many complications of identification, social ordering and "mixing" on island colonies (first on Cuba and Hispaniola) where Spanish concepts of the mestizo had already arisen, along with resistance by maroons and internal rebellion by enslaved African and Indigenous alliances, under shifting European dominance as colonizers.

Great wealth albeit in national treasuries collected in what Marx and others have termed "primitive accumulation" had already made Spain the premier world power colonizer, through extracting valuable minerals (gold, silver) creating large plantations for agricultural commodities (such as sugar) to Europe, and using the entire ecosphere as natural resources (first timber, etc.), solely for profit. Competitive European colonizers, often taken up at wars over these sources of wealth as well as hegemony over growing systems of transoceanic bio-power (see the Spanish armada sent against England as an example, with privateers such as Francis Drake raiding ports to benefit the Crown), had problems of labor and landed populations later in towns and cities.

In moving toward Protestantism, the English had embraced a growing separation of state, church and trade economy, which interfaced exceptionally well with transoceanic colonizing, trading company's relationship with capital, and the global slave trade. The Portuguese had maximized their tripartite trading systems — colonial extraction, enslavement by race (African), wealth accumulation — through the southern Atlantic, by controlling most of the coastal regions of South America (Brazil). Their manpower development was entirely created on race-based enslavement (first Indians, then Blacks).

The Spanish had extended both their large island colonies and their coastal control over the Caribbean, Central and South America regions, also in a tripartite system — extraction of resources and agricultural systems, wealth accumulation and enslavement by race or enforced servitude by ethnicity. This led to manpower labor problems, because they had limited "settler" population for such vast lands, and they had formally, but not in practice, divested themselves of race-based enslavement. Hispaniola growth and devolution into a colonial backwater becomes the perfect case to observe these problems, since Spain had allowed more African enslavers over the western half, and mixed-race mestizo population on the eastern half.

Buccaneers and pirating exploded out of windward passage conflicts, leading to Spain selling its interest in the west, to France as San Domingue that became Haiti, centerpiece to the triple island colonies — Martinique, Guadeloupe and Haiti — and a launching pad or port for colonial interests in Louisiana. Right up until the Haitian revolution, France considered this to be the wealthiest colonial holdings in the world, with its rich plantations, forests and coastal lands.

The French and the English had entered into explorative reconnaissance and invasion of North America, where massive depopulation from colonial destruction (as the initial predator introducing the pandemic pathogen) and disease from epidemics unknown to the continent, with concomitant social disordering, had weakened great civilizations, confederated nations and individual tribes. Now called the Great Dying (Koch, Brierley, Maslin,

Company Towns – Jamestown and Plymouth (B1-5)
Crown Colonies – Virginia and Massachusetts
(settlers, savages, slaves, supremacists)
Focus – Virginia Company (of London)

American racism was borne out of two English start-up colonies, Jamestown and Plymouth, with capital investment from London based companies involved in setting up transoceanic–transcontinental enterprises, controlled by the Crown. The first start-up at Jamestown, and the plantations that followed on it, were private, for-profit operations backed by venture capitalists in England. Half the original colonists died in the first year, with high death rates continuing for the next twenty or thirty years for so-called settlers.

The English had landed in the "middle of a small but rapidly expanding Indian empire called Tsenacomoco… Three decades before, Tsenacomoco had been a collection of six separate chiefdoms. By the time the foreigners came from overseas, its paramount chief, (from the) Powhatan, had tripled its size to about 8,000 square miles and [much] more than 14,000 people… (Powhatan) sphere of influence stretched from the Potomac to Cape Henry." (Mann, 2007:37) Forests were managed by controlled burns, villages tended to mixed field crops rotated every few years, always near fresh water sources, without need for enclosures as no large domesticated animals foraged among smaller animals, that all fed off the coastal rich resources from the sea and land.

Soldier of fortune John Smith took control of the early colony as "starving time" devastated the colonists, becoming more belligerent in seeking food, coming into conflict with the confederation leaders, who did not yet perceive the colonists as a serious threat. Two relief convoys, funded by Virginia Company investors, kept a basic population in place, but survival was in question, with famine, bad water and disease (malaria) taking their toll, some colonists said to have resorted to cannibalism. Local natives reported to their leaders of the conditions, probably saving the colony, that held on until 1610 with the shipwrecked group including John Rolfe appearing a year late, wanting return to England. Luckily (for them, not Native Nations) a large reinforcement arrived under Thomas West, DeLaWar who proceeded to rebuild Jamestown, extend plantations, and conduct raids into Powhatan lands, leading to wars where Matoaka and many Natives were taken hostage.

The Crown and Virginia Company investors lost hope of plunder wealth from gold and silver, and directed the expanding colony to grow tobacco or other trade to cash crops for growing European markets, destroying the balanced ecosphere of the region in forest clear-cutting, monocrop plantings, new voracious animals such as pigs and cattle, fortified private property sites, and introduction of invasive species, rats and honeybees. The land literally transformed into a semblance of England, endangering life for Native peoples.

1619 brought trading for captured slaves to buoy the indentured servant labor, and celebrating Thanksgiving at the Berkeley Hundred plantation 30 miles west of Jamestown, where private venture capitalists had issued the new colonists deeds to the land, setting up the second Powhatan war of 1622 over Land. Newly drawn well-armed militias defended plantations and the taking of even more land from Native nations. Full scale colonization had arrived in the Americas.

Figure 3.2 Jamestown, Virginia – company town, crown colony (B1-5) (text box).

and Lewis, 2019), evidenced in Cortes' taking of Tenochtitlan, followed by smallpox and related pandemics depopulating Mexico, and expeditions such as DeSoto spreading deadly diseases into North America proper, with waves of disease and death weakening Native nations throughout the continent, providing opportunity for new forms of colonization (global cooling, forestation, colonial reinvasion, deforestation and the plantationocene (Murphy and Schroering, 2020).[17]

The lovely and talented Matoaka of the Powhatan people, known to the western world as Pocahontas, makes for a perfect case in point (for how colonizing histories have distorted perceptions that lead to denial of the racial domination in their past social relations now found in contemporary relations). This contributes to a further dehumanization of Indigenous peoples, and erasure of their accomplishments and agency in traditional societies.

The English settlers had arrived at and built Jamestown Fort when Matoaka was 9 or 10, given some leeway as a favored daughter of Wahunsenaca, paramount leader of the Confederation. Matoaka may have befriended the soldier-governor John Smith when he was being held by the Powhatan, and she definitely helped with food supplies and victuals to the early colony when they were suffering famine from their inability to feed their people from the local environment. As a child, elders might have had her approach the fearful colonists, as many other Indigenous peoples continue to do today. When conflicts led to war, her father moved her to nearby peoples so that the English would not go after her, with the colonist-settlers, as John Smith did earlier, threatening leaders to fill boats with "dead carcasses" unless they provided food.

Attempts to recognize each other's sovereignty were at first reciprocal, although the English tried to be deceptive in crowning Wahunsenaca, who refused to bow and thus was their equal. However, London Company directives were to get more land for growing crops and search for gold and timber. English militia decided to take prisoners of the Powhatan, and targeted the well-known Matoaka, who had been partnered in the Indigenous way to a fine young man, Kocoum, who was killed trying to defend her from kidnapping.

Two versions of her captivity emerged, poignantly after the Powhatan released English prisoners in exchange for colonists to reciprocate, who refused to release Matoaka, claiming she became Christian. Later she would marry a colonist, John Rolfe, who named their nonaggression period *Peace of Pocahontas*, Princess of the Powhatan. The colonial histories said she bore him a child, they then traveled to England where she was feted as Indian royalty, meeting aristocrats, paraded for potential investors and to show peace for the Virginia Company. Mysteriously, she died on the return trip, never to see her father or her homelands again.

Some Mattaponi from her birthplace at *Werowocomoco*, tell a very different story. They say she was violently kidnapped, and then sexually assaulted during her lengthy captivity, becoming impregnated by the governor.[18] Needing her for negotiations, they arranged for her to be married to Rolfe after being baptized, thus legitimizing her child. The colonists staged the trip to England to impress both the Crown authority and Company investors with their success – Indian Princess marries English commoner – which they put in press and sold to mainstream history told to this very day. Not needing her return where she could tell her own story, she was poisoned en-route and buried in secret.

John Rolfe and John Smith, sexual braggarts writing fictionalized histories of colonial pioneers, wrote of Pocahontas, typified in media as virginal beauty in nature falling for Anglo colonists, just as Anacaona and many other Indigenous women had been and would be over the centuries, with her sacrificing herself for Smith as a girl, and agreeing to be a peace treaty prop for Rolfe. Indeed, until recently the highly regarded PBS site stated the biggest issue of Race for Native Peoples in the colonies was connected to that of class, in that the English thought the marriage of a Native "princess" was mostly a problem because it was with a "commoner" which denies the initial position of very violent superiority of colonists in Virginia – Rolfe – and deeply inferior position of Natives in North America – Pocahontas – evidenced in the Indigenous stories told about Jamestown and Plymouth.

Rather than an invasive colony expanding over lands and peoples in a Virginia territory, with sexualizing violence in romantic depictions, or conversely with stereotyping imagery in hostile savagery, dominant history romanticizes Indigenous women, thus dismissing them as having agency over their own lives. The same dominant history stereotypes Indigenous men as noble or hostile savages, but always as tribes needing civilization, thus not recognizing their preinvasion societies. We actually see how this works in dominant ideologies when a President of the United States can casually, with racist intent, refer to a U.S. Senator as "Pocahontas" in order to demean her very fractionated descent claims to lift desirable patriarchal dominance, in front of Navajo Nation leaders and the country itself.[19] The racial stereotype held, the actual history did not.

Moreover, we see how deeply mythical this romanticized history becomes in the telling of an American story, one that allows for the disappearance of the Powhatan not as genocidal, but as natural in Native women coupling with Settler-Colonist men, and assimilating by taking on the religion and value structures of the colonial society. If one doubts this, simply go to the capitol rotunda and view the oversize painting The Baptism of Pocahontas, depicted as if taking place in a Protestant cathedral or Parliamentary Hall, with Native and English dignitaries in attendance. Other paintings or drawings have her marriage taking place outside near the colony, or in simpler buildings more

Figure 3.3 Painting in halls of Congress "The Baptism of Pocahontas".

likely to have been early colonial structures. We also note that her baby Thomas was not entered into the colonial birth registry, although John Rolfe was colony secretary and historian for Jamestown. Later, as pointed out by scholars, Native mixed descent (settler fathers) children were considered and registered as White, the polar opposite of Black mixed descent (slave-holding settler fathers) children. This racialization becomes enshrined in the U.S. law and social policy, befuddling most race scholars for the last two centuries.

John Gadsby Chapman (photograph courtesy Architect of the Capitol)[20]

We see similar imposition of patriarchal, racialized terms of colonization in the other colony, Plymouth leading to Massachusetts Bay of a New England envisioned without Native Nations. Gradually, the Pilgrims and Puritans asserted their European laws and culture upon the very Indigenous peoples who had saved them from starvation and death, creating such religious mediating institutions as "praying towns" where Native people were to learn to be Christian, supposedly gaining knowledge and skills that would allow them to make a livelihood in the new colony. Of course, these Indians had to earn their keep, so they would act as servants to good colonial Anglo households, creating conditions later called coercive assimilation into or under superior colonists or settlers, thereby underscoring the cultural and sociopolitical supremacy of English society. And, importantly in opposition to the "Good Indian" were the unconstrained Native Nations, such as most Wampanoag or the embattled Narragansett and Pequot, usually thought of as "Hostile" to the colonies, and philosophically referred to as the Savage.

All of these terms and social institutions would be built into the New England society hardwired into the civilizational discourse already advanced

Company Towns – Jamestown and Plymouth (B2-6)
Crown Colonies – Virginia and Massachusetts
(settlers, savages, slaves, supremacists)
Focus – Plymouth Bay Company (Massachusetts)

Wampanoag peoples lived and prospered along the southeastern territories of what is now called Massachusetts (the people who lived just north of them) including coastal islands directly south, in well adapted communities headed by sachem who coordinated decision-making through councils headed by a massassoit, interactive with an ecosphere that provided for their confederation. Pandemics had recently swept through their lands, wiping out some villages such as the Patuxet, that had interaction with European ships, including interested locals who were kidnapped and sold into slavery, as reported by Tisquantum after his incredible escape from Spanish and English monks leading to his return to an emptied village.

Religious dissidents originally from England who left Holland to make a living in the New World colonies of Virginia, landed near Patuxet in 1620 and proceeded to build a settlement that nearly failed over a winter they lost half their number, and were saved by a diplomat intervention who brought the English-speaking Tisquantum to teach them about the local ecology and arranged alliance with nearby Native nations. Within a few years, they were reinforced by English colonists, became Plymouth colony, later Massachusetts Bay colony, expanding over the region, coming into conflict over land and religion. Their Puritan foundation was intolerant of Natives, while their Company investors wanted more return through large plantations, increased fur trade, and dominance over contested areas. Wars with Native nations erupted as a New England Confederation became stronger in taking over other colonies, and suppressing Indigenous culture and political representation. The English Crown supported racial enslavement and a growing transatlantic market of natural resources and agricultural products, that seemed to require destruction of Native nations, including the Wampanoag who had saved the initial Pilgrims, culminating in the 1676 wars ending Indigenous sovereignty in the region.

New England – Protestant and Caucasian – began its prominence among colonies as a Company driven operation, authorized by Crown authority with Church legitimation, designed to reinforce Colonists in permanent towns and cities, technically at war with all competitive claims by Native nations or other European colonizing (Dutch in New York) forces in the expanding region of control. Colonists became settlers, Indians were typified as savages, Blacks were slaves or non-citizens, and later Christian Europeans operated as ethno-national supremacists. The dye was cast for a north American colonization process that would command Atlantic shipping markets, build agricultural industrial economies, suppress Native nations as Indians, and enslave Africans as Blacks.

Figure 3.4 Plymouth, Massachusetts – company/crown colony (B2-6) (text box).

in Caribbean colonization. Ultimately, the resisting, uncivilizable hostile icon would be transported into colonial frontier wars that were critically important to colonial expansion to northwest territories and the American revolutionary ideologies found in the Declaration of Independence of "merciless Indian savages" that Britain failed to protect the colonists from, that proved to be little more than rhetorical cover for further land-taking and colonial wars for regional hegemony. But, once again, we get ahead of ourselves and must first focus on the initial colonial developments in the northeast.

Return to Merry Mount and Origins of Manifest Destiny

Writing about a theater production,[21] Drinnon (1997) describes how the previously described character Thomas Morton (from Wessagusett of Plymouth and the Massachusetts Bay Colony) with "pleasure-loving" abandon pretended to believe the 'blue-assed Puritans' hated him for his Book of Common Prayer, with an Anglican priest choking:

> ...on Morton's salacious doggerel about having free maids, white or red, in the forest or in bed, declaring in revulsion... "There must be some boundary between the Indian and English subjects." ...the invading Puritan captain agreeing... that was why Endicott had marched his expedition from Salem – to establish such a boundary, to stop the infernal Maypole dancing... to put an end to the horror of drunken whites mating with red women... The expedition's chaplain, Elder Palfrey, warned Endicott not to consider these Indians harmless nor to underestimate the threat they posed:
>
> "There are three thousand miles of wilderness behind these Indians, enough solid land to drown the sea from here to England. We must free our land of strangers, even if each mile is a marsh of blood."
>
> To this man of God the Indians were a plague that "must be smothered if we want our children to live in freedom." He demanded they be taken out of sight and shot. Endicott so ordered, with the promise that after his men had finished with the Indians, they might start burning down the houses of Merry Mount. Tomorrow would be soon enough to burn down the native village itself.
>
> (Drinnon, 1997: 1–4)

After making connections to Vietnam's My Lai killings, Drinnon works backwards to Nathaniel Hawthorne's 1830s short story "The Maypole of Merry Mount" that he connects to Jackson's search and kill missions against the Seminoles in Florida, and the Trail of Tears in quoting "Their weapons were always at hand to shoot down the straggling savage," he wrote of the Saints, "...to proclaim bounties on the heads of wolves and the scalps of Indians." Followed by the future of the national character "Jollity and gloom were contending for an empire" (pg 5).

Drinnon attributes to Hawthorne that Puritans took pleasure and satisfaction at these killings, along with "whippings" to control their bestial nature. Then he shows how Morton was charged with non-existing crimes of fraternizing with the Indians, three times being taken into custody and twice shipped back to England (ironically on the ship *Handmaid*), where he was acquitted for lack of charging laws, but each time imprisoned and whipped on his return to the colony.

Finally, Drinnon (pg 13) shows John Adam's preoccupation with Merry Mount and Morton's relationship with Indians in terms of the "dangers of frontier life" ending that passage with:[22]

> I venture, from 1628 to 1883 and after, the unwritten code assumed Indians **not to be persons**, who might be responsive to kindness and fair dealing, but "savages," who would inevitably use any available weapon to strike at the lives of newcomers, those bearers of "civilization."

We find that scholars of law, the humanities, social sciences, literature and of course politicians spend an inordinate amount of time and energy in rationalizing away American Indian issues, premier among them a loss of their lands. Academics need to discuss the many supremacist[23] ideologies arising around Merry Mount to Plymouth and Powhatan (Pocahontas) to Jamestown, while ignoring or hiding central conflicts between Native Nations and invasive and expanding colonies. Instead (a hundred or more years later), historians, politicians and even many scholars, build mythical constructions of partly friendly relations – a stereotypical Pocahontas and shared defense pact of Thanksgiving being exceptional events or practices engineered by the colonists, which allow a dominant narrative to emerge in American schools and curriculum. To American schoolchildren, of all races and backgrounds, the mythical tales become part of a much larger set of social constructs – Christian civilization, Boy Scouts, sports mascotry, building democracy – that becomes nearly impossible to root out of the minds of adults. It is easier to hold on to simple justifications and positive imagery than to assess a critical and often violent origins of our nation and peoples. From the east coast's rising sun, the Wampanoag in this chapter, to the west coast's setting of the day in California, the Tongva and Tolowa at the end of the chapter, we observe an unbroken string of invasions, colonizing culturicides and genocidal taking of land, representing in the curriculum from elementary school to the most advanced universities, a mistaken mythical story of the unexplained disappearance of more than 500 Nations of Native America.

Here we not only describe the early Plymouth colonial relationships with the Wampanoag, but their 1621 Treaty agreement and its contestation around what would have been Thanksgiving, also a deeply mythologized historical event recreated hundreds of years later to deny or dismiss the fratricidal and genocidal war that ended Native Nations claim to sovereignty and the Land. During these same years from 1640 on, we see the Massachusetts colony develop racist laws for Blacks institutionalized earlier than those in Virginia. We also observe the intentional destruction of Indian Nations and confederations, well into the creation of the United States north (Chapter 4) where Blacks are less critical to agricultural and early industrial capitalism. As in the Virginia colony later becoming an important state government supporting racial enslavement of Blacks, without recognition of Indians as nations or people, we observe that racialized laws and policies grow out of the social structures, rather than the converse.

Colonial Colleges and Culturicide (Hegemonic Education)

The founding of Harvard College, for education of Indian as well as English youths, is instructive of differing perceptions of Native Nations. Their official mascot is John Harvard, named after a Puritan minister who arrived in New England 1636 and died the next year (1637) after providing the University with an endowment.[24] Harvard was established in 1636 by the Massachusetts Bay Colony as a corporation. In order to get England's consent, the 1650 original charter read it was for "education of the English and Indian youth of this country in knowledge and godlynes" since otherwise colonists were to send their young men to English universities. Such hegemonic education was rejected at the time, and continued to be so until Canassatego's famous 1744 speech to Virginia and Maryland delegates at treaty talks in Pennsylvania, as prelude to U.S. revolutionary formation denying education once offered by colonialists. This institutional domination was replicated through creation of the University of California in the 1870s.[25]

Moving from Colleges and Curriculum to Violent Colonization in Chapter 3

The Mystic river massacre was conducted in May of 1637, during what is called the Pequot War, when Connecticut colonists under Captain John Mason with Narragansett and Mohegan allies, surrounded and set fire to the Pequot town where more than 700 people lived, with much of the leadership and warrior age men away in fights and treaty negotiations to the north. The English-led forces set fire to the hutches and palisades, brutally executing everyone trying to escape the flames, including women and children. Witnesses say only a few boys managed to escape by hiding. The colonists gave Mass and tribute to God for helping them with the genocidal victory, much as many notables would in coming years, such as Cotton Mather's relatives conducting Mass before and after massacres in the years up to, during and after the war they started to finish off Wampanoag resistance, the literal people who saved the original Mayflower Puritans noted in the Thanksgiving myths. When the Narragansett saw what had transpired they felt sickened, retired from the battle, offered sanctuary, only to face their own fight for survival years later.

The English Puritans and pilgrim settler populations swelling into the territories renamed New England conducted raids and wars in suppressing Native resistance, building Praying Towns where Indians were abused much like indentured servants without any recourse to the law or any accorded rights. When the great Massasoit of the Wampanoag passed, his sons tried to negotiate a new treaty, but the elder was poisoned in conference, so Metacom the younger led a resistance fight called the First Indian War (though the many above had already transpired) and the most destructive in colonial history, only ending when a turncoat was bribed so that Metacom, called King Phillip, was killed, with his head being placed on a pole outside Plymouth for 20 years, and his family members said to be sold into slavery in the West Indies. Around the same time, the Colonial Governor over Maine territories issued a bounty for scalps of dead Indians in that region, with body parts often substituting for payment. Families were hunted down and killed, much as had occurred in Hispaniola by the Spanish, for total extermination of resistance.

In the upcoming chapters, we will further document such practices done by Protestant Christians, sometimes acting like gangs as the Paxton Boys killing Indians in prelude to the 1763 agreement, or the Gnadenhutten massacre (Moravian massacre), as colonial White American militia forces killed nearly a hundred Christian Lenape in 1782 at a Moravian missionary village in Ohio, prelude to the 1783 ending of the American Revolutionary War. Ritual killings of men included scalping to death, while women and children were mullet stunned before being cutup, resembling English and Protestant methods of public torture and execution. Tecumseh would refer to these victims as martyrs of Jesus Indians and used it as one reason not to negotiate with Americans (showing knowledge of the linked colonizing violence).

We can fast forward to the Indian Removals and other genocidal actions taken by the federal and state governments, and often in the name of settlers. General and President Washington ordered full-scale destruction of Onondaga well-developed villages, as President Jefferson called for the extermination of Native peoples. During the California genocide, one of the most extensive on record (Fenelon and Trafzer, 2014), Tolowa Deneii were slaughtered during their Winter Solstice ceremony at Yontocket, between 450 and 600, where both scalps and heads were taken for bounty purposes, and in a grand fire after the killings, live babies thrown into the flames, completing a journey of hundreds of years as the testimony above states. During Sand Creek militia soldiers took body parts and live prisoners back with them to Denver and put many on display, selling scalps as momentos in the streets for weeks to come, and of course soldiers posed at Wounded Knee kill site and mass grave in 1890 South Dakota, considered the end of the "Indian Wars." We observe a continuous line of extrajudicial and state-ordered killings, massacres and even executions with remarkable symmetry with the previous centuries' wholesale attacks, partly predicated on Native people not being Christian nor fully human and thus outside the obligation of civilized society. In many if not most of these cases, the leaders offered prayers to their God for the strength to do His Will and complete the Manifest Destiny of their people.

What resonates in the American mindset is precisely this historical rendering of Supremacy – first as Christians, then Anglo, free and ultimately with the Euro-American as White – versus savage non-Christian Indians, as uncivilized, extending to African Blacks as enslaved peoples, and further extended back to Africa and colonies around the world. History exemplifies these in the great hypocrisy of Kipling's White Man's Burden, rather than an imposition of a racial order benefiting Euro-Americans. This conflation allows the historical differences between Catholics and Protestants, and the un-racialized other non-Christians, to be put into simple racial binaries or boxes. Jews became penultimate examples of how a racialized ordering of elite supremacy is both fluid and scripted or bordered, within the Nazi genocide being re-narrativized as cultural/religious (racial) in places such as Israel versus the West Bank and Gaza, or the Apartheid of South Africa, or so on it goes in a long litany of world struggles found in the recent ASA Presidential address by Eduardo Bonilla-Silva in that "*settler colonialism, colonialism that is not past history but a contemporary social force, is a racist project.*"

We see how "western European" education systems stand opposed to most indigenous paradigms and world views (Deloria and Wildcat, 2001), from the initial colonial culturicide patterns in creating Harvard College through the treaty conferences as prelude to the United States declaring independence, only to replicate the pattern (Fenelon and LeBeau, 2006).

> *You, who are wise must know that different Nations have different Conceptions of things and you will therefore not take it amiss, if our Ideas of this kind of Education happen not to be the same as yours.*

Canassatego, 1744, Leaders of the Six Nations, Lancaster, Pennsylvania

Our work (2006) illustrates these issues through emphasizing indigenous cultures, curricula, conflicts over social justice, historical perspectives and "voice" of Native Nations/people, existing long before and certainly since Columbus and Europeans first arrived in the Americas (Cleary and Peacock, 1998). Underlying themes show previous education in the United States and colonial North America were for the purposes of cultural destruction (Adams, 1995) and social domination that included institutional racism (Huff, 1997) along with deep struggles over the meaning of life itself (Locust, 1988).

Observing Gnadenhutten Massacre (the American Revolutionary War) monument, located next to a reconstructed mission house in the center of the original village, becomes exemplary of a nation conflicted over race and religion. Dedicated in 1872: "Here triumphed in death ninety Christian Indians, March 8, 1782." Gnadenhutten, or Moravian massacre, was the killing of 96 Christian Lenape (Delaware) men, women and children **as they prayed**, by white American militia from Pennsylvania at a missionary village of Ohio.

Touted as a Revolutionary War action, more than a century later, President Roosevelt called it "a stain on the frontier character that time cannot wash away." But, once again, we are ahead of ourselves and the societies under analysis.

Blacks and Indians in the Colonies – Creation of Religious Race Laws and Institutions

From 1619 to racialized state and religion – One problem I was alerted to is that of 1619 where new historians challenged mainstream perspectives (Hannah-Jones, 2019; versus Magness, 2020) where at first I thought, in reference to the Atlantic critique (2019) of the *New York Times* 1619 project (Project), the problem lay in whether 20 Africans bartered or sold that year at Jamestown were slaves or were more like the indentured Europeans, English colonists known as settlers.

Of course, it is a bit naïve to think that all the enslavement going on in the Caribbean was not known to English colonists, especially since the ship captains who delivered them, as original colonists to American shores, had been deeply involved in slave trading – Christopher Newport – as had been their predecessors Francis Drake and Hawkins. One fifth of the profits had been going to the Crown – Elizabeth then James – which implicates (inculcates) English authority. And John Smith himself saw the potential for profits from slavery and genocide:

> Deliberately emulating the Spanish, Smith argued that with enough military force, any colonists to the region could subdue the Indians, use them for labor, and supplement those forced laborers with Africans.
>
> (Hardesty, 2019: 6)

Even more important is there had been "wars" with the Powhatan in 1610, kidnappings (Matoaka, Pocahontas) and ransom treaties, with Wahunsenaca, paramount chief of a Powhatan confederation who had negotiated the treaties, passing in 1618 the year before, thus upending nonaggression pacts or agreements between the colonists and the "Indians" collectively defined.

The racial triad of (white) settler-colonists (red Indian), native-Indigenous (tribe-nations) and (Black or Red) enslaved/indentured servile workers was well underway in 1619 although overall small numbers of settlers meant adding servile Black Africans to the mix was relatively unimportant in a greater scheme of things. As the combined slave and servile laborers increased, (in relation) to the overall number of colonists (settlers?) and in relationship to the growing elite landowners class, who were bringing great Native land invasions in early colonial expansion, institutionalization (particularly severe) of racial separation and stratification, was perceived to be necessary by the controlling parties and companies still sponsoring colonial trade relations. These social institutions elicited considerable resistance from those the colonizers subordinated, oppressed and destroyed.

Figure 3.5 Great leaders of the resistance in the Americas around 1620–1790. (a) Ousamequin – Massasoit, Wampanoag. Sculptor Cyrus E. Dallin (1861–1944), Public domain, via Wikimedia Commons. (b) Po'pay – Pueblo revolt leader (conquista). US Capitol, Public domain, via Wikimedia Commons. (c) Touissaint Louverture – Ayiti revolt leader. From: Alexandre-François-Louis, comte de Girardin, Public domain, via Wikimedia Commons. (d) Toypurina – Tongva revolt. Courtesy James Fenelon, photo taken of street mural on Indian Alley wall, Los Angeles (2019).

Figure 3.6 Leaders and icons of North American colonization around 1620–1790. (a) Nathaniel Bacon's burning Jamestown. Howard Pyle, Public domain, via Wikimedia Commons. (b) Matoaka (Pocahontas) – Powhatan. Matoaka, or Pocahontas: Wikimedia Commons, accessed October 30, 2021 (by Simon van de Passe 1616). (c) Baron Jeffrey Amherst – English General. File: Jeffrey Amherst, 1st Baron Amherst.jpg. (2020, January 22). *Wikimedia Commons, the free media repository.* Retrieved 19:23, October 30, 2021 (from painting by Thomas Gainsborough, National Portrait Gallery) from https://commons.wikimedia.org/w/index.php?title=File:Jeffrey_Amherst,_1st_Baron_Amherst.jpg&oldid=389270528. (d) Junipero Serra – Founder Priest, Missions. Burkhard Mücke, CC BY-SA 4.0 https://creativecommons.org/licenses/by-sa/4.0, via Wikimedia Commons.

The Black Colonial Formation Period – Continuance of Indian, Creation of Settler-White

Following our theoretical observations, we can observe racial formation, or racist formulation (system put into place is deeply discriminatory and exploitive, it produces a set of practices that roughly conform to developed formulas with laws and policies), dominated by racial categories of Black, Indian and Anglo (White) settler-colonists (indentured white ethnics as a subset). The Black racial category is developed for enslavement, racialized labor and migration population controls, while the already existing Indian racial category is carried forward for land-takings, destruction of nation-tribe status and the removal or extermination of resisting Native peoples. Settler-Colonists were at first Anglo immigrants into the colonies, which with survival became the dominant racial-ethnic group made up of Europeans, increasingly referred to as White. Many Euro-Mediterranean immigrants come as indentured racialized labor, either by limited choices, or direct coercion, and have an intermediate status, usually for an extendable contract period, after which they become part of the settler class.

First, we must identify the creation of the Black under English colonization patterns, since the transatlantic slave markets had become racialized as entirely African, although slaves were still commonly taken from Native populations, as discussed in Chapter 2, and as would continue in the English colonies when convenient to do so. The primary problem that has befuddled many analysts is the institutionalization of these racist practices, since none existed within English society. Even so, policies had been compartmentalized and legalized for those indentured as servants, with the Irish Catholics as ethno-national domination, for some time, further applied to plantation systems, such as those at Ulster and generally throughout Ireland. We will identify those exact policies, however, the status of Blacks starting about 1619 and in cycles throughout the 17th century, needs to be identified before analyzing a building of institutionalized social policy toward Africans as Blacks.

About 1619 or 1620 the soon-to-be privileged class of colonist-settlers was developing, rather sharply differentiated from "indentured servants" whose labor was under contract, for a predetermined period, and sometimes the types and terms of that labor (i.e. skilled, field, or the number of hours per day, relationships such as marriage or children, Christian honor of Sabbath) that was mostly done on an individual basis. Thus, the "servant" category was all inclusive. Since the governors and ships captains, and by 1619 the Crown of England, all had direct experience with Africans as slaves (as discussed in Chapter 2 and already found in North America in Florida, the Carolinas and in northern meso-America), we must assume that the colonial authorities were well aware of the racialized slave status of Africans, who were enslaved while in Africa, brought to the Americas and then either deposited as chattel slaves in the Caribbean or were in transit to be sold at other slave market ports. Moreover, the initial 20 or so Africans bartered for in 1619 were taken from a British-run privateer that had taken them as booty from an actual slave ship (with a Dutch flag), and thus had started out as enslaved (versions of these arguments would be made all the way to the taking of the Amistad in the 1830s United States, see the next book).

Conniff and Davis (1994: 126) analyze the differing status of racialized labor for Blacks sold or delivered to Jamestown, and in other English colonies, and find they were indeed slaves, even if listed as "servants" as a general term, which had migrated to the colonies from England when poor people were "indented" into "servitude" and thus servants (Hardesty, 2019: 4).

> Virginia colonists officially listed captive Africans as "servants," but such an appellation should confuse no one about the **slave status of the Africans in the colonies**. English-language usage in the 1600s conceived of slave as a category of servant. So the use of the word "servant" in documents such as the Virginia censuses of 1623 and 1624 in no way denied the slave status of Africans. Nothing could deny the **reality of their slavery**. Africans in bondage in Virginia were captives, coerced in presence and in effort. They were bought and sold as **chattel**, made by law movable **property**; they occupied a **heritable** status; and they were liable to service for an indefinite term extending to life.
>
> (Conniff and Davis, 1994: 126–127)

However, since status was unclear in many ways, as in relation to indentured servitude, and as "Africans had already been in the Caribbean region for over one hundred years" with a presence in the area of South Carolina since 1526 (Asante, 2021: 9) and a continued presence, even interracial marriage in Spanish Florida since 1565, we must observe both the exceptional individual that breaks free from bondage, however identified, and how racialized boundaries are gradually, ever so firmly, put in place under English colonial laws of Jamestown, Virginia, that reflect early combinations of church and racial supremacy. Oluo (2021) points out a 1630 court that orders a white colonist to be publicly whipped for having sex with an African woman, "polluting whiteness – his own and that of his community" to ensure the purity and "exclusivity" of whiteness (a word not used, rather church sense of "heathen" not Christian; Wilkerson, 2020).

Rolfe is shown to have traded the twin sister of his enslaved African Bermuda woman, Go-Go, for valuable tobacco seeds along with Native and African knowledge how to grow it, (Hill, 2021) becoming horribly ironic when her granddaughter is sold to pay a 1639 tobacco tax demanded by the English King from the colonies. The Church of England mandated similar measures through a 1643 (Virginia) General Assembly policy of payments of tobacco and corn to Ministers for all "tithable" persons, and for "all negro women at the age of sixteen year" (Stevenson, 2021), putting pressures on both enslaved and free Black women to pay the taxes.

In other circumstances, the lack of status or contract of indenture-hood could work against claimants or those accused of criminal offenses, as it did with John Punch who escaped with two (white) servants, but were caught by their Virginia owner, who brought them to court in 1640. The white servants were whipped with years added to their indentured service, while Punch was ordered to "serve his said master or his assigns for the time of his natural Life" (Parker, 2021) since no contract applied, becoming the first Black person to become a slave for life in Virginia (arguably, others had this status but not noted or stated by courts or colonies). In a famous case, Anthony Johnson, who had been enslaved in Angola, worked hard to get freedom from servitude in the colony, married and had children on his farmstead, seeming to defy the enslavement of so many other Africans (Parker, 2021). Yet, when another African man working as a servant on his farm, John Casor, claimed his contract period was finished, there was a dispute with Casor going to work for a white neighbor. After a year, Johnson brought suit in 1655 claiming that Casor was never indentured, and so was a slave for life. The courts sided with Johnson, making Casor slave for his life, even as other cases arose in various states with differing outcomes. Virginia finally passed a 1662 law declaring that (African) children followed the legal status of the mother, in contradiction to English law following the father, establishing heritability for Blacks that went through formation of the United States.[26]

Nonetheless, the vagueness of the laws caused openings for some African families to gain freedom from understood indenture periods, or through baptism as Christians that would allow them or other family members to get freedom. These legal loopholes were soon closed, with other systems like the Dutch producing status like "half-freedom" for Black slaves who fought against Native nations, had to pay taxes for their free existence that could not be passed on to their children (Parker, 2021: 33). The 1662 law on mother's heritability had implications for what would otherwise be sex crimes as well, since Elizabeth Keye was the daughter of an African woman, and her English owner, and was then sold, along with her son, to another Englishman. By 1667, the Virginia Assembly was ready to close the baptism loophole in Black enslavement, declaring "baptisme doth not alter the condition of their person as to his bondage or freedom" (Tisby, 2021). The English colony of Virginia thus superseded both English homeland law and using Supremacy Acts went far beyond what the Spanish and Catholic Church had pushed.

One set of analytical problems creating this confusion, which many scholars have decided means the first Africans were not slaves, is use of settler colonialism frames, since it excludes analysis of Indian nations, another category of humans in distinct racialized position, and it collapses all others into an undefined "settler" class, that does not delineate how indentured status is applied, or its English legal origins (Hardesty, 2019: 3–4). However, as we proceed to identify the racial laws and policies that were created in the English colonies, over time and place, under contracts and charters (King James as Crown had already issued slave charters) we do see that existing institutional factors do operate, and so would be applied to Africans. While noting the general practices below, we also note there were exceptions, some Africans operating in freedom.[27]

> Nothing could rationally support any conclusion other than that the captive Africans were slaves from the first. They occupied no status as indentured servants who had entered contracts voluntarily. Africans had no contracts for service, and for sure they had not entered service voluntarily. As it was in Virginia, so it was elsewhere in the thirteen colonies. Captivity enslaved Africans, coercion kept them enslaved, and social controls held them and their descendants separate as slaves and as nonslaves. The dominant society put them in a position distinct from all others. Specifically, the slave was salable, and no other persons were. An indentured servant's contract and, thus, labor was salable, but the person was not. Slavery was heritable, and no other personal labor obligation was. No others were marked from birth as unfree labor. Even recognition at birth marked Africans apart. Among settlers in the dominant society, heritability followed the father's line; among captive Africans, in contrast, heritability followed the mother's line. So a person was a slave if his or her mother was a slave, despite the father's status. In every crucial feature, settler stood apart from slave.
>
> (Conniff and Davis, 1994: 127)[28]

Laws and policies and practices about racialized slavery and social relations between races were developed from social structures already in place, just not formally fixed and unregulated. This means that both slavery and racial suppression for purposes of labor exploitation were already present in the early English colonies, but were not yet codified, or as Conniff and Davis tell it: "Law did not create slavery; law merely recognized slavery," moving the relationships into the "sphere of public policy." And these relationships were also the result of changing demographics and stratification by race in the growing colony.[29]

> The Chesapeake colonies initiated the law of slavery in the 1650's as they moved from a labor force of mostly white servants to one of mostly black slaves. The transition saw Africans in Virginia multiply from about **300 in 1650 to 12,000 in 1708**, when blacks formed about **40 percent of the colony's 30,000** residents. By **1756 Virginia had 120,156 blacks**, ten times as many as in 1708. But the percentage changed little: **Blacks in 1740 made up 40.9 percent** of the colony's total population. By 1750 Maryland, too, had a substantial black population

numbering about 43,000 and forming 30.8 percent of its population
the increased numbers themselves suggested a need for a more formal
structure within the slavery relationship.

(Conniff and Davis, 1994: 127–128)

The plantations were growing at a similar rate as the importation and potential reproduction of Blacks as slaves during this time period. Labor stratification was being introduced into contract law and for Blacks into public policy
race laws. Individual planters and other labor providers, needed to provide
clarification, especially as some Blacks had gained their freedom and were
owning homes, getting into professions, creating some wealth if not capital and even owning slaves (since they were unrestricted at the time). Even
before Bacon's rebellion obviated these ethnic-racial-class divisions, local
governments worried about reproducing their labor groups. English and
Virginia (colony) laws created two central means of redressing the issues –
making race (for Blacks) heritable through their mothers irrespective of
status, forming colonial militias, and later enacting statutes that all Blacks
were slaves at birth.

> Virginia exhibited its sense of distinction between blacks and whites in
> service in a 1661 statute that provided differing punishments for fugi-
> tive white servants and black slaves. The law referred to "negroes who
> are incapable of making satisfaction by addition of time." Such a diffe-
> rence in tenure of service formed a **cornerstone of the practice of
> slavery**, as it would also for the **legal institution of slavery**. In **1662
> Virginia enacted a law to recognize the heritable slave status**
> through the mother. **Maryland** more than Virginia revealed the per-
> vasive colonial presumption equating African-ness with slavery when
> in **1663 it enacted a statute defining all blacks as slaves at birth**
> whatever the status of their mothers. In 1681 the colony revised the act
> to accord with practice elsewhere that mandated a child's following his
> or her mother's status.
>
> (Conniff and Davis, 1994: 128)

Similarly, courts had distinguished important legal and punishment issues for
Blacks (versus white ethnics), especially in family formation and marriage
laws. Wilkerson shows (2020: 110) that one such situation involved a
European man, Hugh Davis, who was accused and convicted (1630 Virginia
General Assembly) of having sexual relations with an African woman servant
(slave) and punished with a public whipping that other offenders observed.
Wilkerson attributes this to an early racial miscegenation (without the laws,
see Oluo 2020 above) in the colonies, yet, one can just as easily assign it to
Church accords, Oluo's "pollution" that we see practiced with even greater
severity in Plymouth, Massachusetts Bay Colony. Anglican church authority

was indeed taking hold in the House of Burgess, General Assembly of Virginia, as it would through the American Revolution and in race-based slavery as Protestantism in the southern states.

English Colonial Race Laws in Massachusetts and New England

However, there were two main original English colonies in North America, and as it turns out Plymouth Colony, growing into Massachusetts Bay Colony and later as the United Colonies of New England, with Connecticut and New Haven, created the first formalized laws concerning Blacks and slavery, some before those in Virginia. And, many of these laws and policies rather explicitly designated some, if not at other times all, Indian tribal nations as enemies to be killed, driven off the land, or taken captive and traded into slavery in the Caribbean, for Black slaves. Coming after militias fought genocidal wars against the Pequot and Native Nations, the United Colonies formed a New England Confederation in 1643, for military actions against Indians seen as a primary threat to colonial domination, along with the Dutch and other colonial competitors. Moreover, Indian captives sold or bartered into slavery and Black slaves brought back to New England required laws for intercolonial trading, creating effective legislation for two races.[30] Thus, as we discuss in the first introductory and subsequent chapters, we must look at the entire system and all the colonies in order to determine what is really going on, and the level of sharing or learning from policies of other systems. This turns out to be critical in understanding racism, early mercantile capitalism, and the three pointed human race systems in formation. Let us first review the interactive race laws for slavery in conjunction with the New England Indian wars, which share a symmetry with the Virginia Colony in late 17th-century colonialism.

We observe above, the close connections between Colony, Crown, Company and Church (4 Cs) with developing the two, or three, racist systems of (a) enslaving Blacks under colonial authority, and (b) conducting genocidal Indian wars over land under Crown authority, while (c) forming the White-ethnic settler population under Church authority, where all three systems are connected to or controlled by Company (authority) for profiteering and economic development. One critical component of these triadic race systems and quadratic political economies of colonizing powers is the growing world-system of mercantile capitalism embracing race-based slavery for its labor, and utilizing racial genocide for land-taking under Church policies, first Catholic then Protestant. Both systems – racial genocide and race-based slavery – were heavily debated in European courts and capitols (Spanish Catholic see Chapter 2; English Protestant, Chapter 3), never fully resolved, yet were driven by the search for and accumulation of wealth and power.

1624–1629 Samuel Maverick brought "Negro slaves" to Massachusetts (later, more)
1630 Mass Bay Colony established – created to be a plantation with compulsory labor
1631 Colony freemen elect own governor, has to be from same church (religious
   law supreme)
1634 Pequot war starts; Indians restrictions; colonists elect magistrates to enforce laws
1636 and 1637 – First militias form, Pequot war survivors enslaved, women and
   children kept, men taken on slave ship *Desire*, traded for Caribbean Blacks
   (Nicaraguan Negroes)[a]
1638 Slave ship *Desire* returns to land at Salem, discharge enslaved Blacks[b]
1641 "Body of Liberties" – official recognition of chattel slavery (Warren, 2016;
   Pleck, 2018)[c]
1643 Slavery legalized in New Plymouth and Connecticut under New England
   Confederation
1641–1645 Boston Puritan slavers (while in Africa) found guilty of "man-stealing" and
   doing business on Sunday (slaves released in Boston area, allowed to return to Africa)
1651 Rhode Island follows suit, with full formal legal slavery in New England
1660s New York and New Jersey follow New England line and legalize slavery,
   "converted" Indian townships grow in Massachusetts and throughout the region,
   used as labor.
1662 Virginia enacts law of hereditary slavery (through mother if Black slave)
1664 Maryland declares all Blacks to be in bondage, passing slave laws
1663-65 Virginia follows suit and declares slavery for Blacks
1675–78 Wampanoag resistance war, Massachusetts/New England barters for Black
   slaves
1676 Indian wars, Virginia colony frontier, Bacon's Rebellion (mixed race) assaults House

Figure 3.7 Race slavery laws, practices – Massachusetts Bay Colony (chart).

a "Such exchanges became routine during subsequent Indian wars, for the danger of
  keeping revengeful warriors in the colony far outweighed the value of their labor."
  (McManus, 1973)
b The *Desire* arrived back in Massachusetts in 1638, after exchanging its cargo, according to
  Winthrop, loaded with "Salt, cotton, tobacco and Negroes."
c Interestingly, this law was based on the "just war" reasoning that de Las Casas and the
  Dominicans used.

This last observation becomes critical in New England's peculiar orientation toward race-based slavery and land takings, in that profiteering shifted from plantation economics, local industry and natural resource extraction, to the trade and transportation of all three. During the 1640s, Puritans from New England began operations in shipping and trading slaves, Black and Indian, which they had learned from their profitable post Pequot war survivors slave swap experience, utilizing intra-colonial networks in Barbados and other English Caribbean islands with slaves[31] (Warren, 2016). Entrepreneurial captains quickly expanded this to direct enslaving operations in Africa in addition to trading Black slaves in other ports in the Americas, operating under Crown charters that in the next decades were expanded to the Royal African Company (RAC) (chartered 1672), in competition with existing Portuguese, Dutch and other European countries (Danes, French, France, etc.)[32] for transatlantic slave trading. This lucrative business, with Crown investment, expanded very quickly over the next century to an adapted Circuit or Triangular Trade (in Chapter 2), with inter-American slave and commodity trading, that recent scholars have called the Atlantic System, with fleets operating out of New England going directly to Africa, then the West Indies and back home to New England (Warren, 2016) where profits accumulated.

By 1650s, Massachusetts Colony planned ways to control escaped slaves and resisting Indians, in many ways similar to what the Spanish did on Hispaniola during Enrique's rebellion and the maroons who had left the plantations. Much of this was predicated on their Pequot War experience, realizing that Native men attached to families were especially strong in resistance, and enslaved peoples are more likely to strongly resist and escape when kept on their own lands. Virginia followed suit, creating a fugitive slave law in 1657, heritability in 1662, slave identity laws in late 1660s, and in both colonies established militia paramilitary forces, including Rangers. Virginia made a Casual Killing Act 1669 to protect masters who killed (more on this later).

Crown authorities in London, when not preoccupied with profiteering and fighting other colonial powers, created strategies and projects for converting slaves and servants to forms of Christianity, again with similarity to the Burgos Laws and the slavery debates at Valladolid, through a Council of Foreign Plantations.[33] For the English it was Crown authority that reigned supreme, although individual plantations and communities often had Church denominations in charge of local practices. Trading companies often exerted control over colonies as we have seen in Plymouth and at Jamestown, usually by demanding that debt be repaid or investments be fully compensated, which with large resisting, revolutionary nations, such as Haiti in the next chapter, meant international pressures to recover slave labor and initial land costs (so France demanded reimbursements before recognition in treaties). Ironically, both could be considered stolen lands, worked by stolen hands. This is another reason why slavery and genocidal conquest are denied, with additional concerns on rationale and legal justification for colonial conquest and labor. For the Puritans, the primary rationale was seeing themselves as the Elect, as a matter of God's will, while the Calvinists had predestination from their religious reasoning, and both had the depraved (the damned) as rationale for the dehumanization inherent in enslavement and extermination of humans.

Racist Systems Profiting from Enslavement and the Transatlantic Slave Trade

Crown, Colony, Church and Company come together in the latter half of the 17th century with a perfect fusion of transoceanic and transcontinental systems for enslavement of Africans, transportation to the Caribbean slave markets and spread of slavery to the American mainland. The New England fleets profited from providing the ships and the investment capital for slaves to Virginia and the southern colonies of North America. The system was becoming increasingly less dependent, or even independent of the English that now controlled the transatlantic slave markets through government enforced monopoly. Taxes could be applied along with many other commodities and agricultural resources, but they could also be contested, without any effective political representation by the colonial forces, now including regional banking and shipping.

Moreover, corporate formation of companies (noted in Chapter 2) that were controlling and bankrolling all elements of the transatlantic slave marketing, as well as the growing internal enslavement systems, had borrowed from early Roman law enhanced by Mediterranean contracts and services, notions of **legal personhood** – that companies or corporate entities had rights,[34] including the making of contracts, protection form certain liabilities, ability to be represented in court and state proceedings, and a host of other legal privileges that were accorded to a limited citizenry. This was becoming most important in the colonial holdings and initial investments, protecting the corporate groups from colonial failures, wars and individuals bringing lawsuits. This would continue to evolve, as a mainstay in growing capitalism and the future backbone of transnational capitalism of the 20th century, with the United States (subject of the next book). Most important for our analysis is that companies were developing rights and protections that were systematically denied Native Nations and American Indians, and were institutionalized for Blacks under enslavement in the English colonies. This would come to a perfect, and deniable, head in the constitutional formation of the United States in protecting corporations while denying rights to targeted racial groups, Blacks and Indians (in Chapter 4 and further in the next book). This bifurcation of rights – corporate as if legal persons versus citizen persons without including racial groups the same rights – became and is a central contradiction of modern world-systems.

Property Rights versus Human Rights

The rights of property owners, operating under a Christian framework of denying moral laws, responsibilities and rights under a sense of ownership, trumps all and any human rights, within the colonial legislative mindset, extending privilege and power to those who owned both people and property. This is clearly, and ostentatiously, demonstrated in many of the Virginia slave codes of the late 17th century, until they are compacted into a single set of laws in the 1705 Slave Codes. Some of these later codes bear repeating:

Thus, we see colonial laws of Virginia create, over time, the most draconian race laws that forced Black and other persons of color (often mentioning mulattos and Indians) into being property, owned and controlled by English

March 1661/62. Act CII: Run-aways

Wherein people seen as property (slaves and servants) were to be returned to their owners in order to restore legal economic relations (meaning both masters and corporate holders could enjoin run-aways under whatever means necessary). "Christian in company" could be duly fined or forced labor service when joining with escaped slaves, primarily to restore the losses of owners.

December, 1662. Act VI: Women servants got with child by their masters after their time expired to be sold by the Churchwardens for two years for the good of the parish

Wherein women (or girls) impregnated by their masters would have to compensate (usually in service to their owners or the church) to make up for lost time and profits, delivered in tobacco to the churches.

December, 1662. Act XII: Negro women's children to serve according to the condition of the mother

Children would be held in bond or service (slavery) based on the mother's race and place, whether as property or people (interestingly, "Christians" fornicating with negroes paid double fines by this act). Reversing precedent English law, this racial descent law underscored hereditary enslavement for Blacks.

September, 1667. Act III: An act declaring that baptism of slaves doth not exempt them from bondage

As discussed earlier, and noted above, the loophole of slaves (Black) being baptized no longer precluded them from primarily being seen as property in the eyes of colonial law (rationalized that this freed up masters to propagate Christianity among slaves, without fear of losing them as property).

October, 1669. Act I: An act about the casual killing of slaves

Act that allowed even under "extremity of the correction should chance to die" masters undertaking punishment not to be held accountable under the law as a felony (rationalized as presumed lack of malice since no "man to destroy his own estate" held slaves as property) rather than as people (perhaps, the most ominous code, appears to preempt all previous Christian law on killing or murder of humans).

June, 1680. Act X: An act for preventing Negroes Insurrections

Where colonial law banned meetings without "certificates" and all weapons as the frequent meeting of considerable numbers of "negroe slaves under pretence" was offending by lifting "his hand in opposition against any Christian" would "receive thirty lashes" and if in resistance lawful for "persons to kill the said negroe or slave" [by 1682 the law was "ordered read aloud in church twice a year], and masters were fined 200 lbs tobacco if another master's slaves stayed on their plantation without owner's permission.

Figure 3.8 Virginia slave codes development: 1660–1705 (+ sources, Henning 1823). Excerpts taken from William W. Henning, The Statutes at Large; Being a Collection of all the Laws of Virginia, v.2 (1823). Some language modernized, then further edited June 16–July 14, 2022.

April, 1691. Act XVI: An act for suppressing outlying slaves

Law allowing "negroes, mulattoes and other slaves unlawfully absent, to be taken by majesties justices of the peace... shall be empowered to arrest runaways] and in case any negroes, mulattoes or other slaves… shall resist… or refuse to surrender... it shall lawful ... to kill and destroy such negroes"… and "owners of such negro or mulatto" slave were to be compensated, especially over "that **abominable mixture** and spurious issue" with "**negroes, mulattoes, and Indians intermarrying**" with white women… making "such marriage be banished and removed from this dominion forever." Violations were to pay for such persons "to be transported out of the country, and remainder" to be given to the parish.

And finally the comprehensive act beginning the 18th-century racist slave laws.

October, 1705. Chap. Act XLIX: An act concerning servants and slaves

This last set of acts took "all servants imported and brought into this country, by sea or land, who were not Christians in their native country… …shall be accounted and be slaves, and as such be here bought and sold not withstanding a conversion to Christianity afterwards." This act prohibited "immoderate correction" or not to "whip a Christian white servant naked" or else suffer forfeit, and further banned "That no **negros, mullatos, or Indians**, although Christians, or Jews, Moors, Mahometans, or other infidels, shall, at any time, purchase any Christian servant, nor any other, except of their own complexion, or such as are declared slaves by this act" that allowed such so "**purchase any Christian white** servant, the said servant shall, ipso facto, **become free** and acquit from any service."

The act was for the "prevention of that abominable mixture and spurious issue" by English, and other white men and women intermarrying with negros and mulattos, as by their unlawful coition with them, be it enacted – That whatsoever English or other white man, being free, **shall intermarry with a negro** or mulatto man or woman, bond or free, shall, by judgment of the county court, be **committed to prison**, and there remain, **without bail**; and shall forfeit pay… "That no minister of the church of England, or other minister, or person whatsoever, within this colony and dominion, shall hereafter wittingly presume to **marry a white man with a negro** or mulatto woman; or to **marry a white woman with a negro** or mulatto man, upon pain of forfeiting and paying, for every such marriage the sum of ten thousand pounds of tobacco."

Figure 3.8 (Continued)

or other white Christians, whose correction could be taken to the legal killing of Black slaves without being reprobate, except to compensate property owners (white Christians or corporate entities). We see Church rationalizations on baptism, inheritance, compensation and racial murder as correction, written into colonial laws reinforcing capitalist relations of private property (including people and companies) or economic growth (plantations) that dehumanized Africans as slaves and alienated Natives as Indians, and thereby hostile aliens. Institutionalization of racist laws or codes for enslavement labor and extermination land takings was relatively complete in the English colonies by the onset of the 18th century. Racial constructions of Indians, Blacks and Whites were going in opposing directions and taking on their final formations in the colonial growth and development leading to the social revolution of the United States where they would be replicated and hardened.

Returning to Virginia, and the critical juncture of broad social rebellion, we begin to see where some previous scholarship is insufficient in considering a complete big picture unfolding in what we can call world-system time, which includes the growing transatlantic slave markets, by this time entirely racialized as Africans becoming Negroes or Blacks. We also need to consider growing needs for labor, especially enslaved for grueling sugar, tobacco or cotton plantations, which create racist formulation in terms of sale, treatment, disposition and tax values of enslaved Blacks as property. With all our cases, uniquely in Virginia, this is created in direct relation to the growing claims for land, especially that connected to colonial expansion and the new plantation system, meaning conflict and wars with Native Nations, reduced to genocidal suppression by militias, and removal from land going to settlers, all under the racial construct of Indians.

We already observed this in a conflict Nathaniel Bacon, colonial planter and entrepreneur for the fur trade and land speculation after Indian wars, had with Governor Berkeley and House of Burgess, more interested in generating profits on existing plantations in Virginia for their host Company investors in London. Recall Bacon's written grievances were calling into question:

1– taxes, 2- government appointments, 3- interference in fur trade, 4- governor being **pro-Indian**

When he was denied satisfaction with these, and thus economic curtailment of such, he engaged with **intertribal warfare** in order to achieve his ends, for which he was censured by Berkeley in the government House, wherein he got other planters and a mixed force of settlers, indentured servants and slaves in ambiguous legal terms, and marched on Jamestown. When challenged he burned the colony community to the ground. Ship's captains, loyal to the Crown as incorporated, sent in military units to put down the rebellion, later reinforced by both Crown and Company forces out of London, who reestablished the House of Burgess. In addition to hanging rebellion leaders, the governor (for the companies) responded by clarifying their responses:

1 – lenient tax laws, 2- fair appointments, 3- regulated (fur) trade relations, and 4- strong **attacks on Indians** (nations, tribes, collectively) with **land dispositions after wars** were resolved.

Thus, we see no discussion or distinction of indentured labor (though that did begin to transition) connected to race relations with Blacks, or reformulation of contract systems (those did change). Using Occam's razor analysis, the simplest explanation for the changing race status of Blacks **and Indians**, which most analysts forget to mention, is their status change is mainly over greater **need for slave labor** and land, clearly borne out in the following decades. A gradual dissolving of contractual "indentured" labor status is mainly the creation of a dominant group (as White) controllable and invested in a racialized social structure of the growing colony. And racialized practices of warring with militias and alienating Indians (really Native Nations) would be over land seizures and suppression of resistance, which is also borne out for the next two centuries, well into U.S. policies (see Chapter 4).

Furthermore, and important for the next chapter and creation of the United States, is New England race and racism, which actually predates that in Virginia (or Maryland for that matter). We have already shown that strict, formal race laws were developed in Massachusetts in the first half of the 17th century, and were enhanced or refined during the Pequot and Indian wars. During the genocidal resistance wars with the Wampanoag and other Tribes in the region under colonial domination, called King Phillip's (Metacom) War by most historians, captive prisoners and families were sent to Caribbean slavery. Pequots had been traded for Black slaves in 1637–1639, referred to as Negroes in the billing items upon sale or barter to merchants and the wealthy. Wampanoag were straight up sold, since the growing slave shipping business of New England was increasing the Black or Negro population of New England colonies,[35] all the way to New York when taken from the Dutch, meeting the need for servile labor, free and slave.

The systems developed by the English Massachusetts Bay Colony and extended to the United Colonies and firmed up in the New England Confederation, incorporated elements from all interested parties – Crown, Church, Colonists and Company – in a mercantilist style economy that maximized racist exploitation. The Crown provided governance with a centrality of laws and customs from England that oversaw international relations, taxing systems and political guidance for the colony. The Church provided justification for the racialized social life in the colony by finding bible passages – i.e. curse of Ham – which rationalized the dehumanizing treatment of Blacks or Indians – i.e. red Devils – that allowed rights to be denied. These systems developed "just war" reasoning that codified enslavement of peoples, with remarkable similarity to the Spanish systems (Chapter 2). Colonists and Company gained valuable land and resources, and further profited from developing regional shipping fleets. For two hundred years, variations of these practices – violent genocidal taking of Native land that used enslaved Black labor – were to continue in the early United States and all the way west to California (Chapter 4).

Indian slavery also paved the way for African slavery. Embedded...
is the assertion that Narragansett captives could be exchanged for
enslaved blacks. Downing wrote in the immediate aftermath of the
Pequot War (1636-1638). During this conflict, the Pequot of modern-
day Connecticut went to war[36] against settlers in New Haven, Rhode
Island, Plymouth and Massachusetts Bay. After crushing the Pequot in
a gruesome massacre, colonists sold many of them into slavery. New
England war leaders sent captives to the Puritan colony of Providence
Island in the western Caribbean, where they in turn exchanged the
Indians for African slaves. Those Africans, the first explicitly trafficked
to New England, arrived in Massachusetts in 1638. ...this nefarious
swap, aftermath of the Pequot War created a unique and awful system
of exchange of Indian slaves for Africans. Thereafter, in almost every
conflict between Europeans and Indians in the region, settlers would
capture Indian men, women and children to trade. The more significant
the conflict, the larger the commerce. In the aftermath of the apocalyp-
tically violent King Philip's War (1675-1676) colonists sold nearly one
thousand Indian captives, some of them Christian converts, into slavery.
So numerous and rebellious were these Indians that both Barbados and
Jamaica – English West Indian colonies that were among the largest
purchases of Indian slaves – prohibited the further importation of indigenous New Englanders. Nevertheless, Indian captives were a lucrative
trade commodity that allowed settlers to acquire African slaves. It was
such an effective strategy that many leading Puritans... ...advocated
war to procure prisoners.

(Hardesty, 2019:11–12)

The transatlantic slave trade systems created vast dislocations of people as
slaves, economic growth on the American side and large infusions of capital investments, which were interactive with colonial wars over land and
the growth of plantation systems along with the resource extraction from
expansive mining, all requiring huge infusion of cheap labor. Thus, slave
trading from Africa to America took off for the following two centuries,
causing race laws to grow racist colonies, enforced by Crown authority
issuing charters to trading Companies, with meteoric rise in slave voyages
and numbers of Africans enslaved for the American markets.

Note in the below chart Total Known Voyages by Decade (Manning and
Liu, 2020) that a rough bell curve in the growth of slave voyages, mostly
transatlantic, starts rising in a linear fashion after 1650 and continues that
way until 1760 (with a small depression around 1740) with a short plateau
until another high point is reached in 1790 that begins a series of drop offs
each decade, rather constant except for, predictably, 1810 and again in 1850
after which it goes to near zero.

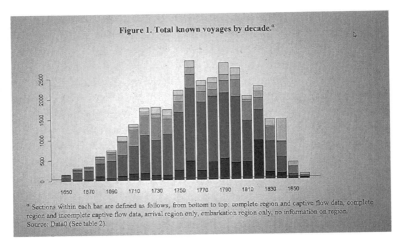

Figure 1. Total known voyages by decade.[a]

[a] Sections within each bar are defined as follows, from bottom to top: complete region and captive flow data, complete region and incomplete captive flow data, arrival region only, embarkation region only, no information on region. Source: Data0 (See table 2).

Figure 3.9 Transatlantic Slave Voyages by decade 1650–1850 (barchart).

Manning, P., & Liu, Y. (2020). Research Note on Captive Atlantic Flows: Estimating Missing Data by Slave-Voyage Routes. *Journal of World-Systems Research, 26*(1), 103–125. https://doi.org/10.5195/jwsr.2020.971 (used with permission).

We also observe that the number of captive flows follows the same pattern, with Lost at Sea percentages[37] running from 11% to 17%, dropping off the tails on either end.[38] (#1) – Growth of these transoceanic slave trade systems have other strong effects on the societies and geopolitical landscapes at both ends of the trading systems; (#2) development of ports and economies in colonies receiving the captive labor versus reduction of nations and kingdoms in African areas where slave trading is maximal; (#3) increased field labor and skilled biopower within receiving colonies that is accompanied by population growth (and replacement) versus siphoning decrease in both labor and skilled populace in sending regions; (#4) increased capitalization and corporate development in both receiving colonies and in colonizer countries versus decreased economic activity in sending regions of Africa; (#5) racist dehumanization systems alongside racial superordination of dominant groups and elites in control, for both sending and receiving colonies and countries, with a more complex racist ordering arising in colonizer nations. This now hemispheric, global and universal system of colonization becomes the heart of capitalism around the world, and quite specifically becomes responsible for the socioeconomic growth and political prowess of colonies, gradually dominated by the English in North America and accompanied by territorial expansion over land bases once entirely under control of Native Nations. Indigenous societies were quickly decimated, many disappearing altogether under forms of racist genocide, including biological warfare (see Amherst, Chapter 4).[39]

Besides the already noted developments in the English colonies of the eastern seaboard of North America, these effects were altering geopolitical struggles for dominance and hegemony in the Caribbean, Atlantic and Pacific oceanic regions. The Spanish found it ever more difficult to hold and profit from its Caribbean colonies, even as the English and French were expanding their land and island bases. We will consider the continental effects of these forces in Chapter 4 (concluding on White ethnic), also instigating massive wars and conflicts such as the so-called Louisiana territories, increasingly thought of as under whichever European power had held claim to such territory, irrespective of existing and still strong Native Nations. We will also consider the expanding Spanish incursions into the southwestern and western seaboards of North America later in this chapter, with a focus on California, which will stay in focus for Chapter 4. For now, we can use a single case study we are already familiar with – Ayiti or Hispaniola – that became critical in racist slave-holding and colonial conflicts (wars) over regional hegemonic dominance in the Caribbean, American continental and European theaters of operation.

France wanted a colonial base near the windward passage (Hispaniola and Cuba), so it could reinforce its land claims north of New Orleans, and to transit its growing slave populations in colonies throughout the region, already holding Martinique and other West Indies islands. Spain had made disastrous choices about population movement, because of the Netherlands' war for independence, and so lost much influence, along with internecine colonial coastal wars. French forces had made landings near Santo Domingo while taking the pirate areas on Tortuga (*Ile de Tortue*) and in the western areas from 1625 through 1660s and beyond gaining lands. The French Colony of Saint-Domingue was moved from Tortuga to Port-de-Paix on the mainland of Hispaniola in 1676, and after ongoing invasions by British and Spanish forces, they established the colony as a slave-holding sugar and coffee plantation society, with Spanish cession in 1697.

France started building up the Black slave labor force with the 18th century, also in creating their capitol city of Cap-Français later moved to Port-au-Prince in the largest bay area. Enslaved Africans were imported in ever greater numbers, perhaps totaling around 750,000 but about 500,000 around 1789, with Europeans around 32,000. Haiti as Saint-Domingue became the premier destination for enslaved Africans, and richest colony in the Caribbean if not the world, with international repercussions for slave-holding colonies in all the Americas. Sugar trade from Haiti quickly became dominant in world trade, fueling French interests throughout the region, even as they began to lose to British–American forces along the St. Lawrence riverway that became Canada and in southeastern areas of North America. As late as the 1763 Treaty of Paris, France actually traded Quebec for a hold on Martinique plantations. The economic developments were important to the political and military wars raging throughout the Americas between

England and France, along with sociopolitical changes in the European origin countries. Even as colonists and settlers, increasingly racially defined in the English colonies of North America, were demanding the "rights of man" and of representation by the Crown instead of the colony, with a remarkable symmetry with what Bacon's rebellion had demanded in Virginia, citizens on the continent, premier among them the French, were demanding rights completely separate from royal or Crown control. England's Civil War may have been partly predicated on Catholic land ownership, and was certainly seen so by a rising Protestant elite, but was turned into a proxy war against the Dutch over the slave trade. And, important for our analysis, and soon critical for all American conflicts, is that African-descent peoples held as slaves, many of them having hooked up with Native forces in resistance (interestingly around St. Augustine in Spanish held Florida), were keenly aware and informed of the movements for freedom, poignantly and powerfully in the mostly Black populated western half of Hispaniola where it all began, Haiti.

International social forces were contributing to race laws in Virginia and the Americas, including the transoceanic transcontinental slave trade. New ports and plantation societies were hailed as progressive developments, at least until one got close to life on the slave plantations. Haiti had been taken by France, who shared a Christian background though not quite as Catholic, often mixing faith systems with British settlers or colonizers already present, usually Protestant. Enslaved Africans with a brutal life expectancy of less than 7 (to 10) years[40] were constantly replaced with newly taken peoples bringing belief systems from their home societies of Guinea, Congo and Dahomey among others. These African cultural elements mixed with a folk-religion rising from interactions with what was left of Taino culture commingled with Catholic practices that had become known as *Vaudon* (voodoo), transcending language and tribal orientations.

Other slave societies and islands in the Caribbean developed similar hybrid cultural practices, along with languages such as Haitian Creole, with deep understandings that could be transmitted across geographic and sociopolitical boundaries through freedmen and mixed-race servants and sailors traveling between communities, nations and islands. In places such as Haiti, these became official identities, like *gens-de-couleur*, with intermediate positions on plantations and in various social settings, including travel to the metropole such as France (or as noted in English colonies between plantation and slaving trade ports on Barbados all the way to New England ports). This complex set of social-racial-cultural settings led to periodic uprisings along with manumissions, which as early as 1685 and beyond, were constrained for the French in a *Code Noir* (by Louis XIV) that established rights and responsibilities, but more importantly forms of corporal punishment that could be terribly brutal in pursuit of total subordination. As these increased with a

Ayiti – Haiti to San Domingue – K3 B3 – 7

The Ayiti large island of 1492 renamed to Hispaniola during the Spanish colonization conquest, had fallen from its initially prominent placement in the Caribbean, eclipsed by Cuba, Mexico and South America. The French challenged Spanish holdings in the early 1600's with the English of course, hovering in the nearby seas. Slaves and sugar became secondary to mining and land grants, with Spain slacking off in areas over-extended in terms of colonial control. English, French and even Danish privateers on Tortuga operated pirate bases with mestizos trading people and goods. The Western half – Haiti – used more slaves with greater economic development than the eastern region.

The 3 to 5 million Taíno people of the five nations in 1492, had been reduced to immigrant settler and African slave populations, of much lower numbers, one reason why revisionist estimates are accepted much later. Spain had put attention on its richer plunder colonies in Latin and South America, so to many Hispaniola had become a backwater country. With the rise of other regional powers though, the rich lands of the western half were appealing to newly invasive colonizers, along with interest in controlling the windward passage with Cuba. Privateers and pirates changed hands in the north, as the French moved in overall, increasing the African slave population and building strength in sugar production. Saint Domingue had become a colonial powerhouse with repercussions all the way to America.

By the mid 1700's African slave importation had increased to between 10,000 to 15,000 yearly, rising along with sugar, coffee and spice trade. By the 1780's slave imports were up to 28,000 plus, and the island accounted for nearly a third of the Atlantic slave trade. Free gens de couleur and mulatre and a colonial elite were in the mid 30,000 range each, with Black population estimated at over 500,000, making African-born slaves a majority. Besides infusing new labor into brutal conditions on the plantations with short life spans, these peoples were bringing vitality into Vaudon, now an ingrained resistance even among slaves under French control, with Catholic overtones covering the Indigenous spirituality.

The reality of Haiti though partly resides in the resistance movements started by Enrique, where a central part of the peace treaty concerned the return of African slaves, which there is no available evidence ever happened in serious numbers. The forces in the mountains were mixed Native, African and some mestizo, where ceremonial life intensified around communities of resistance in the long sixteenth century. During transition from Spanish to French control, these areas developed creole communication networks, that transformed into Haitian creole with a French base during the great plantation development of the 18th century, including religious life. These were critical to anti-slavery rebellion of late 1700's and perfectly exemplified in the networks Boukman called up in the initial uprising. All the conditions for race freedom struggles were in place by the time of French revolution.

Figure 3.10 Ayiti – Haiti to San Domingue – K3 (Text box K3 – B3).

growing slave population in the 18th century, so did potential resistance by entrenched slave forces that would ultimately lead to the systems' undoing, noted later by a Haitian chronicler:

> Have they not hung up men with heads downward, drowned them in sacks, crucified them on planks, buried them alive, crushed them in mortars? Have they not forced them to eat excrement? And, having flayed them with the lash, have they not cast them alive to be devoured by worms, or onto anthills, or lashed them to stakes in the swamp to be devoured by mosquitoes? Have they not thrown them into boiling cauldrons of cane syrup? Have they not put men and women inside barrels studded with spikes and rolled them down mountainsides into the abyss? Have they not consigned these miserable blacks to man-eating dogs until the latter, sated by human flesh, left the mangled victims to be finished off with bayonet and poniard?[41]
>
> (Heinl, 1996)

Irrespective of the Code Noir put into place, suppression and oppression of Black slaves on Haiti rose to almost unheard of levels. Besides the above, there are documented instances of "white" slave owners seeing how many Blacks could be killed with a single bullet as a betting activity, and dipping uncompliant Blacks partway into shark-infested waters off Cap Haitian, gambling on how long they might last during their gruesome deaths. When C.L.R. James describes some of these practices in *The Black Jacobins*, scholars and denialists from across the Euro-American world criticize and attack his work, just as de Las Casas is accused of feeding the Black Legend when describing similar practices by the Spanish in the exact same location (Chapter 2). We also see this when early rights activists describe brutal suppression techniques used during slavery and removal in a southern United States (next book on Whites) and even later well into the 20th century with the utter brutality of lynching and tortures of the Jim Crow south and indeed throughout the United States (next book on global). We observe in the case study Haiti, continuous dehumanization in conquest, colonization, enslavement and domination that extends into the early and late United States, and indeed is under strong inspection in the urban uprisings of 2020 as illustrated by Black Lives Matter, American Indian Movement and La Raza actions. We specifically note sexual predatory oppression often accompanying this racism, as found in Mission systems in California, or the Missing and Murdered Indigenous Women and Girls legislative actions brought to the United Nations (next book). But, as before, we are getting ahead of ourselves.

Both enslaved and free Black, and *mulatre*, Haitians were taken up in the revolutionary discourse that arose from France, with great effect on the uprisings in Haiti and Hispaniola, and arguably even greater effect on racist constructions and developments in the new United States. We will return to this discussion briefly near the end of this chapter, and more again in Chapter 4, since it ended up being one of three major revolutions associated with the European–American colonies revolting, and perhaps the greatest in terms of social change, although easily least well-known, in comparison to the American and French revolutions taking place before the Haitian.

Religion and race were still critical to the colonization going on in the Americas, and in relation to the political economies under development, all using slave labor to build agricultural capitalism. French Catholics broadly rationalized race-based slavery in the Caribbean, so when the French Revolution banned the Catholic church from government, the investment house began to justify its use in practical rather than political terms, reasoning that later appeared in the U.S. conflicts over the same issues. Napoleon reinstated the Catholic church, as much for its ideological authority to defend racism, and to later give him king-like powers as an Emperor.

Religion, Racism and Colonialism

Spanish explorers acting as expeditionary forces were claiming the southern coastline of North America in the early 1500s. When Álvar Núñez Cabeza de Vaca was shipwrecked from one such expedition (1527 under Narváez), he with four others survived over eight years of travels throughout what became Texas and New Mexico, later claiming lands in the name of Christian discovery. Another survivor, Juan Rodríguez Cabrillo, went on expeditions out of Guatemala,[42] and Mexico, being the first European to land in southern California in 1542, dying there in 1543.

Spanish forces were creating a New Mexico with expanding borderlands that would later encompass California, including many invaders, explorers and conquistadors, such as de Vaca, or Coronado with mixed Spanish–Indian forces rivaling those of Cortez a few decades earlier, and last of the colonizing conquistadors, Juan de Oñate, who brutalized the Pueblos with killings and amputations on a very large scale to suppress the resistance from communities like Acoma, "sky city" where more than 800 people were slaughtered. Other governors continued the violent suppression, attacking many religious structures like the kivas. Ultimately this led to the largest, planned uprising of any unified Native peoples in 1680 led by religious warrior leader Pópay, where Indian Nations destroyed the colonial townships and drove the Spanish out of the region.

Along with the encomienda system and forced slavery for mines throughout New Spain, the Catholic hierarchy instituted repression and culturicide toward the Puebloan religious society, imprisoning and publicly whipping known leaders, such as the strong spiritually minded Pópay, who they accused of "witchcraft" and deviltry. After the rebellion, the Puebloan forces repelled two Spanish armies sent to retake the entire region, and word spread to other Native resistance, north to the mountains, east to many peoples resisting the armed Missions invading their land, south to those already conquered and west to strong networks just being penetrated, including the Kumeyaay extending from Baja to what would be southern California, inspiring resistance, rebellion and rejection of the Spanish Mission systems.

As discussed earlier, contemporary and historical analysis continues to act as if these systems are not interconnected, passing on knowledge of invasive newcomers and the conflicts. We will look at the tripartite invasion of California, using the Catholic Missions, military forces and imposed governance (presidios), in these next chapters, noting there were uprisings and/or rebellions at every Mission, starting at the first in San Diego, well-coordinated for the Chumash in three missions around Santa Barbara, and nearly successful revolts around Los Angeles areas led by the magnificent Toypurina representing families and traditional values.

Slavery under Spanish Conquest Colonization

The laws making slavery technically illegal by the Spanish–Catholic conferences – originating in the "rights" of Indians in the laws of Burgos in 1512, reiterated in the New Laws (of Burgos) in 1542 where slavery was banned and the encomienda system questioned (again) – were instrumental in religious authorities resisting some of the Spanish depredations in Mexico, and throughout Latin America.

Spanish Catholics in the colonies had employed race-based slave labor throughout their colonial developments over two centuries, often in open disregard for the church laws that were opposed to such, and in using corvée systems to provide unpaid, unfree labor. These coalesced around the Catholic missions set up in northern New Spain (Mexico) and southwestern regions, which culminated in the militarily enforced mission systems in California. Early mission schools were used in Mexico, first by the Spanish over Nahua speaking elites, resembling residential or boarding schools later in North America.

Further south, racialized uprisings coordinated Africans with mestizo and Native peoples, such as the successful Gaspar Yanga revolts, spreading throughout Central America. Catholic and later Protestant missions both evangelized and subordinated otherwise resisting Indians. Networks among Blacks and Indians grew in particular places, as in the Garifuna of Honduras – mixing Indigenous descent with enslaved Africans displaced along the Atlantic coast of Mexico.

Mestizo forced labor and debt peonage of Indians and mixed-race people were exploited in local systems throughout the Spanish systems, creating an unregulated and ethnically complex system over emerging political economies (see Miskito in Nicaragua and Honduras, the next book).

Waves of conquest colonization had penetrated all of Mexico and most of central and western coastlands of South America. Slave labor, often without specific naming of practices, was critical to wealth extraction, especially in silver mining, that both followed and preceded many epidemics, decimating resistance and decreasing people to be used for slave labor, thus increasing their value. Resendez found "slave corridors" from areas we know as the southwest, around the Pueblo townships down through northern Mexico to the silver mines, such as at Parral and down to Polosi. Although technically illegal, Indian slavery gradually moved toward debt peonage as the encomienda system was also outlawed.

This is why the Spanish portioned out the slave trade to the United Provinces (Dutch, Netherlands) for banking and investment purposes. Much of the wealth being extracted from Spanish America was making its way back to banking and investment houses in the Netherlands. It is also partly why the Dutch begin to traffic in slaves from Africa to the Americas, along with the Portuguese well-developed market in the south Atlantic. This is also why English privateers – working for Crown and Company in the first transoceanic corporations – would periodically raid slave ships, and have difficulty selling their human booty in some Caribbean ports.

For the long 16th century, these colonizing powers were finding religious, philosophic and epistemological conflicts in their legal and social structures concerning slavery, conquest, colonization, home-rule and belief systems about Christian civilization and principles of democracy. When England – through privateers, trading companies, joint stock investments, colonial governments and selective use of militaries – violently expanded into the Americas, they divorced their religious beliefs from state-controlled colonies.[43]

This trifecta – separating the state from religious authority and company investment – allowed England to ignore the inhumanity of slave markets and the brutal treatment of colonists as settlers, coupled with genocidal expansion over Native lands. Where they needed slave labor – on Caribbean islands and southern plantations – they simply ignored its legal or moral basis with a singular focus on profit-making. Where England did not require slavery – northeastern America and parts of the world that did not have epidemic depopulation, they adapted to labor needs by importing, or immigrating, large numbers of indebted and often criminalized excess populations (surplus – expendable – often inflammatory) as settlers, usually under indentured conditions with provisions to attaining freedom at the end of their contracts – free to colonize through private property appropriation of Native lands, whom they blithely destroyed.

There is very little major contention in religious, legal or philosophic circles over this massive destruction of human society. In fact, the grand rationalizations of bringing God and civilization are extended into slavery.

Not only do the ideologies of racism arise from the social structures they create – wilderness and savagery of Native peoples as Indians – with brutish insensibility of African people as Blacks – but the new stratification systems by race and ethnic origins develop new economic relations and political structures such as private property, wage-labor and citizenship – that further race, gender and class systems with differential access to wealth creating social institutions (we should note that some U.S. Christian sects, such as the Quakers, did protest enslavement as ungodly, leading to abolitionist tendencies that did not influence any state or major economic structure, until other conditions arose, noted in upcoming chapters).

The stage was set for a racialized hierarchy within a capitalist economy using selective, gendered citizenship for democratic participation of a few, a minority, seeing their benefit or privilege as ruled by an Elite (less visible), that would become the United States of America.

Dehumanization – Slave Voyages – Second-Class Citizenship

It is clear that forms of dehumanization, commonly referred to as racial oppression in slavery, include both a **micro** or individual component – producing an identity that will accept enslaved conditions that deny any normal set of social interactions – and a larger or **macro**-level system – developing and controlling racially defined groups of people under heritable racial positions for maximal labor production at the lowest investment cost that sublimate or deny social access, mobility or any of a myriad set of desirable positions within a dominant society. Dehumanization is also linked to rationalizations of genocidal destruction of populations over land and labor.

We will set aside discussion of an individual level of analysis, although there is a rich, deep literature replete with a plethora of examples of how this works, and how many enslaved individuals resist and revitalize internalized identity, to adapt, accept or escape from slavery. Further, understanding such processes is necessary to effectively describe emancipatory actions ranging from individual consciousness rising to supporting religious and social institutions. However, it is precisely because of large, systemic levels of dehumanization needed to maintain, control and reproduce enslaved populations, that we must put our focus on the societal or sociopolitical levels of slavery, which includes a healthy decolonization perspective and liberation mentalities (Fanon, 1952; DuBois, 1933; Grosfuguel, 2011; Quijano, 2000).

In this work, we have studied and described the colonization processes that created transatlantic enslavement systems in conjunction with enslaving-destroying systems in the Americas, through the late 17th and half of the 18th centuries of European colonizers over Native and African peoples in colonies based on mercantile capitalism. We considered these systems through a lens of four revolutionary resistance movements, and their leaders, in the Americas in 1620–1790.

Ousamequin – Massasoit, Wampanoag; the Powhatan – English colonizers of 1670s

Pópay – Puebloan revolt leader (conquista) – Spanish conquistadors around 1680

Touissaint Louverture – Ayiti revolt leader – French enslavers from 1770s to 90s

Toypurina – Tongva revolt leader – Spanish Mexican Mission system, 1780s to 90s

Turn of the century California also makes an excellent case analysis for this book:

The people who make up *Tovangaar* – the greater Los Angeles region from San Fernando valley, north to the south around Long Beach, east from Rancho Cucamonga to west ocean and Catalina – have been called Gabrielenos from the San Gabriel Mission built in the center of Los Angeles. Since about 1900 many call themselves Tongva, while others find their name to be Kizh, which means something like village. Rather than see people living in isolated groups, we see they lived within interconnected networks throughout the valleys, and over the ocean-ways, that included recognition with their adjacent nations, as the *Chumash* (north), *Acjachemen* (south), *Cahuilla*, Luiseno, Serrano (east) and on the channel islands and Catalina (west).

Even setting aside the depredations and cultural destruction in creating Mission Indians, what must be noted is Spanish intention for total dominance, reinforced by a regional presidio, the government and with soldiers to enforce a new order. More than 21 missions were created, based on Indian labor of course, that rationalized their religious mission, but in fact developed outposts along the Camino Real along the entire coast of California, and much of the interior. Revolts were common, with the *monjerío* sexual predations often the cause. Women often led these, with medicine woman Toypurina famously organizing a rebellion, and when put on trial stated:

[she despised] the padres and all of you, for living here on my native soil, for trespassing upon the land of my forefathers and despoiling our tribal domains. ... I came [to the mission] to inspire [cowards] to fight, and not to quail at the sight of Spanish sticks that spit fire and death, nor [to] retch at the evil smell of gunsmoke—and be done with you white invaders![44]

Mexico – California – K 4

The large number of tribes or nations in what becomes California, extending north through Oregon and Washington, had existed in close relations to their environs – coastal lands, deserts, mountains, great forested areas, rolling semi-arid plains – for thousands of years. Most of the indigenous societies were small to mid-level size, although they retained close relations to neighboring peoples even in large territories like Los Angeles and Santa Ana river basins (Fenelon, Bogany and Madrigal 2021) cupped between oceans and mountains.

Scholars and Native peoples themselves disagree on size and demography of pre-invasion tribal peoples, but by any measure they were expansive and diverse over the entire region. Powers (1876) was first to estimate the Native population, coming in around 1.5 million, which was roundly rejected, so he revised the numbers to 750,000, and again to 705,000. (this discussion should sound familiar, with the estimates by Las Casas over Hispaniola) Later, just as was done in the Caribbean and overall in the Americas, western scholars kept reducing the estimated pre-conquest numbers, down to some 320,00 and lower, based on their post-genocide analysis (see my next Book on this). At any rate, Indigenous peoples in the region were numerous and diverse, ranging from the extensive Kumeyaay (the Tipai Ipai peoples) to the south, internal tribes like the Cahuilla, great coastal peoples like the Chumash or Tongva, to the many, many peoples of central to northern California lands. I estimate there were close to 1 million people in the greater territory, representing over 40 tribal nations, with diverse, beautiful languages and cultures (Fenelon and Trafzer, 2014).

Cabrillo is the first European to make land-fall in 1542, with luminaries like Drake also touring the coastal lands to the north. The formidable deserts to the east and the Pacific ocean breadth continued to shield California, until the Spanish made inroads in 1760's with a pre-planned Mission system comprised of Church, Colonizer and military forces. There is a vast and growing literature on this, most singularly focused on the missions, which argues over the dominance of Serra and Catholics, forgetting that the revolt at San Saba in Texas (where Serra was supposed to be positioned) caused planning groups to form in Mexico, so that each Mission was apportioned a military garrison and presidio, making it a tripartite invasion. While there was some acceptance at first, the Missions quickly became brutal work-force regimes, demanding total Catholic religious piety, shortening Indian lives and exposing families to sexual and social abuse at all levels. There were revolts at every mission, starting in San Diego, with collective resistance such as the Chumash at each of their three missions. The result was devastating to the Native peoples, with population loss from 60 to 80 percent, and even greater cultural destruction. Many analysts and Indigenous scholars typify the period as genocide, although it would be dwarfed by the coming of Anglo Americans invading mid-1800's with government run policies and intention to make California the most western project of Protestant America.

Between the Spanish Church and Colony mission 60% depopulation loss above and 80% loss by the United States take-over, this is one of the larger genocides in world history.

Figure 3.11 Mexico – California – K4 (text box).

Clearly, the Spanish were using religion (Catholic Church) to subordinate and suppress all Indigenous resistance and cultural practices, including community dances, not remonstrating before a patriarchy of Crown and Colony. In the next book, we see Mexico secularizing missions, leaving dislocated Mission Indians to fend as vagrants on their own land, ending with most of them vulnerable to ideologies of private property rights and Protestant icons of damned or depraved.

Religion, Racism, Colonialism and State – Part 2 (Disclaimer[45])

The rise of Protestantism included a core set of values that offered a redirection of Christianity that was simultaneously beautiful and humanly oriented. The changing social structure arising from Protestant systems also provided powerful forces within northern European nations – a new elite and capital growth – the opportunity to take advantage of the reformed institutions to redirect wealth and power to themselves and the organizations they developed. In this work, we will focus on these forces leading to a deep capitalism that produced racially framed inequality and injustice to the benefit of an elite few. Exploitation of entire groups or races of people, along with religious justification, became central to the larger world system under development.[46]

There are at least four reasons why Calvinism as Protestantism needs to be understood in critical inquiry for this or any work that purports to analyze the social conditions of racism – (slavery, genocide and/or domination) – with the political-economic foundations of capitalism – (capital accumulation in taking surplus, institutional banking, insurance and corporate investments). These are legally separated yet institutionally intertwined relationships of the state with capitalist corporations/companies (please note these are not related to being Christian, per se).

1   One reason (foremost) is a systemic critique, rejection or a reforming against Roman Catholic practices (sanctioned by the state and the Vatican), as in: – (a) indulgences as corrupt,[47] (b) bureaucratic hierarchies in priesthood, (c) wealth in aristocracies controlling monarchy, (d) sanctity descended from Vatican and church rather than from individuals (spirit, work effort, destiny) therefore – in church–state (intertwined) relationships, wealth and power are mixed.[48]

These critiques as protest demands, cloaked as reformation, result in – seeing holiness (sanctity)/purity, as naturally given or predestined for individuals; need for separation of church and state, and separation of financial institutions from church and state (banks, trading corporations, companies, insurance); individuals in predestined or ordained groups

(Elect, congregations, etc.); and\or as above Others who are in total depravity (compare this with the Valladolid debates arguing over whether Indians had souls), with some depraved not-Christian Pagans (Natives), have no Rights, are not eligible to participate in Covenant, in society, or to accumulate wealth, which the Elect see as church sanctioned.[49] (Blacks become property, Indians are alienated.)

2   Second, this reasoning allows both Church and State to treat whole groups, populations of people as being less than, or not as deserving (racialized peoples, the poor, savages, Indians) who therefore can be ignored, or denied religious favors (free will, citizenship), and/or rights of the Covenant (with Protestant churches), or any sense of having a Soul (which hampered late-stage Spanish colonization). All this explains how Protest-ant Euro-Americans can accept genocide in New England, and race-based slavery in the colonies as "natural" or as "God's will" ().[50]

3   Third, the rise of trading companies or corporations accumulating wealth (that can be taxed by the state), giving power to non-state and non-church entities (though both are regulated or controlled by the state or colonizer), and ability to coerce colonies and racialized populations, that in order to increase or secure profits, both for international relations between colonizing powers and a church "pass" (or allowance) can be or are seen as Natural (over savage Native) God-given rights or destiny (the elect).[51] This analysis is needed in genocide studies and for understanding enslavement systems, so when states deny intentionality, and companies avoid Christian compassion or shared values,[52] responsibility or reciprocity – leading to completely dispassionate or uncaring transnational corporations[53] – we can explain how dehumanization works in a "civil" society where some (racial) groups were eliminated from social covenants.

4   Fourth, and perhaps most important in the long-run or *longue durée*, the exigencies of capital (being divorced from church and state) can transform (nature of) community, family, extended kinship and collective responsibility, reciprocity or respect of Other humans, in noted forms of: slave populations; Indian reservations; industrial cities labor; and other segregated social groups; without the slightest nod to human beings as such (predestination of the Elect), civil society and/or inequality (racist separation), religious or spiritual values (being "saved" as individuals), or to some sense of Nationhood, in relationship to the broader environment (Fenelon and Alford, 2020). This is done in a transition from Catholic ideologies of "savage" to Protestant (Calvinist) ideologies (beliefs)[54] including the concepts Total Depravity and Unconditional Election.

Inquisition, Witchcraft and Heresy

Herein we can make comparisons between the Spanish Inquisition and heretic execution, and thereby in Hispaniola as noted by de Las Casas (often called a Black Legend by his critics) and other Church versions of that, such as the Marian Persecutions of the Guernsey martyrs burned to death with infants in 1556, or later, in its reverse, of Catholics in England and Ireland, such as drawing, torturing and quartering of dissidents before, during and after the Gunpowder plot, culminating in 1605, and transported to colonies in the 17th century. At the same time, many Spanish incursions into the southwestern areas of New Spain (Puebloan peoples in what would be New Mexico) led to brutal torture executions by the Governor Juan de Oñate during 1598–1602.

The first Europeans to come "settle" America's northern shores were Protestants,[55] (Calvinist) therefore, they could easily create ideas of religious freedom, or individual free will, democratic "elections" and a socioeconomic political order that excluded Native nations and peoples (leading to colonialism that could move in and out of religiously justified genocide). Witchcraft acts arose in England around 1542 extended into the 1600s burnings in hundreds, or thousands of women in Scotland. Priest practitioners, like Junipero Serra, often noted participation in church backed trials under an Inquisition to determine witchery of mixed-race Native women, dark-skinned "mulata" of African descent (Beebe and Senkewicz, 2015: 92, 91). Terms like depraved could be used (Toypurina was called a witch), similar to Catholic interpretation of race and religion, borrowing from either of these systems in a "new" world.

Here we observe the religious underpinnings of racial exclusion in modern capitalism – (and its Biblical basis) in English colonies restated as Covenant in the U.S. Constitution and Bill of Rights. While there are five tenets of Calvinist religious thought – Total Depravity,[56] Unconditional Election, Limited Atonement, Irresistible Grace and Perseverance of the Saints – it is primarily the first two that we analyze as underpinning racial formation within capitalism as it emerges in new North American colonies and struggles against Europe to become independent politically while relying on these religious philosophies to guide them. Although considerable variations and exceptions begin to arise from disparate factions and schisms (as with Quakers abolition), the essence of Total Depravity extends to non-Christian Indians, Africans, Muslims and non-European Others, and becomes dominant religious thought of New England, with predestination accorded European immigrants (some Catholics) to the Americas during racial formation of the White American. This is one short step from Catholic images of Savages.[57]

The Spanish struggled with this in enslaving Indian peoples after the Church decided they had souls and could be saved or converted. In the debates at Valladolid, they allow encomienda-like systems to continue without formal slave laws, and this continued in various forms through the 16th, 17th and 18th centuries. This became central to creating a mestizo intermediary category (Hall and Fenelon, 2009), not being Indian but also not fully included in elite dominant groups. Protestants also deal with this religiously, deciding in the Virginia Colony that even when Blacks converted to being Christian, this did not free them as slaves, nor did it give them civil rights, later not extended to citizenship. Thus religiously justified race laws were institutionalized in English colonies, later transferred whole into U.S. racial orders and jurisprudence.[58]

As we have already observed in New England, new laws and policies, such as the 1641 "Body of Liberties" – that includes an official recognition of chattel slavery (Warren, 2016:12) – are based on Magna Carta rights, that orders "never be any bond-slavery, villenage or captivitie amongst us; unless it be lawfull captives, taken in just wars, and such strangers as willingly sell themselves, or are solde to us" (34–35). This creates three different ways to set up legitimate ways of buying and selling enslaved people, even though it supposedly acknowledged liberty – "lawful captives" meaning purchased (with an owner's bill of sale) or taken in "just wars" that the Spanish used extensively under Catholic law sometimes extended to colonial Indian wars, and the notion of "strangers" that has a basis in various biblical passages, refers to alien nations, cultures and tribes, and is proscribed by voluntary servitude, and herein phrased as "sold to us" operating under Church legitimacy, under Crown and Colony authority. Warren notes George Henry Moore saw the act as "sanctioning the slave-trade, and the perpetual bondage of Indians and negroes, their children and their children's children" (pg 35).

Although the Spanish courts and the Catholic church had debated this endlessly to find theocratic reasoning for their structural use of slavery, and failed, the New England courts and Puritan-Protestant church had created a way to have their cake and eat it too – creating a body of laws that would carry through the colonial expansion using slavery, the creation of the United States (whose Constitution also did not state sanctioning of racialized slavery), various decisions by courts (Amistad, Cherokee Nation) and many policies (the 3/5ths clause, fugitive slave acts, California Indian policy and more) and even the reasoning behind the 13th Amendment (14th and 15th arguably). This required use of all the above – who is lawful captive, were they legally sold, what is a just war and most poignantly are they strangers of their own accords, with no rights. Amazingly, when conceptualized with God's predestination of the Anglo (White) American, along with the depravity of the savage and uncivilized Indian and Black from other places, thereby strangers, systems of slavery and removal (extirpation) were completely legitimized (slavery of various types did exist in many Indigenous societies, but usually included them in community; see Graeber and Wengrow, 2021, allowing most to become full societal members). (This is why we called our ASA session "Aliens on Our Own Lands" on Indigenous struggles). We also see how supremacy is achieved and reproduced – English (Crown) law over Church; Colonist (settler) over Indian and Black; Company (corporation) over stranger populations, racially defined as the Other, with many, many allusions to their inherited depravity.

Following these initial laws, is Connecticut in 1650 referring to Indian and African slavery as punishment for wrongdoing (Warren, 2016) where magistrates could order English to an Indian town and "seize and bring away any of that plantation of Indians that interteine, protect, or rescue the offendor, onely women and children to be sparingly seized, unless known to bee some way guilty" (pg 35). These laws meted out many punishments for Indians, including to be "exchanged for neagers, as the case will justly beare." Virginia followed suit, creating a fugitive slave laws and heritability in slave identity during the 1660s, and in an ostentatious use in the Casual Killing Act of 1669, that protected owners and overseers, and later literally any member of the dominant race, to brutally punish and inadvertently kill slaves who disobeyed. These become the laws under colonial slavery in the South, in the U.S. plantations, (next book) and the basis for Jim Crow lynchings in the 20th century, along with a mindset of police and paramilitary actions incarceration and counterinsurgency for Blacks and Indians over the century marker (next book), up to the Blacks Lives Matter marches from 2014 to 2020, Standing Rock and other movements from 2016 to 2020, and many would say the supremacist grievances and rationale in the storming of the U.S. capitol in the insurrection of 2021.

Understanding deep ideologies of Christian heresy as it became associated with deviltry (savagery), witchcraft (sexuality) and uncivilized barbarity (Native spirituality) is also critical to understanding a later American mindset of race, gender and class positioning in jurisprudence. This was perfectly realized in the so-called mass hysteria of the Salem Witch Trials (1692-93) supposedly started by a mixed-race Native–African woman Tituba (likely Arawakan from South America enslaved on Barbados) where racist, sexist fears of the Indian were linked to colonial governance by Church and Crown, further influenced by genocidal forays by Governor Phipps over the territory of Maine, his birthplace. The same Increase Mather and his son Cotton Mather who had prayed over the dead bodies of Pequot and Wampanoag Natives in bloody massacres, had published books on spiritual malfeasance attributed to Native and African influences taking over Puritan Christian sensibilities, pertinently the sexual control over women and supremacist position of Christian (white) English men. These were published in England, taught at Harvard, and distributed to churches throughout the Massachusetts Bay Colony and around New England. When an enslaved Native woman was accused by local constables and her owner Samuel Parrish of witchery, probably coming from a sexual liaison that Tituba's husband John Indian found out, Parrish's children blamed spirits and potions on Tituba who, upon being beaten and imprisoned, admitted "spectral" influences such as the Mathers had been railing about for some years then. Fears of Native and increasingly African primitive beliefs blew up the township into the Salem witch trials, leading to a series of executions, imprisonments, confessions and general hysteria, which I attribute to deep conflicted convictions over sexuality, social justice and religious race. Governor Phips, who had become wealthy and politically powerful in retrieving Spanish galleon wealth (probably much of it illegally) both manipulated and then downplayed the colonial fears. Later, in 1755, his adopted son Spencer, as Lt. Governor of Massachusetts Bay, issued the Phips Proclamation for the "pursing, captivating, killing and Destroying all and every of the Indians" that included a bounty for men (50 pounds alive, 40 scalps of dead males), women (25 scalps), and children (20 for scalps under age of 12), continuing the religious inspired political genocide over Native peoples (Penobscot were destroyed along with the Wabanaki Confederacy).[59]

As we move into the sections of the next chapter – with a focus on comparative colonies, development of racism in revolutionary discourse, and new nation building – let us revisit two mainstay arguments in our analysis of the English colonies: growth of the transatlantic African slave trade with England's participatory profits, and the racial separation of Indians and Blacks within the American colonies as they begin transition to an independent country. The RAC was rechartered in 1672 under the 1660 Navigation Act to become the sole monopoly trader of "Negroes, slaves, goods, wares, merchandise" to the Caribbean ports it identified and the English ports from which the ships originated, especially Liverpool and Bristol with direct links to commercial centers and banking interests of their joint stock company RAC operating out of London (where the colonial charters had also begun). This had a direct, strong and sustaining effect on the slave trade and its endpoints in the Caribbean and North America. Through this company (RAC):

> England developed its infrastructure of human trafficking and supplied Africans to meet the labor demands of the lucrative Caribbean sugar plantations. Between 1673 and 1683, England's share of the slave trade increased from 33 percent to three-quarters of the market – rendering the nation the global leader of the slave trade at the expense of the Dutch and the French. A precursor to British imperialism and colonialism, the trading company expanded England's role in the African continent, exploiting the gold and later the human resources…

…Ships from Liverpool carried 1.5 million enslaved Africans, or half the human cargo kidnapped and transported by Britain.

(Love, 2021: 47–50)

On the other end of the highly profitable transatlantic slave trade was the Virginia colony, also developing a legal infrastructure for enslavement of Africans and destroying Native Nations, about the same time as England was taking over circuit or triangular trade. In a remarkable bout of analytical honesty, Heather McGhee takes on an oft-pictured coalition of indentured servants, Africans and bonded slaves in Bacon's Rebellion typified as a "class-based, multi-racial uprising against slavery, landlessness and servitude" as problematic in that:

I found few if any references to class, land, or bondage. What Bacon sought was all-out war with neighboring Indigenous tribes. He rebelled because Berkeley had made alliances with some tribes and preferred negotiation to war. Bacon's anti-Native fervor was indiscriminate; his followers betrayed and massacred the Occaneechi people who helped to fight the Susquehannocks and relentlessly pursued Pamunkey men, women and children.

…But the governing white elite had their minds set on reinforcing slavery after putting down the rebellion. In 1680, four years after the rebellion, Virginia passed the Law for Preventing Negro Insurrections. It restricted the movement of enslaved people outside plantations; anyone found without a pass would be tortured with twenty lashes 'well laid on' before being returned.

(McGhee, 2021: 51–54)

The local and regional markets for African slaves were growing in colonial America, alongside the racialization of Christian Europeans as Whites and the utter alienation of Natives, for the purposes of taking their lands and ways of life. The African slave trade was growing in Atlantic markets that violently retrieved peoples from their homelands, brutally transferred them to the Americas for huge profits, where English ships took on natural and agricultural resources, back to England (or Europe) where they were made into commodities or underwent industrial transformation (cotton, iron products, etc.) that were transported as trade items to African and American colonies. Each of these stages was a highly profitable leg of developing capitalism, with the slave trade, plantation systems and genocidal destruction of Native nations requiring great violence, orchestrated by the Crown, operated by the Company and each Colony, and fully justified by the Church.

We observe a nearly straight line of maximized violence used for state interests, using religious rationale to enslave and kill on a large-scale members of other religions, other races, other nationalities and from non-Christian societies viewed as less or uncivilized. This started during the French religious wars between Catholics and Huguenots until 1600 or so, with three million fatalities, partly over emerging colonization patterns of creating wealth from resource extraction and enslaved labor plantations, and extended into the Thirty Years War until 1650, with eight million casualties, also directly linked to colonial developments in North America, where extreme violence in enslavement practices and land-taking wars became endemic.[60]

We also observe a singular centralized sovereign authority, the Crown of England, controlling the new colonies through direct intervention and the use of charters from stock-holder companies based in London, having supremacy over the Church (of England), along with banking and investment also out of London, and under the sovereign. These companies (RAC) develop and operate transatlantic slave trading of African peoples, with markets at both ends of the trade networks, developing mercantile capitalism into commercial trade capitalism with its profiteering from the taking of valuable lands away from Native nations, commodification of resources and agricultural products, and the reduction of labor costs to an absolute minimum through race-based slavery. Finally, and notably important for the lands called New England, capital revenue and investment is kept within the country, maximizing profits and capital gain. We will now turn to seeing how large transoceanic and transcontinental systems came to be.

First, we need to observe the connections between these phenomena, including the Salem spectral forces associated with savagery and pagan idolatry, with the rise of racism as connected to religious ideologies and mass hysteria – we have Kant along with Blumenbach and Linnaeus, reinforcing animism associated with deviltry, a legacy of witchcraft, an entrenched dominant version of ethnic-racial hierarchies and fear of the other. The rise of scientific racism coinciding with political treatise and European philosophy forms the structural basis for the founding of what becomes the United States of America.

Second, we must observe how colonization process develop under differing situations, especially in terms of reconstructed racial structures. This is difficult to measure as there are large, transcontinental and transoceanic systems in place and rapidly growing, so we use a much more limited or observable colonization process taking place on large islands, where we identify, analyze and to an extent measure demographic and socioeconomic changes in the colony. Two most disparate of these examples, nearly polar opposites in terms of Race and geopolitical place, would be the first colony of Hispaniola in the New World, and ongoing colonization of Ireland, in the ("old") European world (further developed in comparative analysis in Chapter 4).

Third, we observe revolutions that are the product of these increasingly global changes, those where the English colonies arose in North America, those in Europe where citizens' rights were being racially defined as blowback from American colonies, and lastly those revolutionary across races in the Caribbean. We use the truly transatlantic revolutions, quickly following one another – the American, the French and the Haitian Revolution, which also marks the transition period (1783 the United States; 1789 France's Rights of Man to 1794 abolition of slavery; 1791–1797 early Haitian slave revolts; 1797–1802 Haitian declaration of Independence and Rights) over all of Europe and the Americas toward the world-system we now have.

Fourth and finally, we observe a great transition from the Europe-dominated Atlantic toward a Euro-American dominance over market capitalism, racial and ethno-national controls, and ultimately hegemony over international trade and development, marking the modern world. Ideologies of free market capitalism, racialized democracies and evolutionary social systems, initiated in the Iberian period we call Indian, brought to global forbearance in the English period we are calling Black, and institutionalized in the American national development we call White, ethnic or Irish, or just American, become central to global dominance and militaristic hegemony. That is the world we live in today.

Later, in next book's end, we see mass hysteria, fear of dark forces attacking children, Q-Anon child trafficking and baby blood as devil worship, turning to violent assaults on the capitol, coming out of 2020 with remarkable symmetry of armed movement and racist ideologies. Much of the academy and most scholars thought we had put the worst of this behind us, utilizing social science concepts such as Bonilla-Silva's (2009) color-blind racism, or modern neocolonization, white privilege, people of color, cultural erasure or the like.

However, the self-serving ideologies arising from the social structures of enslavement, genocide and racial stratification, remained in American society, and can rear their ugly head, when called upon by political reactionaries and misguided populism. Rationalizations from the long arc of the doctrine of Discovery, scientific racism and enlightenment half-truths, found in comparing colonies such as Haiti and Ireland with Virginia and Plymouth, reveal that invasion, colonization, racism and capitalism have been and are interactive processes. We also observe three great revolutions – United States (America), France (Europe) and Haiti (Caribbean) – produced world-systemic transitions from a Europe-dominated Atlantic to a Euro-American dominance over the following two hundred forty years, focus of Chapter 4 and the next book.

Notes

1 Wahunsenawek was a Pamunkey headsman and a paramount chief of the Powhatan Confederacy of nations, many historians refer to him as Powhatan (not his name), as they would later with the Massasoit of Wampanoag.

2   These are the simple facts, but historians and social science analysts have argued, endlessly, about conditions surrounding these "facts" ever since (see later this chapter, and in the conclusions in Chapter 6), with basic invisibility and denial creating a hegemonic discourse that is countered by a Native centered discourse. Of course, these icons are so powerful that the sitting president of the United States often refers to Pocahontas and the Indians in derision (see note 20 below for Trump Twitter on Pocahontas and even Wounded Knee).

3   The first African slaves in what is now Georgia arrived in mid-September 1526 with Lucas Vázquez de Ayllón's attempted community San Miguel de Gualdape on the current Georgia coast. They rebelled and went to live with local Native people, leaving behind a destroyed colony after only a couple months.

4   Both the original Waterhouse testimony, and the ethnohistorian analyst, likely mean to show colonist friendly toward the people of the Powhatan, and therefore unreasonable in their following attacks. However, it is just as reasonable to show the Natives (who outnumbered the colonists) as being friendly, even as their land was being subdivided by plantations, and periodic militia forays for food destroyed the ripened corn and other provisions of the local Indian communities whenever conflict ensued – Grizzard, Frank E.; Smith, D. Boyd (2007). Jamestown Colony: a political, social, and cultural history. Santa Barbara, CA: ABC-CLIO.

5   While one of the Captains and musketeers met with Opechancanough in a Powhatan village along the Potomac, Governor and Doctor John Potts prepared poisoned wine for ceremonial toasts, where more than 200 Powhatans died after drinking the wine in an offering to peace (think of effects of getting this news during negotiations).

6   "It was given them by the Plymouth Company (the 70 venture capitalists) in 1621. Later, in 1627, the Pilgrims bought all of the stock of the company of adventurers, to avoid the friction caused by a divergence in aim and principle between themselves and their backers. By 1633 the Pilgrims had paid out, and were in unencumbered possession of the territory covered by the original grant." (Markham, 1909:160)

7   Sharing lodges at Wessaguset and overnights at Jamestown strongly suggest sexual fraternization, which is taken to suggest non-hetero relations at Merrymount where sharing beds directly states intimate sexual relations, all that is prohibited and punished by the Puritans of Plymouth, and often punished in Virginia colony (Wilkerson, 2019). Both romantic sources (Markham, 1909) and critical historians (Jennings, 1975) identify looser morals in London and other English communities, as origins of the problem, suggesting it is the start of hetero patriarchal dominance.

8   St. Augustine already existed permanently, and numerous other attempts and mixed-race communities mostly populated by Spanish colonizing settlers, as noted in Chapter 2, and there had been two attempts by English forces, one called the "lost colony" at Roanoke, which had been reinforced by Francis Drake and even John Smith after raiding galleons and slaves in the Caribbean to bring as reinforcement labor, who mysteriously disappear after desertion of one colony near Nag's Head, and being left off with the people who become lost.

9 Nearly, the exact same processes occur after Massachusetts Bay Colony forms the United Colonies of New England launching wars against various Indian Nations as they hardened racial slave laws for Blacks.

10 We have seen an agricultural based precapitalist mode of sugar plantation slavery, on Madeira by the Portuguese, and the more formal plantations on Hispaniola and other Caribbean islands by the Spanish, where initial enslavement and wholesale Indian labor exploitation in mining and natural resource extraction provided great colonial profits and wealth transfers to Spain on a scale never seen before. The primary racist ideologies linked to the colonization for this hundred year period were against the uncivilized savage Indian (even when invading great empires like the Aztecs, the Inca or societies like the Taino), and increasingly the Black African imported for the sugar plantations of the Americas... France and the Netherlands were beginning to compete in these markets and develop the Circuit trade for resources flowing to Europe, then colonizing goods shipped to Africa where enslavement markets were sending Blacks to the Americas. England also pushed to compete, forming international trading companies for the Asian trade of Russia (Muscovy) and India (London).

11 This becomes the first of many treacherous acts by the English, of course cumulative for Native political leaders, historians of the time and for later conflicts, see Alden T. Vaughan, "Expulsion of the Savages": English Policy and the Virginia Massacre of 1622, *The William and Mary Quarterly* 35, no. 1 (January 1978), 57–84.

12 The timeline is still a little unclear here to me. Once we understand that while fighting broke out in 1609, but it was Gates betrayal and slaughter of people of the Powhatan that really started the first War, we can revisit 1622 seeing a similar buildup of fights and skirmishing from 1621 to 1622, with timing of the advisor's assassination in question. When we put the often sidelined description of the treacherous poisoning of Powhatan in a peace conference, we can ask exactly when and how Nemattanew was killed, perhaps during those negotiations? How many other leaders were poisoned in the meeting, an ultimate act of treachery, where the English present must have known not to drink the wine to celebrate the peace? Was this part of a larger plan, similar to what happened in Plymouth?

13 Noting the Susquehannock all but disappear as their lands, peoples and villages are decimated, with those left subject to genocidal militia attacks, such as done by the Paxton boys (see next chapter), all the way to Ohio.

14 Sir William Berkeley refused to retaliate against the Native Americans, farmers gathered around a raiding party. Nathaniel Bacon arrived with brandy and was elected leader. Against Berkeley's orders, the group struck south until they came to the Occaneechi people. After convincing the Occaneechi to attack the Susquehannock, Bacon and his men followed by killing most of the men, women and children at the village. Upon their return, they discovered that Berkeley had called for new elections to the Burgesses to address the Native American raids.

15 "Illegal" land seizures from Native peoples is both terribly ironic and robustly hypocritical, since the colonies themselves were founded on taking of land from Indian Nations, rarely if ever with consent other than after wars.

16 "The fear of civil war among whites frightened Virginia's ruling elite, who took steps to consolidate power and improve their image: for example, restoration of property qualifications for voting, reducing taxes, and adoption of a more aggressive American Indian policy." (Eric Foner, *Give Me Liberty!: An American History* (New York: W. W. Norton & Company, 2009), p. 100). Indentured servants both black and white joined the frontier rebellion. Seeing them united in a cause alarmed the ruling class. Historians believe the rebellion hastened the hardening of racial lines associated with slavery, as a way for planters and the colony to control some of the poor. (Cooper, William J., Liberty and Slavery: Southern Politics to 1860, Univ of South Carolina Press, 2001, p. 9.)

17 Note the French unofficially and the English formally restricted racial enslavement as offshore or colonial enterprises. Also the colonies were being centralized in capitalism processes that devalued the "contributions" of colonized nations, through processes known as (ecological) unequal exchange, that attempts to evaluate land, labor and trade only through monetary systems (see Hornberg in JWSR, 2020).

18 There is interesting evidence supporting this, in that John Rolfe never registers the birth of her son, Thomas, even though he was the colony secretary and religious registrar.

19 Donald J. Trump Twitter: "If Elizabeth Warren, often referred to by me as Pocahontas, did this commercial from Bighorn or Wounded Knee instead of her kitchen, with her husband dressed in full Indian garb, it would have been a smash!" ✓ @realDonaldTrump 40.6K 6:52 PM – Jan 13, 2019.

20 John Gadsby Chapman (photograph courtesy Architect of the Capitol), Public domain, via Wikimedia Commons.

21 Robert Lowell's play *Endecott and the Red Cross* in 1968 New York theaters, Drinnon (1997: 1–3)

22 John Adam's hometown of Quincy is the location of the original colony, and thus he spends effort at converting them to a more rational position in destroying the local Native population.

23 Many scholars and historians have noted hetero patriarchal norms were not being observed at Merrymount, and the suppression of all licentious behaviors and acts was at this time becoming legalized into anti-homosexual debate that also was institutionalized and would command American normative jurisprudence to this very day in 2021.

24 With some 17,000 Puritans migrating to New England by 1636, Harvard was founded in anticipation of the need for training clergy for the new commonwealth, a "church in the wilderness." Harvard was established in 1636 by vote of the Great and General Court of the Massachusetts Bay Colony. In order to get England's consent, the 1650 original charter is for the "education of the English and Indian youth of this country in knowledge and godlynes."

25 The University of California at Berkeley (and later UCLA) was forced to deal with the racist background of the Southerners that founded and were the first presidents of the University, as well as the genocidal takings of land, upon which the university now sits. This was acknowledged in conferences held in 2020 and important ones in 2021 where administrators accepted some responsibility, as was happening across the nation. This is discussed in the next book covering 1776 or 1790 to 2020.

26 Johnson was first enslaved as "Antonio the Negro" but with hard work and a benevolent Master, gained freedom and built up a 250-acre tobacco farm. However, the institutions and laws were catching up with him, so after he died a court ruled he was, indeed, a "negro" and therefore an "alien" to the land. His properties were forfeited.

27 It is precisely the lack of institutional laws that allowed for some exceptional individuals in particular situations to operate freely, even own homes or property (although in most cases where they appeared to "own" slaves these were their own relatives, even family). Some of these practices for free Blacks continued into the U.S. era.

28 We note that Indians disappear in this dichotomous discourse, which continues to be important for another 250 years. Native people did not experience any colonist settler privileges, and initially were enslaved in some places, such as the Carolinas, and non-contractually indentured in others, such as Plymouth.

29 Conniff, Michael L. and Thomas J. Davis. 1994. Africans in the Americas: a History of the Black Diaspora. New York: St. Martin's Press.

30 Hardesty (2019) and Warren (2016) among others have recently identified this dual racial development.

31 Emanuel Downing, Winthrop's brother-in-law, wrote in 1645 longing for a "juste warre" with the Pequots, so the colonists might capture enough Indian men, women and children to exchange in Barbados for black slaves, because the colony would never thrive "untill we gett ... a stock of slaves sufficient to doe all our business" (Greene, 1942).

32 "In 1660, the English government chartered a company called the 'Company of Royal Adventurers Trading to Africa.' At first the company was mismanaged, but in 1663 it was reorganized. A new objective clearly stated that the company would engage in the slave trade. To the great dissatisfaction of England's merchants, only the Company of Royal Adventurers could now engage in the trade. ...The Company did not fare well, due mainly to the war with Holland, and in 1667, it collapsed. But out of its ashes emerged a new company: The Royal African Company. Founded in 1672, the Royal African Company was granted a similar monopoly in the slave trade... Between 1680 and 1686, the Company transported an average of 5,000 slaves a year. Between 1680 and 1688, it sponsored 249 voyages to Africa... Still, rival English merchants were not amused. In 1698, Parliament yielded to their demands and opened the slave trade to all. With the end of the monopoly, the number of slaves transported on English ships would increase dramatically -- to an average of over 20,000 a year." (PBS SoCalAfricans in America/Part 1/Royal African Company established (pbs.org) retrieved 10/18/21) By the end of the 17th century, England led the world in the trafficking of slaves.

33 The Council of Foreign Plantations has a corollary in contemporary U.S. governance, of the President's Council of Economic Advisors.

34 We might note that such corporate rights were gleaned from Roman law about the time that Supremacy arose in state recognition of the Catholic Church in Constantinople, Avignon, then back to Rome (see Chapter 2 supremacy).

35 The Wampanoag and other Native men and boys were pretty much the last Indians sold to the Barbados, since they caused such a set of problems, were "unruly" and hard to tame, or make domestic. What is interesting is that those

were the same claims that Ovando made in 1502 and 1503 about Blacks directly from Africa – it seems that having a sense of nationhood and belonging before enslavement makes one more likely to resist.

36 I must note the problem here in saying the Pequot "went to war" and thus seeing it as an Indian war, when all the available evidence shows that the colonists confederations started, and finished, the war to their benefit.

37 Passive terms such as Lost at Sea are another way that dominant societies and scholarship have of softening utterly horrible statistics, since most of these are due to disease, malnutrition starving, punishment and executions (some to save food costs, other after resistance or rebellion), that are part of the slaveholder calculations on profits.

38 There is an increase from 1830 to 1850, sharply in the 1840 decade, which may be attributed to an increased enforcement (since 1809) against transatlantic trade by the United States, following Britain of course.

39 This is one of those places where I feel I should almost spend some words describing the great increase in both labor power production in general, the rise of life expectancy and falling death rates around cities, and other positive developments along with leadership from democratizing countries with better living conditions (for some people), however, general or mainstream histories and social narratives do that job quite well, so that this work is something of a corrective that balances what is otherwise a dominant, hegemonic perspective.

40 Some historians have the life expectancy of newly arrived enslaved Africans at 4–7 years in Haiti.

41 From Henri Christophe's personal secretary who had been enslaved on French plantation. Heinl, Robert. (1996). *Written in Blood: The Story of the Haitian People, 1492–1995.* Lantham, Maryland: University Press of America.

42 By 1530s, Cabrillo was operating out of Guatemala (Santiago) where he profited from the "encomienda" system, using Indian labor on lands reserved for (services to the crown) Spanish power brokers over farmlands and mines. Cabrillo's resulting wealth – depended on slave labor of Indigenous Guatemalans – which transferred to his wife, Beatriz Sanchez de Ortega from Spain, because his children with an Indigenous woman could not inherit his wealth, Spain requiring landowners to be white Spaniards.

43 Like any good, or bad, divorce, both parties retain interest in the distribution and ownership of property as well as control over minors, or in the case of European colonization what would be called racial/ethnic minorities.

44 From Thomas Workman Temple II's article "Toypurina the Witch and the Indian Uprising at San Gabriel" (some scholars doubt the intensity of this, preferring a soldier's report of simple revile). However, a more tempered version by McLaughlin (2022) infers the same heartfelt intent: "Toypurina… said she had told … the village to join in revolt "to encourage the men to be brave and fight." She declaring she did all this "because I am angry with the fathers and with all the others at this mission for living on Tongva land." (Toypurina: The California Stories, California Missions, Keeping the Past Present. David J. McLaughlin (retrieved July 7, 2022: Toypurina-Final.pdf (missionscalifornia.com; www.missionscalifornia.com/wp-content/uploads/2022/01/Toypurina-Final.pdf).

45 I would be well-advised not to have this section, since religious sensibilities are more powerful and polarized than ever, but instead will offer a disclaimer: being

Christian can (and often does) mean living with morals, ethics and practices we associate with Jesus of Nazareth and early Christians being suppressed by the state (Rome, etc.). When corporations and state structures employ religious arguments and create institutions, they often do this for tactical or even strategic objectives, not related to any true practice of being Christian. As I write here, colonizing and then capitalist forces are products of an enlarging world-system, especially over the Americas, and justify their participation in genocide and systems of slavery, from which they are profiting, using religious doctrines. This is one area where Weber wandered from the social-institutional structures he identified, as in the Protestant Ethic, which embodies capitalist values (or the lack of them) which are the near antipathy of Christian life.

46 If the reader finds this unacceptable reasoning or analysis, we encourage them to flip to the next section of this chapter. We can still conduct class analysis of the growing urban stratification and industrial capitalism (without this analytical regime). In fact, much social theory has been predicated on just that approach, leading to a kind of societal schizophrenia unresolved to this day. In northern America, we are surrounded by this deep, un-abiding conflict of competing theories and observed societal realities, seemingly every day. And as these forces come to a head in the downgrading of our lived environment in the Anthropocene, we are left with stark choices on how to continue…

47 The indulgences may not include the selling of bloodline purity − *limpieza de sangre* − in the protest demands, although this was assuredly implied. More importantly, Protestant English were on the verge of working out these relationships in a completely new way − creating essentialized notions of race with a clear predestination of those Elects of the dominant racial-ethnic order (whites) to be successful in God's eyes.

48 [one example would be the taxing of Black slaves in Virginia]

49 I realize many true believers will have problems with this, as many religious scholars who determine dogma is the same as theocratic reasoning. In this, I must remind the reader that in Catholic reasoning this is Original Sin, which is washed away in baptism and subsequent Christian ceremonies, so introducing a new kind of infallibility in (utterly) depraved (more pejorative than being born in sin) with God (rather than man, like pope or priest) deciding. Of course, the problem is not in philosophical underpinnings, but in determining who gets to interpret God's word.

50 Again, I apologize to true believers, this is not a theocracy but an evaluation of the social structures put in place. For instance, see Casual Killing Act (1669) protections and use of "savages" in declaring these as "natural."

51 Actually, the very language of "natural" as in rights or responsibilities, and in philosophic relationship to people, are literally used that way in the Declaration of Independence and parts of the U.S. Constitution.

52 When getting the PhD at Northwestern, I entered into debate with an assistant professor over Simmel's theory that there is a grand division between Man and Nature, with civilizing discourse accorded to man outside nature. Indigenous thinking is just the opposite, man and nature are one, although man tries to control or dominate nature.

53 Slave trading shipping companies across the Atlantic are clearly operating as transnational corporations through the 16th, 17th and 18th centuries, shifting

modalities for slave, indentured and wage-labor exploitation processes through the 19th and 20th centuries, into modern times.

54 We note here how we often say some tribal group (Lakota) "believe such and such" but never say Americans, Germans or even Christians "believe" they were created in seven days with woman created from a man's rib (bone), which is or should be directly comparable to creation stories or origin myths of Indigenous peoples (Deloria, 1995).

55 Huguenots (also Calvinists) fleeing the French wars were first in landing failed colonies in the Carolinas, 1562, and Florida, 1564 (destroyed by the Spanish in order to found St. Augustine nearby). Later Huguenots joined Dutch colonists in founding the New Netherlands that became New York after English colonists took over.

56 Total depravity supposedly affects all men, who are unable to save themselves, even by individual will. This uses the worst or strongest idioms or language to identify non-Christians but also infers their inability or inferiority to change their position, or status. This conceptually relates to Limited Atonement in that only certain ones should be saved as a result of God's unconditional election, making that Christ died for the elect alone, who are the only ones who will be saved (rather than Christ dying for all men).

Unconditional election means only God can determine (as predestination) whether men or a man can be "saved" – thus leading Calvinists to identify these people (all Europeans initially) as the "Elect" (superordination of groups and individuals). After years of arguing that successful church leaders and other prominent citizens were this Elect, many thinkers began to use this ideology to support or rationalize why some members become wealthy or powerful. Thus, religion can be used to claim that God made manifest a destiny of ethnically/racially defined people as worthy.

57 Interestingly, one faction called Four-point Calvinists (see Unlimited Atonement as global acceptance by God of all Humans), supposedly rejected by mainstream Calvinism since anyone could "choose" God and therefore become Elect, who could end up in Hell (based on their mis-deeds), though I suspect the real reason is in reverse, non-destined or non-Elect people could be in Heaven, thus Indians, Blacks, Jews and Muslims could be saved – creating less of an excuse for genocide, slavery and domination.

58 Note: I felt I had to conduct this historical-comparative analysis in order to be able to explain certain inexplicable phenomena, such as predisposition of settler colonial people (i.e. English colonies) toward conducting brutal forms of genocide, often in the name of a Christian God, while preaching peace and love, which explains the California state-sponsored genocide in places like Tolowa people at Yontocket, completely missing from history and textbooks on California. Also, it is these tendencies that are reformed in lynchings and killings in post–Civil War America, religiously sanctioned in a variety of ways (see without Sanctuary photos, large gatherings at kill sites).

59 1755, lieutenant governor of the Province of Massachusetts Bay, issued a proclamation that declared the Penobscot people enemies, rebels and traitors to King George II, calling "his Majesty's Subjects... Embrace all opportunities of

pursuing, captivating, killing, and Destroying all and every... " Penobscot and "Indians" of the Wabanaki Confederacy. Bounty hunters were paid 50 pounds for living captive Penobscot males 12 years and older, 40 pounds for the scalps of dead Penobscot males age 12 and over, 25 pounds for the scalps of women, and 20 pounds for the scalps of children under the age of 12. https://upstanderproj ect.org/firstlight/phips.

60 During the period before and during formal colonization, England engaged in protracted war and internal struggle with Catholics in France and other European states, reflected in the competitive and violent struggles for control of the Caribbean. This was an outgrowth of what has been called the French Wars of Religion that were a prolonged period of violent, popular unrest between Catholics and Huguenots (Reformed/Calvinist Protestants) in France between 1562 and 1598, estimated to cause three million people to perish from violence, famine, disease and the deadliest religious wars in European history, preceding the Thirty Years' War that took eight million lives, the most destructive religious war until the 20th century.

Personal Statement as Preface to Chapter 4

Walking Race and Empire in America

I first went to the Irish boroughs and African American sections of greater Boston with a friend, a direct descendent of the not-so-blue-blood enslaved workers of Massachusetts Bay Colony. Upon touring the cemetery at the Burying Grounds near the Old North Church, she noted: …where the grave markers demonstrate the making of this American city, are – Mary Dwyer who kept up her Quaker preaching in the face of intolerant Puritan men – Crispus Attucks who escaped enslavement of African-Native ethnicity yet served aboard ships bound for the Caribbean and challenged Redcoats law-and-order. Both of them defied a growing racial patriarchy of New England and paid for it with their lives, becoming unsung patriots of movement, creating a new nation that would deny similar freedoms for some 200 years, including against the Wampanoag who first allowed the Pilgrims to survive on the new land. The more famed patriots hid their identity, masquerading as Indians when dumping an overly taxed Asian tea into Boston harbor, launching a revolutionary fervor over which the British could not figure the perpetrators. We must ask who the real martyrs are in this story.

Afterwards, we went to Philadelphia, city of brotherly love where our nation's first treaty was struck with the Lenape – named after colonizer Thomas West DeLaWar who beat down their relatives in the Virginia colony. Like the Boston Tea Party, with armed opposition toward taxation 'without representation' – we questioned who did the nation represent? (Certainly not Christian women, enslaved African-Natives, or the futures of First Nations across this land).

Later I would walk the streets of Port-au-Prince, Haiti, where statues of revolutionary leaders stood in the shadow of a newly independent Black nation forced to pay Reparations to France for having taken their property 'illegally' (freed themselves as slaves). I would write a poem on *La Belle Ennery* and another –*Passing Urine Cans on the Boat to Jeremie* – to reconstruct

DOI: 10.4324/9781003315087-6

the great treachery of Napoleon in deceiving Toussaint Louverture, with brutal blockades held against Haiti by slave trading powers of the West. Earlier (when I graduated from LMU) we took theater to London, seeing the Tempest at Stratford on Avon, preparing our cross Channel trip to Paris, viewing paintings in the Louvre of Empire, Revolution – liberté, egalité, fraternité (but for all?) – versus the marbled museum columns of England's treasures also taken from colonized peoples of their Empire. These interwoven thoughts would come tumbling back over the winter of my discontent in North Dakota, when I shuttled between Standing Rock and the Bismarck state capitol where my grandparents still lived in a small house on East Avenue E, where I wrote *Wind From the West Indies* encapsulating my conflicted experiences across the Americas.

Yet, the strangest feelings were later after visiting an ancestral family farm in MyShall parish of County Carlow, Ireland, where the empty pews of a grand Protestant Cathedral looked down upon an impoverished Catholic church, overcrowded with Sunday worshippers. I had come to attend the Congress on Violence and Human Co-existence, held at University College Dublin, gathering to tell of historical struggles, including the I.R.A. against England, perfectly seen in a Troubles Murals at Falls Road or Sandy Row, Belfast, or at the bottoms – Free Derry civil rights marches, over into 1968, also seen in Sniper's Promise signs posted outside Crossmaglen.[1]

Alas, I was reminded that Custer's troops were playing the Irish fighting song Garry Owen as they rode out of Fort Abraham Lincoln on their death march to glory on the banks of the Greasy Grass at the Battle of the Little Big Horn (America's empire wars). I like to think I had relatives on both sides of that fight, marking the U.S. centennial in a great military loss finally revenged at the 1890 Wounded Knee massacre, giving an epic finale to two centuries of development and domination in the New World.

Note

1   Crossmaglen (from Irish: Crois Mhic Lionnáin, meaning 'Mac Lionnáin's cross') is a village and townland in County Armagh, Northern Ireland.

Chapter 4

Three Revolutions
1776–1790 Three Races in a New State

Introduction

Critical scholars have long noted "around 1776 certain important people in the English colonies found that by creating a nation, a legal unity called the United States, they could take over land, profits and political power from favorites of the British Empire." These new leaders could hold back "potential rebellions and create support for the rule of a new, privileged leadership. The American Revolution… was a work of genius which created (an) effective system of national control," showing future generations the advantage of …racial paternalism (Howard Zinn, 1977).

> We are black, it is true, but tell us, gentlemen, you who are so judicious, what is the law that says that the black man must belong to and be the property of the white man?
> (Toussaint Louverture, Letter to General Assembly, 1792)

> I was born a slave, but nature gave me the soul of a free man…
> (Toussaint Louverture)

> For too long we have borne your chains without thinking of shaking them off, but any authority which is not founded on virtue and humanity, and which only tends to subject one's fellow man to slavery, must come to an end, and that end is yours.
> (Toussaint Louverture Letter to the General Assembly, 1792)

Other African scholars noted: "all the crimes that have been committed under pretext of justice. People robbed native inhabitants of their land, made slaves of them, let loose scum of mankind upon them… atrocities were perpetrated upon people made subservient to us, systematically we

DOI: 10.4324/9781003315087-7

ruined them with alcoholic 'gifts'...We decimate them, by the stroke of
a pen, we take their land so they have nothing left at all...

(Chinua Achebe, 1977: v)[1]

The secret of freedom lies in educating people, whereas the secret of
tyranny is in keeping them ignorant... The king must die so that the
country can live... To punish the oppressors of humanity is clemency;
to forgive them is cruelty.

(Maximilien Robespierre)

I heard that paper read yesterday, that says, all men are created equal, and
that every man has a right to freedom. I'm not a dumb *critter*, won't the
law give me my freedom?

(MumBet)

Any time, any time while I was a slave, if one minute's freedom had been
offered to me, and I had been told I must die at the end of that minute,
I would have taken it—just to stand one minute on God's *airth* [sic] a
free woman— I would.

(Elizabeth Freeman (aka MumBet))

They came with a Bible and their religion- stole our land, crushed our
spirit. and now tell us we should be thankful to the 'Lord' for being
saved.

(Chief Pontiac (*Obwandiyag*, Odawa))

Grandfathers from tribal nations of the four directions – Mohawk the northeast, Lenape the east, Shawnee to the west, Cherokee to the south, Odawa
to north and west – instructed their sons and daughters how to prepare for
resistance, and war, against Europeans who were destroying lands through
fur trades in the north, and dividing confederations through enslaving in the
south.[2] Grandmothers from the same nations instructed daughters and sons
how to keep good relations and strong families in the face of culturicide[3]
against the peoples, to maintain respect, reciprocity, generosity and spiritual
recognition as keepers of the lodges and for passing their values and traditional
knowledge to the next generation. Colonizing militias, armies enforced the
new systems, creating temporary allegiances with European nations that pit
many tribes against one another, seen in the French and Indian war, and in
the march toward the western territories.[4] Lenape, a.k.a. DelaWare Indians,
are exemplar of the treaty-making or breaking, removal and ethnic cleansing
in Pennsylvania as a century-long continuity, a story we tell a little later.

Creation of 13 original English colonies, from 1620 to their completion in 1783, or 1787, marks the finished racial project of colonization by

supremacist European powers, and their coordinated intent to grow as a solidified new country outward over the new Promised Land. The imposition of European colonizing forces over North America was met by resistance from Native nations and peoples already living on the land in well-adapted communities and societies. Chief Pontiac (*Obwandiyag*) represents this resistance, leading the Odawa to join many Native nations in a confederated movement 1763–1766 that almost defeated combined colonial forces, ranging from frontier armies reinforced by England, irregular militias against local communities, often genocidal and always supremacist, and the disparate French trading forts.

By the mid-1700s significant numbers of Africans were also living in resistance to enslavement and racial subordination (Horne, 2014). Plantation economies had grown using enslaved Black people, as a central part of profit-making production, and structured many laws and policies around this violent slave system. The colonies had European powers as backers, nations also in competition, and sometimes at war with one another. This is evident in both the 1763 and 1783 Treaty of Paris, where Europeans laid claim to territories, without fully acknowledging Native nations pre-Treaty presence on the land (Hill, 2014),[5] instead calling territories New Spain, New France, or under English claim, and so on. At the same time, enslavement systems and markets were critically important in negotiations, including trade-offs for France to control Martinique's sugar plantations and retain control over San Domingue (Haiti) in the Caribbean. St. Augustine, a city within Spanish held Florida, was a major draw for Africans due to its lack of formal slave laws. Actually the Stono Rebellion in the 1739 Carolinas is also a strong example of resistance.

All of these international and national developments produced transcontinental colonial wars, in which Native Nations were removed as soon as possible, through brutal conquests justified by adaptations of the Discovery doctrine, or to colonize by trading economies using international capitalism as integral to treaty agreements, such as France regaining its Caribbean colonies of Martinique and Guadeloupe along with Haiti, using massive African slave labor, while England had built up Black slave labor as a basis of its economic trade, which needed denial or dismissal of any Native nation claim to sovereignty over territories recently seized. Interesting to note that it took English colonies about the same amount of time (1620 to 1670s), to institutionalize slave and indentured labor systems within American colonies, as Spain did (1500–1550). Both colonizers extinguished Native Nations histories and sovereignty, rendering them an invisibility to future historians. As the colonizing powers eyed the conquest over North America, they also realized the possibilities of colonies revolting in social revolutions built partly on slave labor dynamics and partly on wealth by conquest, both of which they deny.

That is the important observation in this concluding chapter on the great transition to the modern world of this book, and its development and spread over North America, and the world, in my next book for another 240 years. We turn toward that discussion, in noting the three great racial constructions coming into full shape in the period – the Indian who must be driven from the land, after enslavement, without recording a claim to sovereignty – the Black (African) who is to be enslaved as stranger in the new land, or otherwise subordinated, without recognizing human rights; and – the White (ethnic or Irish) who are to become citizens of the new country, after a work proving period, with potential for full citizenship and privileges within the society. Both the new political system – ostensibly democratic – and the new economic system – elite-driven capitalism – would exploit and reinforce racial orderings of the United States (Figure 4.1).

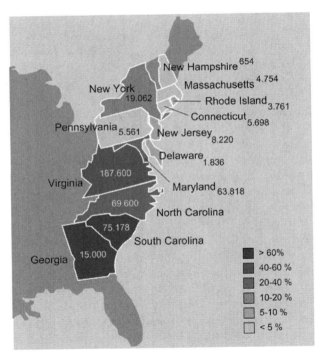

Figure 4.1 Map of 1770 Colonial America with number of (African) Black slaves. Stilfehler, CC BY-SA 3.0 https://creativecommons.org/licenses/by-sa/3.0, via Wikimedia Commons. Also in: Ira Berlin: *Generations of Captivity: A History of African-American Slaves* (2003).

Problematics and Distortions of a Binary View of Racial Orders

We must observe the concomitant development of three great and terrible systems of race, and racism, at or about the same time, as described previously, and in the literature. However, very deep distortions and analytical problematics have plagued most socio-historical descriptions of racial orders, either through vaunting the dominant group, Caucasian Europeans, or through an overly singular focus on one of the subordinated peoples, usually either Africans or Native Americans. Let us turn to a strong example of how this works, even among knowledgeable academics.

One wonderfully informed series on African Americans, narrated by university professors,[6] shows how important such a binary is. While acknowledging participation of African nations in the enslaving systems that fed the great markets across the Atlantic to/in the Americas, the series skirts the participation, and resistance of/by Native Nations in their conquest and colonization, including slavery before and during the African enslavement period, and forms of resistance.

The documentary also states that African enslavement enriched and built the nation, at times saying the great colonies, the war of Independence, the expansion of territory and capitalism itself, due to industrial cotton production (all) would not have occurred without Black slaves… In making that assertion, the documentary misses another important pillar, or leg of the stool holding up the country – wealth of land (and labor) taken from Native Nations.

Similarly, many Indigenous scholars have advanced notions of settler colonialism to the extent they explain the entire national development along those lines, referring to 'settler ideologies' and logics, even a settler state and place these in opposition to an essentialized Indigenous or Natives set of descriptions. Besides missing the larger discussion of Elites, and the Colonizers, much less the capital-driven economies, these scholars tend to dismiss or downplay the powerful forces of market racism that are at play with Black enslavement, as well as Indian Nations.[7]

Finally, both groups essentialize or even avoid discussion of the third major group – Whites, or settlers and colonists, and the Elite interests (the rich and powerful) who form and direct these groups, most often working class or agricultural labor, in order to produce national economies.

It is precisely at the point of national construction, or creation, that this third racial group is[8] formalized and placed in their structural position of dominance – although we should note class and ethnic divisions among the European descent people who are becoming known as White, and later Caucasian (a term that didn't yet exist). In fact, although many scholars say that most indentured servitude ended after Bacon's Rebellion, immigrant white ethnics were still being sold aboard ships as late as 1750 when disembarking in eastern ports such as Philadelphia:

> Rotterdam and in Amsterdam the people are packed densely, like herrings... Children from 1 to 7 years rarely survive the voyage. I witnessed miserly in no less than 32 children in our ship, all of whom were thrown into the sea... When the ships have landed (in Philadelphia)... ...no one is permitted to leave except those who pay... ...others must remain on board the ships till they are purchased... The sale of human beings in the market on board the ship is carried on... every day ...offers for sale passengers... and select... healthy persons... bargain with them how long they will serve... ...adult persons bind themselves in writing to serve 3, 4, 5 or 6 years for the amount due...[9]
> (Mittelberger, 1754: 72–76)

Children are sold, families broken and indentured servitude is replicated as a capital transaction, which was technically banned in the new colonies, saving this treatment for Blacks and Indians. This demographic construction becomes the heart of White Supremacy, or white nationalism, that provides a third leg of the racial group stool upon which the nation is built. It is evident in the Declaration of Independence, the Constitution of the United States and an overtly (covertly, too) emphasized racism seen in the first U.S. Census only noting the White racial category (Figure 4.2).

Pennsylvania – Treaty-Making – Ethnic Cleansing and the United States

The William Penn treaty of Shackamaxon[10] transitioned from Quaker inspired fair-dealings of a Peaceable Kingdom to fraudulent land-takings of the Walking Purchase in order to get valuable holdings such as the land-corridor to New York, which heated up other takings, negotiated under Indian treaty cover with the Iroquois League, itself under pressure. The Lenape (Delaware) were pushed westward from their Lenni-Lenape origins, into the Susquehannock valley (where ethnic cleansing operations were underway against tribal nations; Silver, 2008) even as racial struggles start up in the growing capitol, Philadelphia, where household slavery of Africans was common, and settler colonialism was expanding westward to greater Pennsylvania.

Settlements grew under clear anti-Indian sentiments, flaring conflicts across borders into Ohio with local leaders, including intellects such as Benjamin Franklin, political entrepreneurs like Robert Morris (soon to be acting or deputy governor) and young militia officers like George Washington. These leaders became experienced at dividing Indian Nations between benefactors, the crown of England, and enemy colonizer forces,

(Pennsylvania) – American Dominance – Lenape:hoking 4–1

Lenni Lenape communities extended from upper Schuylkill to the Atlantic coast, and from Delaware Bay to the borders of the Haudenosaunee to the north, in highly traversed riverine regions connected through informal tribal relationships of chiefdoms. Dutch trading posts, mostly off tributaries of the Hudson, Swedish settlements, and English incursions, marked early colonization, as Lenape regularly met in councils along the Delaware over such issues.

William Penn's landing and 1682 treaty of Shackamaxon with the great Tamanend (kitakima) friendship of the Lenape (Nations) with Quakers and the birth of Philadelphia, was quickly followed by Penn's sons creating fraudulent "oral" agreements taking land corridors along the Delaware leading to New York, then virtually all the eastern lands of Pennsylvania, with settler-colonial violence against the Lenape and other Indian Nations of the western regions, enforced by the Scalp Act of 1756 and numerous militia killings for bounties and settlements, reaching full ethnic cleansing into the Revolutionary War.

While the first Treaty of Paris in 1763 ended the French and Indian War and acknowledged tribal nations in western frontiers in the Royal Proclamation, the 1783 Treaty of Paris ending the Revolutionary War left Native Nations out of the negotiations, ignoring the first United States Treaty of Fort Pitt with Delawares in 1778. Future treaty negotiations were centered in Philadelphia and Washington DC, setting up exclusions of Indian Nations in the Constitution and Bill of Rights, while reinforcing enslavement of Africans as Blacks.

Militias operating along Pennsylvania's western frontier with Ohio conducted genocidal raids reinforced by the 1787 Northwest Ordnance legitimizing land takings. General / President Washington ordered militaries to destroy the Haudenosaunee and suppress Native Nations throughout the region, solidifying the United States and establishing taxation of the lands. By 1790 Native peoples not contained on the reservations, were considered enemies of the state. Pennsylvania had been cleared of the Nations who first negotiated treaties with the English, even as great literary, political and philosophical societies were being formed in Philadelphia.

Leading intellectuals such as Benjamin Franklin and political entrepreneurs as Robert Morris, would come to personify the new country, even as they worked for an elimination of Natives, expunging their living histories from the land they now considered God given to themselves. Revolutionary dialogues and politicized rhetoric arose in Constitutional Hall where members of the Haudenosaunee Confederation were advising them of how the five nations developed, with pluri-nationality and blended sovereignty as a means of democratic representation.

Capitalism as economic necessity, and a representative republic with democratic tendencies, arose in a racialized society noted throughout the constitutional meetings in Philadelphia, home to the Lenape who agreed to friendship pacts and a Peaceable Kingdom that never had a chance in the coming years for the new United States of America. Treaties for a hundred years would follow in the decades of expansion for empire and trade, with many abolitionists leading freedom struggles for Black Americans, in the city of brotherly love.

Figure 4.2 American (U.S.) Dominance in Pennsylvania (Lenape – Delaware nations).

France, and attacking any Native Nations that resisted taking sides, later eliminating even those who did side with English descent Americans.

Although a series of treaties were made over the first half of the 18th century (1737 and 1758),[11] they were quickly broken in the mad rush for more lands, driving the original treaty Lenape Delaware mostly into Ohio, or northward into alliances in Canada. Governor Morris responded to settlements in western Pennsylvania calling for Indian Wars with a series of acts and policies, culminating in the Scalp Act of 1756 calling for bounties on Indian men, women and children (men highest; Silver, 2008). The Act caused a series of killings by militias like the Paxton Boys, even against Christian Indians which supposedly caused outrage by religious groups but no legal action against the murderers (Young, 1957), becoming the heart of White Supremacy continuing over two centuries into the 21st century, by then mostly targeting Africans as Blacks.

We can observe direct evidence of colonial government intentionality, and crown involvement in funding the ethnic cleansing by paying for scalps as proof of kill; the targeting of men, women and children; and genocidal expansion in taking over new lands, in the Scalp Act of 1756.

> *Whereas the Delaware Tribe of Indians, and others in Confederacy with them, have, for some Time past, without the least provocation, and contrary to their most solemn Treaties, fallen upon this Province, and in a most cruel, savage and perfidious Manner, killed and butchered great Numbers of the Inhabitants, and carried others in barbarous Captivity, burning and destroying Habitations, and laying waste the Country… I HAVE THEREFORE… and do **hereby declare the said Delaware Indians, and all others… to be Enemies, Rebels and Traitors** to His Most Sacred Majesty. AND I do herby require all His Majesty's Subjects of this Province, and earnestly invite those of the neighbouring Provinces to embrace all **Opportunities of pursuing, taking, killing and destroying** the said Delaware Indians… AND WHEREAS the Commissioners appointed with me to dispose of the **Sixty Thousand Pounds**, lately granted by Act of General Assembly for His Majesty's Use… agreed to pay out of the same the several Rewards for Prisoners and Scalps herein after specified ; FOR every Male Indian Enemy, above Twelve Years old, who shall be taken Prisoner… the Sum of One Hundred and Fifty Spanish Dollars or Pieces of Eight. FOR the **Scalp of every Male Indian Enemy**, above the age of Twelve Years, the Sum of One Hundred and Thirty Spanish Dollars Pieces of Eight. FOR every **Female Indian, taken Prisoner**… and for every Male Indian Prisoner **under the Age of Twelve Years**… One Hundred and Thirty Pieces of Eight. FOR the **Scalp of every Indian Woman**, produced as **Evidence of their being killed**, the Sum of Fifty Pieces of Eight.…*
>
> (The *Pennsylvania Gazette* [1756] from:
> Silver, 2008: 270 [bolding mine])

As earlier colonial expansions in Virginia and Massachusetts had so moved, the Pennsylvania General Assembly and the colonists ranged from early friendship agreements to fraudulent land takings, and after resistance, to armed conflict that devolved into outright calls for extermination. Once Native nations were removed, or eliminated, histories were rewritten, collective memory was reconstructed to say that understandable 'mistakes' were made by colonists, and American frontiersmen, that had to be supported by governments protecting their citizenry, lamentable as that may be. Here we have the first documented cases of 'friendly' Indians mistakenly killed as 'hostile' enemies under the color of law, scalp bounties collected, discounted to for fighting 'spirit.' This is the perfect case study for phenomena that was deployed across North America, extending to the genocides in California and final military suppression on the Great Plains (Figure 4.3).[12]

Even though there are historic paintings and written descriptions of this event (see Benjamin West's *Penn's Treaty with the Indians*, painted 1771/ 1772) that place the Europeans and Native Nation leaders on equitable terms, both scholars and popular historians discount the wampum belt as 'proof' representing treaty agreement on fair and equitable terms, between Tamanend (one of grand clan chiefs representing Lenape) and William Penn (representing English Quakers). With fraudulent 'treaties' and ethnic cleansing of most of eastern Pennsylvania that followed, disavowal of Lenape oral tradition understanding of the physically represented wampum belt, amounts to a denial of historical colonization, theft of lands and genocidal suppression which continues for another 200 years through United States formation and expansion. As we discussed previously, the colony and then the United States move from mutual friendship treaties, to land takings (Walking Purchase extended north), Indian removal policies from Susquehannock valley to the Ohio frontier, genocidal scalping legislation (1756–1777) and disingenuous treaty agreements (1778) with the United States that amount to full ethnic cleansing. Essentially the Lenape go from 'Peaceable Kingdom' treaty-making with the Quaker colonists, through removals and ethnic wars to a first treaty made with the new U.S. government, to complete removal – elimination from their homelands, resulting in literally no Native Nation representation in Pennsylvania during the 21st century, nor any in Philadelphia.[13] Colonial wars of conquest, treaty betrayals and genocidal expulsion were written out of history.

Figure 4.3 Wampum Belt (Lenape) of the 'Great Treaty' of Shackamaxon in 1682 (photo courtesy: James Fenelon, taken at Philadelphia Museum of Modern Art, November 2021).

Leaders such as Pontiac (*Obwandiyag*) tried to rally Native Nations, by then the betrayed Lenape pushed into Ohio River country, into resistance wars, that played critical parts in the so-called French and Indian War (really the colonizing powers England and France with Native alliances) destroying traditional life and council agreements of the divided Indian Nations by internecine fratricide, weakening them to being vulnerable to the victorious colonizer, whether they were aligned with the winning power or not. The devastated and relocated Lenape represent colonial violence and genocidal destruction, in that after the 1763 Treaty of Paris ended colonial warfare (but not scalping) they were subject to English domination which flared into further warfare with American settlers. Supposedly banned by Royal Proclamation in the treaties, this was prelude to Revolutionary War erupting a few years later. The United States engaged the Lenape (Delaware) in its very first treaty, meant to form alliances with Indian Nations against the British in 1778, but just as their colonial forebears had (in fact the very same leaders) Franklin, Morris (one of two signers of all three constitutional documents), and Washington, almost immediately broke treaty provisions when unleashing frontier militias against Indian settlements. The Lenape attempted to form state-like governance (Deloria, 2022; Silver, 2008) with Native Nations in the region, only to realize they had negotiated away their true sovereign claim earlier, which the Americans understood all too well. This is why that first treaty was struck at Fort Pitt, far west of traditional Lenapehoking, over areas called 'Indian Reserve' and other terms by 1763 Royal Proclamation. The 1781 U.S. Articles of Confederation seemed to recognize this, but legalized takings, frontier violence and expanding settlements increased after the 1783 Treaty ended Revolutionary War. By 1784 and in 1785 Land Ordnances, settlers were taking Native lands with implied authority, formalized in the 1787 Northwest Ordnance, with land grants looking like Crown and Company land charters in the Virginia colony, described in Chapter 3 the Black.

In fact, processes throughout North America resemble the colonial invasions or intrusions of Jamestown and Plymouth, not to mention U.S. expansions into Northwest territories of Indiana and Ohio, southern regions of Alabama and Mississippi, or even Montreal and Detroit in Canada, in four steps – (1) establish forts in regions of strong Indian nations, (2) bring in settler-colonists on the heels of expanded trade networks or extraction operations (treaty-making, corporate formation, i.e. Hudson's Bay Company), (3) create settlements that expand over Native lands coming into sharp conflict with Anglo settlers protected by policing military forces, leading to colonial violence, war (including over changing ecological landscapes) and (4) establish a dominant sovereignty by the invading society over reduced if not eliminated (historically 'erased') Indigenous nations or tribes, negotiating with regional (state, provincial) governments operating under a federal (or crown) sovereign authority with plenary power. In other words, colonization reduced nations and societies into tribal groups answering to dominant governments representing larger, mainstream populations of White, Anglo or European settlers. The United States would replicate this process over and over again, while calling itself a new independent country (entirely formed on Native Nation lands) and calling its immigrating/invading peoples pioneer 'settlers' and itself as revolutionary against colonizer governments (England), which befuddles many historians and social theory to this day. Once the continental takeover was relatively complete, and Native Nation resistance had been eliminated by the turn of the century (circa 1890 next book) with race-based slavery driven into history, the United States could and did present itself as a democratic, freedom loving country with individual citizenship rights and a competitive market-based economy. It is transition from colonial governance to a newly independent government that facilitates this. To that discussion we now turn, using the new nation as a fulcrum toward the following two and a half centuries, into the 21st century (Figure 4.4).

The English colonies of America were well on the way toward breaking from the motherland during the French and Indian War. The proclamation line of 1763 was practical and political. With the French driven out of the Saint Lawrence River region, the British had only their own colonials to contest control or sovereignty over the region. Although Native Nations were strong and capable of winning battles, they were unable to successfully resist hegemonic invasion of their lands. Yet it is the 1790 census, the nation's first, that tells us the real story, in connection to the creation of the new country over Native traditional lands. We return to this later.

We must consider two socio-political developments during the constitutional formation period of the U.S. government: first, the structure of the new government, and second, the racial separation of powers built into that structure. These developments that are by choice, by design, become important elements of the new society – politically, economically, culturally.

First, we consider the people's House (of Representatives) with direct ties to a segment of the population – white male property owners. This would appear to be the most democratic political assembly – with comparison to the House of Commons in England. Rowdy and difficult for Elite to control, initial legislation starts here (the Haudenosaunee Confederation influenced this too).

Then we have the Senate with an elite tie to state governments, each ex-colony getting two seats, regardless of size. This body is also, of course, elected by white men. Here interplay is between power brokers in the states and the federal acceptance of legislation, guaranteeing that elite and state interests are always taken into consideration. The Senate has a corollary with the House of Lords in England (at least historically), with its ties to peerage, land ownership and property.[14]

The Long Arc of the Doctrine of Discovery – Part 3: The Making of WASP America

Transition toward European-Christian laws, social policies, political structures in the United States denies its colonial roots and its racist orientation toward labor and land.

5 – English colonies rise up – challenge England's supremacy and sovereignty.

1763 Treaty of Paris – settling French and Indian War, designating sovereign lands as English Crown Colonies (others as Spain, France, Netherlands) without recognizing Native Nations[a] (like the Westphalia treaty, European nations were only full sovereign in treaties with Natives).

1763 Royal Proclamation – restricting Virginia Land companies and other settlements from land grants as colonial expansion westward (Indian Reserve) especially Ohio and Canada.[b]

1776 Declaration of Independence – authorizing militias/armies, declare continental elites in charge, no specific reference to slavery or Native Nations only to 'merciless Indian Savages' designating them non-Christian (pagans), outside civilized moral laws, invisible as non-citizens.

1778 Treaty of Fort Pitt – first Treaty (with Delawares, or Lenape) by the United States.

6 – Discovery, Dehumanizing, Dominance – Supremacy and Sovereignty.

1781 Articles of Confederation – Supremacy to Congress, Sovereignty to States (ex-colonies) – Discovery background, recognizes Native Nations through Treaties[c] but not Africans.

1783 Treaty of Paris – authorizing **independent United States as coastal America – France, Spain and England** to retain lands in North America (without Native Nations or Africans).[d] (later three-fifths apportionment for [Black] slaves for political representation, tax purposes).[e]

1784–1785 Land Ordinance – creates mechanism for land transfers/takings.

1787 Northwest Ordnance – puts Territory controls on Native Nations (added Southwest 1790) – operationalizes American settlement rights to claim lands, form new states (Indians not taxed).

1787–1789 Constitutional Convention(s)[f] (establishes electoral college, states rights) – institutes elite control of presidency, whites vote over Blacks (3/5 clause),[g] excluding Indians 'not taxed' (therefore not represented), regulates Indian trade in the Commerce Clause.

1790 Naturalization Act limits citizenship to 'free white person …of good character' (men) **Census** nominalizes only Whites, Slaves and Other Free Persons (holds for another 70 years).

1790 Constitutional Authority in Three Powers (seats the Supreme Court) cements new nation – total Race (white) Gender (male) Class (property owner) domination of politics and law.

(1776–1792) Scientific Racism Notes Inferior Sub-species (enumerates population slavery, genocide) – provides rationale for holding people as property and seizing land as civilizational domains, along with plantation agriculture and capital investment, helps launch modern world-system.

Figure 4.4 Chart – Long Arc of Doctrine of Discovery: Part (3)–5 and 6.

a The quest to take the northwest territories, with multiple colonies claiming it as their own, led England to set aside the region, ostensibly for tribal nations to have for their own, but in reality because they could no longer defend it, with France no longer in competition with the English colonists and Indian Nations, freeing up the colonial elites to support settlers and militias invading the territory and claiming it for their own, which is precisely what they did.

b Many scholars and Native Nations view the Royal Proclamation and the Treaty of Niagara of 1764 as establishing 'covenant chain' upon which all laws between England and the Nations named in the treaties would be respected; however in the northern 13 colonies of the soon to be United States, leaders like Washington always viewed it as a temporary appeasement of the Indians. Certainly Washington's attacks during and after the Revolutionary War bore this out, so that England and Canada did recognize these relations, while the early United States did not. I take a different interpretation of how this was playing out, in that with France out of the picture with the 1763 Treaty of Paris, it was abundantly clear that the colonies wanted to expand over the territory, and were increasingly independent in making those claims. Consider Ohio, Loyal and Mississippi land Companies (operating under Virginia Company charter) that had lost land grant settlements in the 1763 Treaty and Proclamation, the Ohio Company having direct ties to Virginia aristocratic elites; Eugene M. Del Papa, "The Royal Proclamation of 1763: Its Effect upon Virginia Land Companies" *The Virginia Magazine of History and Biography*, Vol. 83, No. 4 (Oct., 1975), pp. 406–411.

c Maryland delayed the final signing or ratification, holding out that other colonial States would not have rights to land west of the Ohio river, the same territory both Treaties of Paris were concerned about.

d England did insist that the territories around Ohio, west and north of the river, and indeed all territory east of the Mississippi, would be under the control of Indian tribes, who would be shown the utmost respect. Remember, this is the same England conducting genocidal wars in New England, who was 'quitting' the region, unable to dominate.

e White southerners controlled the 3/5 representation for Black slaves, White northerners benefited from taxing Black slaves as property – neither north nor south was in the interest of Blacks as people or property.

f It is interesting to compare the Electoral College and the 3/5 compromise with The New Laws and the decades-old *Leyes de Burgos* (Laws of Burgos), issued by King Ferdinand II of Aragon on December 27, 1512. These laws were intended to control relations between Spaniards and recently conquered indigenous peoples of the New World. These are regarded as the first humanitarian laws in the New World (since they gave any rights at all, but they were not fully implemented because of opposition by powerful colonists, similar to the slave-holding South of the United States).

g Article I, Section 2 of the U.S. Constitution states:

> Representatives and direct Taxes shall be apportioned among the several States which may be included within this Union, according to their respective Numbers, which shall be determined by adding to the whole Number of free Persons, including those bound to Service for a Term of Years, and excluding Indians not taxed, three fifths of all other Persons.

The 'other Persons' were slaves... The 1787 Constitutional Convention addressed apportionment in the House of Representatives and the number of electoral votes each state would have in presidential elections based on a state's population. The Southern states wanted to count the entire slave population to increase their number of members of Congress. The Northern delegates and others opposed to slavery wanted to count only free persons, including free blacks in the North and South. (we must remember that White owners controlled the 3/5 votes in the South, working against the interest of Blacks)

Figure 4.4 (Continued)

Then there is an Executive (President) – which becomes the true power broker of the new nation, taking control similar to parliamentary monarchs, already contended in European countries.[15]

The framers of the (U.S.) constitution *did not trust* popular election for this most powerful post, even though only white men could vote – for Representatives and Senators, which would create a limited Presidency or Prime Minister – nor did they design a direct vote by 'the people' meaning white men[16] (of property). Instead, the framers constructed an electoral college, based on a mix of both the House of Representatives (population based) as a number of electors (to the college) and a complicated relationship to states through Senators (based on each state naming electors).

We must remember both the House and Senate were entirely constructed by, and made up by (tax-paying) white men. The framers (founding fathers if you will) did not trust even this highly racialized election process to choose the Chief Executive. The electoral college they created provided some critical features for the new government that a 'popular' election would not (avoiding Haudenosaunee five or six nation representative councils). These are as follows:

> First, it allowed state governments a direct hand in presidential elections, protecting "interests" really the elite of those states, through an elector naming process refined over the years. Although only white men could vote (see note *xxiii*, as there were fewer Blacks in the north, and Indians were made invisible) the political-economy of the new nation-state, racially constructed, would further be protected through determining a second crucial feature – whether Black slaves would be represented and by whom. As we will see shortly in the 1790 census, this was a much bigger issue for southern states. (Here it also deviates from Haudenosaunee pluri-nationality)

Second, this system allowed racialized representation to work against the interests of some of the populace, i.e. Blacks, who were also (mainly) property. We underscore the importance to see the electoral college guaranteed reproduction of race-based slavery, and attendant discriminatory institutions, most of which we continue to have with us in one form or another up to today.

Since this was as much an economic endeavor as a political concern, the electoral college allowed for the continued taxation of men and women as property, note the census does not distinguish the gender of slaves, nor of Other Free persons, even while it denied them any and all representation, ignoring the key revolutionary grievance – 'taxation without representation.' This argument (which was always more economic than political) is why the three-fifths compromise, already worked out for Representative purposes in the national government, would be brought back by apportionment (Black

slaves were counted as three-fifth of a whole count for creating electors –
bringing taxes back in, as they were to be counted as three-fifths of property
that could be taxed).[17]

The northern states demanded the taxation clauses, as it was an important
revenue stream for the national government (at a time when there was great
need for it). Although a near total racist construction (at least for the South)
based partly on taxation that was built into the presidential election, the
founding framers did not trust *even* this system to produce leaders for elite
interests, so, they built a back door into the selection process – the electoral
college could elect, or appoint, whoever they wanted (elector votes could
bind, or not, their votes by state mandates).[18]

This last point, based on a racist political-economic construction of the
electoral college process, uncovers hidden purposes of colonial elites about
to take power. The majority of slave owners, the rest beneficiaries of related
profiteering systems, such as the circuit or dual triangle trade, wanted to
assure their interests, racialized capitalism in formation, would be dominant.
Supremacy and sovereignty were both built into the national government
and were surpassed by an Elite (wealthy capitalists) of the day, controlling
every aspect of the nation's governance.

This is also why the President and the Congress were to represent the
now reconstituted colonial elite over a most important political-economic
issue of the day – new territories (north and south) just west of the newly
minted United States, ripe for picking and plunder.

All this was reflected early on in the 1763 treaty, was directly addressed in
the Declaration of Independence and was of paramount concern in the 1783
treaty conventions. The Indian nations, rendered invisible through discovery
and savagery, would need to be conquered and colonized, just as the British
had been doing for the previous 250 years of colonization. The nation would
have to determine if these new states would be slave-holding, or not.[19]
Although the newly constituted United States used the Haudenosaunee
bundled arrows to show strength of one, many peoples standing in unity, *it
failed to produce* inclusive plurinationalism, OR blended sovereignty like the
five or six nations, each with its own fully represented councils.

No better evidence exists, than where we social scientists always begin and
end – the U.S. Census of the population, who is named and who is not, and
for what purposes. We will take a look at the first census in 1790 at the end
of this chapter, and the end of this book that marks a transition toward the
second half of the creation of America and the modern world-system. For
now, let us observe its resonance with what we have seen in the constitutional formation of the country, at its birth. Native Nations essentially don't
exist in the census or constitution, except as Indians not yet fully 'civilized'
and on the way toward elimination or absorption as ethnic minorities.

Africans as such are also disappearing at this time, becoming Blacks whose
centrality to socio-economics noted in the constitution mostly exists as

slaves nominalized in the census by their comparative numbers in states. The founding framers basically dodged the question of whether they are property, or people, and leaves them three-fifth of both, misrepresenting all in the process.

Whites were formally stated as the only people who count, who can vote, and who will be future citizens of the country. The census wants to know the number of men, women and their age if white men. Supremacy by race (not ethnicity, i.e. Irish) and gender are made clear. All struggles for socio-political representation flow from this point of race, gender and class dominance.

Comparative Colonies, Racism, Revolution and Nation-Building

Here we make some rather basic observations about colonies from a comparative method, identifying the use of large systems of racial religious colonization, so-called revolutionary discourse, and the racist Nation-building that resulted in the United States of North America. Hispaniola (Ayiti, Espanola, Dominican Republic/Haiti) and Ireland (undergoing colonization, later separated by Colonizing religions) are our two major cases. Both are large islands, with key differences being between the Colonizers (Spain/ France as Catholic; England as Protestant) and racialization (Haiti as a Black nation, Ireland as Catholic European – in the United States as white).

First there is size, with Ireland (32.5+ square miles) a little larger than Hispaniola (29K+ square miles).[20] Their initial colonizing demographics are near opposite, in 1500 Ireland starts with over a million and by 1700 has nearly three million inhabitants, while around 1500 (1494) Hispaniola starts about 2–3 million and by 1700 has well under a million inhabitants (majority Black slaves) undergoing waves of colonization by Spanish colonial conquest and France's racial colonization, while England moves for a more intense colonial domination over Ireland starting about 1500. Emigration out of Ireland by suppressed Gaelic Catholics starts rising along with the English colonies in the Americas, on Caribbean islands, in Canada and Virginia territories. What we observe is demographic power of highly racialized colonization – with a destructive collapse of the Native population of Hispaniola and their partial replacement with enslaved Africans, under control of a relatively small number of Europeans (first Spanish, then French and others). With Ireland we see an increasingly oppressive colonization by the English, typified by religion (Protestant over Catholic) forcing Gaelic Irish to become part of a large emigration to colonies (whether as indentured servants, penal law labor, or contract labor settlers), that would become a flood in the mid-19th century when famine and war pressures pushed out millions.

The presence of systemic colonial racism was a key difference between the two colonies. Once Africans were enslaved in the Americas as Black, they had little opportunity for mobility or even freedom, since the majority of the colonizing European countries were engaged with or profiting from the great racialization patterns being imposed on a continental scale. However, Irish, English and other Anglo Americans could become settlers, especially in the frontier areas, where they could become landholders with all rights, and later citizens of the new countries. The critical difference with Ireland was being of European origin, not of African or Native peoples. Transoceanic global colonizing initially had violent demographic and geo-physical effects on colonized and colonizer lands alike, with millions dying of famine, war and imposed fealty, across Ireland based on religious affiliation, much like the religious wars of northern Europe, producing millions of casualties. We also see deforestation and natural resource extraction on Ireland and Hispaniola, marked between 1500 and 1700, when the North American colonies were developed as primary producers of timber (ship-building), agricultural commodities, and other resources to fuel the growing industries and economies of Europe, especially England. Settler populations, growing out of the original colonization, became the base skilled labor force who would engage in frontier expansion and creation of the new towns and cities of empire. They also were the 'volunteers' in settler militias, first seen in the New England Indian wars, later also employed to put down slave rebellions. Enslaved labor forces were entirely racialized, mostly African descent as Blacks with some mixed-race, non-white and local Native labor force. These two primary intersections of Race and Class, along with gender in family construction, produced the racial divisions of Indian, Black and Anglo (White) that evolved into the United States.

Comparison of Island Colonies – *Size, Geo-Political Strategy, Demographics, Migrations*

The colonization of Ireland in many ways prefigures that of the Americas with early movement of English settlers into a region where land and control was already alienated from the original inhabitants, Gaelic Irish. Then sub-ordination/supremacy was enacted through institutional discrimination – penal laws over property ownership, church, language, intermarriage and political rights – including the establishment of plantations where land alienation/control moved to English elites with agricultural markets feeding the central economy, or metropole.

The graph[21] in Figure 4.5 shows Ireland's population since 1100.[22]

Emigration was a part of Irish history, more than most other countries in the world.[23]

Besides considerably higher death rates over the Indigenous Catholic Gaelic Irish, these systems also produced large outmigration of Gaelic Irish, further weakening resistance and changing demographics toward English control in capitol areas, i.e. Dublin, and around large plantations, i.e. Ulster.

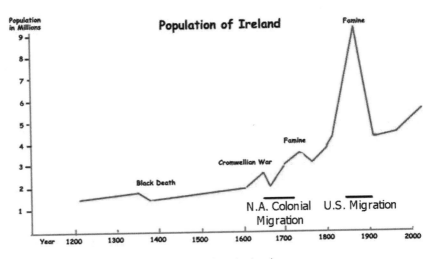

Figure 4.5 Ireland's population since 1100 (graph chart).

Many Gaelic Irish were taken prisoner to Caribbean islands or other English colonies, even as others found ways to the Americas as contract labor and frontier forces against Indians. Another dynamic out of Ulster was middlemen minority managers moving into the new region of race-based plantations, i.e. Scots Irish (acting as Protestant overseers – not initially land-owners) over Africans in the colonies. They played critical parts in militias – slave patrols in the south, Indian raiders in the north. Both of these forces contributed ultimately to racial formation in colonial America and later the United States, congealing these populations under White.

Comparative Colonization – Hayiti and Ireland

We observe two or more basic differences between these colonies: race/racism vs. ethnicity, religious, from a north Atlantic perspective; and demographic collapse/replacement versus settler colonial domination without population replacement.

In other words, advent of at first the Indian (Haiti) – who is to be destroyed to take the land – and secondly the Black – who is to be a manipulated labor force with no claim to the land – demonstrates the de-civilizing/dehumanizing process controlling Race formation in its early stages. Whereas, in comparison to a roughly equivalent island land mass and a comparative (Indigenous) population, the Gaelic Irish (Catholic) undergo ethnic (religious–political) domination including military conquest and colonization but are not effectively fully replaced (without a full collapse from disease). As a fuller Race paradigm emerges in western European – American societies, it could not be effectively deployed to alienate Irish as a lower order Race, though the English did try (Curtis, 1997), through dehumanizing and de-civilizing strategies used against Natives and Africans.[24] The Irish at first have a mid-level position as ethnic Europeans, which moves into a mainstream category by the late 19th early 20th centuries.

The Penal Laws and Plantations of Ireland – Transplanted to Racial Laws of America (U.S.)

English partial colonization of Ireland had developed the Pale – the King's own country under sovereignty not unlike the beachhead colonies of Jamestown or Plymouth, and Anglo Irish lords under English authority, for much of the rest of the countryside expanding over Gaelic lands. With the Tudor conquest colonization of the island, England developed plantations over land, political and church supremacy over forced assimilation by subordinating Gaelic chieftain earls, and suppression of the general populace by a series of laws restricting access and human rights of the broader Catholic Gaelic Irish. Fashioned after pre-colonization Kilkenny laws, following Protestant Ascendancy of pure cultural domination, penal laws circumscribed all social behavior of dominated groups, reducing their political, economic and cultural positions in society. Later, they would be models of colonizing with the added characterization by race.

Some English Penal Laws over Ireland:

Education bans on Catholics, from foreign education, elite universities, leadership, teaching

Exclusion of Catholics from most public offices (90% of population excluded Catholics).

Ban on intermarriage (Catholics with Protestants) and some church services (sinforming)

Catholics barred from holding firearms or serving in the armed forces

Bar from membership in government (Parliament) and legal professions (judiciary, lawyer)

Exclusion from voting (disenfranchising – excluded most of the population)

Ban on Catholic buying and some inheritance (Popery) of lands (taxation imposed)

Ban conversions from Protestant to Catholicism (forfeiture of lands and rights as above)

Ban against custody of orphans, and owning property of higher value (and horses)

Registration of priests, limitations to church building (of wood, away from main roads)

Clearly these forms of institutional discrimination could be, and were, adapted to the highly racialized systems in the American colonies, and later inculcated into U.S. race laws. Just as with the plantation system, English colonial overlords and Anglo-Irish overseers also determined agricultural crops, market prices and individual consumption (O'Hearn, 2001), leading to starvation, extreme poverty and famine (Figures 4.6).[25]

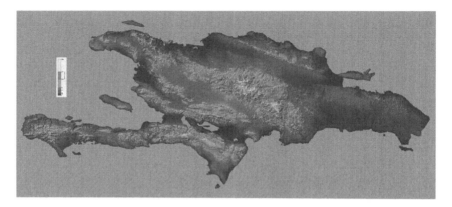

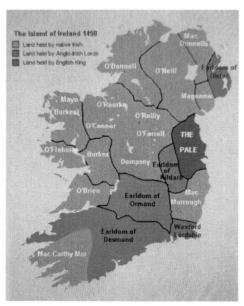

Figure 4.6 (a) Map of Hispaniola (topographic) and (b) map of Ireland – 1450 (political).

Hispaniola (Ayiti, San Domingue, Haiti) – Dominican Republic Eastern Half of island[26]

Ireland -1450 – note Ulster in the northeast quadrant where some of the first plantations were later developed and employed; the Pale where the Crown of England was sovereign (where Dublin is today) and Anglo-Irish control of the southern, lowland regions. Treaties like Etaples (1492) freed up English forces to expand over the entire island, after that armies under Lords like Cromwell had used scorched earth against the resistance, putting English domination as tantamount, with great loss of life of Catholics, increasing ethnic emigration that continued for hundreds of years, culminating in 19th century waves to America where racialization took hold in identity shifts to becoming White. The opposite unfolded in Haiti and other Caribbean countries where race slavery caused immigrants to be labeled Black thus inferior, or ex-colons as White (dominants), in addition to slave-holding states cutting off global trade.[27]

Not only were the Gaelic Irish Catholics of the same religious origins as all of Europe, but phenotypically and socio-culturally they were not, in any meaningful way, different from the colonizer – England. This may be the most important, since England passed discriminatory laws.

Within the Penal Laws, which are based solely on one's ethnic descent, a means or method of legal and societal discrimination and stratification arose for a primary purpose of raising a super-ordinated colonizer/settler elite while maintaining an ethnically subordinated (Indigenous) population, as servile and incompetent at keeping land and liberty. Essentially, the Penal Laws are resurrected from their earlier, pre-Columbian formation, and used in all the colonies, then undergoing intense racialization. Of course, they cannot hold in Ireland, lasting longer in the northern (Ulster) provinces with Scots middlemen, than on the main island central regions. Resistance to and rebellion against the Penal Laws played a major part in the English Civil War that dethroned and executed the King of England, and forced parliamentary controls over taxes, elections, and constitutional rule by the monarch.

Similar penal laws were applied in heavily racialized forms in Virginia and New England colonies, where they took firm hold lasting into the U.S. formation period, becoming draconian, violent and severe, especially in the militias. Based on race in the Caribbean, none were more evident than the western European powers of the Dutch, French and English who began to harden them into racism, as France did in a Code Noir which covered more than three-quarters of the land base now called Haiti. There is a perfect comparative case in its neighbor, the Dominican Republic, where Spanish Catholic systems failed to use the full long-term power of Race (although highly oppressive as documented in this and previous chapters). While compelling, we must turn to the North American mainland to see the full intersectional power of race laws, capitalist economy, sovereignty and ethno-religious patriarchal domination.

Territorial Expansion – Ordnances over Land, Slavery, Labor, Citizenship

Almost from the onset of colonial expansion since the early 1700s, it was obvious that England would be a fading power with less influence in the region south of the Great Lakes, while the fledgling United States literally bordered the region and was making claims by individual states. The 1763 Proclamation line by England was an ironic attempt to control the colonies from taking over, which the English even referred to as Indian Reserve, requiring respect for Native nations, whose lands could not (supposedly) be entered (or settled) without permission (see Figure 4.12).

This is the primary rationale for the Declaration of Independence (written by Thomas Jefferson), calling Native peoples 'merciless Indian savages' supported by their uncivilized way of warfare, which in fact was how English colonists eliminated Native resistance, starting with John Smith's 'dead carcasses' through the Pequot and later Wampanoag wars in the north, that laid to waste entire villages regardless of gender or age. American authors were calling upon the Discovery claims of Papal bulls and Caribbean conquest, over non-Christian 'savages' without civilized discourse or diplomacy, to give credence for breaking treaties or agreements, which continued through the Indian wars right up to Wounded Knee one hundred years later.

With the United States constitutional construction complete, the Northwest Ordnance invoked the constitution to legitimate a land grab with language remarkably similar to the 1763 English proclamations decades earlier:

> With utmost good faith shall always be observed toward the Indians; their lands and property shall never be taken from them without their consent; and in their property, rights, and liberty they never shall be invaded or disturbed unless in just and lawful wars authorized by Congress; but laws founded in justice and humanity shall, from time to time, be made, for preventing wrongs being done to them and for preserving peace and friendship with them.
>
> (Northwest Ordnance, enacted by Congress in 1787)

This act of supremacy over Native nations was created, like the Requerimiento by the Spanish, working in conjunction with Church authority, to declare sovereignty over the land and people. Led by the now modern American militias, originally formed under George Rogers Clark as the rangers who often wiped out entire Native communities, these special forces ravaged lands from the Ohio river to the Illinois valleys, preparing for a more formal neo-colonization and invasion.

What is less known is its counterpart 1790 Southwest Ordnance, passed a few years later. Again, sovereignty and supremacy lay at the heart of expansion, except this time a critical issue was allowing African peoples to be turned into Black slaves, who would provide the cheap labor for a new country. Extension of the Southwest Ordnance[28] then reproduced race-based slavery, with a full scale apparatus of building up slave populations for large-scale plantations on land violently wrested from Native nations – Barber's *stolen hands on stolen lands*. Racial supremacy was key to this system, over Africans and Natives, and so state sovereignty was tantamount to the deeply racist ex-colony, becoming part of a larger system alluding to freedom and democracy for its dominant population, guaranteeing the South to become the home of White Supremacy.

Whereas we see Pennsylvania and even Massachusetts trying to claim the Ohio territory for themselves, and the deeply contested region that became Kentucky attempted takeover by Virginia (along with what became Tennessee, they declared nation independence as Franklin, which could not stand under the United States expansion), further south of the Ohio river into the mountains and forests, both Georgia and Carolina attempted claims westward, even to the Mississippi river. The map in Figure 4.7 draws out some of these claims as cessions, which otherwise have Spanish and British 'possessions' as the other sovereigns. Nowhere are any Native nations even mentioned, much less accorded the rights to cede land, even when under treaty obligations. The two Ordnances set up the means for (newly acquired) territory to become states, in the north as burgeoning industry, and in the south as agricultural economies with (slave) plantations.

Two key issues are illustrated in Figure 4.7: the new states were trying to expand westward and lay claim to lands contested with Native nations, without even mentioning them; and main European colonizing countries were allocated 'possession' of vast tracts of lands where Native nations continued to exist in strong numbers. In other words, the U.S. and European countries were engaged in colonial warfare and conquest over North America, conveniently leaving out or ignoring the most important part of their actions – Native Americans as nations with pre-existing claims to the land, with or without cessions. Additionally, the southeastern nations were quickly moving toward plantation economies, which seemed to require enslaving Africans as Blacks.

Critical to all land appropriation occurring west of the colonies, now the fledgling United States, were the means of legitimizing the takings, and their transfer from Native Nations control to U.S. individual control or ownership, realized through the Land Ordinance of 1785, based on the 1784 Ordnances, by the Continental Congress. These ordnances essentially were legalized land grabs, mechanisms for creating land titles for individual

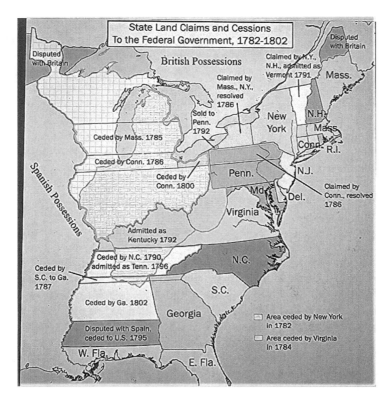

Figure 4.7 Eastern North America with U.S. claims 1782–1802. United States, States, European colonizers, claims and 'cessions' 1790 in 10 years. Note: Wikimedia commons, by Kmusser "This map showing state land claims and cessions from 1782 to 1802."

American citizens that provided taxable sales for the national treasury and effectively occupied what would otherwise be contested territories. They began an organized taking of land for individual plantation-based occupation in the south (first by frontiersman 'sales' followed by consolidation into larger holdings) and for community-based 'townships' in the north,[29] driving westward expansion of the United States after the American Revolution. The 1787 Northwest and 1790 Southwest Ordnances were the political mechanism or legal rationalization for taking vast territories away from Native Nations already holding the land (and broader ecosphere) and transferring title and occupation rights to the United States that produced a revenue stream (monetizing land values) for the new government. Ultimately, Land Ordnance laws would survey territories and entire regions, transferring occupancy rights from Native Nations to the United States covering more than three quarters of the continental land-base of the growing country, amounting to a vast wealth transfer, or extraction, designed and based on earlier colonial laws, especially the land grants from English-based companies. This discussion is advanced in the my next book, from 1776 to 2020 with a special focus on the great 19th century land-takings across the 'western' United States (like the frontier, always a moving boundary, with Ohio territory being the Midwest at first, likewise Mississippi in the south, going to and crossing the great river by the same name).

Dehumanization – *From Slave Voyages to Plantations, from Nations to Disappearing Tribes*

Dehumanization is usually accomplished through a process for particular purposes, such as the denial of Human rights in taking and creating slaves, followed by their forced labor on plantations, or in mines. Venture Smith tells his own story of being enslaved in Africa, how this used 'seasoning' and death on a middle passage voyage and how many if not most of his rights were violated in American slave systems (though he did win his freedom).[30] Another system was used against Native peoples by denying their nationalism, cutting rights to freedom, land and self-determination, without access to courts or adjudication because of their racial status. Together, the larger dehumanization processes of genocide and culturicide are also important to understand as they legitimate, or sometimes make invisible, the systemic nature of enslavement, genocidal land takings and a legal system that honors no claims for those enslaved or removed. The Black is dehumanized into bondage, the Indian as the savage original habitant – neither can be Citizens for different reasons in a new United States continuing practices of dehumanization.

As the old adage goes, Possession is nine-tenths of the law. The other tenth is denial of the rights of Africans and Native peoples, swept up in a process of nation –building. Examples of places where such a denial of rights did not occur, would include St. Augustine, held by Spain, earlier embattled, already intercultural, multiracial, important as a place for fugitive ex-slaves, along with much of Florida where otherwise escaped slaves often hooked up with Indian nations in complex ways, especially resistance camps against forays from the new U.S. forces. This had already occurred in Hispaniola with the Tainos in the mountains, and other islands, proving to be a problem in the American South, where racial divisions were already implanted, leaving – Indian, Black, White – as three critically important racial constructions, each codified against mulattos (as in Haiti, and among the French), as early essentialist racist constructions.

As late as the 1730s and on to mid-century, immigrants were being tendered both as bondage on their journey, and in some cases as indentured servants or indebted settlers who were not released until payment was made, such as the German Dutch shippees 'sold' in the 1750 port of Philadelphia, future constitution city, that also regularly discharged enslaved Africans.[31]

Lord General Amherst famously moved on calls for the extirpation of Native peoples resisting frontier expansion using biological warfare by giving out smallpox infected blankets.[32]

Within 12 years, the colonial definitions of race for enslavement and suppression, hardened into three main groups – Indian, Black and White. By the 1763 English proclamation colonials were distinguished by race, specifically for interior areas ongoing colonization, and later by the United States in the Northwest and then Southwest Ordnances. By 1790 the U.S. Constitution delineated who could be racially dehumanized by perceived race – restricting citizenship to white males – not having the privileged status of an ethnically, racially homogenous homeland population.[33]

The Haitian revolution was underway but still far away from any success that seemed threatening to slave societies such as the United States. As already observed, racist systems can and do develop in democratic oriented societies, such as the United States. These societies tend to rationalize how their systems came about, that it was through deep colonial transformation. The reproduction of those systems was to create a single independent union, simply accepting the intense social stratification of racist systems, especially in slavery and an exclusion of citizenship by race, as being both natural and religiously ordained. It is patently obvious that constitutional political philosophy contributed to denial and distorted perversion of human rights, using language that would grow into Manifest Destiny and straight-out genocide in California. So, here we have considered some of an array of practices and policies implemented during, before and after founding of the United States to illustrate this point.

As we say in both of the chapters preceding this, race-based slavery began in a 'New World' conquest, initially over newly invaded and conquered Indigenous peoples, and was quickly extended to Africans as Blacks, although rarely tightly categorized. In fact both of these systems were seen in their most extreme in Brazil by the Portuguese, and yet no clearly demarcated system of race stratification emerged in that country, although racial and ethnic groups experience systemic wide stratification with porous boundaries that generated considerable inequality. White ethnic immigrants were pouring into the new country with ideas of freedom, and to an extent, the hope of gaining land and rights unavailable in their home nations.

By now in English colonies and later afterbirth of the United States and Canada, phobias characterized[34] North American attitudes toward intermarriage with people of African ancestry. This would be made into miscegenation laws in the colonies, in the early United States, and many states of the United States, taking sundry shapes against other 'people of color' such as in California proscribing against Asians and Mexicans.

Various Christian groups, significantly harkening back to Bartolome de Las Cases in the 1550s, also began to criticize racial slavery, with expected reactions and rationalizations in defense of its practices. In the United

States explicit racism as an ideology of inherent black inferiority re-emerged in reaction to rising northern abolitionism in the 1830s. Deeper institutionalization of racism toward Blacks was further found in various laws and statutes that refused to give the freedoms of citizenship and other 'men' throughout the United States, finally nationalized in the Dred Scott decision (brought 1846, decided 1857) which found that free blacks could not be citizens of the United States. Of course, Indians were not citizens either, unless they renounced their tribal heritage, and sometimes even that didn't work out. By this time, the deepest ideologies of racism toward Blacks, initially found in anti-Indian Nation racism and discrimination, had become (and would stay for another 100 years) foundational to the entire system. Blacks were associated in the Western (white) mind with "the primitive, backwards, savagery of Africa, as an inherently unprogressive race" (Frederickson, 2002).

Of course, this is a false association with the societies and civilizations of Africa. Black people were stigmatized by the 17th-century Virginia laws as servile and inferior, effectively changing legal rationales for slavery from heathenism to heathen ancestry with racist functions, such as blood purity. More explicit and autonomous racism emerged in the 18th and 19th centuries because the 'popular mind' tended to conflate religion and race (as rationale for slavery; Fredrickson, 2002). Thus culture, in guise of religion and ideologies of the origins of civilization, combined to reinforce the deepest mindsets of racist thinking. A counterpoint is explained in examples of the Spanish Inquisition and colonization of America, where this movement had already been made, under Church Authority found in the Papal Bulls and states (or Prince's) Rights to Conquest, reaffirmed in Westphalia (as treaty). While it is true the popular 'mind' or mainstream ideologies did need to conflate religion and race (as argued by Spain in the Burgos Laws, and formally at Valladolid), what Virginia did was to fully institutionalize the social practices of slavery as racism, and allow religion to avoid the central problem of the humanity of Black slaves, which Spain and the Catholic Church had already addressed with Indians. So, government (institutions and the state), society (popular and elite) and religion (Protestant, Catholic, basic Christian) conspired in a new country, the United States, to rationalize racial slavery and genocidal conquest. As the country, and indeed all of Europe, matured, the U.S. and European society had to find a way to make these otherwise noxious practices reasonable. This was done through concepts we now call scientific racism.

The Rise of Scientific Racism – An American Story

Another aspect of the contemporary world-system that has grown out of this century or two of colonial development leading to the United States (of America) is the co-inciding of science and society in terms of creating race and systemic racism, with the added category of *Americanus* (American Indian).

Many scholars placed the critical juncture for this scientific progress at or around the time of Darwin and mainstream thoughts around the evolution of species, somewhat separate from the societal sophistication often attributed to the same or similar dynamic. However, this thinking, and its aberrations, occurs much earlier, and is critically present at the creation of the United States. Carl Linnaeus is among the first biologists to attempt to classify a taxonomy of species (1735) and schematize or geographically identify different Races (1758), as problematic as that turned out to be.[35] An exceptional student follower Johann Blumenbach contributed to the scientific misidentification of a racial 'origin of species' with an implied hierarchy of 'taste' (Bourdieu, 1984) and geographic 'place' through identifying characteristic traits of 5 Races of mankind (clearly inductive in nature) that are in all actuality based on the colonial domination and deep Eurocentrism of the time (Painter, 2011).[36]

> Caucasian variety. I have taken the name of this variety from Mount Caucasus, both because its neighborhood, and especially its southern slope, produces the most beautiful race of men, I mean the Georgian; and because ... in that region, if anywhere, it seems we ought with the greatest probability to place the autochthones [original forms] of mankind.
> (Blumenback, 1795)[37]

His first work allows (late) enlightenment thinkers and socio-political philosophers to reify existing (and growing) inequalities and systems of domination (supremacist) clearly evident in the North American colonization by northern European powers, premier among them England. It is published in 1775–1776 and read by a new class of American thinkers, including Thomas Jefferson. Some years later, 1787, as if to follow a supremacist ordering of his first work, Blumenbach adds identification of European peoples as being Caucasian, a terms he simply creates. He extends Caucasian to the origins of the Races (species?) as the first (in 1795), with (lower order) races following outward as if in rough approximation of their distance from empire and Europe. Blumenbach, of course, had it exactly wrong on all counts. There are no clear differences between the so-called Races of man, and if one was to determine their origin points it would likely be central Africa with travels throughout Eurasia, Micronesia and even the Americas. This reasoning, incorrectly linked to growing colonial societies by the likes of Gould (1981) proved epic in its influence and application around the world, and notably New England. As Gould deceptively infers this to the creation and growth of freedom and democracy in America colonially and racially constructed, we observe the same conundrum as with the early Enlightenment – for whom?

Certainly there is no freedom and democracy for Native societies undergoing colonization, including the highly developed meso-American civilizations or the socio-politically advanced social systems that had grown out of North America. And, undeniably there is and would not be freedom and democracy for the African peoples enslaved and taken to the Americas to be exploited for their labor, racially identified as Blacks on the bottom of the newly created racial hierarchies, which proved to be so essential to the recent and coming revolutions on the continents and islands flanking the Atlantic (Figure 4.8).

Agency and Rationality, Race and Enlightenment

Figure 4.8 Leaders and icons of Resistance and Euro-American Revolution 1760–1790. (a) Pontiac (Obwandiyag)-Odawa resistance leader. John Mix Stanley, Public domain, via Wikimedia Commons. (b) Le Negre Incconu-Black Maroon (PauP Haiti). Created by Haitian sculptor Albert Mangonès. See Ira Berlin: *Generations of Captivity: A History of African-American Slaves* (2003) ['75,178'] Wikimedia Commons, CC BY 2.0 Creative Commons CC0 License. (c) Elizabeth Freeman – Mumbet. Susan Anne Ridley Sedgwick, Public domain, via Wikimedia Commons. (d) Thomas Paine – Common Sense. Wikimedia Commons: Auguste Millière, Public domain, via Wikimedia Commons-original at National Portrait Gallery: NPG 897 Thomas Paine in the National Portrait Gallery (anonymous).

Figure 4.8 (Continued)

Rationalization of Race, Capital and Politics: The Power of Mind and Society

The power of the mind (individuals) and society (groups in social systems) to rationalize their existence is all encompassing, and is perfect representation in the elite philosophic leaders of American Revolutionary thinking. The two great racial constructs at the time of formation of the country – Indian and Black – are rationalized in the enlightenment thinking in quite different ways. The Indian had to be cleverly subsumed into Native non-nations, who were without rationale thought in the original colonies, and as a threat, so the country could be prepared for ongoing invasion and destruction for their country. The United States had to deny Indian nations in order for it, the new nation, to expand its own land-base. The 'merciless Indian savages' referred to in the Declaration of Independence achieves these goals in one swift and terrible moniker. All wars – past and present – become 'just' and conducted in the name of civilization (Graeber and Wengrow, 2021). This inexorably leads to the ideologies of Manifest Destiny.

For the Black, the need (perceived) to retain social institutions of slavery while creating language of freedom and democracy, was met by simply ignoring their existence while creating laws and policies that would maintain their status of uncompensated labor and non-political participation. Thus enlightened thinkers created a system where Blacks could be treated as property, not people, and could be discounted and mis-represented in the infamous three-fifths rule. This brilliant but dehumanizing rationale act would come to be a central problem in the ongoing expansion of the United States for the next hundred years – with Haiti a simple 'denial' that the country or the revolution even existed (L. DuBois, 2004: 303).

These two systems of dehumanization would come to characterize internal struggle of the country then creating and hardening its third great racial construct – the White as dominant – that also undermines any rationale for democracy and freedom 'for all men' (continuing patriarchy) by super-ordination of the European male as superior in all society. This is also the foundation of white supremacy, which survives for 200 years in various guises – Reconstruction and Jim Crow south, support for Nazi Germany, apartheid colonization in South Africa, and has reared its ugly head once again in response to the BLM racial equity marches and demands of 2020. As before, though, we are getting ahead of ourselves.[38]

Carl Degler (Out of Our Past): "**No new social class came to power** through the door of the American Revolution. The men who engineered the revolt were largely members of **the colonial ruling class**." George Washington was the richest man in America. John Hancock was a prosperous Boston merchant. Benjamin Franklin was a wealthy printer. And so on …

(Zinn, 1977)

And they either held enslaved peoples or profited from markets and products of slavery. They all called for, or tolerated, the near total destruction of American Indian nations. Finally, not a one spoke for the full rights of women, except as they were 'represented' by the race and class position of their husbands and fathers, the patriarchy inherited from England. These were the Founding Fathers (well-off white men) who declared in their Declaration of Independence that the new country was founded on the 'Laws of Nature and of Nature's God entitle them' toward their freedom and a 'decent respect' to impel their separation from England. Of course, this independence was not accorded to African descent peoples or to the very Native Nations who had allowed them to settle upon the lands they now claimed.[39] Elizabeth Freeman (Mumbet) makes for a compelling example here, in challenging her own slavery, without any formal education or even literacy, and winning the case which upended Massachusetts race and slavery laws, vaulting it to the high abolition states.

With this in mind, and the colonial developments and upcoming conquest colonization headed westward, let us revisit the actual revolutions that produced the modern world-system, including a hegemonic rise first of England through world colonizing strategies, and the United States as its like-minded inheritance, through global neo-colonizing or neo-liberalism forms of economic and political control. The American Revolution was closely followed by the French Revolution (a 'real' revolution that eliminated the Old Guard and simple Monarchy, getting rid of slavery mostly as a by-product, then re-establishing it in the colonies) which led to the Haitian Revolution directly challenging European colonization and American racialization systems.

Three Revolutions

Three revolutions ushered in the great social change, supposedly about freedom, democracy, equality and fraternity for all men, women, from all cultures and peoples; yet the profound transition that brought this period into the modern world, is still dominated by capitalism, colonization past and present, and a ubiquitous patriarchal racism. We must revisit these revolutions to uncover this problem.

The United States of America – freedom from England, but reproduced Race, Gender, Class systems

The French Republic – universal citizenship, barred slavery with human rights, yet gave us Napoleon[40]

The Haitian Revolution – upending racist enslavement system, recoding race, yet ending in poverty

-----

Each revolution was accompanied with or followed by reactionary uprisings – where the status quo reproduced its preceding conditions – the United States with an Anglo elite, France with an imperial leader and a very complicated Haiti with race revenge killings. We will consider the United States, below in depth. France and the rise of Napoleon are connected to the windward passage of San Domingue (Haiti and Cuba) as colonial wealth holdings and in conjunction with the Louisiana territories of North America. Both phenomena were driven by ideologies and myths of 'purchase' including Protestant reasoning for a coming world order, and were held back by a Catholic Spanish-dominated colonization. These conditions set up the foundations for capitalism and the rules to the road of early colonizing. First, the United States is discussed, in taking English Protestant colonies and declaring Independence.

The United States institutionalized race-based slavery and a new scientific racism that delineated different races, deeply stratifying American society. By the latter 18th century one had to be black to be a slave in the American colonies. The United States reproduced the same system, so when Johann F. Blumenbach in 1776 (following Linnaeus in 1735) described all the 'varieties of mankind' as divided into fivefold subspecies, this was readily accepted by socio-political leaders and scientists alike.

Even so, the two great (American and French) revolutions had little other incentive to elaborate a systematic racist ideology for the purposes of maintaining domination. However, these countries would institute or constitute laws that kept subordinated groups from being full citizens of the new state[41] especially those of racial lines already existing in their societies (it was the reverse in Haiti's case).

Blumenbach had contributed to ideological and scientific racism by concluding that Caucasians were the original (beautiful) people, that all others 'degenerated' from. Among his early readers were the like of Thomas Jefferson, accepting a ready-made rationale for his plantations. Such 'scientific' evidence supported the (United States) country's three main races (species) as – whites, blacks, and American Indians.[42] Enlightenment thinking, with its delusions of universal freedoms and rights, would underscore a quasi-evolutionary perspective on Race as separate species and would develop supremacist ideologies and practices, where a single species perspective would underline social divisions – as in slavery, citizenship, and for conquest (genocidal) – which dominant thinking found to be unacceptable (even as the arguments raged). Thus, justifications for slavery and genocide institutionalized both the social practices as good for economies, and application into social thought and the sciences, even when early colleges, such as Harvard, were implicated in this strangest of all rationales, existing within its own charter, but now in conflict with the 'merciless savages' of the declaration of independence, or on Benjamin Franklin's 'hostiles' in press after the Scalp Act. Thinkers such as Thomas Jefferson embraced Blumenbach's separation of races as both foundational in the early biological sciences and a rationale for supremacist domination.

The reasoning was basically: if all peoples are descendant from the same ancestors – then, they are somewhat equal, or equitable in the eyes of the scientist; however, if these were different sub-species, separate 'human' lines of descent, that justifies a hierarchical construction of society, including slavery, conquest and colonization, with their subsequent domination and underlying supremacy. This became the intellectual heart of systemic racism (Figure 4.9).

What, to the American slave, is your 4th of July? I answer: a day that reveals to him, more than all other days in the year, the gross injustice and cruelty to which he is the constant victim. To him, your celebration is a sham; your boasted liberty, an unholy license; your national greatness, swelling vanity; your sounds of rejoicing are empty and heartless; your denunciations of tyrants, brass fronted impudence; your shouts of liberty and equality, hollow mockery; your prayers and hymns, your sermons and thanksgivings, with all your religious parade, and solemnity, are, to

(United States) – American – Revolution 4 – 2

There is much to praise and prevaricate over with the Patriots of the American Revolution, with the founding (fathers) of the Constitution, and the creation of a flexible yet grounded government over a set of fairly disparate colonies, in the face of European threats of wars. However, the pathways of the new country were well worn in racial domination and elites.

The United States form of government was not all that new, with tripartite forces already existing in the United Kingdom having pretty direct corollary – the House of Representatives with the House of Commons; a (House of) Lords with the Senate; the Executive (president) with a monarch, constrained by an English Civil War and deferring to Parliament under law. (Parliament's forces had defeated / executed Charles I, creating a constitutional monarchy.)

The United States was entirely formed by race, class, and gender – white men of property – which produced racialized capitalism. The founding framers were also deeply influenced by the Haudenosaunee Confederation of five nations, that also had a type of bicameral legal structures, with Younger brothers (Oneida and Cayuga nations) debating laws sent to Elder brothers (Mohawk and Seneca nations) who upon assent would pass on to the Central Fire Peacekeepers (Onondaga nation, modern forms have the Onondaga as Elder brothers too). While England had a dominant monoculture, the Haudenosaunee had a diversity of nations, producing a more democratic consensus governance than the elite, racialized United States. The U.S. revolution replaced English colonial structures with more flexible American forms, but also reproduced the racist economy and citizenship laws from colonial to U.S.A. rule. (whereas England always kept its enslavement systems external to the homelands, the United States internalized race-based slave labor and genocidal expansion, as legitimized structures.)

What became foundational to the new country (we could argue it did not have to go this way) was perfectly reflected in the final grievance of the Declaration of Independence – where it said King George (He) "has excited domestic insurrections amongst us, and has endeavored to bring on the inhabitants of our frontiers, the merciless Indian Savages, whose known rule of warfare, is an undistinguished destruction of all ages, sexes and conditions." Domestic referred to enslaved Blacks potentially revolting for "their" freedom with insurrections, quite carefully not named since so many, including Jefferson had railed against the evils of slavery, yet in referring to "their" frontiers, they do name the people as merciless Indian Savages. The frontier is the Northwest territory (first brought to bear in 1763 passed 1787) and Southwest territory (brought to bear in 1783 and passed 1790 extended to Mississippi territory in 1798) that would realize expansion of the country, again requiring, from the founders point of view, destruction of existing Native Nations and enslaved Black labor for plantations. We put this into the discourse in order to re-humanize both Africans and Natives, and as a comparative point in considering the other two revolutions that would also be critical to the development of capitalism and the modern world-system, the French and Haitian revolutions that truly pushed the boundaries of freedom and democracy.

Figure 4.9 American (U.S.) Revolution (text box).

him, mere bombast, fraud, deception, impiety, and hypocrisy — a thin veil to cover up crimes which would disgrace a nation of savages. There is not a nation on the earth guilty of practices, more shocking and bloody, than are the people of these United States, at this very hour.

(Frederick Douglass, 4th of July speech, 1852)

To the person of African descent born into slavery, the total lack of freedom and independence, and to the Native American who heralds from many nations destroyed in order to build a country upon their lands, holidays like Independence Day or Thanksgiving are complicated, jarring celebrations that demonstrate schizoid divisions of history and heritage.

The opportunity to realize actual freedom and some form of workable democracy for all the human beings in the new society that the United States supposedly represented, was decidedly there, even if slave-holding southern states and westward looking larger states felt constrained by their economic concerns of profiteering from labor and land exploitation. However, we must remember that Thomas Jefferson and George Washington held their plantations in the state of Virginia, the most populous new state (of slaves as well as citizens) with the strongest gaze westward facing resisting Native Nations. Neither of these wealthy landowners would consider giving up their property, even if it was people; both would become powerful first and early Presidents wielding authority over these very issues.[43]

Let us look at another revolution, much influenced by connections to the American experience and with primary players – Thomas Jefferson and Thomas Paine – integral to its development. A bloody internal struggle punctuated by executions and radical ideologies (the Paris Commune) produced 'rights of man' and nominative freedoms for all, with end results greater in the New World than the Ancien Régime (Figure 4.10).

When the French Assembly declared all men to be citizens, including those of color in the colonies,[44] news spread to the Caribbean like wildfire whether slave or servant, none more ready to hear uplifting and radically new platforms for humanity than resistance spiritual leaders on Ha(Ay)iti. By the 1790s Haitians were well aware that the American Revolution simply didn't apply to them, because they were Black and increasingly seen as Native to the lands. France as a colonizing master country mattered more simply because they controlled the colonies, but also as nearly all learned men and free thinkers looked to the French revolution for inspiration and as intellectual philosophy for freedom struggles.

Even as the Assembly then the Convention and the Directory, each slid into regimes of internal terror (none worse than everyday life for African-descent peoples in Haiti) the populace held out hope that was nurtured by resistance leaders, themselves in close connection to Taino resistance war survivors. The British periodically invaded or occupied Martinique and Guadeloupe, supposedly freeing the slaves, yet real freedom never took hold,

(European) – French – Revolution 4 – 2

The storming of the Bastille and the fall of the Ancien Régime in 1789 France, leading to a newly socially independent nation led by a National Assembly rather than a monarch and their nobility, was as much influenced by the events from the colonies, notably the new United States even if English based, as it was the rise of a radical leadership drawing up a new social order.

Declaration of the Rights of Man and Citizen, was a key point in the French Revolution, adopted by the National Constituent Assembly as part of the new French constitution. For the colonies and all those excluded for legal or nationalist status, the rights for all free men to be citizens was huge, pushed by a parliamentarian writing by the legislative assembly, and border warfare, 1791-1792.

Executions of enemies of the state increased during this period, at its height the beheading of King Louis and then of Marie Antoinette seemed to indicate the full end of the monarchy, increasing pressures for power grabbing along ideological lines, emanating from the Paris Commune and then special committees and self-selected political groups. Extension of citizenship to all free men of color in the colonies, was a critical point in this development, following quickly on heels of open revolution in Haiti. However, the national convention began a reign of terror, 1792-1795. Ideologies of revolutionary fervor spun out of control, along with the execution of anyone trying to espouse criticism or narrowing of the revolution that had spread to the colonies, who erupted in their own revolutionary discord. The Directory (1795-1799) re-established social controls in many ways, but its counter-revolutionary backing brought the military, now under Napoleon, back into kingmaker roles. Haiti under Louverture made great advances, even as other European forces were pressuring or invading French territory, and their colonies in the Caribbean.

It is interesting to observe the rise of extreme ideologies, from the left, against monarchy and of nobility controls, yet the leaders resort to becoming ideologues themselves, either consumed by or directed by the reins of power, as happened in many revolutionary movements before and since. Scholars note that such leaders as Robespierre were swept up in the lethal ideological internecine warfare, yet succumbed to it themselves when faced with compromise with bureaucratic systems. Ultimately, France was beset by power struggles, historically the case, leading to a dictatorship of Napoleon to establish Codes or laws that could be applied in courts rather than committees, 1799-1815, but in the process crowning himself Emperor, in the historic fashion of taking power, thus countering the initial driving forces of the revolution and principles of the First French Republic.

We have the conflicted dualities of European western civilization – thinking and belief (systems) needing and seeking out affirmation and support for its philosophies and political origins – against or with the anciens or the ancillary, the indigenous and idolatrous, the heuristic and the heresy of world history. They once again led back to elite (racist) political economy of hegemony and power of the purse, supported by the gun. Like the American revolution, the French did inspire reforms and correctives that became more democratic and participatory over time, but it would take those who were marginalized the most, the ex-slave supported by surviving Natives, to realize the truer revolution overthrowing the old order and replacing it with social change from the bottom.

Figure 4.10 European (France) Revolution (text box).

much like the English colonies themselves. It was Haiti, then and now, that held on to hope and revolutionary thought, precisely because of its long-fought independence wars starting with Enrique's 14-year rebellion against the Spanish, ending in a negotiated settlement that allowed mixed-race communities to exist, mostly in mountainous areas of the Xaraguan peninsula, highlands above Kenscoff (that I would walk with the marchandes, over trails to the beach at Jacmel), and through the Artibonite valley, where Dessalines noted the *Rouges* or Incas (referring to Natives) knew of places to hide next to secret burial grounds, from where they could conduct resistance war. Although both dominants (Spanish, French and European-American historians) and critical scholars often refer to a complete genocide (by overall numbers it certainly was) and imply the Taino-Arawak were eliminated to the last one, in fact many were assimilated into communities that were mixed-race as well in the above stated areas, while others lived in mountainous or forest redoubts that held on to their own histories, shared with Africans in ceremony adapted to Vaudoun.[45] Underground networks connected slave resistance and maroon communities with the surviving Arawaks, fueling the rebellion, and giving it a spiritual and cultural basis in the land itself. I was assured after landing in Jeremie, city of poets and revolutionaries at the end of the long, often isolated southern peninsula, that these practices still existed in 1982 as we traveled inland, with road-building crews, finally driving through a candle lit region where the drumming from the hillside announced our presence. This was a 450-year continuity of resistance, revitalization and cultural adaptation, marked in our story herein about 250 years (or halfway) from its start with Guarocuya.

On the flip side, suppression and execution of African Haitian leaders like Mackandal mid-century, or Boukman and other houngan spiritual healers, appeared to reinforce the French position of racial-cultural supremacy throughout the islands. When Josephine, from a Martinique plantation family, rose in the courts of France, ultimately marrying Napoleon Bonaparte, she, like other *colons*, demanded that slave-master supremacy relations be restored. In Haiti, a marriage between state colonizer with local elites was countered by Black African resistance communities, mostly far in the mountains. When Toussaint Louverture was betrayed and imprisoned, and ultimately killed like too many had before, these communities rose up even stronger, and the western part of the island that had been taken over by resistance forces began fomenting their own revolutionary discourse, many white planters fled to American places like Louisiana where French or Cajun speaking overseers ran slave labor plantations, carrying on the profitable operations, similar to the earlier slavery demands in France. When Boukman had led the Bois Caïman ceremony in the interior, the African ex-slave rebellion was on.

Almost immediately the French metropole and military responded, not only to the freedom fighters in Saint Domingue and the revolution spreading to other French slave colonies, but to the international trade dynamics (precipitous drop in sugar exports) throughout the Caribbean and in particular the growing port New Orleans linking to Louisiana territory. Many ex-colons and plantation owners had moved operations to the French speaking area, with the United States moving toward incorporation of fertile lands, eliminating Native resistance, followed by creating plantation economies based on slave labor of Africans. Slave-holding powers of the Caribbean, including the United States, feared Black independence movements, and contributed to counter-revolutionary forces in their countries and back in Haiti, that continued for a hundred years.

Toussaint Louverture as one of the original and most famous of the anti-slavery freedom fighting forces, was always one to compromise for the good of the country, and yet was so charismatic that French and Spanish officers served under him, sometimes switching sides to do so. We can only wonder what might have arisen for the country if the treaty like agreements made with him would have been followed, but like Indigenous leaders but as an African nation, Europeans were only going to honor treaties or agreements made with other Europeans, and sometimes not even those. After Haiti declared independence (1804) all slave-holding states and colonies worked against the development or progress of Haiti, invading and occupying it on multiple occasions over the next two hundred years. French colons to Louisiana could no longer depend on France's unwavering support and played into the hands of a forced 'sale' to the United States (L. DuBois, 2004: 304) over North American territory entailing a largest leap or land grab in world history. But as we have said earlier, that is a story for our next book (1790–2020)... (Figure 4.11).

We also see how both social theory and jurisprudence follow, rather than precede or construct, societal development of slavery, genocidal conquest, racialized colonizing and racist hierarchies. This coincides with the American Revolution and the creation of the United States, with leading philosopher-politicians such as Thomas Jefferson taking Enlightenment thinking to a natural end of observing peoples on top as deserving of their privileged location[46] – supported by Crown (government) Church (Christian), Company/Corporation (economic stratification) and Colonist (settler) ideologies, perfectly evidenced in Manifest Destiny. This will be the subject of the next substantive chapter – the White (Ethnic) or Irish – in my following book (chapter 2).

Throughout the 19th century, the ideologies of races as separate sub-species with differing traits were used to underscore and support existing racial practices, social policies, religious thinking and even early scientists following the lead of social Darwinism and supremacist thinking, launched at the time that the United States was being formed. After the U.S. Civil War these efforts actually increased in the South, with a rise of racist militias and of terrorist organizations, accompanied by segregation by race, within the

(Afro-Caribbean) – Haitian – Revolution 4 – 3

The historical (mixed) Races of Ayiti created the true Haitian revolution from 1519 to 1799.

The French declaration on the Rights of Man extended as freedom, equality and brotherhood to all peoples (even slaves), kick-started a nascent slave rebellion or movement in San Domingue, Haiti, that had been percolating in the mountains under earlier resistance leaders as Mackandal, spiritual leaders like Boukman who led the Bois Caïman ceremony, in the legendary tradition of Enrique, (Guarocuya) the first such rebellion on Hispaniola. The French colons had allowed the system to become ever more repressive and brutal, with sugar production as its only operative goal, at all costs, human and environmental. A generation or two of Caribbean born managers and overseers, often of mixed race themselves, worked in conjunction with the gens de couleur, and merchants, small and large, to produce a vibrant economy with trade networks throughout the islands, based on brutal slave labor conditions. Native communities (resistance) traded from mountain areas too.

As more Black Haitians left plantations, many with their own memories of freedom in Africa, or at least a somewhat more humane system of servitude / slavery, leaders arose among their children, none more eloquent and charismatic than Toussaint Louverture, who embodied the revolution. European powers resisted – hated and feared – the movements and what it portends, so there was much switching of allegiances over the years, between the Spanish (who controlled the eastern half of the island), the French of course, and often the British (who contended for other islands). In all those years, Native Taino "indien esclaves" (5,000 or so living openly), and "indiens sauvages" (thousands living in mountain resistance communities, esp the southern peninsula) worked closely with Black maroons and revolutionary forces, so Dessalines later called them "rouges" and "Incas" that coordinated military action and gave sanctuary and hiding places, leading to birth of (h)Ayiti.

After an initial bloody uprising in 1791 following the French Assembly assigning citizenship to all, (where plantations were overrun, many owners and overseers killed) battles waged back and forth, mostly won by Black Haitian fighters, until the entry of Napoleon's invasion forces looked to tip the balance; but the betrayal, imprisonment and death of Louverture in Gonaive, enraged the Black revolutionary ex-slave forces, and they took the capital and major ports. This betrayal is also why Dessalines and Christophe entered into total Race war, killing most French colonials on the island.

Freedom from slavery was always the key to the Haitian revolution, from start to finish. When the corvée system of forced labor was re-established to rebuild the economy, existing factions split off and fought between themselves, which both local leaders and European powers ignited and divided to weaken central governance. In many ways, a Haitian rebellion was the only truly revolutionary change in the world, but could never recover from reactionary internal and external racist forces to become the intra-racial, pluri-national model to end genocide and slavery, it could have been…

Figure 4.11 Caribbean (Haitian) Revolution (text box).

justice system and then affirmed by the U.S. Courts. But again, we are ahead of ourselves, into the province of my next book.

Colony–Company–Capitalism: Land and Labor Exploitation by the State (Crown)

These two primary forces – Crown authority and Company (corporate) economy – were established in the English colonial beachheads at Jamestown and Plymouth, and maintained in the colonizing processes set in place and extended out for the following 400 years. They are found in, and referenced in the Constitutional framing for the United States (including the 1763 Proclamation, the 1783 Treaty of Paris) definition of Territories, the 1787 Northwest Ordnance, and a 1790 passing nod to sovereignty; and, are foundational in governmental law dictated by SCOTUS in the Marshall Trilogy (esp. Johnson v. McIntosh on 'Discovery doctrine' in Cherokee Nation 'domestic dependent nations' and in Worcester with the alienation of titular land possession, even if by 'consent'), where the United States, using European jurisprudence, found ways to deny tribal sovereignty, while pursuing Indian (racialized) policies (Fenelon, 2002). Trajectories for other Races were also in place at this time – Africans as Blacks for labor exploitation, settlers as Whites for the dominant or mainstream population base.

Southeastern slave systems using Natives (the Spanish developed massive slave systems in the Caribbean first) were

> the drive to control Indian labor – which extended to every nook and cranny of the South – was inextricably connected to the growth of the plantations, and trade in Indian slaves was at the center of the English empire's development in the American South. Trading of Indian slaves was the most important factor affecting the South in the period of 1670 to 1715 – its impact was felt from Arkansas to the Carolinas and south to the Florida Keys.
>
> (Gallay, 2015: 7)

It would continue in new forms, strictly racist, into the United States.

Political Economy of the World-System (PEWS Effects)

Similar to what developed in the North American fur trade expansion, Native nations were destabilized by other native nations against (each other) in the slave trade under threat from well-armed European invaders and the first colonies. We observe negative effects, especially social disruption and changing relationships with the environment, far beyond the initial penetration by invasive colonial forces. This continues on a continental scale and can be seen in other parts of the world, such as in Africa or Southeast Asia, within the context of colonization.

This takes a form quite different from the Spanish systems in the mainland areas of Latin America, precisely because of the formal bans against legalized slavery by Catholic orders. Reviewing these relationships from a world-systems historical perspective, we see that advances and declines of Dutch hegemony versus the failure of the French (Mississippi Company bubble) and rise of British colonial hegemony (trading companies – Hudson's Bay, beyond East India, including Plymouth, Massachusetts, Northwest Passage) as key junctures in destroying Native Nations and the rise of global systemic racism with capitalism. This observation underscores how important it is to see colonial armed intrusions as **invasions** sponsored by state apparatus, versus accepting economic determinism of investment and control by companies as a sole cause.

The so-called Mississippi Bubble is a good case to make this observation. *Compagnie du Mississippi* was originally chartered in 1684 (following the English models) supported by France with a large expedition intending on founding a colony at the Mississippi River's mouth. Not too successful, it was renamed Company of the West from 1717, and Company of the Indies from 1719 on, under Controller General of Finances of France, John Law, who tied it to French currency by creating the *Banque Générale Privée,* the first use of paper money by a financial institution. Although ostensibly to support the Louisiana colony, it was lauded as such a great investment, that speculation in French financial circles went wild. Consequently Louisiana territorial land development became frenzied, as it was connected to consolidation of French trading companies (the Orient) and was detached from economic reality. The company absorbed the *Compagnie des Indes Orientales* and the *Compagnie de Chine* (China), and other rival trading companies and became the *Compagnie Perpétuelle des Indes* in 1719 with a monopoly on French commerce. Stock fell precipitously, and along with it currency devaluation, crippling the French economy, private investors and the use of Company colonial interests. This scheme was a first example of economic bubbles, but more importantly had hindered future French development by not allowing trading companies to operate independently (theoretically, legally) that became an iron law of capitalism (following companies operated independent of the state).

Ultimately, long-term effects weakened French control of the larger colonial territories, leading to treaties with the United States, discussed in my next book as the Louisiana Purchase and other lands held by Spanish Mexico that did not mention Native nations or tribes.

The fledgling United States learned from this experience, in exactly the same territories, also discussed at length in my next book as an integral part of the development of capitalism (Desmond, 2019). For now, let us observe that the plantation system built on Mississippi lands was partially leveraged through slave valuation collateral (further dehumanization, depreciation) more so than land, financed by private banks authorized but separated from the state, so market fluctuations were tied to the trading companies, banking investments and insurance corporations, rather than government itself. When these periodically failed, as they did in the Panic of 1837 (Desmond, 2019) the state itself was not threatened, race-based slavery for plantations not only survived but actually thrived by moving unto new lands, often taken through war, such as Texas (eastern half) and the lower plains states (then becoming Indian Country).

We learn from all these cases, and the spatial-temporal context in which they develop and exist, that prime social structural characteristics such as deep racism, patriarchy or economic domination are also embedded within larger international systems, such as colonialism and/or industrial capitalism. These systems shape micro- and macro- mini-systems in geographically defined regions such as 'the South' operating within larger systems, such as the United-States, or the economies of the north Atlantic countries. Therefore, analysis of structural configurations within the systems – racial slavery, economies of plantations, banking investment or loans, political dynamics – can only be done effectively when understood by their placement to and relationship within continental or global forces. European ethno-national stratification, international currency and trade flows, labor struggles, or differential citizenry construction often offer little real political choice, however great the very real economic consequences might be. So in addition to asking where socio-economic assets are derived from (i.e. trans-atlantic slavery, vast land takings), the cases must be assessed for the part they play in the much larger political-economy of empire, colony or countries (i.e. circuit trade from America(s) to England, European banking systems creating global economies). Only then can we apply a further moral lens on colonizing processes, social structural domination or hegemonic trade capitalism, which create the societal behaviors. Our last point is precisely on the convergence of powerful socio-economic forces and racialized social elites, in that racial dynamics of the South cohere to growing industrial capitalism in the North and international trade relations in factories and in banking systems of Europe, observed in world-system time. As discussed earlier, larger systems (Jim Crow South, Nazism, South African Apartheid) not only interact, but borrow from other, earlier systems. Understanding the larger systems helps us to frame the American experience, where incredible intellects (Benjamin Franklin) many noted political leaders (Robert Morris) and great military governor heroes (George Washington), often referred to as Founding Fathers, can be seen as contributing to ethnic cleansing (the Scalp Act) systemic racism (owning slaves) or rampant elitism (money/capital/property accumulation).

Understanding world history in the context of overarching systems of capitalism, racism and socio-political domination means that we must include the larger systems in which they exist. As polarized points of view are debated by scholars (Desmond, 2019 v. Coclanis, 2022) global or world-systemic perspectives often get set aside. Plantation systems are viewed through a lens of race, or cotton production, even as capitalism is viewed similarly in these contexts, or in regional/continental frameworks. Let us review what we have found in this work so far, when considering the world-system developing over two centuries in the North Atlantic, leading to the formation of the United States out of English colonies of the eastern seaboard and economic systems on the verge of cementing racialized capitalism in place.

Banks and trading companies arose out of northern Europe, especially the Netherlands, with the rise of great fleets of merchants (armed themselves, but further backed up by military navies in support), all requiring great financial credit and types of insurance, that predated on the resources – labor and land – taken out of the Americas. State coffers and holdings were privy to political intrusion, markedly so by kings and royal families, thus becoming greater risk at loss, weakening the excessive institutional growth from extractive resources and agricultural holdings in what became Latin America. The growing commercial circuit trade to Africa violently forced people into race-based slavery and transported them as true human capital to the Americas, where they would be subjected to a life of brutal labor. Here the slaves were sold, creating another market, and goods and resources were shipped or traded for transport to Europe, notably England where early industrialization took hold. This Triangular Trade system required capital investment in ships, for initial layouts for slaves in Africa or for valuable (mineral) resources in America, and for early industrial production in the northern cities and countries of Europe. Banking became critical to development of the new system, along with insurance (companies) and national military systems to protect the deep investments of nation-state economies of trade. However, noted above, company investments had to be divorced from state manipulation.

Later, freedom of the seas, touted by England's global trade network empowered by a merchant marine force and enforced by its battleship Navy, would be taken to ever greater lengths by U.S. hegemonic domination of the global economy. Much of that activity is oil based, requiring great ocean networks with arterial links such as the Suez and Panama canals, enforced by the hegemon's military forces, in the name of the state, but controlled by private money. This also is discussed in the next book as related to capitalist development in the United States.

Transition toward religious ideologies increasingly divorced from the state, rationalizing new systems of capitalist profit tied to banking credit, investment and insurance, were structured into the Protestant revolution. The transition disentangled monetary holdings from state religions that allowed direct control by political elites, skirting the Catholicism and Spanish–Portuguese forms of dominance from the first 100 years of colonization, and under change for the next 100 with growing English dominance. Thus capitalism embraced and developed two key elements of human bondage systems – slavery and genocide – along with a growth of global systems that depended on private capital and large trading companies, where banks operated independently of states that sponsored them in their home countries. This is what the United States positioned in its political economy structures over the next 200 years.

> The wealth of the imperial countries is our wealth too. …For in a very concrete way Europe has stuffed herself inordinately with the gold and raw materials of the colonial countries: Latin America, China, and Africa. From all these continents, under whose eyes Europe today raises up her tower of opulence, there has flowed out for centuries toward that same Europe diamonds and oil, silk and cotton, wood and exotic products. Europe is literally the creation of the Third World. The wealth which smothers her is that which was stolen from the underdeveloped peoples. The ports of Holland, the docks of Bordeaux and Liverpool were specialized in the Negro slave trade, and owe their renown to millions of deported slaves. So when we hear the head of a European state declare with his hand on his heart that he must come to the aid of the poor underdeveloped peoples, we do not tremble with gratitude. Quite the contrary; we say to ourselves: "It's a just reparation which will be paid to us."
>
> (Frantz Fanon, The Wretched of the Earth)

I note for this first three hundred years, it is the centrality of Hispaniola/Haiti in the Caribbean, the third great social revolution of the 18th century, that demonstrates capitalist supremacy:

> Haiti was the first country to liberate itself against slavery — the first successful anti-slavery revolution in the world. Since the Haitian Revolution, masters of the capital system never accepted that Haiti showed the way for the progress… because the Haitian Revolution was beyond class, gender, and race.
>
> (Jean Eddy Saint Paul)[47]

From the Paxton Boys to the Proud Boys – A Straight-Line Development of White Supremacy Groups, or Gangs, across the Time and Space of North America

As noted, the Paxton Boys were formed in relation to creating and maintaining racial dominance over the expanding frontier of the English colonies. More importantly, we can see a response by England in forming the 1763 Proclamation (over Indian Territory), since this expansion will work against English containment of the colonial forces and toward growing independence (or lack of dependence) of the American militias control in what was being called Indian Territory. Certainly, the initial expansion of the English colonies took very similar forms in wiping out Native Nations and any sovereign claim to the land they had, or espoused. Reviewing Bacon's Rebellion we observe the same form of local militias expanding genocidal takings of land, while the Crown/Colony want to retain control over peoples and taxation. Many historians and social (science) analysts get this a little skewed, because they believe a political hyperbole that emerges later about the American independence war, which is more about self-determination and internal institution-building during westward expansion than simple taxation without representation (keeping money in the homeland). Nation-building propensity toward breaking from Britain is exactly why England suddenly decides to recognize the boundaries and rights of Indian Nations, and lack of them for the Massachusetts Bay, now New England, colonies. The racial formation of home-grown Whites – the colloquial 'Boys' – was essential to their background ideologies. Thus for 100 years homeland militias would be formed to contain and destroy Indians in the expansion westward, including slave suppression in the South, ending in Oregon, where genocidal policies and practices would turn over the territory into a state. Like its southern neighbor California, progressive (liberal) agendas were built on this racial dominance agenda, and so its rejection of systemic racism in late 20th-century politics seems groundless and hypocritical to the racist militias formed to patrol its borders, geographically and socially.

So, whereas colonial militias initially have the express intent of defending the expanding crown boundaries of two major colonial incursions into North America, Virginia and Massachusetts, under the United States, both in formation and its early and later years of development, armed militias become driven by supremacist ideologies. We see it in the 1763 Pennsylvania militias, 1782 Ohio at Gnadenhutten; in 1830's Creek wars by Andrew Jackson and the Indian Removals (annotated map, Figure 4.12) in 1862 Minnesota uprisings with Mankato hangings. Further, we see the prelude and aftermath of the 1868 Treaty with the Lakota, punctuated by South Dakota killings at Wounded Knee in 1890, in militias and when newspapers consistently referred to Indian 'savage' threats to the 'civilized' women, and children, of white settler families.

As closely documented in my next book, and extensively elsewhere, similar militia supremacist ideologies continue through the Tulsa killings in 1921, lynchings of Blacks throughout the 20th century Jim Crow south until the Civil Rights movement of the 1960s, and periodically in both northern cities like Chicago and western cities like Los Angeles through the 1990s, replicated in various urban environs in the 21st century, all the way to an outright rejuvenation of racist groups or their armed militias in

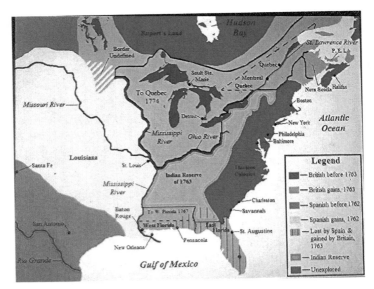

Figure 4.12 Map of eastern North America 1763–1790 (expansion, racial state (ex-colonies)) violent westward frontier (1763–1783) un-legal land takings (Map 4.7) over 'Indian Reserve' lands of the Royal Proclamation of 1763, after 1783 Ohio and west territories of the Northwest Ordnance to 1787, southern Indian Reserve 1763 (Tennessee, Kentucky, northern Mississippi) taken in the Southwest Ordnance to 1790, completing the march to the Mississippi River. Note: Commons Wikimedia – Jon Platek, 2008 as NorthAmerica1762-83.png; description as "North America after the Seven Years' War. France ceded Louisiana to Spain before surrender; this kept Britain out of the trans-Mississippi West. Spain traded Florida for Cuba. Britain created two colonies with capitals at Pensacola and St. Augustine."

2020 – Michigan, Missouri, Minnesota and many southern states – culminating for the next book in well-armed truckloads of Proud Boys driving into Portland, Oregon, Fall of 2020, displaying White Power, militia and Confederate flags next to American US flags, or Trump MAGA banners. Oregon is a state built on genocidal killings and Indigenous nations removals (Lewis, 2016; Keeler, 2021) and banning of Black immigration as state policy (Semuels, 2016). Thus we observe a straight-line continuum of U.S. white supremacy militias, creating the racist exclusion and discriminatory treatment of both Indians and Blacks, Native and African-descent Americans, from the East to the West coasts of North America, from 1763/1783 (Figure 4.14) through two centuries and four decades (central theme in the next book).

In the map in Figure 4.12, stressing the sources of supremacist ideologies from their colonial roots, observe colonies becoming states, that expand over

'Indian Reserve of 1763' (Proclamation) after 1783 through 1787 North and 1790 South west ordnances, to the Mississippi river.

Demography and the First United States Census – 1790

In reviewing entries to the editions of otherwise brilliant Introductory Sociology texts,[48] one immediately observes the previously identified distortion effect, of not seeing the whole, global development of systems of race and racism over at least the last 500 years of the conquest and colonization of the Americas. The resulting world-system, with transnational capitalism at least partially developed from the racial exploitation of different peoples in North America and the United States, is much harder to identify without fully humanizing all living people.

Under their race and racism chapters, authors typically identify the expansion into the Caribbean America, noting Columbus's mis-identification of Native (Americans) as Indians and discussing ethnic diversity of the Americas, especially the United States. These textbooks bring up Native American examples of being an extreme minority of only 1% without mentioning that initially these societies were 100% of existing population of two continents and major oceanic regions. Full humanization would discuss removal of Indigenous people and replacement with Europeans.

Similarly when discussing the colonial population of North America, many texts state people as being immigrants (not mentioning coerced indentured servitude or forced migration for slavery) and some claim that nearly all people were of Anglo-Saxon or British descent, most Protestant. Such a statement does not identify pre-existing Native populations, many who had undergone enslavement, suppression, extermination and removal westward. Even more problematically these texts do not analyze the large numbers of racially enslaved peoples, making up one fourth to a third of the population in some states, such as Virginia, North/South Carolina or Maryland.

These basic texts (authored by sociological theorists or general institutional analysts) make an example of how social science scholars can essentially miss many basic racialized facts rising from the colonial development of the United States.[49]

First, it is as if Native Americans just disappear and are later the most minoritized of peoples. Although we can see how the authors might avoid the central problem of genocide and or of brutal conquest modalities of the Spanish and the French (leaving a denial of the English settler colonialism), the destruction of Native Nations and Indigenous societies is closely documented through treaties and wars during both colonial and later nationalist creation of the United States. In viewing maps of the times, one easily observes how the Western mindset is only considering peoples in the original colonies. Most of the rest of the continent's population is set aside under labels such as Spanish possession, French territories, England when that is denied, and in what creates a 1763 northwest territorial compromise, called 'reserved for Indians' (when it's not).

In hegemonic description solely concerned with settler immigration, the extensive Black slave population is often also ignored and dehumanized, through reference of immigrant settlers over the early English colonies. Again, it is as if they are not visible, which of course is how these peoples were isolated from socio-political constructions of colonial society. This is clearly emblematic of what Patterson (1982) calls Social Death,[50] which Wolf and others see as a denial of their histories. While in fact, the growing capitalist system partly grew from the wealth created by genocidal taking of Native lands and resources, and the highly profitable labor exploitation of Black enslavement. It's as if they simply don't count.

Which of course, they don't – that is the primary social problem, evident in the sophisticated presentation by leading social scientists from a wide variety of background specialties. This also explains an evidentiary error of often undercounting, then over-counting Black slaves in 1780, although by any statement of the population, as shown in the 1790 Census, there are only about 4 million non-Indigenous people, including colonists and slaves, in the entire colonial complex.

What we can transmute from this text then are not only the vast and egregious omissions of a great many peoples – Native Nations who will disappear under extermination, Black slaves who simply don't matter to the dominant group of racialized immigrant settlers – but how both mental trickery and racially distorted frames can invert and transpose demographic numbers in mis-analyzed temporal and spatial forms that further contribute toward a deeply flawed (later) mis-representation of racial and ethnic systems of discrimination.[51]

In Figure 4.13 we observe a proximate number of Blacks, listed under Slaves (before the United States, there were significant number of Indian slaves, until at least 1730 mostly in southern colonies), and demographic relationships with Whites (broken down by Gender and Age for Males, mostly for voting purposes) noting the highest number being in Virginia, also the most populous state, followed by South Carolina, Maryland and North Carolina (also see relatively high numbers in New York and New Jersey, later declining to 0). Only white people count in this census.

The other uncounted number is so-called Native Americans, who are really members of Nations, Tribes and/or other collectives and amalgamated groups of refugees and isolated families. This poses two very significant problems in trying to ascertain the actual Human Beings much less societies in the early United States, one being the actual count of Natives including on lands not yet fully incorporated into the new country (see Georgia and New York here) and the other number of Native peoples as Nations or

District	Free white males of 16 years and upward, including heads of families	Free white males under 16 years	Free white females, including heads of families	All other free persons	Slaves	Total
Vermont	22,435	22,328	40,505	255	16	85,539
New Hampshire	36,086	34,851	70,160	630	158	141,885
Maine	24,384	24,748	46,870	538	0	96,540
Massachusetts	95,453	87,289	190,582	5,463	0	378,787
Rhode Island	16,019	15,799	32,652	3,407	948	68,825
Connecticut	60,523	54,403	117,448	2,808	2,764	237,946
New York	83,700	78,122	152,320	4,654	21,324	340,120
New Jersey	45,251	41,416	83,287	2,762	11,423	184,139
Pennsylvania	110,788	106,948	206,363	6,537	3,737	434,373
Delaware	11,783	12,143	22,384	3,899	8,887	59,094
Maryland	55,915	51,339	101,395	8,043	103,036	319,728
Virginia	110,936	116,135	215,046	12,866	292,627	747,610
Kentucky	15,154	17,057	28,922	114	12,430	73,677
North Carolina	69,988	77,506	140,710	4,975	100,572	393,751
South Carolina	35,576	37,722	66,880	1,801	107,094	249,073
Georgia	13,103	14,044	25,739	398	29,264	82,548
Total	807,094	791,850	1,541,263	59,150	694,280	3,893,635

Figure 4.13 United States Census of 1790. August 2, 1790, enumerated to be 3,929,214.

The census of 1790, published in 1791.

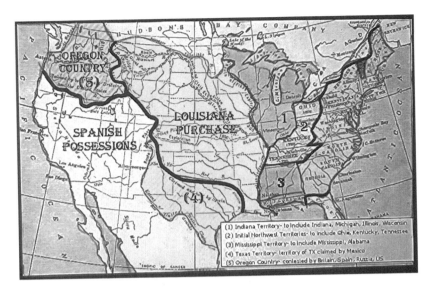

Figure 4.14 Colonized America.

Tribes in areas vaguely defined as Indian Reserve, in some maps simply left to Territories (see Indiana, Mississippi). And, there is the rest of the continent… (it's as if Native peoples and nations have disappeared in North America).

In Figure 4.14 see the first expansion of the early United States over the initial western territories that later become slave states in the Lower South and become settler-worker states in the north, all predicated upon the much greater expansion over the Louisiana 'Purchase' territories, where Indian Nations are to be removed and racial enslavement with ethnic subordination are replicated in complicated numbers. This sets up Jacksonian takeover of lower south (western) states via genocidal removal of Native nations and development of race-based slave plantations focus on cotton production, for an increasingly textile-based industrial capitalism (Desmond, 2019). Both north and south are characterized by un-legal or fictional land 'cessions' by states (Figure 4.7).

Property Laws and Relations to Land

Property laws and relations of private ownership are/were instrumental in the colonizing process, especially by the English employing settler colonists. While this is basically a set of replacement operations where mostly communal or community-based Indigenous systems were replaced by a combination of crown/state and individual/corporate ownership by private parties, exceptional people and highly adaptive families managed to maintain their position or even grow within the newly dominant system. We can see how some Powhatan people have survived for hundreds of years to re-emerge as community and reclaim sovereign relations in the 21st century. In the same region, we have seen cases like ex-slave Anthony Johnson build Virginia farmlands (that were lost in succeeding generations to repressive colonial laws of race and ownership). We have seen many such cases. The Aquinnah Wampanoag managed to achieve recognition in the 20th century, as the Mashpee re-emerged to struggle for and win sovereignty recognition, in places where intermarriage with Blacks disqualified them in the eyes and laws of the dominant society. The primary difference between these peoples is having community-based stewardship over the land, as opposed to private (therefore exclusive) ownership of land. An outstanding example of how difficult this was would be some of the Lenape who remained during the great land takings and ethnic cleansing of the 1700s up to and then including formation of the United States and Pennsylvania. We can see the real dangers in the Gazette reporting by Franklin's press of the murdered 'Friend Indian' during the scalping policy times, where families that had managed to finesse staying on their historical lands were under constant threat from settler dominants over their valuable property. Many individuals identified as being Indian or believed that over time, facilitating their often hidden existence, making for complicated legacy issues of Indigenous identity centuries later, when, as California Natives were wont to say – "We are still here!"

United States Neo-Colonization of the Continent

With the creation of the United States, transplantation of mostly English-dominated European colonization was complete. The ex-colony (or colonies) becoming states were well positioned to become a burgeoning global power over time, precisely because of its:

- continuing expansion of neo-colonization[52] (Bhambra and Holmwood, 2021) westward, under military-legal frameworks of the 1787 Northwest and 1790 Southwest Ordnance (s)
- ideological elimination of treaty-making responsibilities with Native Nations by employing 'merciless Indian savage' and tribal war-like societies tropes; leading to Manifest Destiny
- racist legal and social structures allowing for enslavement for profiting off Blacks and the labor of new immigrant Europeans now termed White
- separation yet coordination of central components of the new State – banking and taxation, political and citizenry, judicial and law-making, executive and military – through a two tiered layered

sovereignty (denying Native Nations and other ethnic groups their own nationalism)

- constructing an 'elected' executive authority for command and control of conditions (above) over the state's expansion
- creating a racist, classist and intersectional sexist society for the purposes of capitalist (elite) accumulation, wealth (re-) production and stratified growth
- structuring race–gender–class systems through new state (ex-colony) formations, an Electoral College, manipulating an Executive (President) reproducing racist separation, and representation via the dehumanizing three-fifth rule over people and/or property (replicated in tax systems).

Even as England reinforced global colonization, with Spanish, Portuguese, French and Dutch colonies controlling much world commerce, the fledgling United States stood poised, after and along with its nationalist continental expansion, to join European world powers in their quest for global hegemony. The Founding Fathers of the United States developed their revolutionary government in Philadelphia, where ethnic cleansing over the Pennsylvania state, drove Native Nations to destruction and despair, and where African descent peoples commonly slaved as house servants, literally for the authors framing the Declaration of Independence, Articles of Confederation and United States Constitution calling for freedom and democracy.

Epilogue for the Next Book – A Two Centuries Rise to Racialized Capitalism

"God Is Red"
"Custer Died For Your Sins"
"The Metaphysics of Modern Existence"
Three books by Vine Deloria, Jr. on the Western Europe divide with American Indians[53]

And what of agency of individuals and their societies that we began this book narrative with?

Anacaona's people were all but extinguished by 1790 with some Xaraguans and other Ayiti'n descendants mixing with Spanish and African peoples for more than 270 years, as in Enrique's resistance camps.[54] Native and African-descent women had lost all rights with the new slave and servant society, and most common European descent women fared little better, except upon the patriarchal pleasures of the white men in their family's lives.

Mochtezuma's people had been toppled as an empire, followed by a dominating colonial spread of the Spanish over what would become Mexico and

Central America, with pockets of resistance everywhere, especially among the Mayan holdouts in mountainous regions. While some Native communities retained their identity and culture, most were falling to Spanish cultural domination and intermarriage producing an intermediate population, neither Indigenous nor European, called *mestizo* in popular parlance, with a deep and sustaining racial patriarchy.

Ayenwatha's peoples had been systematically attacked by the British, French and then the Americans, breaking the unity of the confederation, disrespecting the Grandmother's control over meeting lodges and appointments to councils. Surviving towns and nations were surrounded by Euro-Americans who treated women as objects under law and refused to recognize traditional boundaries of the five or six nations that had once stood as one. However, they did maintain limited sovereignty and survivance throughout the 20th century, emerging as an example of how contemporary Native Nations stand in resilience and revitalization to the present.

The Oceti Sakowin leaders of the northern Great Plains and Woodlands tribes had been fractionated by the colonial economic forces yet to fully invade their lands, causing divisions among the nations that would deepen and worsen over the next century, so the older councils coming to consensus agreement would seem fictional to the Europeans taking over the country. Their resistance wars were fought in the long 19th century, especially Lakota and Dakota, part of the discussions going into the next book, explicated in my first book (Fenelon, 1998).

Toqui Lautaro's Mapuches would also be broken up, with women Machi's disrespected at every turn, reflective of the Conquistador and Spanish patriarchies even in religion. Their rivals the Inka, Túpac Yupanqui's vast civilization, were effectively destroyed in ways similar to the Aztecs to the north, where cultures and families survived in the face of violent assimilation, later referred to the language (Quechua) they still spoke rather than the nations they were.

Columbus as Spain's progenitor of fantastic imperial growth from colonizing, fell into disrepute, was jailed briefly but managed to get the courts to partially reinstate his estate. Like the Spanish rise to wealth and global power in the 16th century, he and his heirs, Spain and its influence, would begin to falter in the 17th century, and fall into a lesser power in the 18th and 19th centuries, losing in global yet regional wars to England, France and the United States, never to regain its prominence and power in world affairs.

The Borgias continued in their corruption in the seats of power based on Mediterranean societies, but the Vatican slowly faded into purely religious authority, still powerful, but more indirectly, first with the rise of the super wealthy colonizing states of Spain and Portugal, partially eclipsing the need for Papal Bulls, then in the religious wars of northern Europe with the rise of Protestantism and separation of church and state, morality and company profiteering, and any need of justification for racializing colonization. All this was realized in the Supremacy Acts of England, the subordination of church to state, and its pure extension and development, within the English settler colonies of North America, institutionally reproduced in the formation of the United States.

King of France Charles VIII Valois would maintain his central power base in Europe, although greatly weakened by religious wars, and in ongoing debate as a mostly Catholic country with the 'rights of man' challenging monarchy, while the King of England (Henry VII Tudor) did re-establish goals of finishing the colonization of Ireland,[55] although the Irish rebellion and rise of Cromwell during struggles over Parliament's power presaged King Charles' execution, passing Crown authority down to a long line of Kings and Queens better positioned to develop, control and profit from colonies around the world, especially North America.

Sonni Ali, like many royal leaders of African nations, found 1492[56] (1500) to be a high point for their nations, with slave trade markets weakening the coastal kingdoms and indirectly down the line effects over interior countries as well. Colonization would wreak havoc pretty much over all of West Africa and produce global racialization that overtook the entire continent, ultimately overthrown in decolonization and independence wars of the 20th century. That is the province of the next book, with direct correlation to the rise of racism in colonial structures, none more obvious than South Africa, also falling under settler colonization by the English.

African-descent Americans, mostly living under enslavement, would periodically rise in revolt, yet otherwise were riding out the terrible conditions of plantation slavery with every law working against any attempt at freedom and democracy. They were manipulated by all parties during the revolutionary war and promised greater freedoms to join military forces, which were, of course, mostly betrayed at the end of the war. It would be another 80 years before slavery was nominally ended, even as strong socio-economic conditions were replicated in the new society. That too is the province of the next book.

Irish or white ethnic Americans continued to immigrate in large numbers to the North American English colonies, especially when faced with devastating wars and famine at home, becoming an important part of the creation of a dominant group in the new nation, racially defined as White. Most of these people experienced 'optional ethnicity' into the 20th century, that is also a key part of the next book. Ireland as a colonized people only won their freedoms well into the 20th century and have still not achieved that in North Ireland.

The epicenter of growing global domination had moved from its European origins to the Americas, subsuming the African continent in its wake of slavery and subordination through colonization, finding its center in the newly formed United States of North America. Once racial and gendered class domination of the continent was complete in another couple hundred years, racialized capitalism and ethnic cleansing colonialism would be home grown and exported out of and by the United States in its quest for global domination.

The United States, as a constitutional government, took the essential thoughts and social structures of European colonizers to its logical extension, or ends. The democratic tendencies toward a participatory and/or elected government without effective presence of a monarchy were put into place through a bicameral legislature and an executive who could be constrained by the Supreme Court and an elected body of all elected legislators, House and Senate combined, to reflect, supposedly, the will of the people. But like enlightenment questions in this first book, we must ask – who are the 'people' and who exactly represents them, or us, as the case may be?

This is a root of the problem, transplanted from European colonizers who systematically destroyed Native Nations, enslaved millions of African people and made the position of women tenable on their race and family, headed up by men (who did have full citizenship). White men of property (race, gender, class) were the only participating people in the government, and they were circumspect – controlled by the Electoral College for the Executive and a state mandated system for the legislators. It is necessary to have this understanding before moving on to my next book where these issues come into conflict, and indeed arise in the early 21st century. Hiding in background racism of the new country is considerable institutional discrimination against Jewish and Muslim people, with periodic pogroms in Europe (culminating in 20th-century genocide), depicted against race domination in America, where Jews could join the Irish as white ethnics.

English settler colonialism in the American colonies had many opportunities to turn out differently than the genocidal expansion out of the east coast westward that became the pattern. Shared beds and lodging, with celebration, at Merrymount near the Plymouth Colony was put down in violence, as were many outlying settlements at Jamestown, reported in Chapter 3. More directly, the Peaceable Kingdom for mutual understanding and fair dealings proposed by William Penn and the Quakers, were overtaken by fraudulent land deals by Penn's own sons, followed by frontier wars and colonial genocidal policies of scalp bounties and ethnic cleansing, culminating in the first disingenuous Treaty of 1778 by the United States with removed Lenape, furthering violent expansion into the frontier. It simply didn't have to happen the way it did.

Great American heroes such as George Washington, extremely brave as war commander, and wise as the first president who steps down from power can also be seen as an unremittent slave holder who sent armies to destroy the Onondaga central peace-keepers of Haudenosaunee confederation keeping the Great Law of Peace. Truly remarkable political documents such as the U.S. Constitution with its focus on political freedom and economic mobility, also reinforced race-based slavery through a three-fifths compromise and supported genocidal land theft through the 1785 and 1787 Ordnances taking land and entire territories from Native nations.

The guise of the new country was decidedly westward where its pioneer settlers would build the nation, even as they took Black slaves on their journey south and fought Indian nations in the north. And the ironic conflicts were about to create new ethno-national divisions over the wealth from lands and labor exploitation – warring with Mexico in the southwest and forcing (suppressing) Mexicans and Asians into labor exploitation in the far west. Perhaps most powerfully, a fast developing capitalist economy began to strengthen industrialism in ever larger cities, where race, gender and class stratification would be reproduced in new formations with urban segregation and Indian reservations. If we are to love this country and work for a more just America, then we must consider these dialectical realities and their continuity to the 20th and 21st centuries where they intersect with global climate change.

The other defining feature of the new country was its political geography, made up of thirteen centrally English colonies along the eastern seaboard of North America. Having clawed and carved these colonial societies out of existing Indian nations (for Land), and so established racially subordinated enslaved worker population (for Labor), a governing elite looked westward to lands claimed by European countries – Britain, France, Spain – where Native Nations were not yet subdued by genocidal warfare. To the north, England held sway after the 1783 Treaty of Paris, while to the south lay Florida, a racially diverse region held by Spain,[57] and complex Caribbean colonized islands, still under internecine warfare and deeply racist systems – exemplified by where it all started – Ayiti/Kiskeya called Hispaniola divided into Spanish and French holdings already under internal and external attacks, especially by Black freedom forces demanding their own revolutionary independence. The exigencies of capital and growing global capitalism would demand the reproduction of systemic racism, and expansion of the racial state, however democratic and freedom-oriented it was toward its central demographic, white men. Hundreds of Indian Nations stood in the way of this expansion, their societies filled with a great diversity and deep appreciation for cultures they wished to keep and protect against invasion. The dye was set and cast for the next 240 years of armed racial struggle in the Americas…

Notes

1   Chinua Achebe. "An Image of Africa: Racism in Conrad's Heart of Darkness." Archived 18 January 2006 at the Wayback Machine – the Massachusetts Review. 1977 (c/o North Carolina State University).

2   In the north, fur trading increased gun violence and competition leading to warfare between neighboring tribes, decimating respect for elders and national

trading agreements. In the south, massive enslavement operations run out of the Carolinas and other port colonies from 1680 to its peak in 1730 when populations were declining and ability to defend land interests fell off, increasing divisions among the nations, exploitable during wars and trading times.

3 Fenelon, 1998. "Culturicide, resistance and survival of the Lakota (Sioux Nation)"

4 Note how both the fledgling United States and England name this French and Indian war, when in reality it was France and England colonizing powers creating and betraying alliances with Indian nations, all the while demarking territory only by colonizer claim – New England, France or Spain – without any recognition of Native Nations.

5 Treaties had been struck with the colonizing nations, most potently with the English, before and even during the Revolutionary War, with the Haudenosaunee formally recognizing a 'Covenant Chain' carrying over with the new governments, based on the previous treaties (Hill, 2014). This was done in direct treaties with the United States.

6 I want to give great praise to this series, and how it reframes and humanizes the African American experience, from first enslavement, through the Middle Passage, plantation slave systems, resilience, resistance and adaptation, the Civil War, Reconstruction and its demise, the Jim Crow South and on into the 20th century. Interviews and historical statements humanize the African descent people in this documentary. Which, of course, is its limitation when considering the larger, global interconnected world-system, the point of this book.

7 Importantly, these scholars have advanced the discussion of long-term effects of settler colonialism, and their interaction with Indigenous peoples everywhere in the world. The critical point here is that we can essentialize our depictions of peoples called 'settlers' and lose their diversity and struggles, as well as the bigger picture. There is also a tendency to essentialize Indigenous peoples – as tribes, generalized nations or collectives – rather than the complex and often contradictory realities of separate Native nations and peoples, with their own conflicts.

8 Map showing the carving up of North America, especially the **1763 Proclamation Line**, with 13 colonies of course, rest is **New Spain, New France** and The **1783 Paris of Treaty agreement**.

9

> Rotterdam and in Amsterdam the people are packed densely, like herrings… one person receives a place of scarcely 2 feet width and 6 feet length in the bedstead, while many a ship carries four to six hundred souls… the ships most often sail 8, 9, 10 to 12 weeks before they reach Philadelphia. …No one can have an idea of the sufferings which women in confinement have to bear with their innocent children… Children from 1 to 7 years rarely survive the voyage. I witnessed miserly in no less than 32 children in our ship, all of whom were thrown into the sea… When the ships have landed…
> …no one is permitted to leave except those who pay for their voyage… the others who cannot pay, must remain on board the ships till they are purchased… The sale of human beings in the market on board the ship is carried on… every day Englishmen, Dutchmen and High-Germans… go on board… and offers for sale passengers from Europe, and select among the healthy persons such as they deem suitable… and bargain with them

how long they will serve for their passage money, which most of them are still in debt for. ...adult persons bind themselves in writing to serve 3, 4, 5 or 6 years for the amount due... Many parents must sell and trade away children like so many head of cattle; for if their children take the debt upon themselves, the parents can leave the ship free (many do not see each for many years, perhaps no more in all their lives) When both parents have died over half-way at sea, their children... ...must stand for their own and their parents' passage, and serve till they are 21 years old. When a serf has an opportunity to marry in this country, he or she must pay for each year ... have yet to serve... If some one in this country runs away from his master... he cannot get far. Good provision has been made for such cases, so the run-away is soon recovered... If such a runaway has been away from his master one day, he must serve for it as a punishment a week, for a week a month, and for a month half a year.

(Mittelberger, 1754: 72–76)

10 From the Lenape term 'Sakimauchheen Ing' (pronounced Sak-i-mauch-heen Ing) which means 'to make a chief or king place'; called 'Shackamaxon' by the English, Dutch, and Swedes. It was where the Lenapi 'crowned' their many family 'sakima' (chief) or their three clan 'kitakima' (big or clan chief) of the Lenape Nation. (Wikipedia, https://en.wikipedia.org/wiki/Treaty_of_Shackamaxon retrieved 6/6/2022).

11 Treaty of Easton 1758 signed by Teedyuscung as the 'King of the Delawares' to establish a permanent Lenape (Delaware) home in eastern Pennsylvania in the Lehigh, Susquehanna and Delaware River valleys, but resulting in the surrender of Lenape claims to all lands in Pennsylvania. Interestingly, this was two years after the Scalp Act, ethnic cleansing in the territory under treaty. Teedyuscung was assassinated during the 1763 Royal Proclamation.

12 Note that the Scalp Act does not distinguish between 'friendly' and 'hostile' Indians, terms later used in policy formation, by Benjamin Franklin in press analysis (Pennsylvania Gazette story in 1756 reporting on a 'murdered' family of 'friendly' Indians (therefore not deserving of bounties) all the way to U.S. congressional acts in the 1876 wars against 'hostiles' not reporting to Indian agencies in the Dakotas established in 1868 Fort Laramie treaty.

13 This becomes a penultimate irony and hypocrisy, when the Penn sons of liberty (later western white supremacists) falsify an 'oral' treaty called the Walking Purchase, distort boundaries even of that fraud, which are employed for a hundred years in genocidal takings of lands, as they deny the clear oral tradition of Lenape wampum belts.

14 When Cromwell seizes power over England after finishing the brutal colonization of Ireland, they all but dismiss the House of Lords, and begin stacking it with various nobility and assumed peerage, increasing the overall number thus diluting individual members powers, resolved in the U.S. Senate by strictly limiting each state to two positions.

15 Actually, with the take down and execution of King Charles in England and the subsequent rise of the House of Commons (and periodic fall of the House of Lords) we have a 'lesson learned' experience that the colonists were well aware of, including the rise of Cromwell (the same Commander of Ireland's extreme

colonization) to become 'Lord Protector of England, Scotland and Ireland' who ultimately restored a more chastened monarch.

16 The U.S. Constitution gave all power over voting requirements to the states, which overwhelmingly limited it to property-owning or tax-paying white males (ranging from 6% to 11% of the population). Interesting some states did allow Black males (if propertied) to vote, although like New Jersey by 1807 they revoked the right later. Unmarried women (if propertied, which married women could not meet) could technically vote as well. This means that states varied across voting rights, with tax-paying white males foundational to all states until well after the Civil War.

17 Southern states would assuredly vote against Black interests in freedom from slavery, even as northern states were consumed by taxation interests, for themselves, meaning math adding up to two times 3/5 or 6/5 of a property, really is zero as a person (debates have raged recently about three-fifths of a person, rather than the economic gains).

18 Some scholars may disagree on this, with laws and statuary changes made in the coming years (1803 and on) leading to a more modern electoral college, rather than a 'smoke-filled back room' making the selections. It is interesting to note the 2020 elections being challenged in just this way, with some Trump and Republican bosses replacing electors, both in state governments and in the January 6 assault and conspiracy of 2021.

19 This is another major point of deviation from the Haudenosaunee confederation, which was inclusive by its formative properties of representing the 5 and then 6 tribal nations of the pluralistic constituted peoples.

20 **Hispaniola** is the second-largest island in the Caribbean (after Cuba), with an area of 76,192 square kilometers (29,418 square miles), 48,440 square kilometers (18,700 square miles) under Dominican Republic sovereignty (the eastern part) and 27,750 square kilometers (10,710 square miles) under Haitian sovereignty (the western part). The Republic of Ireland measures 70,273 square kilometers/ 27,132 square miles while six counties that make up Northern Ireland measure 14,136 square kilometers/5,467 square miles, so **Ireland** island (North Atlantic) has a total area of 84,421 square kilometers (32,595 square miles).

21 Population of Ireland 1500–2000 – Genealogy of the Grantonline: Population of Ireland 1500–2000 (grantonline.com) www.grantonline.com/grant-family-genealogy/Records/population/population-ireland.htm retrieved in 2020 and again November 20, 2021.

22 Ireland's population are estimated around 1 million around 1500, rose slowly from 3 million in 1700 until the last half of the 18th century when it reached 4 million. The increase in the population was not smooth during this century, having reached 3.25 million by 1740, the famine at that time wiped out 400,000 people, or about 1 in 8. Then population increased until it reached around 4 million by 1800. It then entered a rapid increase that slowed by 1830. In 1841, people had reached 8.2 million (total might have been 8.5 million), that would have gotten to 9 million, except famine beginning in 1845, accompanied by English pressure to emigrate.

23 5 million people live in Ireland, yet an estimated 55 million people worldwide trace their ancestry back to Ireland. Emigration went up and on during and after the famine, but there was mass emigration from Ireland long before the famine.

Irish accounted for a third of all voluntary traffic across the Atlantic. These emigrants were mainly from Ulster and Leinster, fewer coming from poorer areas of Connaught and Munster.

24 A fascinating comparison can be and is made with racial caricatures of Africans (Curtis, 1997), in Apes and Angels, the Irishman in Victorian Caricature (Washington DC: Smithsonian Institution).

25 Some Irish scholars see connections to share-cropping in post-Civil War America, while others see the system as maximally oppressive in determining market prices and practices; indeed, during the potato famine some elite food was exported to London and other sites in Europe.

26 NASA/JPL/SRTM, Public domain, via Wikimedia Commons

27 Wikipedia., Public domain, via Wikimedia Commons: Stilfehler from Ira Berlin: *Generations of Captivity: A History of African-American Slaves* (2003)

28 The Southwest Ordnance is initially explicit over the Southwest Territory that becomes Tennessee as 'ceded' by North Carolina claims (since Kentucky was already being claimed, first as the country Franklin). Mississippi Territory was still not defined, contested by Spain and England, both having alliances with strong Indian Nations. (These lands were 'ceded' by Georgia in 1798 to the United States.) What was clear is that the region would be slave-holding, which set up the southern slave plantation system (using the Southwest Ordnance as legalization for taking land).

29 More than half of New York (western half and most of the far north) had already been taken or seized without legalized cession through the genocidal 'Indian Expedition' ordered by General (soon to be president) Washington during the Revolutionary War in 1779 and subsequent campaigns after the United States was formed (Smith, 2020).

30 A Note on the Voyage of Venture Smith – [A Note on the Voyage of Venture Smith (voyageid 36067) and the Historical Record of Transatlantic Slave Trading] by David Eltis and Paul Lachance; under Slave Voyages www.slave voyages.org/voyage/essays#interpretation/a-note-on-the-voyage-of-venture-smith/3/en/

31 We might note, discussed in the previous chapter 3 Blacks, that many indentured or indebted servile immigrants did escape or flee their situation, with many staying free and often getting land of their own. Of course, this was not possible, with rare exception, to non-Europeans who were not viewed as part of the settler class.

32 Lord Jeffrey Amherst, Commander-in-Chief of British expeditionary forces during the French and Indian War, wrote in a letter to Colonel Henry Bouquet (July 7, 1763): "Could it not be contrived to send the Small Pox among those disaffected tribes of Indians?" and later replied his intentions: "You will Do well to try to Innoculate the Indians by means of Blankets, as well as to try Every other method that can serve to Extirpate this Execrable Race."

33 France had of course achieved its' liberation, for all peoples, in their revolution and subsequent policies; whereas England had not allowed slave laws in their country, even as they were master ship-builders and engaged in the huge cross-Atlantic slave marketing system; while Spain was stuck with their philosophical meanderings and policies. All the European countries did not have to construct internal enslavement systems, a critical point for the United States.

34 See Chapter 3 (Black) Figure 3.8:Virginia Slave Codes development: 1660–1705 that brings up 'abominable mixture' of the races if intermarriage with white women is allowed, extended to all non-whites (Indians) by 1705.

35 *Europaeus albus:* European white; *Americanus rubescens:* American reddish; *Asiaticus fuscus:* Asian tawny; *Africanus niger:* African black (1735); later added 'humors' or temperaments, six attributes, by (1758) adding: (1) Skin color, medical temperament (corresponding to the four medieval humors) and body posture; (2) physical traits relating to hair color and form, eye color and distinctive facial traits; (3) behavior; (4) manner of clothing; (5) form of government; and an ambiguous six of monstrous with Africans at the bottom of the order.

36 Blumenback described racial taxonomies taken from Linnaeus, that introduced ideas of more or less 'beautiful' with implied origins of hierarchy in his influential 1776 book, and later found five classifications of human races: Caucasian, Mongolian, Malayan, Ethiopian, and American (where he created the Caucasoid category as first origin), using 'degenerative' causation for other, lower order races (Gould 1989 disagrees, but both beauty and first origin connect with degeneration to clearly delineate hierarchies), in his 1787 and subsequent works (1790 on), also highly influential in the taxonomy of humans as species in racial hierarchy.

37 One might ask what the standards of this 'beauty' are, or where Blumenbach got such a fantasticized notion, that scholars have at times debated. Besides the earlier documented depictions of European men as being strong, handsome figures that Native women were supposedly drawn toward, a deeper reading of his works shows places where he praises Caucasian women as having breasts that are beautiful 'white orbs tipped with vermillion' which implies a fascination with a woman probably from Georgia or thereabouts, in contrast to the cloistered lifestyle that Gould believes protects him from claims of racism (I find his racism intersectional, sprinkled with sexism).

38 Actually, we are both before and after our analysis of the creation of a revolutionary America that would reify racial slavery and genocidal destruction within its very constitution. We must remember that the people versus property paradigm introduced to maintain Blacks as slaves, had its counterpart in the personhood extended to corporations, becoming the basis of laws circumscribing capitalism, and later abused to extend to incorporated companies rights (such as freedom of speech) that it denied much of its own human population – Blacks and Indians.

39 One rarely sees this referenced in scholarly literature, yet it is essential in the European rationales later called the Enlightenment that is brought up by Graeber and Wengrow (2021) as the Indigenous Critique – in other words just what is 'natural' and how does one rationalize that with dehumanization of Indians, Blacks and the poor. This Nature versus Civilization paradigm is very deep in Euro-American consciousness, noted by Deloria (1979, 1995).

40 Arising from the military, Napoleon was a regressive, counterrevolutionary who ultimately became a dictator.

41 Fredrickson (2002).

42 This of course is the landed discourse under colonial and later U.S. laws, reflected as I state herein this chapter in the census and the constitution. However, academia took many turns through the 19th and 20th centuries, finding in the

anthropology of the 1940s there were "only 3 races – caucasoid, mongoloid, negroid – in that order" (Nell Irvin Painter, lecture at Rhodes College on March 3, 2015, notes taken July 18, 2022 [Dr. Nell Irvin Painter – "The History of White People" – Bing video] YouTube).

43 Washington (and Jefferson) allowed some or all of their slaves to be freed upon their death, or their wife's death, which is hardly emancipation except in the sense of losing the privilege of their property usage. Jefferson is given credit for this with two of his own children, by Sally Hemings who was never freed, where his estate sold many of their enslaved people, to pay off debts and settle financial inheritance.

44 Initially, the Assembly stated that citizens included all men, those of color were said to be among the 'free' men (an attempt to thread the needle on slavery in the colonies), however, Haitians interpreted it as both slave or servant, incendiary thought to the rebellion, and a model to other Caribbean peoples.

45 In fact Leclerc calls for killing all 'Blacks of the mountains' as the primary site of resistance and revolution (L. DuBois, 2004: 290–291) men and women above the age of 12 even though it would reduce plantation profits.

46 As noted earlier, contradictory information was simply ignored or denied, as in African revolutionary thought creating Haiti as the world's first successful slave revolt and Black nation in the Americas (DuBois, 2004: 303).

47 "To Rebuild, Haiti Needs a Break From Neocolonialism" (Interview with Jean Eddy Saint Paul), by Gabby Birenbaum, Vox August 20, 2021.

48 For example, see: Essentials of Sociology (by Giddens, Appelbaum, Duneier and Carr).

49 For instance, neither Native Nations nor peoples are included in the population counts in the ex-colonial states (whose boundaries are changing) nor are they represented in the north and southwest territories.

50 Better called societal death, or in theory sociological death, in they disappear without rights of representation.

51 I suspect this is at the heart of the 1619 debates, still raging across academia and into the public discourse, often under cover of other analytical approaches, such as Critical Race Theory. Basically, generalists and mainstream historians and social theorists either don't see these large intersectional population shifts as dehumanization by and for the academy, or don't want to make the connection to these vast forces of migration and dominance critically important to the construction of the United States, as observed in the first census and constitutional frameworks.

52 The ex-colony, now independent, replicates the colonial invasion and take-over of lands and resources, mostly through an elimination of the Native. In terms of processes, the United States differs little from the colonizers, especially England, that operated out of Europe. In fact, race-based slavery fully institutionalized in the southern colonies (Virginia and the Carolinas) were near exact copies of what England was doing elsewhere, while a strong racialized class stratification system in the northern colonies (Massachusetts, Connecticut, New York) lending itself to urban and industrial development, grew with great similarity as urban centers in England (Manchester, Leeds).

53 Deloria, Jr. Vine, 1973. *God is Red: A Native View of Religion*. Golden, CO: Fulcrum Publishing. Deloria, Jr. Vine. 1979. *The Metaphysics of Modern Existence*.

New York: Harper & Rowe. (See 2012 edition with preface by Daniel Wildcat for effective introduction to this work, that stands today.) Deloria, Jr. Vine, 1995. *Red Earth, White Lies, Native Americans and the Myth of Scientific Fact* (New York: Scribner, 1995).

54 Taino Arawakan people on what became the Dominican Republic half of the island, were melded into mestizo, African and dominant Spanish groups, keeping identity alive through familial stories of descendancy. Interestingly, this also occurred on Puerto Rico and other Spanish held territories, while the Black – White binary diminished Native ancestry under French and English colonization systems, similar to what developed in the United States.

55 During much of this period, most of Ireland was technically under control by the Vatican as being Catholic, which was effectively repealed during the Union of the Crowns in 1603 followed by the Cromwellian expansion wars, Acts of Union 1707 forming Great Britain, completing English domination and transfer under Crown authority, later made official in 1800 Acts of Union becoming the United Kingdom of Great Britain and Ireland.

56 Sonni Ali passed in November 1492 ironically as the Columbus expedition approached Hispaniola island. While he was the first of the Songhai kings, establishing an inland empire that rivaled Mali or ancient Ghana, the year 1500 introduced the Portuguese to Brazil and Spain began the transfer of African slaves to the Americas, so the century mark, over time and historical analysis, reflected a high point of what West Africa had come to be, and what it could have been without the transatlantic slave trade.

57 The colonial interchange, or trading, of colonies after wars, exemplifies what happened to the Floridian territories. After the French and Indian War ends in the Treaty of Paris in 1763 and the British had seized Havana, part of very complex set of colonial trades included the historical La Florida held by Spain (raided by French and British forces) which England took over and declared East Florida (England also traded the larger territories of Quebec and Canada for France to retain control over Martinique, Guadeloupe and the conflict in San Domingue – Haiti) as West Florida controlled the southern coast to the Mississippi River. When England negotiated the second Treaty of Paris in 1783 (losing the revolutionary war to the United States) East Florida returned to Spanish control, where it would remain, under high conflict with escaped slaves from the United States, until 1821 invasions and takings. West Florida was more or less contained in the Mississippi territories later becoming Alabama and Mississippi under state formation, and racial slave plantations, found throughout the Caribbean and notably Haiti.

Bibliography

Abbott, Andrew. 2016. *Processual Sociology*. Chicago: University of Chicago Press.

Abrahamson, Mark. 1996. *Urban Enclaves, Identity and Place in America*. New York: St. Martin's Press.

Achebe, Chinua. 1977. "An Image of Africa: Racism in Conrad's Heart of Darkness." Archived January 18, 2006 at the Wayback Machine – the Massachusetts Review (c/o North Carolina State University).

Aguirre, Adalberto and Jonathan H. Turner. 1995. *American Ethnicity, the Dynamics and Consequences of Discrimination*. New York: McGraw-Hill.

Alatas, Syed Farid and Vineeta Sinha (Eds). 2018. *Sociological Theory beyond the Canon*. London: Palgrave Macmillan.

Alexander, Michelle. 2010. *The New Jim Crow: Mass Incarceration in the Age of Colorblindness*. New York: The New Press.

Allen, Theodore W. 1994. *The Invention of the White Race: Racial Oppression and Social Control*. New York: Verso Books.

Altman, Ida. 2007. "The Revolt of Enriquillo and the Historiography of Early Spanish America." *The Americas*, 63:4 April 2007, 587–614 (Academy of American Franciscan History).

Aronson, Marc and Marina Budhos, 2010. *Sugar Changed the World: A Story of Magic, Spice, Slavery, Freedom, and Science*. Boston, MA: Clarion Books.

Arrighi, G. 1994. *The Long Twentieth Century*. London: Verso.

Asante, Molefi Kete. 2021. "Africa." In *Four Hundred Souls: A Community History of African-Americans 1619–2019*, Ibram X. Kendi and Keisha N. Blain (Eds). New York: One World Press (Random House).

Back, Les and John Solomos (Eds). 2000. *Theories of Race and Racism: a Reader*. New York: Routledge.

Barber, Rev. Dr. William, II. 2020. Stolen Hands, Stolen Lands, from 1619 to a Just Future, 400 Years of Inequality, A People's Observance. Lecture Celebration at Riverside Church, October 20, 2019, streamed youtube, https://www.youtube.com/watch?v=4vjEKq-QwAM. Retrieved January 28, 2023.

Barrett, Ward. 1990 "World Bullion Flows, 1450–1800." In *The Rise of Merchant Empires*, J.D. Tracy (Ed.). Cambridge: Cambridge University Press, 224–254.

Beatty, Aidan, Sharae Deckard, Maurice Coakley and Denis O'Hearn. 2016 "Ireland in the World-System: An Interview with Denis O'Hearn." *Journal of World-Systems Research*, 22(1): 202–213.

Beebe, Rose Marie and Robert M. Senkewicz. 2015. *Junípero Serra: California, Indians, and the Transformation of a Missionary*. Norman, OK: University of Oklahoma Press.

Bell, Derrick. 1973. *Race Racism and American Law*. Boston, MA: Little, Brown & Company.

Bell, Derrick A. 1995. "Who's Afraid of Critical Race Theory?" *University of Illinois Law Review*, 4: 893–910.

Bethencourt, Francisco. 2013 *Racisms: From the Crusades to the Twentieth Century*. Princeton, NJ: Princeton University Press.

Bhambra, Gurminder K. 2007. *Rethinking Modernity: Postcolonialism and the Sociological Imagination*. Basingstoke, UK: Palgrave Macmillan.

Bhambra, Gurminder K. and John Holmwood. 2021. *Colonialism and Modern Social Theory*. Cambridge, UK: Polity Press.

Birenbaum, Gabby. 2021. "To Rebuild, Haiti Needs a Break from Neocolonialism" (Interview with Jean Eddy Saint Paul), *Vox*. 20 August 21.

Blackhawk, Ned. 2006. *Violence over the Land: Indians and Empires in the Early American West*. Cambridge, MA: Harvard University Press.

Blauner, Bob. 1989. *Black Lives, White Lives: Three Decades of Race Relations in America*. Berkeley, CA: University of California Press.

Blaut, James M. 1993. *The Colonizer's Model of the World: Geographical Diffusionism and Eurocentric History*. New York: Guilford.

Bonfil Batalla, Guillermo. 1996. *Mexico Profundo – Reclaiming a Civilization*. Phillip A. Dennis (Trans.). Austin, TX: University of Texas Press.

Bonilla-Silva, Eduardo. 1997. "Rethinking Racism: Toward a Structural Interpretation." *American Sociological Review*, 62(3): 465–480.

Bonilla-Silva, Eduardo. 2009. *Racism without Racists: Color Blind Racism and the Persistence of Racial Inequality in the United States*. Lanham, MD: Rowman and Littlefield.

Bonilla-Silva, Eduardo. 2015. "More than Prejudice: Restatement, Reflections, and New Directions in Critical Race Theory." *Sociology of Race and Ethnicity*, 1(1): 73–87.

Bourdieu, Pierre. 1984. *Distinction: A Social Critique of the Judgement of Taste*. London: Routledge.

Box-Steffensmeier, Janet M. and Bradford S. Jones, 2004. *Event History Analysis Modeling: A Guide for Social Scientists*. New York: Cambridge University Press.

Braudel, Fernand. 1972. *The Mediterranean and the Mediterranean World in the Age of Philip II*, Vol. I,. S. Reynolds (Trans.). New York: Harper & Row.

Brodkin, Karen. 1999. *How Jews Became White and What That Says about Race in America*. New Brunswick, NJ: Rutgers University Press.

Brown, Karida. 2021. "Theorizing Racial and Colonial Capitalism: The Thought of W.E.B. Du Bois and Cedric Robinson." Presented at American Sociological Association Conference (virtual), August 2021.

Burawoy, Michael. 2013. "Living Theory." *Contemporary Sociology: A Journal of Reviews*, 42(6): 779–783.

Burawoy, Michael. 2021. "Why Is Classical Theory Classical? Theorizing the Canon and Canonizing Du Bois." *Journal of Classical Sociology*, 21(3–4): 245–259. https://doi.org/10.1177/1468795X211036955.

Bush, Roderick. 1999. *We Are Not What We Seem: Black Nationalism and Class Struggle in the American Century*. New York: New York University Press.

Bush, Roderick. 2009. *The End of White World Supremacy: Black Internationalism and the Problem of the Color Line*. Philadelphia, PA: Temple University Press.

Carnoy, Martin. 1994. *Faded Dreams: The Politics and Economic of Race in America*. New York: Cambridge University Press.

Castells, Manuel. 1989. *The Informational City: Information Technology, Economic Restructuring, and the Urban Regional Process*. Oxford, UK: Blackwell.

Castells, Manuel. 2000. "Grassrooting the Space of Flows." in *Cities in the Telecommunications Age: The Fracturing of Geographies*, J. Wheeler, Y. Aoyama and B. Warf (Eds). London: Routledge, 18–30, https://handwiki.org/wiki/Social:Space_of_flows. Retrieved February 1, 2023.

Césaire, Aimé. 1955. *Discourse on Colonialism. Discours sur le colonialisme*, Paris: Présence Africaine.

Champagne, Duane. 1994. *Native America, Portrait of the Peoples*. Detroit, MI: Visible Ink Press.

Chase-Dunn, Christopher and Peter Grimes. 1995. "World-Systems Analysis." *Annual Review of Sociology*, 21: 387–417.

Chase-Dunn, Christopher and Thomas D. Hall. 1997. *Rise and Demise, Comparing World-Systems*. Boulder, CO: Westview Press.

Chilisa, Bagele. 2020. *Indigenous Research Methodologies*. 2nd ed. London, UK: SAGE Publications,

Chomsky, Noam and Pollin, Robert. 2020. *The Climate Crisis and the Global Green New Deal: The Political Economy of Saving the Planet*. Verso.

Coates, Ta-Nehisi. 2019. "Reparations Are Not Just About Slavery but Also Centuries of Theft & Racial Terror," *Democracy Now* (Youtube), www.youtube.com/watch?v=ml_VAWFHHps. Retrieved June 24, 2022.

Cook-Lynn, Elizabeth. 2007. *New Indians, Old Wars*. Champaigne, IL: University of Illinois Press.

Collins, Patricia H. and Sirma Bilge. 2016. *Intersectionality*. Cambridge, UK: Polity.

Collins, Randall. 2008. *Violence: A Micro-Sociological Theory*. Princeton, NJ: Princeton University Press.

Connell, Raewyn. 2018. "Decolonizing Sociology." *Contemporary Sociology*, 47(4): 399–407.

Conniff, Michael and Thomas Davis. 1994. *Africans in the Americas*. New York: St. Martin's Press.

Costo, Rupert and Jeannette Costo. 1987. *The Missions of California: A Legacy of Genocide*. San Francisco, CA: Indian Historian Press.

Coulthard, G. 2014. *Red Skin, White Masks*. Minneapolis, MN: University of Minnesota Press.

Cox, Oliver. 1948. *Caste, Class, and Race: A Study in Social Dynamics*. New York: Monthly Review Press.

Cox, Oliver C. 1948. *Caste, Class, and Race*. Garden City, NY: Doubleday, 332–333.

Cox, Oliver Cromwell. 1959. *Foundations of Capitalism*. London: Peter Owen Limited, 384–385.

Crenshaw, K. 1991. "Mapping the Margins: Intersectionality, Identity Politics, and Violence against Women of Color." *Stanford Law Review*, 43(6): 1241–1299.

Crenshaw, Kimberlé, Neil Gotanda, Gary Peller and Kendall Thomas (Eds). 1995. *Critical Race Theory: The Key Writings that Formed the Movement*. New York: The New Press.

Crosby, Alfred W. 1972. *The Columbian Exchange: Biological and Cultural Consequences of 1492*. Westport, CT: Greenwood Press.

Crosby, Alfred W. 1986. *Ecological Imperialism: The Biological Expansion of Europe, 900–1900*. New York: Cambridge University Press.

Curtis, L. Perry Jr. 1997. *Apes and Angels, the Irishman in Victorian caricature*, 2nd ed. Washington, DC: Smithsonian Institution Press.

d'Errico, Peter. May 24, 2017. Northwest Ordinance and Slavery: White Supremacy in the Foundation of the US. *Indian Country Today* (media network). Retrieved May 24, 2017.

Dalrymple, William. 2019. *The Anarchy: The East India Company, Corporate Violence, and the Pillage of an Empire*. London: Bloomsbury Publishing.

Darity, Jr. William A. March 14–17, 2017. "The State of Black America 150 Years After Emancipation" presentation at Reflections on the Impact of the Reconstruction Amendments, a Research Symposium on the Social and Economic Outcomes of the 13th, 14th, and 15th Amendments, Smithsonian National Museum of African American History and Culture.

David, Strang. 1990. "From Dependency to Sovereignty: An Event History Analysis of Decolonization 1870–1987." *American Sociological Review*, 55(6): 846–860.

Davidson, Basil. 1980 (1961). *The African Slave Trade*. Rev. ed. Boston, MA: Back Bay Books, Little, Brown and Company.

de Las Casas, B. 1974. *The Devastation of the Indies: A Brief Account*. H. Briffault (Trans.). New York, NY: Seabury Press (Original work published 1538).

Degler, Carl N. 1959. *Out of Our Past: The Forces that Shaped Modern America*. New York: Harper & Brothers.

Delgado, Richard and Jean Stefancic. 2012. *Critical Race Theory: An Introduction*. 2nd ed. New York: New York University Press.

Delgado, Richard and Jean Stefancic (Eds). 2013. *Critical Race Theory: The Cutting Edge*. 3rd ed. Philadelphia, PA: Temple University Press, 2013.

Deloria, Jr. Vine. 1973. *God Is Red: A Native View of Religion*. Golden, CO: Fulcrum Publishing.

Deloria, Jr. Vine. 1979. *The Metaphysics of Modern Existence*. New York: Harper & Row.

Deloria, Jr. Vine. 1995. *Red Earth, White Lies, Native Americans and the Myth of Scientific Fact* New York: Scribner.

Deloria, Jr. Vine. and Clifford M. Lytle. 1984. *The Nations within, the Past and Future of American Indian sovereignty*. New York: Pantheon Books.

Deloria, Phillip. April 6, 2022. "The Indigenous Constitution, the Greater X, and the Lenape," 4th Annual Paul V. McNutt Lecture, Indiana University.

Deloria, Vine, Jr. and Daniel Wildcat. 2001. *Power and Place: Indian Education in America*. Goldon, CO: Fulcrum Publishing.

Deloria, Vine Jr. and David E. Wilkins. 2000. *Tribes, Treaties, and Constitutional Tribulations*. Austin, TX: University of Texas Press.

Diamond, Jared. 1999. *Guns, Germs and Steel: The Fates of Human Societies*. New York: W.W. Norton.

Dippie, Brian W. 1982. *The Vanishing American: White Attitudes and U.S. Indian Policy*. Middletown, CT: Wesleyan University Press.

Dobyns, Henry F. 1983. *Their Numbers Become Thinned: Native American Population Dynamics in Eastern North America*. Knoxville, TN: The University of Tennessee Press.

Doob, Christopher B. 1996. *Racism, an American Cauldron*. New York: HarperCollins.

Dubois, Laurent. 2004. *A Colony of Citizens: Revolution and Slave Emancipation in the French Caribbean, 1787–1804*. Omohundro Institute of Early American History and Culture, Williamsburg, VA: University of North Carolina Press.

DuBois, W.E.B. 1899. *The Philadelphia Negro*. Oxford: Oxford University Press.

DuBois, W.E.B. 1900. *Problem of the Color Line*. Philadelphia, PA: Temple University Press.

DuBois, W.E.B. 1903a. *The Souls of Black Folk*. Oxford: Oxford University Press.

DuBois, W.E.B. 1915. *The Negro*. Oxford: Oxford University Press.

DuBois, W.E.B. 1920. *Darkwater*. Oxford: Oxford University Press.

DuBois, W.E.B. 1933. *Black Reconstruction*. New York: Harcourt, Brace and Company.

DuBois, W.E.B. 1939. *Black Folk Then and Now*. Oxford: Oxford University Press.

DuBois, W.E.B. 1940. *Dusk of Dawn*. Oxford: Oxford University Press.

DuBois, W.E.B. 1961. *Worlds of Color*. Oxford: Oxford University Press.

DuBois, W.E.B. 1968. *The Autobiography of W.E.B. Du Bois*. Oxford: Oxford University Press.

DuBois, W.E.B. 1989 (1903). *The Souls of Black Folk*. New York: Penguin Books.

Du Bois, W.E.B. 1995 (1923). "The Superior Race." In *A Reader*, D.L. Lewis (Ed.). New York: Henry Holt and Company, 470–477.

Du Bois, W.E.B. 1935. *Black Reconstruction in America*. Oxford: Oxford University Press.

Dunaway, Wilma A. 1996. *The First American Frontier: Transition to Capitalism in Southern Appalachia, 1700–1860*. Chapel Hill, NC: University of North Carolina Press.

Dunbar-Ortiz, R. 2014. *An Indigenous Peoples' History of the United States*. Boston, MA: Beacon Press.

Dunbar-Ortiz, Roxanne. 2015. *An Indigenous Peoples' History of the United States (Revisioning American History)*. Boston, MA: Beacon Press.

Duneier, Mitchell. 2016. *Ghetto: The Invention of a Place, the History of an Idea*. New York: Farrar, Straus & Giroux.

Dunn, Oliver and James E. Kelley, Jr. (Eds). 1989. *The Diario of Christopher Columbus's First Voyage to America, 1492–1493 (abstracted by Fray Bartolome de las Casas)*. Norman, OK: University of Oklahoma Press.

Dupuy, Alex. 2014. *Haiti: From Revolutionary Slaves to Powerless Citizens, Essays on the Politics and Economics of Underdevelopment, 1804–2013*. New York: Routledge.

Duster, Troy. March 2015. "A Post-Genomic Surprise. The Molecular Reinscription of Race in Science, Law and Medicine." *British Journal of Sociology*, 66(1): 1–2.

Elias, Sean and Joe R. Feagin. 2016. *Racial Theories in Social Science: A Systemic Racism Critique*. New York: Routledge.

Eltis, David. 1999. *The Rise of African Slavery in the Americas*. New York: Cambridge University Press.

Estefan, Michel and Josh Seim. 2022. "Teaching Social Theory as Cartography: Toward a Pedagogy of Radical Accessibility." *Teaching Sociology*, 50(3): 269–280.

Fanon, Frantz. 1952. *Black Skin, White Masks*. L. Markmann (Trans.). New York: Grove Press.

Fanon, Frantz. 1963. *The Wretched of the Earth*. New York: Grove Press.

Feagin, Joe. 2001. "Social Justice and Sociology: Agendas for the Twenty-First Century." *American Sociological Review*, 66(1): 1–20.

Feagin, Joe. 2006. *Systemic Racism: A Theory of Oppression*. New York: Routledge.

Feagin, Joe R. 2000. *Racist America: Roots, Current Realities, and Future Reparations*. New York: Routledge.

Feagin, Joe R. 2006. *Systemic Racism: A Theory of Oppression*. New York: Routledge/Taylor & Francis Group.

Feagin, Joe R. 2013. *The White Racial Frame: Centuries of Racial Framing and Counter-Framing.* 2nd ed. New York: Routledge.

Feagin, Joe and K. Ducey. 2018. *Racist America: Roots, Current Realities, and Future Reparations.* New York: Routledge.

Feagin, Joe R. and Clairece Booher Feagin. 1999 (1978). *Racial and Ethnic Relations.* 6th ed. Upper Saddle River, NJ: Prentice Hall.

Feagin, Joe R. and Hernan Vera. 1995. *White Racism.* New York: Routledge.

Feagin, Joe R. and Kimberley Ducey. 2017. *Elite White Men Ruling: Who, What, When, Where, and How.* New York: Routledge.

Feagin, Joe and Sean Elias. 2011. "Rethinking Racial Formation Theory: A Systemic Racism Critique." *Ethnic and Racial Studies,* 36(6): 931–960.

Federici, Sylvia. 2004. *Caliban and the Witch: Women the Body and Primitive Accumulation.* New York: Autonomedia, 17.

Fein, Helen. 1979. *Accounting for Genocide: National Responses and Jewish Victimization during the Holocaust.* New York: Free Press.

Fein, Helen and Joce Freedman-Apsel (Eds). 1998. *Teaching about Genocide: A Guidebook for College and University Teachers.* Washington, DC: American Sociological Association.

Fenelon, James. 2016. "Critique of Glenn on Settler Colonialism and Bonilla-Silva on Critical Race Analysis from Indigenous Perspectives." *Sociology of Race and Ethnicity,* 2(2), 237–242.

Fenelon, James. 2016. "Genocide, Race, Capitalism: Synopsis of Formation within the Modern World-System." *Journal of World-Systems Research,* 22(1): 23–30.

Fenelon, James. 2017. *Standing Rock: Epicenter of Resistance to American Empire,* paper presented at American Sociological Association 2017 annual meeting, Montreal, CA.

Fenelon, James. 2021. "Immigration as Racial Dominance since 1492." In *Migration, Racism and Labor Exploitation in the World-System* (2017 41st Annual Conference, Political Economy of the World-System), Denis O'Hearn and Paul Ciccantell (Eds). New York: Routledge.

Fenelon, James V. 1998. *Culturicide, Resistance, and Survival of the Lakota (Sioux Nation).* New York: Garland Publishing (Routledge).

Fenelon, James V. 2002. "Dual Sovereignty of Native Nations, the United States, & Traditionalists." *Humboldt Journal of Social Relations,* 27(1): 106–145.

Fenelon, James V. 2007. "The Struggle of Indigenous Americans: A Socio-Historical View." In *Handbook of the Sociology of Racial and Ethnic Relations,* Hernan Vera and Joseph Feagin (Eds). New York: Springer Press, chapter 3, 15–38.

Fenelon, James V. 2011. "Indigenous Peoples and World Systems Analysis." In *International Handbook of World-Systems Analysis,* Salvatore Babones and Christopher Chase-Dunn (Eds). New York: Routledge.

Fenelon, James V. and Clifford E. Trafzer. 2014. "From Colonialism to Denial of California Genocide to Mis-Representation: Indigenous Struggles in the Americas." *American Behavioral Scientist,* 58(1): 3–29.

Fenelon, James V. and Mary Louise Defender-Wilson. 2004. "Voyage of Domination, 'Purchase' as Conquest, Sakakawea for Savagery: Distorted Icons from Misrepresentations of the Lewis and Clark Expedition." *Wicazo Sa Review,* 19(1): 85–104.

Fenelon, James V. and Thomas D. Hall. 2005. "Indigenous Struggles over Autonomy, Land and Community: Anti-Globalization and Resistance in World Systems Analysis." In *Latin@s in the World-System: Towards the Decolonization of the US Empire in the 21st Century*, Ramón Grosfoguel, Nelson Maldonado-Torres and Jose David Saldivar (Eds). Boulder, CO: Paradigm Press, 107–122.

Fenelon, James V. and Thomas D. Hall. 2008. "Revitalization and Indigenous Resistance to Globalization and Neoliberalism." *American Behavioral Scientist*, 51(12, Aug): 1867–1901.

Fenelon, James and Dorothy LeBeau. 2006. "Four Directions for Indian Education: Curriculum Models for Lakota/Dakota Teaching and Learning." In *Indigenous Education & Empowerment: International Perspectives*, Ismael Abu-Saad and Duane Champagne (Eds). Walnut Creek, CA: Alta Mira, 21–68.

Fenelon, James and Jennifer Alford. 2020. "Envisioning Indigenous Models for Social and Ecological Change in the Anthropocene." *Journal of World-Systems Research*, 26(2): 372–399.

Fenelon, James, Julia Bogany and Luke Madrigal. 2021. *Indigenous Ethnography for the Santa Ana Watershed Project Report*.

Finkelman, Paul. 2001. *Slavery and the Founders: Race and Liberty in the Age of Jefferson*. Armonk, NY: M.E. Sharpe.

Flynn, Dennis O. and Arturo Giráldez. 1995. "Born with a 'Silver Spoon': The Origin of World Trade in 1571." *Journal of World History*, 6(2, Fall): 201–221.

Flynn, Dennis O. and Arturo Giráldez. 1997. "Introduction: Monetary Substances in Global Perspective." *Metals and Monies in an Emerging Global Economy*, D.O. Flynn and A. Giráldez (Eds). Aldershot, UK: Variorum (Ashgate), xv–xl.

Flynn, Dennis O. and Arturo Giráldez. 2002. "Cycles of Silver: Globalization as Historical Process." *World Economics*, 3(2): 1–16.

Flynn, Dennis O. and Arturo Giráldez. April 2004. "Path Dependence, Time Lags and the Birth of Globalisation: A Critique of O'Rourke and Williamson." *European Review of Economic History*, 8(01): 81–108.

Foley, Neil. 1997. *The White Scourge: Mexicans, Blacks and Poor Whites in Texas Cotton Culture*. Berkeley, CA: University of California Press.

Foster, Roy F. (Ed.) 1989. *The Oxford Illustrated History of Ireland*. Oxford, England: Oxford University Press.

Frank, Andre Gunder. 1998. *ReOrient: Global Economy in the Asian Age*. Berkeley, CA: University of California Press.

Franklin, John Hope and Alfred A. Moss, Jr. 2000. *From Slavery to Freedom: A History of African Americans*. 8th ed. New York: Knopf.

Frederickson, George M. 2002. *Racism: A Short History*. Princeton, NJ: Princeton University Press.

Freeman, Elizabeth (aka MumBet). Elizabeth Freeman Center, Berkshire County Massachusetts. https://elizabethfreemancenter.org/who-we-are/elizabeth-freeman. Retrieved February 1, 2023.

French, Laurence Armand. 1994. *The Winds of Injustice, American Indians and the U.S. Government*. New York: Garland Publishing.

Gallay, Alan. 2015. *Indian Slavery in Colonial America*, edited by Alan Gallay. Lincoln, NE: University of Nebraska Press.

Genovese, Eugene D. 1989. *The Political Economy of Slavery: Studies in the Economy and Society of the Slave South*. Middletown, CT: Wesleyan University Press.

Giddens, Anthony. 2013. *The Consequences of Modernity*. Hoboken, NJ: John Wiley & Sons.

Giddens, Anthony, Mitchell Duneier, Richard P. Appelbaum, and Deborah Carr. 2019. *Essentials of Sociology*. 7th ed. New York: W.W. Norton & Company.

Glenn, E.N. 2015. "Settler Colonialism as Structure: A Framework for Comparative Studies of U.S. Race and Gender Formation. *Sociology of Race and Ethnicity*, 1(1): 52–72.

Go, Julian. 2008. *American Empire and the Politics of Meaning: Elite Political Cultures in the Philippines and Puerto Rico during US Colonialism*. Durham, NC: Duke University Press.

Go, Julian. 2009. "The 'New' Sociology of Empire and Colonialism." *Sociology Compass*, 3(5), 775–788.

Go, Julian. 2011. *Patterns of Empire: The British and American Empires, 1688 to the Present*. New York: Cambridge University Press.

Go, Julian. 2013. "Sociology's Imperial Unconscious: The Emergence of American Sociology in the Context of Empire." In *Sociology and Empire: The Imperial Entanglements of a Discipline*, G. Steinmetz (Ed.). Durham, NC: Duke University Press, 83–105.

Go, Julian. 2016. *Postcolonial Thought and Social Theory*. Oxford, UK: Oxford University Press.

Go, Julian. 2020. "Race, Empire, and Epistemic Exclusion: Or the Structures of Sociological Thought." *Sociological Theory*, 38(2):79–100.

Goatly, Andrew. 2007. *Washing the Brain: Metaphor and Hidden Ideology*. Amsterdam, Netherlands: Benjamins Publishing Company, 194.

Golash-Boza, T. 2016. "A Critical and Comprehensive Sociological Theory of Race and Racism." *Sociology of Race and Ethnicity*, 2(2), 129–141.

Golash-Boza, Tanya. 2012. *Immigration Nation: Raids, Detentions and Deportations in Post-911 America*. Boulder, CO: Paradigm.

Golash-Boza, Tanya. 2015. *Deported: Immigrant Policing, Disposable Labor and Global Capitalism*. New York: New York University Press.

Golash-Boza, Tanya. 2016. "Racialized and Gendered Mass Deportation and the Crisis of Capitalism." *Journal of World-Systems Research*, 22(1): 38–44.

Goldberg, David T. 2002. *The Racial State*. Malden, MA: Blackwell.

Golden, Renny and Michael McConnell, Peggy Mueller, Cindy Poppen and Marilyn Turkovich. 1991. *Dangerous Memories: Invasion and Resistance Since 1492*. Chicago, IL: Chicago Religious Task Force on Central America.

Gould, Stephen Jay. 1981. *The Mismeasure of Man*. New York: Norton.

Graeber, David and David Wengrow. 2021. *The Dawn of Everything: A New History of Humanity*. New York: Farrar, Straus and Giroux (Macmillan).

Greenfield, Patrick. March 21, 2016. "Story of Cities #6: How Silver Turned Potosí into 'the First City of Capitalism'." *The Guardian*. Retrieved May 9, 2020.

Grizzard, Frank E. and Smith, D. Boyd. 2007. *Jamestown Colony: A Political, Social, and Cultural History*. Santa Barbara, CA: ABC-CLIO, 130.

Grosfoguel, Ramon. 2011. "Decolonizing Post-Colonial Studies and Paradigms of Political-Economy: Transmodernity, Decolonial Thinking, and Global Coloniality." *Transmodernity*, 1(1): 1–37.

Grosfoguel, Ramón. 2013. "The Structure of Knowledge in Westernized Universities: Epistemic Racism/Sexism and the Four Genocides/Epistemicides of the Long 16th Century." *Human Architecture: Journal of the Sociology of Self-Knowledge*, XI(1).

Grosfoguel, Ramon. 2016. "What Is Racism?." *Journal of World-Systems Research*, 22(1): 9–15.

Gurr, Ted Robert and Barbara Harff. 1994. *Ethnic Conflict in World Politics*. Boulder, CO: Westview Press.

Hall, Thomas and James Fenelon. 2009. *Indigenous Peoples and Globalization: Resistance and Revitalization*. Boulder, CO: Paradigm.

Hall, Thomas D. 1989. *Social Change in the Southwest, 1350–1880*. Lawrence, KS: University of Kansas Press.

Hannaford, Ivan. 1996. *Race: The History of an Idea in the West*. Baltimore, MD: Johns Hopkins University Press.

Hannah-Jones, Nikole. August 2019. "'America Wasn't a Democracy Until Black Americans Made It One' in 'The 1619 Project'." *The New York Times*. ISSN 0362–4331. Archived from the original on August 17, 2019. Retrieved September 7, 2020.

Hannah-Jones, Nikole. August 14, 2019. "The 1619 Project". *The New York Times*. ISSN 0362-4331. Archived August 17, 2019. Retrieved September 7, 2020.

Hannah-Jones, Nikole and New York Times Company. 2021. *The 1619 Project: A New Origin Story*. New York: The New York Times (One World imprint of Random House).

Hardesty, Jared Ross. 2019. *Black Lives, Native Lands, White Worlds: a history of Slavery in New England*. Amherst, MA: Bright Leaf (University of Massachusetts Press).

Hayes, Floyd W. (Ed.) 1992. *A Turbulent Voyage: Readings in African American Studies*. San Diego, CA: Collegiate Press.

Hechter, Michael. 1999. *Internal Colonialism: The Celtic Fringe in British National Development*. 2nd ed. New York: Routledge.

Heinl, Robert. 1996. *Written in Blood: The Story of the Haitian People, 1492–1995*. Lantham, MD: University Press of America.

Heizer, Robert and Alan Almquist. 1977. *The Other Californians: Prejudice and Discrimination under Spain, Mexico, and the United States to 1920*. Oakland, CA: University of California Press.

Henning, William W. 1823. *The Statutes at Large; Being a Collection of all the Laws of Virginia*, from the first session of the Legislature in the year 1619, published by an act of the General Assembly of Virginia (Richmond 1809), 13 vols. (Richmond, Philadelphia, and New York, 1809–1823). v. 2 (1823). New York: R. & W. & G. Bartow.

Hill, Damaris B. 2021. "Tobacco." In *Four Hundred Souls: A Community History of African-Americans 1619– 2019*, Ibram X. Kendi and Keisha N. Blain (Eds). New York: One World Press (Random House).

Hill, Richard W. 2014. "Linking Arms and Brightening the Chain, Building Relations through Treaties." In *Nation to Nation, Treaties Between the United States & American Indian Nations*, Suzan Shown Harjo (Ed.). Washington, DC: Smithsonian Institution, 36–58.

Hochschild, Jennifer L. 1995. *Facing Up to the American Dream; Race, Class, and the Soul of the Nation*. Princeton, NJ: Princeton University.

Holleman, Hannah. 2016. "De-naturalizing Ecological Disaster: Colonialism, Racism and the Global Dust Bowl of the 1930s." *The Journal of Peasant Studies*, 44(1): 234–260.

Holleman, Hannah. 2018. *Dust Bowls of Empire: Imperialism, Environmental Politics, and the Injustice of Green Capitalism*. New Haven, CT: Yale University Press.

Horne, Gerald. 2014. *The Counter–Revolution of 1776: Slave Resistance and the Origins of the United States of America*. New York: New York University Press.

Horne, Gerald. 2020. *The Dawning of the Apocalypse: The Roots of Slavery, White Supremacy, Settler Colonialism, and Capitalism in the Long Sixteenth Century*. New York: Monthly Review Press.

Horowitz, Irving Louis. 1989. *Taking Lives: Genocide and State Power*. 3rd ed. New Brunswick, NJ: Transaction Publishers.

Howard, John R. 1999. *The Shifting Wind: The Supreme Court and Civil Rights from Reconstruction to Brown*. Albany, NY: State University of New York Press.

Ignatiev, Noel. 1995. *How the Irish Became White*. New York: Routledge.

Itzigsohn, José and Karida L. Brown. 2020. *The Sociology of W. E. B. Du Bois: Racialized Modernity and the Global Color Line*. New York: New York University Press.

Jacobs, Wilbur R. 1985. *Dispossessing the American Indian, Indians and Whites on the Colonial Frontier*. Norman, OK: University of Oklahoma Press.

Jacobson, Matthew Frye. 1998. *Whiteness of a Different Color: European Immigrants and the Alchemy of Race*. Cambridge, MA: Harvard University Press.

James, C.L.R. 1963. *The Black Jacobins*. 2nd ed. New York: Random House.

Jennings, Francis. 1975. *The Invasion of America – Indians, Colonialism and the Cant of Conquest*. New York: W.W. Norton & Company.

Johansen, Bruce E. 1982. *Forgotten Founders, How the Indian Helped Shape Democracy*. Boston, MA: Harvard Common Press.

Jones, Edward L. 1992. "Lucius Septimius Severus: The Black Emperor of the World." in *A Turbulent Voyage, Readings in African American Studies*, edited by Floyd W. Hayes III. Collegiate Press, 96–110.

Josephy, Alvin M. 1992. *America in 1492: The World of the Indian Peoples before the Arrival of Columbus.* New York: Knopf (Random House).

Josephy, Alvin M. 1994 (2002). *500 Nations*. New York: Knopf.

Kendi, Ibram X. 2016. *Stamped from the Beginning, The Definitive History of Racist Ideas in America*. New York: Nation Books.

Kendi, Ibram X. and Keisha N. Blain. 2021. *Four Hundred Souls: A Community History of African-Americans 1619–2019*, Ibram X Kendi and Keisha N Blain (Eds). New York: One World Press (Random House).

Koch, Alexander, Chris Brierley, Mark M. Maslin and Simon L. Lewis. 2019. "Earth System Impacts of the European Arrival and Great Dying in the Americas After 1492." *Quaternary Science Reviews*, 207: 13–36.

Korzeniewicz, Roberto and Payne, Corey. 2019. "Sugar, Slavery, and Creative Destruction: World-Magnates and 'Coreification' in the Longue-Durée." *Journal of World-Systems Research*, 25: 395–419. 10.5195/JWSR.2019.893.

Lachmann, Richard. 2020. *First-Class Passengers on a Sinking Ship: Elite Politics and the Decline of Great Powers*. London: Verso Press.

Lappé, Frances Moore and Joseph Collins, 1977. *Food First: Beyond the Myth of Scarcity*. Boston: Houghton Mifflin, 1977 (New York: Ballantine Books, 1979).

Las (de) Las Casas, Bartolome'. 1974 (1538). *The Devastation of the Indies: A Brief Account*. Herma Briffault (Trans.). New York: Seabury Press.

Lewis, David G. August 2016. "American Complicity in Genocide in Oregon." *Quartux Journal of Indigenous Anthropology* (Salem, OR: Ethnohistory Research).

Lindsay, Brendan C. 2012. *Murder State: California's Native American Genocide, 1846–1873*. Lincoln, NE: University of Nebraska Press.

Louverture, Toussaint. 2008 (1792). *The Haitian Revolution* (#3. Letter to the General Assembly), edited by Nick Nesbitt. London: Verso.

Love, David A. 2021. "The Royal African Company." In *Four Hundred Souls: A Community History of African-Americans 1619–2019*, Ibram X Kendi and Keisha N Blain (Eds). New York: One World Press (Random House).

Lui, Meizhu, Barbara Robles, Betsy Leondar-Wright, Rose Brewer and Rebecca Adamson, 2006. *The Color of Wealth: The Story Behind the U.S. Racial Wealth Divide*. New York: the New Press.

Lunenfeld, Marvin. 1991. *1492: Discovery, Invasion, Encounter*. Lexington, KY: D.C. Heath & Co.

Madley, Benjamin. 2016. *An American Genocide: The United States and the California Indian Catastrophe, 1846–1873*. New Haven, CT: Yale University Press.

Magness, Phillip W. 2020. *1619 Project, a Critique*. Washington, DC: American Institute for Economic Research.

Magubane, Zine. 2004. *Bringing the Empire Home: Race, Class, and Gender in Britain and Colonial South Africa*. Chicago, IL: University of Chicago Press.

Mann, C.R. and Zatz, Marjorie. 1998. *Images of Color, Images of Crime*. Los Angeles, CA: Roxbury. (Paperback ISBN 0-935732-97-7).

Mann, Charles C. May 2007. "Creating America, Found & Lost." *National Geographic*, 211(5): 32–53.

Mann, Charles C. 2011. *1493, Uncovering the New World Columbus Created*. New York: Knopf.

Manning, Patrick and Liu, Y. 2020. "Research Note on Captive Atlantic Flows: Estimating Missing Data by Slave-Voyage Routes." *Journal of World-Systems Research*, 26(1): 103–125. https://doi.org/10.5195/jwsr.2020.971. Retrieved June 22, 2022.

Markham, Edwin. 1909. *The Real America in Romance*. 1st ed. William H. Wise & Co.

Marx, Anthony W. 1998. *Making Race and Nation: A Comparison of the United States, South Africa, and Brazil*. New York: Cambridge University Press.'

Marx, Karl. 1977. *Capital*, Vol. I, Ben Fowkes (Trans.). New York: Vintage Books, 915, 926.

Meredith, Martin. 2014. *The Fortunes of Africa: A 5,000-Year History of Wealth, Greed and Endeavour*. Washington, DC: Public Affairs.

McGee, Heather C. 2021. "Bacon's Rebellion." In *Four Hundred Souls: A Community History of African-Americans 1619–2019*, Ibram X. Kendi and Keisha N. Blain (Eds). New York: One World Press (Random House).

McKay, Dwanna L., Kirsten Vinyeta and Kari Marie Norgaard. September 2020. "Theorizing Race and Settler Colonialism within U.S. Sociology." *Sociology Compass*, 14(9).

McKee, James B. 1993. *Sociology and the Race Problem: The Failure of a Perspective*. Urbana, IL: University of Illinois Press.

McLaughlin, David J. 2022. *Toypurina: The California Stories, California Missions, Keeping the Past Present* (Toypurina-Final.pdf, missionscalifornia.com; www.missionscalifornia.com/wp-content/uploads/2022/01/Toypurina-Final.pdf. Retrieved June 21, 2021)

McManus, Edgar J. 1973. *Black Bondage in the North*. Syracuse, NY: Syracuse University Press.

Meghji, Ali. 2020. *Decolonizing Sociology: A Guide to Theory and Practice*. Medford, MA: Polity Press.

Mignolo, Walter D. 2011. *The Darker Side of Western Modernity: Global Futures, Decolonial Options*. Durham, NC: Duke University Press.

Mittelberger, Gottliev. 1754. "Gottlieb Mittelberger's Journey to Pennsylvania in the Year 1750 and Return to Germany in the Year 1754." In *Voices of a People's History of the United States* (10th anniversary edition), Howard Zinn and Anthony Arnove (Eds). New York: Seven Stories Press. 72–76.

Mills, C. Wright. 1959. *The Sociological Imagination*. New York: Oxford University Press.

Mills, Charles W. 1997. *The Racial Contract*. Ithaca, NY: Cornell University Press.

Mills, Charles W. 1998. *Blackness Visible: Essays on Philosophy and Race*. Ithaca, NY: Cornell University Press.

Mills, Charles W. 2003. *From Class to Race: Essays in White Marxism and Black Radicalism*. New York: Rowman & Littlefield.

Miranda, D. 2013. *Bad Indians*. Berkeley, CA: Heyday Books.

Mirandé, Alfredo. 1987. *Gringo Justice*. Notre Dame, IN: University of Notre Dame Press.

Mittelberger, Gottliev. 1754. "Gottlieb Mittelberger's Journey to Pennsylvania in the Year 1750 and Return to Germany in the Year 1754." In *Voices of a People's History of the United States* (10th anniversary edition), Howard Zinn and Anthony Arnove (Eds). New York: Seven Stories Press, 72–76.

Montague, Ashley. 1997 (1942). *Man's Most Dangerous Myth: The Fallacy of Race*. Walnut Creek, CA: AltaMira Press.

Moore, Jason W. 2009. "Madeira, Sugar, and the Conquest of Nature in the 'First' Sixteenth Century, Part I: From 'Island of Timber' to Sugar Revolution, 1420–1506," *Review XXXII*, 4: 345–390.

Moore, Jason W. 2010. "Madeira, Sugar, and the Conquest of Nature in the 'First' Sixteenth Century, Part II: From Regional Crisis to Commodity Frontier, 1506–1530." *Review (Fernand Braudel Center)*, 33(1): 1–24. www.jstor.org/stable/41427 556.

Moore, Jason W. 2015. *Capitalism in the Web of Life: Ecology and the Accumulation of Capital*. London: Verso.

Morgan, Edmund S. 1995. *American Slavery American Freedom: The Ordeal of Colonial Virginia*. W.W. Norton & Company.

Morris, Aldon. 1984. *The Origins of the Civil Rights Movement*, Free Press: New York.

Morris, Aldon. 2015. *The Scholar Denied: WEB Du Bois and the Birth of Modern Sociology*. Oakland, CA: University of California Press.

Morris, Aldon. 2022. "Alternative View of Modernity: The Subaltern Speaks." *American Sociological Review*, 87(1): 1–16. doi:10.1177/00031224211065719.

Muhammad, Khalil Gibran. August 14, 2019. "The Sugar that Saturates the American Diet Has a Barbaric History as the 'White Gold' That Fueled Slavery in 'the 1619 Project'," *The New York Times*.

Murphy, Michael W. and Caitlin Schroering. 2020. Refiguring the Plantationocene: Racial Capitalism, World-Systems Analysis, and Global Socioecological Transformation. *Journal of World-Systems Research*, 26(2): 400–415. https://doi.org/10.5195/jwsr.2020.983.

Nagel, Joane. 1996. *American Indian Ethnic Renewal: Red Power and the Resurgence of Identity and Culture.* Oxford, UK: Oxford University Press.

Newcomb, Steven. 2008. *Pagans in the Promised Land: Decoding the Doctrine of Christian Discovery.* Golden, CO: Fulcrum Publishing.

Norgaard, Kari M. 2019. *Salmon and Acorns Feed Our People: Nature, Colonialism and Social Action.* Newark, NJ: Rutgers University Press.

Norton, Jack. 1979. *Genocide in Northwestern California: When Our Worlds Cried.* San Francisco, CA: American Historians Press.

Norton, Jack. 2014. "If the Truth Be Told: Revising California History as a Moral Objective." *American Behavioral Scientist,* 58(1): 83–96.

O'Hearn, Denis. 2001. *The Atlantic Economy: Britain, the Us and Ireland.* Manchester, UK: Manchester University Press.

Okihiro, Gary. 2001. *Common Ground: Reimagining American History.* Princeton, NJ: Princeton University Press.

Okihiro, Gary Y. 2016. *Third World Studies: Theorizing Liberation.* Durham, NC: Duke University Press.

Oluo, Ijeoma. 2021. "Whipped for Lying with a Black Woman." In *Four Hundred Souls: A Community History of African-Americans 1619–2019,* Ibram X. Kendi and Keisha N. Blain (Eds). New York: One World Press (Random House).

Omi, Michael and Howard Winant. 1994. *Racial Formation in the United States: From the 1960s to the 1990s.* 2nd ed. New York: Routledge.

Omi, Michael and Howard Winant. 2008. *Racial Formation in the New Millennium.* London, England: Routledge.

Omi, Michael and Howard Winant. 2015. *Racial Formation in the United States.* 3rd ed. New York: Routledge.

Ortiz, Roxanne Dunbar. 1984. *Indians of the Americas, Human Rights and Self-determination.* New York: Praeger.

Paddison, Joshua. 2012. *American Heathen: Religion, Race and Reconstruction in California.* Berkeley, CA: University of California Press.

Painter, Nell Irvin. 2011. *History of White People.* New York: Norton & Company, Incorporated.

Parker, Nakia D. 2021. "Unfree Labor." In *Four Hundred Souls: A Community History of African-Americans 1619–2019,* Ibram X. Kendi and Keisha N. Blain (Eds). New York: One World Press (Random House).

Patterson, Orlando. 1982. *Slavery and Social Death.* Cambridge, MA: Harvard University Press.

Patterson, Orlando. 1992. *Freedom in the Making of Western Culture.* New York: Basic Books.

Payne, Corey R. 2020. "Review Of: First-Class Passengers on a Sinking Ship: Elite Politics and the Decline of Great Powers, by Richard Lachmann." *Journal of World-Systems Research,* 26(2), 424–427. https://doi.org/10.5195/jwsr.2020.1019.

Persaud, Roger. 2021. *America Should Be Grateful to Haiti: Don't Believe the Lie When You See People of Color See Pride.* Fredericksburg, VA: RP Consulting Solutions LLC.

Phelan, Jo C., Bruce G. Link and Naumi M. Feldman. April 2013. The Genomic Revolution and Beliefs about Essential Racial Differences: A Backdoor to Eugenics? *American Sociological Review,* 78(2): 167–191. doi: 10.1177/0003122413476034.

Pleck, Elizabeth. Autumn 2018. *"Slavery in Puritan New England" Review of New England Bound: Slavery and Colonization in Early America.* By Wendy Warren.

New York, Liveright Publishing, 2016, in: *Journal of Interdisciplinary History*, XLIX: 2, 305–313.

Pontiac, Obwandiyag. 2021. *Dictionary of Canadian Biography.* Vol. III (1741–1770), Toronto, CA: University of Toronto/Université Laval. www.biographi.ca/en/bio/pontiac_3E.html. Retrieved November 11, 2021.

Powell, Stephen. 1876 (1976). *Tribes of California*, Introduction by Robert F. Heizer, Berkeley, CA: University of California Press.

Prucha, Francis. 1984. *The Great Father, the United States Government and the American Indians.* Lincoln, NE: University of Nebraska Press.

Pulido, L. 2017. "Geographies of Race and Ethnicity: Environmental Racism, Racial Capitalism and State-Sanctioned Violence." *Progress in Human Geography*, 41(4): 524–533.

Quijano, Anibal and Michael Ennis. 2000. "Coloniality of Power, Eurocentrism, and Latin America." *Nepantla: Views from the South*, 1(3): 533–580.

Ragin, Charles C. 1992. *What Is a Case? Exploring the Foundations of Social Inquiry.* Cambridge University Press.

Ramirez, Gloria Munoz. 2003. *EZLN: 20 y 10, el fuego y la palabra.* Revista *Rebeldia*, Mexico City: Revista Rebeldia.

Reséndez, Andrés. 2016. *The Other Slavery: The Uncovered Story of Indian Enslavement in America.* New York: Houghton Mifflin Harcourt.

Reyes, Victoria and Karin A.C. Johnson. 2020. "Teaching the Veil: Race, Ethnicity, and Gender in Classical Theory Courses." *Sociology of Race and Ethnicity*, 6(4): 1–6.

Richter, David K. 2002. *Facing East from Indian Country: A Native History of Early America.* Cambridge, MA: Harvard University Press.

Ritzer, George. 2010. *Globalization: A Basic Text.* Hoboken, NJ: John Wiley and Sons.

Robespierre, Maxmillian. 2006. See *Robespierre*, in ed. Colin Haydon and William Doyle. Oxford, UK: Cambridge University Press.

Robinson, Cedric. 1980 (2016). *The Terms of Order: Political Science and the Myth of Leadership*, North Carolina: The University of North Carolina Press.

Robinson, Cedric. 1983 (2021). *Black Marxism: The Making of the Black Radical Tradition.* London: Penguin.

Robinson, Cedric. 2001 (2019). *An Anthropology of Marxism.* London: Pluto Press.

Robinson, William I. 2004. *A Theory of Global Capitalism.* Baltimore, MD: Johns Hopkins University Press.

Robinson, William I. 2014. *Global Capitalism and the Crisis of Humanity.* Cambridge, UK: Cambridge University Press.

Robinson, William I. 2016. "Introduction: Globalization and Race in World Capitalism." *Journal of World-Systems Research*, 22(1): 3–8.

Robinson, William I. 2020. "Global Capitalism Post-Pandemic." *Race & Class*, 62(2): 3–13. doi:10.1177/0306396820951999.

Robinson, William I. and Mario Barrera. 2012. "Global Capitalism and Twenty-First Century Fascism: A US Case Study." *Race & Class Institute of Race Relations*, 53(3): 4–29.

Rodriguez, Sandy. 2019. *Codex Rodriguez-Mondragon: You Will Not Be Forgotten.* Los Angeles, CA: Charlie James Gallery.

Roediger, David. 1991. *The Wages of Whiteness: Race and the Making of the American Working Class.* New York: Verso.

Roediger, David R. 2002. *Colored White: Transcending the Racial Past*. Berkeley, CA: University of California Press.

Roediger, David R. 2005. *Working Toward Whiteness: How America's Immigrants Became White*. New York: Basic Books.

Romero, Mary. 2020. "Sociology Engaged in Social Justice." *American Sociological Review*, 85(1): 1–30.

Rosenblum, Karen E. and Toni-Michelle Travis. 1996. *The Meaning of Difference*. New York: McGraw-Hill.

Russell, James. W. 1994. *After the Fifth Sun: Class and Race in North America*. Englewood Cliffs, NJ: Prentice-Hall.

Sáenz, Rogelio and Maria Cristina Morales. 2015. *Latinos in the United States: Diversity and Change*. Boston, MA: Polity Press.

Said, Edward. 1978. *Orientalism*. New York: Pantheon Books, Republished by Vintage Books in 1979.

Said, Edward. 1993. *Culture and Imperialism*. New York: Knopf (Random House), Republished Vintage Books 1994.

Sale, Kirkpatrick. October 22, 1990. "What Columbus Discovered." *The Nation*, 251(13): 444–446.

Sale, Kirkpatrick. 1991. *The Conquest of Paradise: Christopher Columbus and the Columbian Legacy*. New York: Plume.

Santos, Boaventura de Sousa. 2014. *Epistemologies of the South: Justice against Epistemicide*. Boulder, CO: Paradigm Publishers.

Santos, Boaventura de Sousa. 2018. *The End of the Cognitive Empire: The Coming of Age of Epistemologies of the South*. Durham, NC: Duke University Press.

Sassen, Saskia. 2014. *Expulsions: Brutality and Complexity in the Global Economy*. Harvard University Press.

Silver, Peter. 2008. *Our Savage Neighbors: How Indian War Transformed Early America*. New York: W. W. Norton & Company, 158, 162–163.

Simpson, Leanne Betasamosake. 2017. *As We Have Always Done: Indigenous Freedom Through Radical Resistance*. Minneapolis, MN: University of Minnesota Press.

Smedley, Audrey. 1993. *Race in North America, Origins and Evolution of a Worldview*. Boulder, CO: Westview Press

Smedley, Audrey. 1999. *Race in North America, Origins and Evolution of a Worldview*. 2nd ed. Boulder, CO: Westview Press.

Smith, Adam. 1937 (1776). *An Inquiry into the Nature and Causes of the Wealth of Nations*. New York: Random House (Modern Library Edition).

Smith, Andrea Lynn and Nëhdöwes Randy A. John. Winter 2020–2021. "Monuments, Legitimization Ceremonies, and Haudenosaunee Rejection of Sullivan-Clinton Markers." *New York History*, 101(2), 343–365.

Stampp, Kenneth Milton. 1989. *The Peculiar Institution: Slavery in the Ante-Bellum South*. New York: Vintage Books.

Stanford History Education Group (Wineburg, Sam and McGrew, Sarah and Breakstone, Joel and Ortega, Teresa). 2016. *Evaluating Information: The Cornerstone of Civic Online Reasoning*. Stanford Digital Repository. http://purl.stanford.edu/fv751yt5934. Retrieved February 1, 2023.

Stannard, David E. 1992. *American Holocaust, Columbus and the Conquest of the New World*. New York: Oxford University Press.

Steger, Manfred B. 2017. *Globalization: A Very Short Introduction*. 4th ed. Oxford, UK: Oxford University Press.

Steinberg, Stephen. 1989 (1981). *The Ethnic Myth*. Boston, MA: Beacon Press.

Steinberg, Stephen. 1995. *Turning Back, the Retreat from Racial Justice in American Thought and Policy*. Boston, MA: Beacon Press.

Steinman, E. 2016. "Decolonization Not Inclusion: Indigenous Resistance to American Settler Colonialism." *Sociology of Race and Ethnicity*, 2(2): 219–236.

Steinman, Eric. 2012. "Settler Colonial Power and the American Indian Sovereignty Movement: Forms of Domination, Strategies of Transformation." *American Journal of Sociology*, 117(4): 1073–1130.

Steinmetz, George. 2013. "Major Contributions to Sociological Theory and Research on Empire, 1830–Present." In *Sociology & Empire, the Imperial Entanglements of a Discipline*, George Steinmetz (Ed.). Durham, NC: Duke University Press, 1–50.

Steinmetz, George. 2014. "The Sociology of Empires, Colonies, and Postcolonialism." *Annual Review of Sociology*, 40: 77–103.

Stevenson, Brenda E. 2021. "Black Women's Labor." In *Four Hundred Souls: A Community History of African-Americans 1619–2019*, Ibram X Kendi and Keisha N Blain. New York: One World Press (Random House).

Swedberg, Richard. 2016. "Can You Visualize Theory? On the Use of Visual Thinking in Theory Pictures, Theorizing Diagrams, and Visual Sketches." *Sociological Theory* 34(3): 250–275.

Takaki, Ronald. 1994 (1987). *From Different Shores, Perspectives on Race and Ethnicity in America*. 2nd ed. New York: Oxford University Press.

Takaki, Ronald T. 1993. *A Different Mirror: A History of Multicultural American*. Boston, MA: Little, Brown. (Original work published 1979).

TallBear, Kim. 2013. *Native American DNA: Tribal Belonging and the False Promise of Genetic Science*. Minneapolis, MN: University of Minnesota Press.

TallBear, Kimberly. 2014. "Standing with and Speaking as Faith: A Feminist-Indigenous Approach to Inquiry." *Journal of Research Practice*, 10(2). http://jrp.icaap.org/index.php/jrp/article/view/405. Retrieved February 2, 2023.

Telles, Edward. 2014. *Pigmentocracies: Ethnicity, Race, and Color in Latin America*. Chapel Hill, NC: University of North Carolina Press.

Thornton, John. 1998. *Africa and Africans in the Making of the Atlantic World, 1400–1800*. New York: Cambridge University Press.

Thornton, Russell. 1987. *American Indian Holocaust and Survival*. Norman, OK: University of Oklahoma Press.

Thornton, Russell. 1998. *Studying Native America: Problems & Prospects*. Madison, WI: University of Wisconsin Press, 1999.

Tilly, Charles. 1985. "War Making and State Making as Organized Crime." In *Bringing the State Back In*, Peter Evans, Dietrich Rueschemeyer and Theda Skocpol (Eds). Cambridge, MA: Cambridge University Press, 169–191.

Tisby, Jemar. 2021. "The Virginia Law on Baptism." In *Four Hundred Souls: A Community History of African-Americans 1619–2019*, Ibram X. Kendi and Keisha N. Blain (Eds). New York: One World Press (Random House).

Trafzer, Clifford. E. and J. Hyer. 1999. *"Exterminate them!": Written Accounts of Murder, Rape, and Enslavement of Native Americans during the California Gold Rush*. East Lansing, MI: Michigan State University Press.

Trafzer, Clifford E. and Joel R. Hyer (Ed.). 1999. *Exterminate Them: Written Accounts of the Murder, Rape and Slavery of the Native Americans during the California Gold Rush 1848–1868*. East Lansing, MI: Michigan State University Press.

Trafzer, Clifford E. and R.R. McCoy. 2009. *Forgotten Voices: Death Records of the Yakama, 1888–1964*. Lanham, MD: Scarecrow Press.

Tuck, Eve and K.W.Yang. 2012. "Decolonization Is Not a Metaphor." *Decolonization: Indigeneity, Education and Society*, 1(1): 1–40.

Tuck, Eve and M. McKenzie. 2014. *Place in Research: Theory, Methodology, and Methods*. Hoboken, NJ: Taylor and Francis. Routledge advances in research methods.

United Nations. December 9, 1948. *The Crime Against Genocide: A United Nations Convention (Resolution 260(III)A of the General Assembly)*. New York: Author.

Usner, Daniel H. 1992. *Indians, Settlers, and Slaves in a Frontier Exchange Economy: The Lower Mississippi Valley Before 1783*. Williamsburg, VA: Omohundro Institute of Early American History.

Vaughan, Alden T. January 1978. "'Expulsion of the Savages': English Policy and the Virginia Massacre of 1622." *The William and Mary Quarterly*, 35(1): 57–84.

Veracini, L. 2017. "Settler Colonialism as a Distinct Mode of Domination." In The *Routledge Handbook of the History of Settler Colonialism*, E. Cavanagh and L.Veracini (Eds). New York, NY: Routledge, 1–8.

Veracini, Lorenzo. 2010. *Settler Colonialism: A Theoretical Overview*. New York: Palgrave Macmillan.

Veracini, Lorenzo. 2013. "Settler Colonialism: Career of a Concept." *The Journal of Imperial and Commonwealth History*, 41(2): 313–333.

Veracini, Lorenzo. 2016. "Patrick Wolfe's Dialectics." *Aboriginal History*, 40: 249–260.

Wallace, Athony F.C. 1999. *Jefferson and the Indians: The Tragic Fate of the First Americans*. Cambridge, MA: Harvard University Press (Belknap).

Wallerstein, Immanuel. 1974. *The Modern World-System, Vol. I: Capitalist Agriculture and the Origins of the European World-Economy in the Sixteenth Century*. New York: Academic Press.

Wallerstein, Immanuel. 1980. *The Modern World-System, Vol. II: Mercantilism and the Consolidation of the European World-Economy, 1600–1750*. New York: Academic Press.

Wallerstein, Immanuel. 1983. *Historical Capitalism*. New York: Verso.

Wallerstein, Immanuel. 2004. *World-Systems Analysis: An Introduction*. Durham, NC: Duke University Press, 7–8.

Warren, Wendy. 2016. *New England Bound: Slavery and Colonization in Early America*. By Wendy Warren. New York: Liveright Publishing.

Weatherford, Jack. 1988. *Indian Givers, How the Indians of the Americas Transformed the World*. New York: Fawcett Columbine.

Weber, Max. 1961. "The Three Types of Legitimate Rule." In *Complex Organizations*, Hans Gerth (Trans.), Amitai Etzioni (Ed.). New York: Holt, Rinehart and Winston.

White Hat, Albert (John Cunningham: Compiler). 2012. *Life's Journey – Zuya: Oral Teachings from Rosebud*, Salt Lake City, UT: University of Utah Press.

Whyte, Kyle. 2017. "Indigenous Climate Change Studies: Indigenizing Futures, Decolonizing the Anthropocene." *English Language Notes*, 55(1–2): 153–162.

Wilkerson, Isabel. 2020. *Caste: The Origins of Our Discontents*, New York: Random House.

Williams, Robert. 2012. *Savage Anxieties: The Invention of Western Civilization*. New York: Palgrave Macmillan.

Willie, Charles V. 1983. *Race, Ethnicity, and Socioecoomic Status: A Theoretical Analysis of Their Interrelationship.* Bayside, NY: General Hall Inc.

Wilson, Carter A. Wilson. 1996. *Racism: From Slavery to Advanced Capitalism.* New York: SAGE Publications, Inc.

Winant, Howard. 2001. *The World Is a Ghetto: Race and Democracy Since World War II.* Basic Books. New York: Basic Books.

Wolf, Eric R. 1982. *Europe and the People Without History.* Berkeley, CA: University of California Press.

Wolfe, Patrick. 2006. "Settler Colonialism and the Elimination of the Native." *Journal of Genocide Research*, 8(4): 387–409. https://doi.org/10.1080/14623.

Wolfe, Patrick. 2016. *Traces of History: Elementary Structures of Race.* London: Verso Books.

Wong, Eddie L. 2015. *Racial Reconstruction: Black Inclusion, Chinese Exclusion, and the Fictions of Citizenship.* New York: New York University Press.

Wright, Ronald. 1992. *Stolen Continents, the "New World" Through Indian Eyes.* Boston, MA: Houghton Mifflin Company.

Yamashita, Michael. 2006. *Zheng He: Tracing the Epic Voyages of China's Greatest Explorer.* New York: White Star (1st ed.).

Young, Henry J. 1957. "A Note on Scalp Bounties in Pennsylvania". *Pennsylvania History: A Journal of Mid-Atlantic Studies*, 24(3), 207–218. www.jstor.org/stable/27769743.

Zimmerman, Andrew. 2013. "German Sociology and Empire: From Internal Colonization to Overseas Colonialization and Back Again." In *Sociology and Empire: The Imperial Entanglements of a Discipline*, G. Steinmetz (Ed.). Durham, NC: Duke University Press, 166–187.

Zinn, Howard. 1977. *Justice in Everyday Life: The Way It Really Works.* Boston, MA: Beacon Press.

Zinn, Howard. 1980. *A People's History of the United States: 1492 to Present.* New York: Harper & Row.

Index